The
EPHESUS
FRAGMENT

The EPHESUS FRAGMENT

GARY E. PARKER

BETHANY HOUSE PUBLISHERS

MINNEAPOLIS, MINNESOTA 55438

The Ephesus Fragment
Copyright © 1999
Gary E. Parker

Cover by Koechel Peterson

Library of Congress Catalog Number 99–6479

ISBN 0–7642–2256–2

Published by Bethany House Publishers
A Ministry of Bethany Fellowship International
11400 Hampshire Avenue South
Minneapolis, Minnesota 55438
www.bethanyhouse.com

Printed in the United States of America by
Bethany Press International, Minneapolis, Minnesota 55438

I want to dedicate this book
to three spiritual influences—

Richard Moyers,
the man who baptized me and
taught me to love the scriptures;

Jim West,
an English professor who told me long ago
that maybe I had some gift for writing;

and Mrs. Lucy Faile,
a stalwart supporter who helped me
as I began my faith journey and
service in the local church.

ACKNOWLEDGMENTS

As with any writer who relies on specific and particular research, certain key people offered me expert guidance and advice as I authored this manuscript. Chief among those I need to thank are Dr. Mike Fanning, an archeologist who made helpful suggestions regarding that aspect of this story, and the Reverend Monsignor Terry Young, a Catholic priest who read and corrected the part of the work that dealt with Catholic faith and practice. Any mistakes or misunderstandings regarding archeology or Catholicism are mine, not theirs.

In addition, I express appreciation to my editor, Dave Horton, who offered important ideas to make the manuscript better, and Claudia Cross, my agent, who believes in what I do and how I do it.

Finally, I never finish any writing project without recognizing anew and afresh how dependent on my family I truly am. Without the three women in my life, my wife, Melody, and daughters, Andrea and Ashley, I simply couldn't do it. Thanks, girls, for the good gift of home.

Inasmuch as many have taken in hand to set in order a narrative of those things which have been fulfilled among us, just as those who from the beginning were eyewitnesses and ministers of the word delivered them to us . . .

St. Luke 1:1, 2

PART ONE

*Now there stood by the cross of Jesus His mother.
When Jesus therefore saw His mother, and the
disciple whom He loved standing by, He said to His
mother, "Woman, behold your son!"
Then he said to the disciple, "Behold your mother!"
And from that hour that disciple took her to his own
home.*

St. John 19:25–27

*The knowledge of Man is as the waters, some
descending from above, and some springing from
beneath; the one informed by the light of nature, the
other inspired by divine revelation.*

Francis Bacon

ONE

Dr. Hugh McAuley found the document on a Sunday, the day of the Feast of St. Mary for those who, unlike himself, paid attention to such things. He found it in spite of the fact that his current résumé contained a lot of blank spaces where a list of archeological accomplishments should have been written. He found it thirty-one feet inside a cave that measured about eight feet across the front, nine feet from the top to the bottom at its highest point, and almost one hundred fifty-four feet from the entrance to the back corner. He found it, and his life, to that point as empty as a looted Egyptian tomb, changed forever. For that matter, so did a lot of other lives.

He was alone when he found the document. His crew chief, Dr. Martha Hinton, a woman who seemed to spend more time in front of a camera than in a cave, had spirited the rest of the team off to Izmir to spend the day relaxing in a local pub. McAuley didn't mind being alone, though. In fact, he liked it, liked it more and more the older he became.

He had been at work for right at three hours when the discovery occurred. Though the temperature in the cave stayed constant at a chilly fifty-five to sixty degrees, McAuley was sweating profusely. One of his distinguishing character traits, he often chided himself. Enough excess flesh to crush a small pack mule and enough sweat to drown even the most talented of ducks.

With a hand the size of a baseball glove, he wiped a stream of perspiration from his goatee, repositioned the mobile light sitting to his right to augment the one on his helmet, then began to chip away again at the lower quarter of the cavern wall. The limestone rock seemed a bit softer here than in the upper section.

Chisk, chisk, chisk. His trowel, no longer than a hammer and pointed like a pelican's beak, dug into the shadowed surface. Chip the limestone and brush away the dirt, chip the limestone and brush away the dirt.

Gritting his teeth, McAuley shifted his fleshy haunches to the corner of the stool that supported them, his determination digging in as tight as the trowel in his thick hand. He had two bad knees and they hurt like a migraine. No matter how much he hurt, though, he wouldn't stop digging. He loved it too much to do that.

Chisk, chisk, chisk. Pick against rock, pick against rock, pick against rock. Chalky white dust danced in the air as he chipped out another shard of the scaly rock. *Chisk, chisk, chisk.* It was a kind of soothing medicine for a fifty-two-year-old Irish-American with bad skin who loved the dark of a cave and the sound of tool against stone more than breath. He thought of the bottle of aspirin in his belly pack but decided he didn't want to stop to get a couple. His knees would just have to hurt. *Chisk, chisk, chisk.*

Beneath his feet, McAuley sensed a slight quiver. Pausing briefly, he touched his trowel to his lips, puzzled by the sensation. But then the vibration disappeared. He lifted his trowel again, then thought he heard a rumble. His goatee stood on edge. The rumble, though faint, seemed to slide beneath his body, then snake toward the sliver of sunshine that marked the cave entrance to his right. For an instant, McAuley thought of a distant train, but then remembered that no track ran nearby. The rumble dissipated and he relaxed slightly. But then, in less time than it takes to wink, the earth shifted and the wall before him shimmied as if made of gelatin.

Recognizing the sensation now, McAuley pounced from his stool and threw his two hundred and ninety pounds toward the cave entrance. In his headlong rush, his feet banged into the stool and he crashed to the ground, his chin ricocheting up and down, his helmet and its light bouncing away into the dark. From behind, he heard another grumble in the ground, then the sound of rock falling.

A wave of dust washed over his face, and he gagged as the cave went dark. Spitting out the dust, he scrambled to get up, his fingers clawing the ground as he stumbled in the direction of the cave entrance. The ground felt liquid under his boots, slipping and sliding as if someone had waxed the stone floor.

Through the fog of white dust, he saw a stream of light at a distance and staggered toward it. Two steps, five, ten. Another stride or two and he would make it to fresh air and blue sky overhead!

Expecting another tremor at any second, McAuley pushed ahead, gasping for breath. Reaching the exit, he threw himself through it and sagged to the ground. His chest heaved and his knees seemed to have caught fire they hurt so much. But he was alive!

For several moments, he lay flat on the ground, hugging it like a child clinging to its mother, waiting for the next surge of the earth. But nothing moved. A clear sun beamed down on his back, and his breath hovered in the forty-degree air, but it seemed that the whole world had become still, as still as death and just as quiet.

McAuley stayed in place too, only his eyes moving. They darted from side to side, watching for the world to tremble again. But he saw nothing out of place, no cracks in the ground, no uprooted trees, nothing amiss.

His breathing slowing, McAuley cautiously stood and brushed himself off. To his surprise, he still held his trowel in his hand. Smiling slightly, he continued to listen for another rumble. But none came.

Slowly, ever so slowly, he edged back to the cave and peered inside. Amazingly, the dust that had blanketed him just a few moments ago had almost all settled back down. If he didn't know better, he would have sworn that nothing had happened.

Still not trusting the ground, he remained in place for several moments and tried to make a decision. Should he go back to camp and wait for the crew to return from Izmir? Or go back inside the cave and continue his work?

McAuley touched his trowel to his lips. A small tremor like the one he had just experienced could mean nothing at all, just a slight burp of the earth's crust. Or it could signal a larger quake about to erupt. Who knew? Earthquakes were quite common in Turkey, but as far as he could remember, Ephesus itself had none recorded in its recent history. Which made the whole thing most peculiar.

With his right foot firmly planted outside, McAuley eased his left foot back inside the cave. He spotted his helmet less than five feet away, its light washing the ceiling in bright yellow hues. He leaned down, stuck his right foot inside, picked up the helmet, and pointed its light back toward the wall where he had been working. His mouth fell open. He took another step, wanting to make sure his eyes weren't deceiving him, then he stopped.

Unbelievable! He saw a crack in the wall at knee level, a crack the width of a computer keyboard, but jagged at the edges. He leaned closer and his light probed the opening. Though not certain, he thought he saw a bit of white stirring at the edges of the crevice, fanning out from it as if puffed away by moving air.

Fully in the cave now, he put on his helmet, took a step toward the hole, then remembered the tremor and stopped. Should he let the earthquake scare him off or forget the danger and explore the strange orifice?

McAuley tugged at the legs of his khaki shorts. A series of tests with the best ultrasound equipment available had suggested this exact spot as one of three in the cave worthy of careful attention. These spots, marked on the ultrasound like cavities on a dentist's x-ray, revealed the possibility of an open space behind the walls, a space covered by accretions of dirt built up over the centuries. He and the rest of the crew had already explored the other two spots but had found nothing in them.

Was this one any different? Was this the one cavity he had always hoped to find, a crack revealing an inner region behind it? Did the crevice lead to an unknown cave perhaps, a cave that once hid a fugitive or housed an ancient dweller of dark places?

McAuley patted his trowel against his heavy thighs. What he did know was that a previous excavation team had worked through this cave in 1948. That crew had discovered several bits of tattered leather, the remains of an ancient campfire, and three strips of woolen cloth. The pieces, all dated no later than the second century, demonstrated that someone had once inhabited the cave, even if only for a short time. Now, with the advantage of more technologically advanced equipment, he and the rest of Martha Hinton's team had the task of reexamining the site. With funding for the dig running out December 31, he didn't want to leave any possibility unexplored.

McAuley tugged at his khakis again and did a mental review of his less-than-distinguished career, a lackluster track record if ever he saw one. In more than thirty years of excavations, he had not found a single artifact worth noting. When it came to archeological discoveries, he had worse luck than a pig on a barbecue spit on the Fourth of July. Not that he didn't have significant skills. He knew without question that he was as competent as ninety percent of the people who worked with him day by day.

But he never found anything. Which made it all the more remarkable that he still loved what he did, craved it even, the isolation in the bowels of a cave, the shadows and silence he found there.

He stroked his goatee with the trowel and considered the risk facing him. If a full-blown earthquake hit while he was in the cave, he could kiss his big backside good-bye! He twisted back toward the entrance as if to leave but then hesitated. An unusual sense of bravado suddenly overwhelmed him. So what if an earthquake buried him alive? What better way to go? All alone in the dark, doing what he loved the most! *Why not go for it?* he asked himself. *Throw caution to the wind and grab for the gusto just once in your miserable, bland, unremarkable life.*

His decision made, McAuley strode toward the opening in the wall, grabbing his stool as he went. Sitting, he situated the stool beneath him again, then leaned forward and quickly struck at the edges of the hole—top to bottom, side to side. Bit by bit, the opening widened, gradually becoming the size of a steering wheel.

McAuley's breath came faster now, but not from exertion. His backside tingled. He tried to swallow but found it difficult. Any thought of the tremor disappeared as he concentrated on his digging. Fighting to keep his hopes in check, he lowered his face to the gap in the rock, picked up his flashlight, and peered inside. The smell of old air hit him, and he knew that no one had seen this hollow pocket in a long time, if ever. He shifted his flashlight, trying to see more, but couldn't.

Shrugging, he placed the flashlight on the ground, grabbed his trowel, and started hacking away again. A bit more and maybe he could squeeze his shoulders, remarkably thin for a man his size, through the aperture. His knees started to ache again, and a throbbing just over his eyes added to his discomfort. For a second he thought he heard voices outside the cave. He caught his breath, his ears poised toward the noise. Had the crew sucked down enough booze for one day and returned early? He doubted it. The sound from outside disappeared, and he passed it off as an overactive imagination. Glad no one had disturbed him, he went back to work. The hole became a black space the size of a washtub, large enough to squeeze his shoulders through.

McAuley took off his helmet and trained his flashlight directly on the hole. Then, his heart thumping wildly, he crawled through the opening—hands, then head and shoulders. Only his waistline, wider than his shoulders by at least six inches, stopped his penetration. Testing his mobility and giving his eyes a moment to adjust to the darker space, he twisted slightly side to side. A tinge of claustrophobia bit him as the edges of the opening scraped his sides, and he remembered the tremor. Biting his tongue, he pushed back the feeling and played his light straight ahead. From what he could see, the hollow space ended about four feet away.

He swiveled to the right and raised his eyes to the ceiling— no more than five feet above him. He ran the light up and down the right wall, then into the corners. Nothing there but stone and darkness.

McAuley sighed. As usual, he had hit a dead end. If he had been the first person to step into the caves at Qumran in 1947, the Dead Sea Scrolls would have miraculously disappeared. His headache intensified, and his knees felt as though someone had dropped a refrigerator on them. Frustrated, he tried to roll over so he could see the left side of the cave. But his belt buckle hooked in the dirt, stopping his movement.

He tried again but couldn't move. Taking a deep breath, he sucked in his stomach and pushed. His belt snapped out of the dirt, and he rolled over and pointed his light at the left wall of the hollow cavity.

Wha—?!

An earthen jar, about two feet high, stood in the corner about an arm's length away, as prim and proper as if placed on an entry hall table by a housewife with a keen sense of style. Its sides, rounded to about sixteen inches in diameter, narrowed to a dainty flare at the top, and a knob-shaped cap covered it.

McAuley grunted involuntarily and blinked twice. Had he actually found something? He blinked once more, half expecting the artifact to be gone when he looked again, but it wasn't.

Unaccustomed to such circumstances, he tried to figure out his next move. Should he go right now for help? The discovery, of course, would belong to the whole team, but Dr. Hinton, the under-forty darling of the trade journals, the blond but moody "Cave Queen" as television's Discovery Channel called her, would immediately grab the credit. Like a moth drawn to fire, she would step before the cameras, and the limelight that should rightfully fall on Hugh McAuley would never touch his face. Not that it was much of a face.

McAuley knew the proper procedure. All his training told him to leave the jar in place and wait on Hinton. When she arrived, the team would photograph the piece in place, make an artist's drawing of it and plot it with meter sticks. After that, and only after that, they would excavate it. He closed his eyes, his training locked in mortal combat with a just-discovered sense of rebellion. If he handled this according to procedure, his chance for fame would disappear forever.

Grunting, McAuley made a decision most unlike him to make. Hinton would eventually get the artifact, but not just yet. He opened his eyes and surveyed the area, trying to determine the best way to approach the jar. The space cramped him terribly, and he needed to take extreme care. If not, he might harm the jar in some way, chip it or . . .

He pushed away the thought and told himself to stay easy. For another few seconds, he studied his discovery. Though shadowed in the small opening, the jar appeared yellowish and simple in shape. No markings decorated it from what he could see. He started to calculate its age, then decided to refrain from hasty conclusions. Testing would determine those kinds of things later.

Positioning his light to free both hands, he carefully pressed his elbows into the cavern floor and pushed. His stomach wedged against the sides of the opening, not cooperating with his desire to crawl farther. He pushed on his elbows again and gained a couple of inches. Using his left arm as a prop, he stretched as far as he could and touched the top of the jar with his right hand. The artifact tilted toward him.

McAuley's eyes widened in horror as he realized he had tipped it over. Jerking into the cave as far as his girth allowed, he grabbed for the jar. But too late! The jar crashed to the ground, its top piece popping off and rolling into the shadows, its body breaking into two almost identical halves just beyond his grasp. Dust roiled up from the cave floor, momentarily blinding him, and a groan escaped his throat. His one opportunity shattered!

At that moment, the gravity of it all overwhelmed him and McAuley panicked. Frenzied, he raked his hands across the cavern floor in a vain effort to find the jar. His mind played tricks on him, telling him that he had imagined the jar breaking, suggesting that if he could just find it, the artifact would be unharmed. The dirt boiled up higher and higher as he stirred it, and he choked and coughed out a slimy mixture of saliva and cave dust. For a couple of seconds, he thought he would choke to death, a victim of his own incompetence, a fat man of no repute dying within arm's reach of the only important discovery of his life. But then, slowly, inevitably, the gagging began to ebb, and he regained a bit of equilibrium. Like a top winding down, he stopped his frenetic movements and the dust settled.

Okay, he told himself, *okay*. He had cracked the jar, but a craftsman could repair it. Nothing to do now but find out how badly it was broken. Biting his tongue, he forced himself to calm down. Gradually, the air began to clear.

Taking a deep breath, McAuley wondered what he should do next. Pretend the artifact was broken when he found it? Or admit his clumsiness and accept the consequences?

The dust had completely settled now, and he once again studied the jar. Though it was no longer in one piece, his peers would still see it as a good find. He breathed a little easier. He had fouled up, but perhaps not irreparably. He stretched as far as he could and grabbed the top of the jar. With great care, he fingered both halves of the vase and pulled it closer. As the two pieces separated a bit farther, a coiled fragment of parchment fell from between the two halves. McAuley almost swallowed his tongue.

The jar contained a scroll! A scrap of human history, and he had discovered it! He had, of course, read of such good fortune and hoped that it might someday come to him. But never, in his wildest dreams, had he ever really dared to think it might. But here, right here, just a few inches from his acne-scarred face, a piece of ancient literature lay untouched and perhaps unread.

McAuley jerked hard and felt his stomach slide forward. His hand shaking, he ignored the jar and reached for the scroll instead. In the shadows, he couldn't really tell its color. But it looked to be ten to twelve inches wide, wound tightly around a straight thin stick.

Though he knew he should leave things in place and go for help, McAuley ignored his misgivings and grabbed for the scroll. He had followed procedure his entire professional life but had gotten nothing more for it than an assistant's title and a few footnotes in a couple of obscure textbooks.

A tingling sensation ran through his fingers as they touched the scroll. Then, quite surprisingly, they seemed to burn for an instant. Like hot blood, the warmth in his fingers surged through his arms, past his shoulders, and then divided—one stream aimed at his head and another at his lower extremities. Instantly, the throbbing in both knees ceased and his headache disappeared. Just like that, the hurting evaporated. *Adrenaline*, McAuley told himself, adrenaline was masking his pain.

Forgetting all caution now, McAuley yanked the parchment toward his face and quickly unrolled it a couple of inches at the top. As expected, the scroll felt brittle on the edges and a sooty-looking color marked the corners, obvious signs of the decay that inevitably came with age. The edges of the document ran at an upward angle from the left to the right, and McAuley knew immediately that someone had torn the papyrus off from the bottom of another piece, leaving the top of it jagged, like someone tearing a piece of newspaper with their bare hands. For a moment, he wondered about the torn off piece, but then tossed aside the concern. Regardless of what was on the missing piece, he had a huge fragment of it, a fragment large enough to contain something truly incredible. He concentrated on the document in his hands, unrolling it a couple of inches more. He saw writing on it.

He caught his breath as his eyes adjusted to the script on the scroll. It really did contain writing—words penned ages ago by some unknown person, some living, breathing, eating, sleeping human being just like himself!

A strange sense of bonding flooded McAuley's senses. Somehow, in this moment, whoever wrote these words became his kin, the brother or sister his parents never gave him, the wife he never had, the friend who wouldn't criticize or poke fun or, worse still, ignore him.

He exhaled and forced himself to look at the scroll. What was it? An ancient will? A list of a merchant's wares? A government document? He read the first word.

Greek. Good heavens, it was Greek, the language his father had studied all his life, the Koine of the biblical New Testament. The manuscript had to be close to two thousand years old!

McAuley stopped reading, and his hands began to tremble as the burning sensation ran through his fingers once more. He really should go for help. This scroll was incredibly important if authentic. Someone more experienced than he should take it from here.

He grunted, dug his toes into the ground, and tried to push back. But he couldn't. His stomach wedged against the sides, and he discovered he was stuck. He almost laughed, but it was too tragic. Of all the world's imbeciles, he reigned as chief. He clutched the first significant find of his miserable career in his hands but couldn't extricate himself from the cave where he found it. He thought of the tremor once more, and this time he couldn't hold in the laughter. If an earthquake hit now, he was dead meat and there was nothing he could do about it.

Shaking his head, McAuley gave up his efforts to back out of the hole and focused again on the scroll. Apparently fate had decreed that he should read this all by himself.

He unrolled it once more and studied the first line. His eyes widened and then filmed up with moisture. His heart skipped a beat, and he noticed again that his head and knees no longer ached. He read the second line of the scroll, then the third and fourth.

But then he stopped, unable to go on. Gently, ever so gently, he laid the scroll back into one half of the broken jar. For several long moments, he didn't move. Then, still on his stomach, he closed his eyes and rested his face on the ground. Dust filtered into his nostrils as he breathed, but he didn't notice. Sweat dripped off his forehead and mixed with the dirt to form small puddles of gooey mud. But he didn't care. Only one thing filled his thoughts—the beginning words on the scroll.

In the last days of this temporal life, I John, a follower of the Lord Jesus and witness to many signs and wonders that He did, do now undertake to write an accounting of the life of Jesus, as told to me through the words of Mary, mother of our Lord, who lived in my house as the Lord commanded before His death and resurrection.

Though not at all religious, McAuley did what he hadn't done since the last funeral he had attended more than nine years ago. He began to pray, "Our Father, who art in heaven, hallowed be thy name . . ."

Under the circumstances, it seemed the only reasonable thing to do.

TWO

ROME, ITALY

His body wearied by almost three weeks of constant travel and his internal clock confused by the whiplash of more time zones than he cared to count, His Holiness slipped off his white cassock and handed it to the assistant who helped him prepare for bed each evening.

"Forgive me for calling you early," said the pontiff. "But I am exhausted from the Mass, and my body does not know that it is not yet dark."

"You have no need to apologize to me," said the assistant, handing the pope a robe, also of the purest white. "I know the schedule you have followed the last few days, the travel, then the Feast of the Blessed Mother all day today. You deserve a good long rest, and I'm here to make sure you get it."

The pontiff smiled, playfully wagged his finger at the assistant, and handed the white robe back to him. "You never give up, do you?" he asked, pointing to the closet to his right. "You know the robe I want."

"But it's so worn," countered the assistant, stepping to the closet and pulling out a plain, chocolate-colored garment. "You can almost see your elbows through the wool."

The pontiff took the robe, fingered it lovingly for a second, and then slipped into it. "So let my elbows show," he said. "I've had this over fifty years. My mother hand stitched it for me the year before she died. It's—well, you know the story. I suspect I'll wear out before it finally does."

"I'll leave you to your rest, then," said the assistant, the vaguest hint of displeasure around his thin lips.

"And I'll see you in the morning," said the pope.

"Your water is by your bed as always."

His Holiness nodded. "I appreciate your remembrance." Every morning and every night, just as he awoke and just before he went to sleep, he drank almost a quart of cool, clear bottled water. Though not prescribed by any doctor, he thought such a routine one of the keys to his astonishing good health.

"If you need me—"

"I know how to get you," the pope gently interrupted. "You stay awake all night, just outside my door with my Swiss Guard. All I have to do is punch the summons button on the phone by my bed and you'll come running. I know the procedure and I'll call if I need you."

His face solemn in concentration, the assistant nodded slightly, then backed out of the room, the white robe he had wanted the pope to wear hanging like a huge folded napkin over his forearm.

Watching him leave, His Holiness sighed. He knew the man disliked his attachment to battered old keepsakes like the robe. He thought it beneath the papal dignity. And, perhaps it was. But if the wearing of a frayed brown robe at bedtime meant he didn't have enough dignity, then so be it.

The pontiff shook his head. Tomorrow morning at 5:30 a different assistant would take his place, this one carrying a fresh white cassock for the new day; this one equally eager to minister to the needs of the Holy Father. Such constant attention sometimes made him wish for simpler days.

A man of few pretensions, he occasionally grew weary of it all—the protocol of the papacy, the fuss made over him, the pomp and pageantry of his office, the pressure to wear white robes even to bed! In moments like this he found himself yearning for the work of a parish priest again, the down-to-earth ministry that took place in hospitals and schools and around kitchen tables.

Wistful, the pope tossed off his slippers and headed toward his bedroom. His toes gripped the soft surface of the Oriental rug that led into his private quarters, and he smiled as he always did when the rug tickled his feet. It did feel good to get home, out of the limelight and clamor of the crowds. Fifteen thousand miles of cramped jets and strange beds and unusual foods; time zones from Rome to Brazil to Mexico to London to Rome; Mass after Mass and speech after speech. Such travels would sap anyone's strength—how much more a man of his advanced years.

His gaze swept over the bedroom as he entered it. For one

with so much wealth at his disposal, the room wasn't ornate. A few tasteful paintings from the Vatican art museum hung on the walls. Bits and pieces of antique furniture—a substantial bed with a canopy and a rolltop desk from the sixteenth century, a rocking chair from the eighteenth and a wall of bookshelves made of pure mahogany in the nineteenth—served his needs, but not extravagantly. The pontiff liked it this way, an attractive room, but not one to embarrass the Lord Jesus if He should seek it as a place to sleep for a night.

Easing his way toward his bed, he stopped for a second in the corner and took a swipe at the heavy punching bag that hung by a chain from the ceiling. One, two—he popped the leather with his right, then his left hand, and a hint of a mischievous smile crossed his lips. One, two—he punched the bag again, bouncing it about half a foot, not nearly the distance he had moved it back when he fought as a lightweight in his teen years, but still not too bad for an old man. The pontiff reared back one more time. Whap! He slapped the bag with a right cross and rocked it backward before stepping away, satisfied with his effort.

Breathing a bit heavier, he picked up a black leather notebook and a gold pen from his desk. Then he climbed into bed, fluffed his pillow at his back, and opened the notebook. Focusing intently, he reread his jottings from the last four days. Much of it pertained to his own devotional life, a life he hoped pleased God. Of all else that His Holiness wanted, for Mother Church and for the world at large, he sought this more than anything— that his own life might reflect the image of the Lord Jesus and please the blessed Virgin, Mother of the Savior. For most of his life, he had dedicated himself to that one task, and all else paled beside it.

Finished with the review, the pontiff began to scribble in the notebook. But this time he said nothing of his own spiritual pilgrimage. Instead, he reflected on his hopes for the Church. Though others tended to downplay the subject when he brought it up, he knew his days as the Vicar of Christ were numbered. As he saw it, the Lord had already granted him far more years than he deserved and the notion of dying bothered him not at all. Death eventually grabbed for everyone and, in spite of all the power he possessed, he was no different.

He finished one page and started writing on another. Yes, he had a school of secretaries to whom he could have dictated all this, a number of talented helpers who dutifully chronicled practically everything he ever spoke or thought. But on this subject he wanted to keep his own counsel, at least for a bit longer.

The pontiff rubbed his eyes then penned another page of scribbling. Others knew much of what he wanted in this matter. After all, he had spent hours and hours with theologians and church historians discussing the merits of such a decision. Contingencies for action based on multiple possibilities had been drawn up and stored away for future reference. But, in spite of all that, he had not yet told anyone precisely what he wanted. Maybe because he kept fluctuating himself, first with this conviction, then with that one. How could one know exactly what one should do in such a far-reaching issue?

The pontiff sighed. The time to firm up the choices had surely come. If he didn't act soon, the moment to do so would slip by unattended.

The clock to the left of the pontiff's bed chimed the four o'clock hour, and he stopped for a second and stared into space. "Mother of Jesus, bless me," he prayed. "Give me guidance for this that I think I should do. Let my choices please you and make you smile in your soul."

His prayer finished, he laid his pen on the table by the bed and swallowed. His throat felt sore and he rubbed it, feeling the glands for any swelling. Too many speeches, he decided. Reaching for his water glass, he took a huge gulp. The cool water soothed the back of his throat, and he drank it quickly. Placing the glass back on the table, he licked his lips and picked up his pen again. Before he started to write, however, he noticed a bitter taste on his tongue.

The water? Had someone changed the brand of water he drank every day? He started to push the button on his phone but then decided against it. No reason to disturb the attendant for something so insignificant as bad water. Besides, his sore throat might have caused the bitter taste. He would see to it in the morning.

His hands a bit shaky, the pontiff returned to his jottings. A hint of perspiration appeared on his forehead, and he knew he should stop soon and go to sleep. But not just yet. He peered down at his words, then decided to write just a few more lines. His fingers gripped the pen, and he licked his lips. The bitter taste was more noticeable, and his vision was becoming blurred. His head suddenly began to throb, and he shut his eyes against the pain. A shudder passed through his chest, and his right arm suddenly cramped in the forearm and elbow area. He surged back against the headboard of the bed, his shoulders bumping hard into the wood.

Trying to stretch out the cramp in his arm, he lifted both his hands over his head as if reaching for the ceiling, the golden pen in one hand, the black notebook in the other. But then the pen fell from his fingers, and his chin slumped toward his left collarbone.

As his body toppled sideways, the notebook dropped from his hand, wedged between the mattress and the headboard, and stuck there.

His fingers clenching and unclenching spasmodically, the pontiff fought hard against the blackout he knew was coming. With a sudden but short-lived burst of strength, he threw himself toward the telephone, and his right hand collapsed on the summons button and smothered it with a clammy palm. But the pope didn't notice because his eyes were closed, his breath had stopped, and darkness had invaded his mind.

THREE

His biceps gorged with increased blood flow, the honorable Father Michael Del Rio sucked in a quick shot of air and pushed up the iron bar, pressing 210 pounds off his chest. His arms fully extended, he held the weight for a hard count, then slowly lowered it back down. Finished with the tenth repetition of the weight and almost through with his workout, he rolled out from under the bar and sat for a second on the bench. He had been at it for almost an hour—thirty minutes jogging on the treadmill and twenty minutes lifting the free weights—and he felt a bit winded, a good feeling but one that required a little regrouping before he completed his last round with the weights.

Picking up a water bottle, he took a sip and enjoyed the rush the exercise had given him, grateful that even on Sunday in Rome he could find a place to work out. This place, the World Power Club as it was translated into English, was part of a European chain that catered to foreigners who valued hard exercise in an upscale atmosphere. Filled with the latest high-tech equipment—stationary bicycles, treadmills, stair climbers, overhead televisions, and an indoor pool, sauna, steam bath, and health food bar—the club was located about ten minutes southeast of the Vatican, and Michael visited it at least three times a week while visiting Vatican City.

To his left, a shapely brunette walked into the room, her ponytail bobbing up and down as if it had not a care in the world. Before he could look away, she caught his eye and smiled at him, showing lots of good straight teeth. Slightly embarrassed, Michael nodded politely. The woman fluttered her lashes, her smile coy.

Michael's face burned hot. The woman was flirting with him! Hurriedly grabbing a towel, he wiped his forehead and looked away. To his right, three elderly men puffed and sweated through their exercise routines, oblivious to his discomfort.

Standing, Michael wrapped the towel around his neck and wondered if the woman would have responded the same way if she knew he was a priest. Some did. In fact, some women seemed to take a strange pleasure in directing their charms at him. Was she one of those? Would she laugh if she found out? Would she toss her hair back and ask him what all women eventually seemed to ask—why would a man so handsome as he choose to become a priest? He, of course, thought he knew the answer to the question but tried hard to keep it repressed.

Picking up a curling bar, Michael felt guilty just thinking about the matter. After all, vanity wasn't a trait much coveted in the ranks of devout Catholic clerics, and he fought an ongoing battle to keep his own pride buried deep. But, whether he liked it or not, women did want to know. People had reminded him all his life that God had gifted him with more than his share in the looks department. Even though he was almost forty, he still had hair the color of Kentucky coal, eyes as blue as a robin's egg, and dimples the size of dimes. He was tall too, just over six two and shaped from shoulder to waist like an anvil sitting on an ax handle. Michael grunted and straightened his spine. At his next confession he would definitely need to repent for this unbidden outbreak of pride.

Taking a deep breath, he focused on his exercise, curling the bar from the waist up. His forearms tightened from the weight. To his left, he heard a door open and turned to it. To his surprise, the man entering was none other than Cardinal Severiano Roca, head of the Congregation for the Doctrine of the Faith, perhaps the most powerful division in the Catholic Church outside the office of the pope. Even more surprising, Roca had dispensed with the clothes of his office. Instead of a black cassock trimmed in red and topped off with a scarlet skull cap and pectoral cross, Roca had chosen the attire of an affluent Italian businessman— elegant navy suit, white shirt, and gold silk tie.

Confused, Michael laid the curling bar down and wiped his towel across his face. Knowing the cardinal as he did, a knowledge gained because the man was his only uncle, the brother of his deceased mother, he knew he hadn't come to the club to work out.

"You come to pump some iron?" he called playfully as Roca approached.

"The Bible says physical exercise availeth little," teased Roca, trading his native Italian for a lilting form of English.

Michael flexed his biceps. "Then how do you explain these?"

"Steroids, my nephew," said Roca, pecking Michael on both cheeks. "Better bodies through the chemicals."

"You should try it," countered Michael. "Keeps you young."

"And which of your insane pursuits would come next?" asked Roca. "Scuba diving? Rock climbing? A parachute jump? Let them keep you young. I'd rather die in a more peaceful manner."

Michael laughed and studied his uncle. The man constantly badgered him about his love for adventure. No taller than a chest of drawers and almost as wide, Roca had spent far more time in Vatican intrigue than in physical exertion. Scraggly lines crisscrossed his nose and fenced in his eyes, sure signs of too little rest and too much conversation oiled with wine. Age had thinned his hair on top, and in his only concession to physical vanity, Roca always combed it crossways, left to right, to cover as much bald space as possible.

"Is there somewhere we can talk a few minutes?" asked Roca, his face reverting to its normal seriousness.

Still mystified by Roca's presence, Michael nodded, then led him out of the room and into the lounge area of the club. A torrent of Italian pop music flooded the room, but it wasn't too loud for conversation. Ordering two bottles of water from the bar, Michael pointed to a table in the back corner. Sliding into the booth, he handed Roca one of the bottles, then twisted the top off his own. As he did, he noted that Roca still wore his cardinal's ring, the golden symbol by which the Church had identified its leaders for centuries. Given to him by his mentor, the late Cardinal Rossilini Medici, one of the most traditional men ever to wear the cardinal's red, Roca's ring had a blue sapphire center and reminded all who saw it that the wearer held much power.

"For a man going incognito, that's a dead giveaway," Michael said, pointing to the fourth finger on the cardinal's right hand.

Roca shrugged, then rolled the ring around his finger. "I wanted to speak to you without notice," he said. "But this I always wear."

Michael took a sip of water and decided to let his uncle lead the conversation. For several seconds though, nothing happened. Michael leaned back, his wide shoulders against the back of his seat, his long fingers playing with the neck of his water bottle. Roca raised his right eyebrow and stared at him but still said nothing. Michael almost smiled. More than one rival in the Pope's inner circle had buckled under the pressure of Roca's frozen gaze—a stare known in the Curia, the Vatican's ruling council, as "the black ice."

"I have to cancel our dinner plans for tonight," Roca started, breaking the silence. "Church matters, you understand."

"Sure, things come up, no problem."

Roca fidgeted with his water, then rolled his ring again. "But that's not the reason I came to find you," he finally said.

"I didn't expect it was."

Roca placed his water on the table and moved to the point. "You're leaving in the morning," he said, his voice almost a whisper. "So this is our last chance to talk. I think His Holiness is going to press ahead with the Marian Decree."

Pulling the towel off his neck, Michael slowly mopped his face. He and Roca had spent hours and hours over the last few weeks talking of little else. His uncle seemed mesmerized by the issue, unable to leave well enough alone and allow events to unfold naturally. Time and time again Roca had asked Michael what would happen in America if the pontiff pushed ahead with this controversial proclamation.

Michael sighed. "Not much you can do about it if he does," he said.

"But do you believe he will?"

Michael sucked on his water. The door to his right opened, and the brunette from the exercise room stepped through it. She took a seat three tables away, gave her order to the waiter who hustled over, then leaned back and pushed out her chest. Michael took a deep breath, turned away, and gave Roca his attention again.

"You're a lot closer to the situation than I am," he said. "You tell me."

Roca placed his hands on the table and interlocked his fingers. "If His Holiness takes this step, it will change everything."

"What's the word in the inner circle?" asked Michael, trying to lighten the mood. "Anyone taking odds?"

A crooked grin crossed Roca's face, making him appear slightly drunk. But when he spoke, the grin disappeared. "This is too serious for our normal childish wagers, my nephew. You know that. It is not one of your Fighting Irish football games!"

Michael wiped his mouth and scowled. "It's certainly serious in America," he said, his mood shifting to match his uncle's. "If

His Holiness names Mary the Co-Redemptrix with Jesus, we won't be able to get a Protestant within a hundred miles of us. Any hope for ecumenical dialogue will die instantly. Even worse, the political alliances we've formed with the Christian Forum and the Americans United for Life will disappear faster than beer at a frat house."

"And that will splinter our antiabortion efforts, our battles against pornography, and every other project we currently share with our Protestant brothers and sisters."

Michael closed his eyes for several seconds, fighting the tension he felt creeping into his back. On the surface, he and Roca held little in common. Roca was twenty years his senior, stumpy, Italian, and entrenched in papal politics—at times even rumored as a possible successor to the pope. He, on the other hand, was as American as apple pie—a former reserve halfback for the Fighting Irish, a lover of Touchdown Jesus and the Golden Dome. A total outsider to Vatican intrigue.

Yet, in spite of their differences, Roca was his only living relative and the most influential person in his life. Michael had been coming to Italy at least once a year since the summer of his high school graduation—the summer his mom, dad, and younger brother had died. Through college and doctoral studies, through his decision to enter the priesthood, and through his appointment as a professor of New Testament at Notre Dame nine years ago, Roca had counseled him.

In those years, the two had discovered a common bond in one vital area—both loved the exactitude of their faith and the Church that embodied it. On his treks to Rome, he and his uncle spent hours and hours talking about the Church—its history, its sacred writings, and the doctrine that supported it like steel in a skyscraper. Like Roca, Michael had come to understand that his love for the Church was his best connection to any kind of tangible proof of God. In fact, if the hour grew late enough, he usually ended up confessing that if not for the Church, he wasn't sure just where he and God would connect.

But none of that mattered right now. What mattered now was the pope's undying devotion to Mary and his rumored plans to issue a papal decree at the New Year's Eve Mass—a decree that would declare Mary the Co-Redemptrix with Jesus Christ. Such a decree would, in effect, designate her equal to Jesus in the minds of almost every believer on the face of the earth—Catholic or Protestant.

Though many in the Church thought that declaration vital,

Michael felt otherwise. To him, such a decree spelled disaster. Even with the explanation the Church would offer—to call Mary the Co-Redemptrix didn't mean she held equality with Jesus in her nature—the Protestant community would not understand such theological hairsplitting.

Gritting his teeth, Michael opened his eyes. When he spoke, his voice had an edge to it. "Most American scholars believe the pontiff has already decided to issue the decree. Reports have been rampant since 1997."

Roca nodded. "I remember the first American airing of the subject, a *Newsweek* article in August of that year. You faxed me the story. On the cover, if I recall."

"At the time, most people thought it was just media hype, mindless speculation and little more."

"But they don't know this pope like we do, the depth of his love for the Holy Mother."

Michael shook his head, his concern evident. "I applaud his devotion to the Virgin, agree with it even. But this . . . I just can't . . . to name her Co-Redemptrix . . . what does that do to the notion of the Trinity?"

Roca touched Michael's elbow and his smile returned. "Easy, my boy, you'll make your stomach sour. Such a proclamation will certainly require a measure of theological tinkering. But such revision is not unprecedented in our history. You know that as well as I. We have seen the elevation of the Virgin over and over in the Church. At the Council of Ephesus in A.D. 431, the Church officially titled her *'theotokos,'* Mother of God; by the seventh century we called her *'aieiparthenos,'* perpetually a virgin and declared she had no other children than Jesus. In the Middle Ages, the masses saw her more and more as the mediator of God's mercy. By the fourteenth century, the Church had decided she was also immaculate, without sin in her own origin and life. And Pope Pius issued the decree, making it official in 1854. Many see this step as the final completion of what has been happening since the beginning of our faith. At every step, whenever a controversy arose, those who wanted to venerate the Mother always won."

"Which makes it almost certain they will win again."

"Unless something is done to stop it."

"But what—?"

"What can be done about it? I don't know exactly. Perhaps the Congregation for the Doctrine of the Faith will come out against it."

Thinking of the council of officials assigned the task of dealing with doctrinal issues, Michael shook his head. "All but you
are too loyal to the pontiff," he said. "He appointed most of them.
They'll do as he directs."

"But I am the head of the Congregation," said Roca.

"But he is the Vicar of Christ," countered Michael. "They'll
follow his lead."

Roca sighed and yielded the point. "More than likely."

"So nothing can stop it."

Roca sipped his water, then said, "Unless something happens
to the pontiff, God forbid. But he is getting to that age. Even the
Vicar of Christ falls prey to the ravages of time."

Michael studied Roca for several seconds, not sure if he was
reading his uncle correctly. Having watched his machinations in
the power circles of the Vatican for years, he knew Roca was capable of much creativity when it came to accomplishing his ends.

"Does that mean you'll try to postpone the matter . . . slow
things down . . . wait for the pope to—!"

"You misunderstand me," interrupted Roca, his voice measured. "Such a tactic is . . . how shall I say it . . . beneath the high
ideals of our Lord."

Michael fingered his towel. The brunette woman stood to
leave, her bangs falling in her eyes, her smile still in place. Michael pulled his attention away from her and noticed Roca staring at him, a hint of amusement playing around the corners of
his mouth.

"Millions are pushing the pope to make this declaration," Michael said, shifting the conversation. "Why do you think that is?"

Roca shrugged. "It sounds simple, but the masses want a God
who is personal to them. You and I worry about the doctrine of
the Trinity. But few people care about such abstractions. Most
people cannot, how do you say it, 'get a handle on' the Trinity.
They cannot imagine such a thing; can't see it with their eyes,
hold it in their arms, caress it, sing to it, love it. So they choose
the Mother, a common person like themselves, someone with
dirt on her feet and a cheap shawl on her shoulders. In addition,
many people, especially the feminists, see the Trinity as incom-
plete. Too much the masculine image for our more aggressive fe-
males, even those within the Church.

"So, they want the Virgin elevated as high as possible. Then,
well . . . then my boy, God will have at least one face for everyone—Jesus for the men and Mary for the women."

Michael pondered the thought for a moment. Though supportive of women's ministry in the Church, even to the point of ordination, he despised the notion of doing such a thing to please a particular interest group. "But surely His Holiness isn't acting to appease the feminists," he said. "He's tougher than that. Since when does he give in to political pressure?"

Roca patted his hand as if calming a child. "You are right, my friend, this is not to appease anyone. But if the pope does it, and it happens to keep the feminists—who have excoriated him so completely for what they see as his failures on their behalf—at bay until his death, then so much the better."

Michael grunted, but he knew he had to accept the logic of the statement no matter how much he disliked it. The pope would almost certainly follow through with his plans—his last major act before his own imminent demise.

"It's going to blow up in our faces in America," he said. "Our allies won't be able to stomach it."

"But that won't be the worst of it," Roca said, his shoulders slumped.

"No, I expect it won't," Michael said, knowing instantly what Roca implied.

"The statistics on hate crimes get worse every year, don't they?"

Michael finished the last of his water. "The Jews, the Mormons, the Muslims—they're all feeling the pressure. If the pope declares Mary the Co-Redemptrix, the extremists will go nuts."

"Will they lump us with all the others?"

Michael sighed, wishing he had a different answer, but knowing he didn't. Persecuting Catholics had once been part and parcel of America's political landscape. "These are strange times," he said. "Apocalyptic crazies are everywhere. If Mary is named Co-Redemptrix, the notion that the Catholic Church is the home of the Antichrist can't be far behind. Though I wish things were different, nothing says it can't happen—"

A phone beeped, and Michael paused at the interruption. Roca reached inside his suit, pulled out a portable phone, and flipped it open. Within seconds, Roca's black eyes brightened, as if torched from inside, then clouded over.

"I'm ten minutes away," Roca said. "I'll be there in five." Closing the phone, he slipped it back into his jacket, and jerked from his seat. His hands shook as he placed them on Michael's shoulders.

"His Holiness," he whispered. "His Holiness has had a stroke."

"Is he—?"

"He's alive, but not conscious. We must go to him."

Still dressed in his workout togs, Michael wordlessly pushed up from the table and followed his uncle out of the club and into a taxi. A minute later, the taxi swerved recklessly around a corner, its driver pointing it toward the Vatican.

———————

Less than seven miles away from The World Power Club, a slender woman named Valerie Miller pushed her auburn hair out of her eyes, leaned forward at her desk, clicked the computer mouse resting under her right hand, and opened the e-mail her dad had sent her that afternoon from Charlotte.

"Hey," started the message. "It's just a couple of weeks till Christmas. When are you going to send us a list? Santa can't get you anything till you clue us in."

Valerie smiled. Her dad was the oldest "little boy" she had ever seen. She scrolled on down through the e-mail.

"Mom and I are headed to New York next week. More talks with New York Financial about a possible merger. We hope to take in a Broadway show or two between my meetings. Any—"

The sound of footsteps interrupted Valerie's reading, and she glanced up from the computer. To her surprise, she saw Arthur Bremer, the United States ambassador to the Vatican, step through her door, his usually sunny face gray and pale, his immaculately tailored gray suit slouching on his bony shoulders. She automatically thought of the ambassador's health. On two different occasions a doctor had cut him open to repair a leaky valve in his heart.

"Have a seat, Mr. Bremer," she said, standing and stepping around her desk. "You don't look so good." She took his elbow and steered him to the leather executive chair that sat directly opposite her square mahogany desk.

Exhaling heavily, Bremer nodded and accepted the seat.

"I'm fine," he said, his hands cupped over his ears, his fingers massaging the silver streaks that decorated his temples. "Nothing wrong with me. But it's . . . it's here . . . it's happened."

"What's here?" Valerie asked, perching on the desk next to Bremer. "What's happened?"

"The pope," muttered Bremer, still working his temples. "The pope is in the hospital. Had a stroke or something."

Valerie moved off the desk, seated herself before the computer again, and opened an Internet connection.

"Is His Holiness at Gemelli Hospital?" she asked, remembering instantly the name of the hospital that had provided health care for popes for years.

"Don't know yet. Everything's too early, still fluid. I just got a call from the Vatican, nothing official, mind you, but a friend there who wanted me to hear it from him personally."

Valerie clicked the mouse, found her links to Vatican news. Several more clicks brought her to a brief report that the pope wasn't feeling well, and Vatican medical personnel had taken him to the hospital for a thorough checkup. Quickly scanning the entire account, she found few details. Licking her lips, she faced Bremer again.

"Not much here," she said. "You expect the Vatican to take its usual stance? All quiet, no comment, that kind of thing?"

Bremer nodded, his hands off his ears now, folded in his lap. "As always, they'll say as little as possible. They don't major in public relations, not even with us."

"They're more secretive than the New York mob," agreed Valerie. "Keep everybody in the dark."

Bremer stood and went to work on the silver at his temples again. "But I don't want to stay in the dark," he said. "The State Department won't stand for it. What happens in the Catholic community is of urgency to the president."

Valerie nodded and leaned back in her seat. To this point, her sixteen months as media relations envoy to the Vatican had been quieter than a funeral home at midnight and about as exciting as doing nails in a local hair salon, a job she had actually held between her junior and senior years of high school. Nothing of real consequence had happened in Rome, absolutely nothing. The aged pope traveled and made speeches, the cardinals whispered and wondered who would replace him when he died, and the largely unseen but extremely efficient administration of the Vatican kept the small independent state called the Holy See running like a well-oiled machine. Not exactly scintillating work for a twenty-nine-year-old woman who had chosen a career in diplomacy because she loved the challenge of new and unusual circumstances.

"Let me go to the hospital," suggested Valerie. "See what I can find out."

Bremer's brow furrowed as he considered the idea.

"I'll nose around," she said gently, knowing Bremer usually worked slowly, warming to ideas like an electric stove under a pot of water.

Bremer tilted his head. "Security will be tight," he said.

"I'll work around it. Can't hurt anything."

Bremer bit his lip and Valerie held her breath. Though it saddened her to think that the pope, a man she admired in spite of her religious differences with him, had taken ill, she loved the idea of snooping around the hospital to see if she could learn anything more than what the Vatican would inevitably say.

"I guess you're right," Bremer said, finally coming to a decision. "It can't hurt. But keep a low profile. I don't want anyone complaining about you sticking your nose where it doesn't belong."

"Thank you, Mr. Ambassador," gushed Valerie, almost leaping from her seat. "They won't even know I'm there."

"Oh, they'll know you're there," Bremer said, standing also, but much more deliberately.

Grabbing his hand, Valerie shook it and smiled at him, her heart thumping rapidly.

"I'll call as soon as I can," she said, grabbing a waist-length tan jacket from a hat tree by the door and turning back to Bremer. "I'll keep you in the loop."

"You do that," Bremer said. "I want to know exactly what's happening. If the pope is really sick, the whole world is going to turn the spotlight on us. CNN, MSNBC, all the major networks will show up, the—"

"The networks?" asked Valerie, stopping in her tracks.

"You bet, the illness of a pope brings major league attention."

Valerie's arms sagged to her side, her jacket hanging at knee level in her hands. How stupid of her! Of course the media would come! In her rush to get out of the confines of the embassy and actually do something, she hadn't really thought through all the implications of the pope's supposed illness.

She lifted a finger to her cheek and unconsciously began to rub a spot just under her right ear, a scar the width and length of a fingernail. For some reason she couldn't identify, she suddenly remembered the day she had created the scar, the August morning she fell twelve feet from the magnolia tree that bordered the left side of the porch outside her home in Charlotte. The smell of the magnolia welled up in her nostrils again as she faced Bremer, and the same feeling of giddy excitement that bordered on fear washed over her with the fragrance. A tree climber since she was a toddler, she loved the sense of adventure the branches brought, the branches that beckoned her to climb higher and higher, higher and higher until she couldn't climb anymore. She was nine when she fell out of the magnolia and broke her right wrist and jabbed her right cheek on the last branch before she hit the ground, a jab that brought her six stitches and a scar that makeup could never quite completely cover.

"You okay?" asked Bremer, interrupting her musings.

"Oh yeah, just pondering it all."

Bremer grunted, his fingers moving to his temples once more. "A wise move, I'd think. As media relations envoy, you're going to get plenty of business if there's anything to all this. Now, get on over to the hospital." He gave the command as if the idea had been his all along. "And pray to God the pope doesn't die. If he does, you can forget it. Our lives—your life—will never be the same."

Valerie slipped on her jacket and headed from the office, her steps carrying her quickly down the stairs of the two-story renovated home the embassy used as its headquarters. Two minutes later, she hailed a taxi and jumped into the backseat. Perched on the edge, she told the driver to take her to the hospital. Taking a deep breath, she stared out the window and nodded, as if acknowledging the pedestrians as she passed them. The pope's illness, if it turned out to be serious, gave her a chance to climb a tree again. Whether she could do that without falling—as she had so many years ago—she didn't know. But right now she didn't care. A high branch beckoned her, and she planned to grab it.

FOUR

Eight time zones to the west, a peasant woman named Maria Sanchez crossed herself and pulled her thread-bare shawl tight around her head to ward off the damp air of the morning. Sunday had come again, and she had another mile to walk to her village church to celebrate the Mass. Spitting onto the rocky path that led down the mountain, Maria kept her sharp nose pointed south. Mutterings that no one but she and God could understand dribbled from her lips.

"O, sweet Mother of Jesus," she mumbled. "No sons, no sons, no sons." Maria shook her head and felt again the familiar pangs of guilt. Now that she had passed her fifty-fourth summer and her womanly flow had stopped, the days for bearing sons had certainly passed forever.

She shrugged, then spat again. She and Ramon had always wanted sons. But one could not see the plans of God and did not dare to question them. She had birthed five daughters, and that would have to satisfy her.

Her breathing a bit ragged from the two miles she had already traveled, Maria paused for a moment and lifted her eyes heavenward as the trail forked. The sun's warmth began to heat her shoulders, and Maria almost smiled. Though many trials now made dark shadows on her soul, the day of St. Mary's feast always gave her cause for much joy. It seemed that time and time again the Holy Mother had used the day to do memorable things in her life.

Ramon had pledged his love for her thirty-six years ago only a few hours after she had taken the Mass on this blessed day. Then three of her black-eyed daughters squalled for the first time as they came into the world on the evening of the special feast. Named after the Blessed Virgin, Maria felt a special kinship with the Mother and knew to keep her heart open to the next surprise Mary might bring her.

Muttering again, Maria crossed herself and started picking her way down the path once more. She needed the Mother now more than ever. A month ago she had coughed up a clump of blood the size of a river pebble. Though no doctor lived in Las Diegas to verify her conclusion, Maria knew as surely as she knew how to stir the fires in Ramon's loins that a tumor as ugly as a rotting rat grew in her stomach. So far she had told no one but her priest, asking him to pray for her. But someday soon all the others would have to know. Her stomach tightened against the tumor more and more each day, and her legs and arms now grew weary each evening long before she ran out of water to haul and meals to cook and threadbare clothes to stitch. Though she hated to think of it, she suspected this would be her final Mass for the Feast of St. Mary.

Grunting, Maria shook her head and forced herself to think more pleasant thoughts. In only a few more minutes, her priest would offer the Eucharist to the people of his tiny parish. Maria opened her mouth and rolled her tongue across her lips as if to taste the wine and wafer. "Mother of God, bless me," she prayed.

She trudged ahead for several more minutes, and the trail snaked ahead and down, past one curve after another. Just when it seemed that it would never end, it turned one final time around a thicket of lush green vegetation and came to a crease that opened into a clearing in the underbrush. Maria stopped in her tracks. Dead ahead, less than fifty yards farther down the incline, stood her humble village church. The building, no more than a collection of sun-baked bricks and a bare wood floor, jutted up from the ground on one of the few level spots in the forest. A steeple housing a rusty bell reached to the sky, and a porch no wider than a poor man's wagon stretched across its front.

Maria crossed herself and glanced around to see if anyone else had ventured out so early as she, but she saw no one. She pricked her ears but heard nothing. She smiled and her leathery skin seemed to drop a few of its wrinkles. Her teeth, though brown and sparse, caught the morning's sun and reflected it back into the sky. Everything was silent.

Careful not to scrape her feet on the rocky path and so disturb the quiet, Maria eased forward another twenty yards and bowed her head. She loved her church as deeply as she loved

her children. If Ramon had not stirred so much heat in her as a
young woman, she might have become one of the sisters of the
faith. But Ramon's slender body and quick smile dimmed her
thoughts of holiness, and she had traded her desires for the sis-
terhood for the favor of a man and the joy of—

A pain as sharp as a new knife cut through Maria's side, and
she doubled over and clutched her stomach. A piece of her in-
sides coughed into her throat, and she gagged. Another blow
ripped through her chest, and she stumbled to her knees. For a
second her eyes watered, and the taste of blood flooded her
tongue. She spat out the blood, and the stain of it soiled the path
at her feet. She tried to breathe but couldn't. She fell onto her
side and closed her eyes.

Her whole body clenched against the hurt in her stomach,
and she began to roll over and over on the path, the sloped de-
cline carrying her closer and closer to the church. The sun beat
down on her as she rolled, and she suddenly felt hot, so hot it
seemed the sun had decided to bake her like she baked tortillas
for Ramon to eat for supper. Sweat poured off her face, and she
let go of her stomach and yanked her shawl from her head. Her
long gray hair looped out behind her in a ponytail, and the dirt
from the trail caught in it and made it dark. Still rolling forward,
Maria cried out against the morning sky, hoping and praying
that the Blessed Virgin would hear her prayer and let her die so
the pain would stop.

Her right shoulder bounced off a rock as big as a burro's
rump, and her body recoiled, then lurched to a stop against it.
Now a new hurt throbbed in her brain as the rock cracked
against her collarbone. Another cough racked her chest and
shoved blood into her mouth, but she swallowed the clump of
tumor this time instead of spitting it out.

Dimly aware that the rolling had stopped, Maria crossed herself and closed her eyes and waited for several minutes to see if
the Death Man would take her. But she didn't die. Instead, to
her surprise, the coughing that had just wracked her body suddenly ceased, ending just as quickly as it had begun. Glad for
the momentary relief, Maria took a deep breath and silently
thanked the Blessed Mother that she still lived.

Opening her eyes, she found herself staring straight up into
the side of her church. But it wasn't sun-baked brick that she
saw staring back at her. No, it was a vision instead—the upper
half of the body of the Holy Virgin. The Mother held something
in her lap, but, focused on her face, Maria paid her hands little

attention. The Mother's eyes gazed at her, and a loving smile danced across her face.

Maria's head tingled, and the skin on her cheeks seemed to draw tighter. She stayed still, not daring to look away lest the vision disappear. The Blessed Virgin nodded slightly, and Maria read it to mean something significant should happen now. She wondered if she should move, try to get up. But that made no sense, so she remained where she lay. Not sure what else to do, she began to pray.

"Hail Mary, full of grace, the Lord is with thee."

As she finished the sentence, she suddenly realized an astonishing change had occurred in her body.

"Blessed art thou amongst women and blessed is the fruit of thy womb, Jesus."

For the first time in weeks, no pain dug at her from inside her bowels. Maria frowned. What did this mean?

"Holy Mary, Mother of God . . ."

The throb in her collarbone also ceased to pulse. The sweat on her face dried up, and she felt cooled.

"Pray for us sinners, now and at the hour of our death."

Maria started to ask the Mother what it all meant, but then realized such questions were blasphemous. One did not question the Holy Virgin unless invited to do so. One simply waited and listened.

Maria coughed, but no blood rose in her throat. Then the cough ceased and her body relaxed. Without quite knowing how, Maria suddenly understood. The Blessed Mother had healed her—just like that. One moment Maria was a few weeks short of a wooden box, the next she was healed and healthy again.

Closing her eyes, Maria crossed herself and breathed a prayer of thanksgiving. When she looked up again, the Mother had vanished, her presence fleeing faster than a fog burned away by the morning. But Maria didn't mind that the Mother had left her. She didn't mind because she knew that the tumor that had pushed bitter blood into her throat no longer grew in the dark spaces in her belly.

FIVE

Ephesus

His body limp with nervous exhaustion, Hugh McAuley slumped on his bed in the camp barracks, squeezed his head with both hands, and tried to figure out his next step. Fearful of damaging the scroll, he had read no further than the introduction. Then, anxious to report his news, he had placed the fragment back inside the broken jar, left it in the cave, extricated himself and rushed back. To his chagrin, the camp was still empty.

For almost an hour, he hadn't moved. Feeling like someone had opened up his head and stuck his brains on a stick separate from his body, he stared aimlessly at the bare walls of the barracks where he had lived for the last two months. Spartan conditions at best—military-like bunks, small square windows, cobwebs in the corners, and chalky dust on the floor. Most people would deplore such conditions. He, on the other hand, usually found them comforting somehow, the essence of a simple, if undistinguished, life.

Now, though, he found the barracks disconcerting, strange and foreign. Yet, stunned by what he had found, he continued to sit and stare, his body as inert as a tree stump. He knew time was passing, but it seemed beyond his capacity to step back into it. From outside, shadows draped across the room and fell onto his face. The change in the light level jarred him from his inertia, and he glanced at his watch, then stirred and stood up. It was time to eat. Amazingly, though, he didn't feel hungry. His appetite, normally the most active part of his body, seemed to have disappeared, and though he knew he had to be imagining things, he felt thinner than when he woke up that morning.

Standing by his bunk, McAuley wondered again what to do. Continue to wait for Hinton to return? That made sense. He stepped toward the trunk at the foot of his bed, planning to get a candy bar. Might as well eat something, even if he didn't really crave it. A frightening notion suddenly hit him. What if Hinton or someone else from the crew dropped by the excavation site before returning to camp? They would see the opening in the wall, go in and find the scroll! His moment of glory would disappear before it ever arrived!

As if jumpstarted by a bolt of lightning, McAuley shifted into action, quickly gathering several pieces of equipment from his trunk and heading back to the cavern. Once there, the task took almost an hour. But carefully, ever so carefully, he wedged himself back into the hole, picked up the broken jar and scroll, and wrapped them separately in two pieces of clean linen cloth. Then, with equal gentleness, he secured the two items—the scroll in a vacuum-sealed metal cylinder to keep it free from humidity and light and the jar in a square wood box the size of a computer case.

Satisfied that the artifacts were safe, McAuley put them in a green duffel bag, eased the bag out of the cave, and again returned to camp. It was still empty. Good, more time to chart his next move.

Tiptoeing to his barracks, he tucked and locked the treasure in the bottom of his trunk. Then, sitting down on it, he considered his options. One, he could pull Hinton aside the minute she returned and whisper his discovery into her ear. She had gorgeous ears—small and tight against her head, her blond hair pinned discreetly behind them.

For a moment he imagined himself kissing Hinton, but then he stood and walked to the square windows on the left side of the barracks. How ludicrous! Hinton would laugh at the idea of romance with him. Though she would gladly claim his work as her own, she would ignore him in every other way, just as she had since the start of this dig.

McAuley stroked his goatee as another option materialized. Why tell Hinton anything? The scroll was *his* find. He should get to test its authenticity; he should get to call the press conference and announce the verdict. The flashbulbs should pop in his face, and he should receive the lucrative fees the lecture circuit would surely bring. If everyone managed at least fifteen minutes of fame, then his had arrived. Only a fool would hand it over to Martha Hinton—an affirmative action favorite who had feminized her way to more magazine covers and front-line grants than any one human being he had ever seen. But not this time. Not if Hugh McAuley had anything to say about it!

The idea of handing his discovery to Hinton suddenly felt insane, the decision of a simple-minded professor, not the action of a competent, well-esteemed archeologist. A man with any guts at all would handle this himself. But how? What came next?

McAuley straightened his back and glanced at his watch as an unusually assertive idea crystallized in his mind. He needed to test the document before he did anything else. But to do that, he needed to move it to a proper place, a place with the right equipment.

His pulse notching up a beat, he yanked a laptop computer from beneath his bed, took it from its case, and moved to a small desk sitting in the corner of the room. It was almost six o'clock. If he wanted to do this, he needed to move quickly.

Snapping a phone line into the modem, McAuley keyed up his e-mail. Within seconds, he selected the address of one Sarah Stanley Suggs, curator for the Metropolitan Museum of Antiquities in New York City and the only real girl friend Hugh McAuley had ever had. Fortunately, even though Sarah had eventually broken off their romance and married a smart-aleck heir to a jewelry store fortune, she had remained the best friend any man could ever want. McAuley trusted her more than anyone else on earth. She could provide him the equipment he needed to do this whole thing right.

His hands shaking, McAuley fingered the computer keyboard and began to type.

Sarah,
I'm catching a plane to New York as soon as possible in the morning. I've found a piece, a fragment of something that might be outstanding. No one else knows about it. Made a decision (know I shouldn't have, but I did) to handle this myself.

He paused, trying to verbalize his next thought. A sudden inspiration came, and his fingers, more confident by the second, flew over the keyboard.

I've played by the script all my life, but the ending has always left me on the cutting floor. So, this time, I'm writing the story myself.

He really liked the way that sounded!

*I don't want to say too much at this point, but it's a scroll,
related to the Greek New Testament. If it's authentic, it's
astonishing. I've only read the first part (no time to do more),
but if it's genuine, everybody in the world will want to get
their hands on it. I don't want to say too much here, but,
Sarah, it's written from the viewpoint of Mary, the mother of
Jesus. The story of her life, can you believe it? I'm nervous as
a politician turning down a donation. I'll call you as soon as
I get there. I need to go. I'm scared, Sarah.*
                                        Hugh

Finished, he paused just a second and reread the missive. It
sounded good—excited but reasonable. He poised his finger on
the mouse, then clicked the "send" command.

Exhaling heavily, McAuley leaned back and closed his eyes.
Somewhere, deep in the recesses of his gut, under layers of excess weight, he suspected this might be his last day of anonym-
ity. Though he craved the notoriety this document would surely
bring, he feared it too. After today, the silence he loved so much,
the solitude of an empty cave and the *chisk, chisk, chisk* of his
trowel against stone might disappear forever. Ah, the price of
fame.

McAuley opened his eyes and powered down his computer. A
sheepish grin broke out on his face. Fame. The word tickled his
ears. Who cared about solitude and quiet? No magazine covers
in those.

Sitting in a plain wooden chair in a tiny rectangular space at
the back of the church that her priest used as his office, Maria
Sanchez crossed herself and placed her fingers on her belly.
Across from her sat Father Adolpho, a heavy man with a head
as bald as a baby's bottom. With great patience, Maria had
waited for the father to finish both the morning Masses before
she approached him with the story of her healing. The time had
moved as slowly as an old woman making her way up the hill to
the spring to draw water. But, thanks be to God, the minutes had
finally passed, and Maria had approached her priest and poured
out her tale. Now, she rubbed her belly and waited for Father
Adolpho to speak.

His skepticism obvious in his eyes, he scratched his head.
"This morning, you say? The vision of the Virgin appeared on the
side of the church?"

Maria nodded, certain of her facts. "Yes, she came to me, her face as clear as the moon on a night without clouds."

"And you say she smiled at you and you were healed?"

Again Maria nodded. "The Mother smiled and I felt quivery inside, then poof, the tumor disappeared. I know it, as simple as that." She crossed herself again.

"But no doctor ever verified that you were sick."

"You saw the blood I coughed up, Father, you know my illness. I asked you to pray for me months ago."

Father Adolpho scratched his head again, and Maria could see him weighing her words. Her priest, a simple man in the poorest of parishes, was not the kind to get overly excited about many things.

"Visions of the Mother seem to be happening more frequently," he said, dropping his eyes and muttering under his breath. "The nearer we get to the new millennium, here a vision, there a vision, here a healing, there a healing." He lifted his face and spoke to Maria again. "We'll need a doctor to check you," he said.

"The doctor will find nothing."

Adolpho chewed on his lip for a moment. Then a sparkle Maria had never seen flashed into his eyes, and he leaned forward and touched her elbow. Maria read the sparkle and didn't like what it told her.

"I'll need to tell the Bishop immediately," he said. "That's required when anyone reports a miracle. Is there anything else you can tell me about your vision? Anything at all?"

Maria closed her eyes and replayed the experience in her mind, seeing once again the blessed face of Mary. For several minutes, the whole episode returned to her—the fall, the pain in her collarbone, the vision, and the disappearance of the pain in both her shoulder and her belly. It had all happened so fast, but she would never forget it, not one speck of it. She opened her eyes.

"The Mother held something in her hands," she said. "I paid it no mind at the time. But it was round, like a . . . like a . . . like a cloth wrapped up in a circle, not too big."

"The baby Jesus wrapped in warm blankets?"

"No, I saw no baby, I am sure of it. I know a baby in a mother's arms when I see one." She couldn't help but smile.

Father Adolpho rubbed his head. Then he stood and stepped out of the tiny cubicle. A few moments later he reappeared, a roll of paper towels in his hands. He tore off several sheets of the paper and handed them to Maria.

"Show me," he said. "Show me what it looked like."

Maria took the sheets of paper and rolled them into a coil. When she had finished, she held up her creation. The paper, wrapped spherically, looked something like the bread she rolled around the beans she often served Ramon for dinner. Adolpho stared at the paper, the skin on his forehead furrowed right down the center.

"I don't know what this is," he frowned.

"Neither do I," said Maria. "Does it matter?"

"Sure, everything about a vision matters." He jammed his hands onto the top of his head and squeezed shut his eyes. "Is there anything else, anything else about the vision?"

Maria genuflected and said a prayer that she would remember everything. Wanting to please her priest, she again shut her eyes and focused. It all came back to her, every second as plain as if stamped upon the inside of her skull. She watched it all once more, then opened her eyes.

"A stick," she said. "A stick was stuck inside the circled cloth. Like the wood we use on our banners in the church."

"Show me," said Adolpho, scanning the small office, looking for something to use as a prop. He grabbed a pencil from the single drawer in his desk.

"It was longer than a pencil," said Maria. "It stuck out on both ends of the cloth."

"Hold on." Father Adolpho hurriedly left the room, then reappeared within seconds holding a worn broom. With a snap, he wedged the broom against the wall and cracked it with his foot. "Show me now," he said.

"That's too thick," said Maria.

"Use it anyway!" he insisted.

Not wanting to be disrespectful to her priest, Maria took half of the broken broom, inserted it into the wrapped paper, and rolled the paper up around it. Finished, she handed the creation back to Adolpho. For several moments, he studied it but said nothing. Maria waited, still and quiet. Suddenly, Adolpho's eyes sparkled again.

"A scroll," he said. "It looks like a scroll."

Maria nodded, but not from understanding. She knew nothing of such things as scrolls. All she knew was that the Mother had healed her belly. As for the rest, what did that matter?

———

When Hugh McAuley hit the "send" button on his computer,

the e-mail addressed to Sarah Stanley Suggs bored through the electronic cable into a central server for the archeological crew headed by Dr. Martha Hinton. There, a security program picked it up, scanned its contents, then launched it into cyberspace toward Mrs. Suggs.

Unknown to McAuley, however, the same security program that scanned the message also copied it three times. Each of these copies then darted through the electronic world toward preset destinations.

By the time McAuley had showered and changed into clean clothes, packed a few belongings, and climbed with the scroll into a truck, the computers of three people—Martha Hinton, her sponsor for the dig, and the head of the World Archeological Society—had automatically downloaded the message. By the time he arrived at a nondescript hotel about ten miles from the Adnan Menderes Airport, rented a room, made a reservation for a 6:15 A.M. flight that would start him toward New York, and lay down to sleep, someone in each location had read what he intended for Sarah Suggs' eyes only.

As a result, by the time McAuley awoke, dressed, and walked through the still dark morning to his truck for the drive to the airport, the story of his discovery had passed through enough hands and into enough ears to make the idea of keeping it a secret quite silly. Overnight, a number of phones and faxes and computers in the archeological world buzzed with the story that a Dr. Hugh McAuley, heretofore remarkable only for his heft and bad skin, had found something potentially extraordinary.

McAuley, of course, had no clue about any of this. Which explained the really surprised look that broke out on his face when a speck of a man with hands the size of a cat's paws and a mustache as thick as a dark sock stepped from behind his truck, jammed a strange-looking weapon into his fleshy side, and pulled the trigger.

PART TWO

No one, having put his hand to the plow, and looking back, is fit for the kingdom of God.

Jesus, St. Luke 9:62

To say yes, you have to sweat and roll up your sleeves and plunge both hands into life up to the elbows.

Jean Anouilh

SIX

Standing against the wall as still and straight as a palace guard, Father Michael Del Rio sucked in his breath and scanned the extraordinary scene unfolding at a magnificent mahogany table barely twenty feet away. Though he had stayed up almost all night, much of it in conversation with Roca, and it wasn't quite seven A.M. yet, he felt anything but sleepy. His well-toned muscles were juiced with adrenaline, and if someone had asked him to scale the walls of the Sistine Chapel with his bare hands, he felt as if he could have complied.

For obvious reasons, he had decided to postpone his return to America for a few days. With no classes to teach until mid-January, nothing pressing called him home.

Roca had agreed with his decision. "You will learn much through this," he said. "And I may need your help."

Though unsure how Roca might need him, Michael had no doubt he needed to stay. Only an idiot would walk out on such drama, and though he was many things, an idiot wasn't one of them.

Now, his hands tingling with excitement, Michael surveyed the room. A row of high-backed chairs, each of them inlaid with exquisite murals of former popes, surrounded the rectangular, forty-foot table. In each chair sat a man dressed in a black cassock with a scarlet sash, wearing a pectoral cross and a gold ring, some with sapphires and some without. Each also wore the scarlet zucchetto, the famous red hat that came with his station as a cardinal. Most of the men at the table were members of the Curia, and all were cardinals.

Surrounding the cardinals, some in smaller chairs against

the wall and others standing like Michael, a host of assistants and lesser church officials waited for the meeting to officially begin. As if collectively struck mute, no one spoke—least of all Michael. He was too nervous to speak. Roca had not asked anyone whether or not he could attend this meeting.

"You will come as my assistant," said his uncle. "With things in such a state, no one will question you." Anxious about the protocol, Michael stayed still as a mannequin and equally as quiet.

His attention directed to the head of the table, Michael watched as the Secretary of the cardinals, His Eminence Cardinal Nelson Randuhar, the first African secretary in the history of the Church, leafed through a stack of papers on his right. Everything about Randuhar was long—his height of six and a half feet, his wolfish cheeks and chin, and his fingers, thin as the strands in a spider web and longer than pencils.

Studying the man, Michael wondered how he had ascended to the position he held. He knew he couldn't simply write it off as the reward of his race. To do so minimized the mixture of intellect, ambition, and energy that one must surely possess to rise so high in Vatican politics. Though no one spoke of Randuhar as a successor to His Holiness, most did speak of him as a man of significant abilities. His silver-gray hair gave him an air of nobility, and those who knew him well often spoke of his unflappable demeanor and rock-solid devotion to his convictions.

Michael wondered how Randuhar would handle the pressure he undoubtedly felt, the confusing circumstances of the pope's illness. He knew the Church had plans, spelled out in the "apostolic constitution" to deal with the death of a pope. But what about a long incapacitation? Did the Church have an elaborate contingency plan for that? Or would these men handle the situation ad hoc, believing in the leadership of the Spirit of God to see them through the maze of choices that lay ahead?

Michael wasn't sure. Even to one such as he—a veteran of a Catholic childhood in Missouri, a priest for over a decade, and a Biblical scholar of some international reputation—the ways and means of Mother Church often seemed a mystery, a series of twists and intrigues that caused even the most deeply immersed to occasionally lose his way. Could Randuhar, an outsider from Zaire for most of his life, negotiate the corridors of such chaos? Again, Michael had no clue.

Randuhar finished with the papers and raised his head. An assistant to his left lifted a hand. Though no one was talking, the room instantly became even quieter, almost tomblike.

Michael heard a thump, thump, thump, then realized it was the sound of his own heart. He glanced away from Randuhar for a moment and saw Roca just two seats to the Secretary's right, his black eyes blank. He tried to catch his uncle's attention, but Roca ignored him.

Michael allowed himself to take a breath, mentally gearing himself to translate from Italian to English. Randuhar cleared his throat, and Michael shifted his attention back to the regal black man.

"Before wee begin, I mussst ask for our deliberations to remaain under the seal," began the Secretary, his voice deep and measured, each word stretched out, seemingly as long as the man's body. "We don't want the public to become distraught over this newsss. And we don't want the media to begin unwarranted specuuulation. Such nonsense will only create more confuuusion. So the extent of our pontiff's condition remains a seeecret."

He paused to let the gravity of his statement sink deep. To declare their deliberations "under the seal" meant it became as confidential as the words that a priest heard in a confessional.

"But what will we tell the media?" shouted a voice from the end of the room.

"We will do as we always do with them," said Randuhar. "We will tell the truth, but only the truth we want to tell. Our communications officers will put out a simple statement: 'His Holiness is weary from his travels and has postponed his appointments for the next few days.' That's all we will say. Are we agreed?"

Michael watched to see if anyone would challenge Randuhar. No one did. They knew how this worked and kept confidences well. It was part of their training. At times, the Church worked best when it kept quietest.

Seeing no dissent, Randuhar brought the tips of his fingers together in front of his mouth, then the palms. The men in the room faced him directly, their eyes concerned.

"This is a most grave hour," the Secretary began again. "Our beloved pontiff remains critically ill. According to his physician, who is doing all he can, he cannot speak. The physician tells me he has no way to know what the next few hours will bring. So, we have gathered here to make plans for the operation of the Holy Church until we get a clearer picture of the future."

Randuhar paused and looked around the table. No one moved. A grave hour indeed.

Randuhar steepled his hands again, then continued. "Our

concern right now has to focus on our beloved pope. Even the best of our medical technologies have their limits. We know that better than the doctors. But faith has no limits. So, today, and until His Holiness is well again, we will practice faith." He paused to catch his breath. Small beads of sweat welled up below his eyes.

The room remained still, and Michael wondered how so many men could stay so rigid for so long. His nose began to itch, and he wanted to scratch it but dared not. The cardinals all seemed stunned, as immobile as if someone had poured liquid oxygen onto them, turning them into ice crystals. A sense of the absurd came over Michael, and he suddenly wanted to shout, to jump into the center of the room and yell, scream, anything to make someone react. Swallowing the urge, he watched as Cardinal Randuhar shifted in his chair, his gray head tilting up ever so slightly. The movement made his long face seem even longer.

"We will continue our around-the-clock prayer vigil," continued the Secretary. "Please plan your schedules so you can participate. It is my belief that the expertise of the medical community, the strength of our beloved pontiff, the prayers of the believers of the Church, and the intercession of the Blessed Mother will enable our pope to survive this episode and serve the Lord for many years yet to come." He spoke the words matter-of-factly, his tone giving no room for disputation.

To Randuhar's left, a diminutive man in thin-rimmed glasses whose red hat seemed to swallow his head, spoke up in a voice no bigger than his skull. "His Holiness has cheated death more than once already; he can do it again. One of his doctors once told me he's tougher than a piece of English beef."

The remark sparked a wave of laughter, a wave made stronger by the heavy tension in the room. Michael noted the affirming nods the cardinals gave their elfish brother, thankful acknowledgments for the quip that broke the unbearable silence and gave them all permission to relax.

Though he didn't know the diminutive cardinal well, Michael recognized him as Antonio Marchino, archbishop of Milan and one of the most powerful men in the Curia. He had a face as round as a nickel, a nose that seemed to disappear when he talked, and a head of black hair thicker than a shoe brush. Known equally for his liberalism and witticisms, Marchino often clashed with the more traditional members of the pope's inner circle, including Roca.

"God will see him into the new year!" called a cardinal from the end of the table, echoing Marchino's sentiments.

"Our pope is too tough for death to take him!" shouted another. "He's been knocked down a million times, but never out!"

"His Holiness will outlive all of us!" added a fourth.

For several moments, the room sounded more like a football team celebrating a bowl victory than an enclave of the most powerful men in the Catholic Church talking about their leader. Michael, who had stood in three post-season locker rooms after Fighting Irish triumphs, marveled at the willingness of the cardinals to so quickly forget the gravity of the pope's illness. Were these men really so easily dissuaded from their concerns, or did they simply want to deny the realities of what they faced if the pontiff died in the next few hours? Michael shook his head, alternately amused and amazed at the scene.

He turned toward Roca, curious to gage his uncle's reaction. As he expected, Roca sat still and quiet, refusing to participate in the giddy display that had captured the rest of his brothers. Though seemingly alone in his serious demeanor, Roca nonetheless appeared at ease, his body relaxed, attentive, but not anxious. All around him the hubbub dimmed, the room became quiet again, the emotion slowly ebbing from the crowd.

Randuhar cleared his throat as if to begin a new statement. But Roca suddenly interrupted him, rocking forward and placing both elbows on the table. His voice was solid, but not rigid as he spoke.

"I dislike being the one to say this," he began. "I know you will think me too pessimistic. But that seems to be part of my calling." He paused and gave the others enough time to smile at his self-deprecation. His no-nonsense reputation was well known. Calling attention to it showed that he well knew what others thought of him and did not begrudge them their opinions.

"But even at that risk," Roca continued, "let me say what I know all of us feel, at least to some extent. Certainly, we pray for the full recovery of our beloved pontiff. No one else can lead us as he can, especially as we face the monumental work of guiding the Church in this difficult time in history. But . . ." Roca paused and searched the faces of his fellow cardinals. "What if he does not recover? Or perhaps equally as difficult, what if he remains as he is—alive but unable to communicate? In either case, we have huge decisions to make—decisions that will affect the Church for years to come. Though we know we should not make any hurried decisions, we cannot avoid the discussion of these matters. To do so is to be irresponsible. We have to make plans for the worst—as well as for the best."

He stopped talking and scanned the room, his black eyes a probe into the hearts of the men who sat around him. Watching their reactions, Michael knew that the cardinals fell into several camps when it came to an opinion about his uncle. A few deplored him. On the other hand, a slightly greater number loved him. Most, though, fell into a more central block—the group that both feared and admired him. Such was always the case with powerful men.

Regardless of their opinions, though, Michael saw that Roca's words had frozen them all into place. One man cleared his throat. Several studied their hands. A few sighed and sank in their seats.

Randuhar broke the silence, his voice still smooth and slow. "We all share your concern, Cardinal Roca, but perhaps it is a bit premature. Perhaps we should wait a few days until we get a clearer picture of our pontiff's prognosis."

Roca nodded. "Of course, Your Eminence, I am not trying to rush anything. But I simply don't want us to act as if nothing has changed. We have so little time to complete plans for the New Year's Eve Mass. Work for it is already well underway. But now, without the pontiff's participation, many of the plans will have to be put on hold. As we well know, his decisions have a direct bearing—"

"Surely we can plan a Mass!" interrupted Marchino, his high voice tinged with the faintest note of sarcasm. "Even one on this scale, without the full participation of our pope. We already know what he wants—he's made those plans well in advance. With his staff helping, we can—"

"We don't know the most important thing he wants," Roca said, returning the interruption.

Michael sensed the temperature rise in the room. Though not sure, it looked to him as if a bit of red appeared on Roca's cheeks. In an instant he knew what was happening. Roca and Marchino were already at war for the hearts and minds of the cardinals sitting at the table. If the pope died from his illness, these men would join the rest of the cardinals from around the globe in a holy enclave that would elect the next prelate of the Church. The exchange between Roca and Marchino marked the beginning of the struggle to see who would become the next successor to the apostle Peter, the Vicar of Christ on Earth. Though nothing guaranteed that either of the two men would win the papacy, both would certainly play a most significant role in deciding who did.

Roca continued to speak. "We don't know if he plans to issue a papal decree—"

"Of course we know!" insisted Marchino. "We've known for two years. The decree is as good as done. His Holiness has been considering this for—"

"But His Holiness has made no official decision yet," countered the man immediately to Roca's left, a loyal protégé Michael recognized from previous conversations in Roca's chambers. "His mind remains open to—"

"Enough," interrupted Randuhar, his voice firm, but not angry. "This is not the time or place for this discussion. Whether or not the pontiff declares the Holy Mother the official Co-Redemptrix is out of our control. So we will not talk of it further until the Holy Father's condition and prognosis become clear. Are we agreed?"

All eyes turned to Roca. Michael noted the disappearance of the color in his uncle's cheeks. Roca bowed his head only slightly, but it was enough for the other men in the room to see it. Apparently he had decided, at least for the moment, not to challenge Randuhar. No one expected Randuhar, a man who always sought the middle road, to become the successor to the pontiff. Better to show him a certain respect, use him to win over those like him who naturally sought the way of conciliation.

"Agreed," said Roca.

Randuhar faced Marchino. He bowed his smallish head. "Agreed."

Randuhar stood from the table and the others followed. "Then let us conclude our meeting in prayer," he said.

In concert, everyone bowed, the cardinals removing their caps. Michael started to close his eyes, but then felt someone watching him. Instinctively, he glanced toward Roca and saw a crease of a smile on his uncle's face. As Randuhar started to pray, Roca winked at Michael, then closed his eyes.

As Michael followed suit, the meaning of the wink dawned on him. Whether wittingly or not, Randuhar had given Roca precisely what he wanted—a decision to quell official discussion of the Marian Decree. Though Marchino wanted others to see the decree as a *fait accompli*, Roca wanted it stopped in its tracks. And what better way to accomplish that than to forbid others from talking about it? Randuhar had just done exactly that!

Though Randuhar continued to pray, Michael barely noticed.

His mind was fixed on palace intrigue, and he once again found himself marveling at his uncle. Could Roca perhaps become pope? His background and experience certainly fit the profile of what most experts said the next pontiff should bring to the task. An Italian with experience in both the parish and the Curia, he was capable in several languages and young enough to be modern but not so young that his tenure would last forever. Did he truly have the papacy in his sights? Was that what he wanted?

As Randuhar's prayer concluded, Michael wondered just how long Roca, and perhaps even Randuhar as well, had been planning for this exact moment to unfold.

SEVEN

EPHESUS

Her blond hair pushed through the opening in the back of her baseball cap, the collar of her brown leather jacket turned up, and her blue jeans tucked neatly into a pair of black laced boots, Martha Hinton sprinted out of room 117 and rushed to Hugh McAuley's truck.

She jerked open the door, quickly scanned the cab, and ransacked the glove compartment. Finding nothing helpful, she jumped from the truck and faced Buster Ridings, the junior member of her archeological crew and, therefore, the one she had conscripted to serve as her driver. She had been up all night searching for McAuley, and Ridings, obviously wary of her frustration, stepped back a pace.

"Where is he?" she demanded, pulling a filterless cigarette from her jacket, lighting it, and sucking a big puff from it. "You said he was at this hotel!"

Ridings studied his boots. "He *was* at the hotel. Still is as far as the desk clerk is concerned."

On the verge of losing her temper, Hinton glared at him. She didn't have time for any of this wasted motion. Too many hours had passed already, and, for all she knew, McAuley had betrayed her five ways from Sunday.

She had returned to camp just before midnight. More than a little drunk after a day of margaritas and loud music, she had quickly dressed for bed. But then, just when she was snuggled under the covers, Ridings had interrupted her to report that McAuley wasn't in his bunk. Thinking nothing of it at first, she sent Ridings away.

"Check the excavation site," she said. "If there's a cave

nearby, McAuley's usually in it." She dozed off.

Less than thirty minutes later, Ridings returned and woke her. Taking one look at his face, she rolled out of bed. "What is it?" she asked.

"I . . . don't . . . don't exactly know," Ridings stammered. "But . . . well, you need to come to the cave."

Twenty minutes later—royally hacked off but curious, she slid into the hole that McAuley had uncovered earlier in the day. A hurried examination of the space told her all she needed to know. Easing out, she dusted off her pants and blouse, stood, and faced Ridings. "He found something," she said. "Something he thinks is important."

"And now he's gone," agreed Ridings.

"Any idea where?"

"No clue."

"Anybody in particular he might contact if he found something valuable?"

"Nobody he ever mentioned. McAuley isn't exactly the sociable type; you know what I mean?"

"You think he called someone?"

Ridings shrugged, and Hinton made a mental note to go through the phone logs. Though it would probably take a few days to get the information, any calls McAuley made would show up in phone company records.

Hinton checked her watch. Just after one A.M. "You call the airport," she commanded Ridings. "Check the schedules for flights to the States. I can't imagine McAuley going anywhere else. If he's in a hurry to get out of Turkey, he'll need to fly."

"If he hasn't already left."

Hinton snapped her eyes at Ridings, and he backed off, his head down.

Back in camp, she hustled to McAuley's bunk, pulled the neatly tucked corners loose from the bed, ripped off the sheets, and flipped the mattress upside down. But she found nothing. She moved to his trunk and saw it was unlocked.

Her slender fingers moving fast, Hinton plowed through the contents of the trunk, noting that McAuley had left behind several changes of clothes, an extra pair of boots, and a stack of books. Obviously, he had left in a hurry. She spotted a computer battery lying in the bottom of the trunk.

His computer! Hustling to her office, she jerked a chair to her desk and keyed up her computer screen. Within seconds, she brought up the security software she had installed for just such possibilities as this. Never one to leave anything to chance if she could help it, she had loaded the program to copy to her files every e-mail sent by anyone in her crew. Though she knew McAuley didn't use e-mail very much, she still needed to make sure.

Breathing rapidly, she didn't hesitate when the screen asked for McAuley's password. A conscientious boss, she knew the password of every person in her charge. The computer clicked, then beeped and whirred. A second later, the record of Hugh McAuley's e-mail flashed onto her screen.

He had sent only two messages in the last four weeks. One was a response to a question from an archeology student in Phoenix. The second one was a note to Sarah Stanley Suggs. Sucking on a cigarette, Hinton quickly read the message.

She rocked back in her chair and grabbed her ponytail behind her baseball cap. Tugging the ponytail around and under her chin, she felt her stomach flip. Slowly, she shook her head. Of all people, she hadn't expected this from Hugh McAuley. A middle-aged nobody, an elephant minus a trunk and about ten pounds, a—

She heard a knock on her door. "It's open."

Ridings stepped inside. "Did he send an e-mail?" he asked, indicating the computer screen.

Hinton sat up straight, then hit the "close" icon on the program. "Uh, no, nothing here," she lied, pushing herself from her chair. "What did you find out about flights?"

"There's a 6:15 headed to New York," he said. "I told the attendant I was Hugh McAuley and had lost my ticket. Wanted to make sure I was on the passenger list. The woman verified that I was."

Hinton smiled widely. "Good job," she said. "Get the jeep. We'll go to the terminal and stop him before he gets on that plane."

"It's barely two," said Ridings, obviously preferring to wait a couple of hours before leaving, maybe catch a bit of sleep.

Hinton inhaled a long drag of smoke. The airport was no more than an hour and a half away. But she knew she wouldn't sleep if she stayed in camp. Besides, McAuley might be at the airport already, asleep in the terminal, his big carcass taking up half an acre of floor space. The sooner she knew where he was, the better. If he did indeed possess what his e-mail indicated, she wanted to get her hands on it immediately.

"Get the jeep," she said, her mind made up. "If McAuley isn't there when we get there, we'll eat breakfast, then wait for him to show up."

"Any idea what he found?"

"Just get the jeep."

But they didn't find him at the airport—not when they arrived at four A.M. and not at six-fifteen when his flight left either. To Hinton's disbelief, McAuley never showed.

Fighting panic and not sure where else to look, she and Ridings spent the next two hours phoning every hotel within a ten-mile radius of the airport, hoping against hope that McAuley had registered somewhere for the night, thinking that maybe he had simply overslept and missed his flight. To her relief, they finally found one where a Hugh McAuley had registered. The attendant remembered him—a big man with a pock-marked face.

"Yes, he is here," said the clerk over the phone. "Room 117."

But he wasn't in the room when they arrived. Tangled bed covers and a wet sink and shower indicated he had slept there. Apparently though, he had packed his belongings, such as they were, and left. Hinton and Ridings carefully picked through the room, examining it closely. But they found nothing to indicate what had happened to McAuley.

Now, standing by McAuley's truck, Hinton took another puff from her cigarette and stared at her driver.

"I'm open to ideas," she said sarcastically.

"He couldn't have gone far on foot," Ridings offered.

"Maybe he took a taxi."

"But where? He didn't go to the airport."

"When's the next flight to the States?"

"If he's headed to New York, not until three."

"We could call to see if he's on it."

"I already did. He's not ticketed, at least not yet."

Hinton thought a second. "Then we'll just need to wait," she said. "Go back to the terminal about one. Then see if he shows up for the three o'clock plane."

For several moments, neither of them spoke. Then Ridings cleared his throat and shuffled his feet.

"Speak up," Hinton said. "Something's bugging you."

Ridings grunted. "Well, I was just thinking, you know . . . if he found something important, maybe . . . well, maybe someone else knows and . . . well, maybe something happened to him to keep him off his flight."

"I thought of that," she said. "And I guess it's possible. But how could anyone else know that he found something, or what it might be? No one would bother him unless they were sure he had something valuable."

Ridings shrugged. "Just a thought. What now?"

Hinton stared at the sky as if searching the heavens for answers. Her breath, white in the chilly morning, disappeared into the clear air. Did anyone else know about the document McAuley had found? She considered the possibility, then dismissed it.

But what if McAuley had made a phone call? Could someone have tapped into it? But why? Why tap phones on a routine archeological dig? It made no sense. She thought of the security program on her computer. Did anyone else know about it? Had someone hacked into it? But who? And why? No answers came readily to mind, so she focused again on the matter at hand. If McAuley had indeed found what he told Suggs he had found, then she had to locate him. If she didn't, then nothing she had ever done mattered one bit.

This discovery, if authentic, made history. This one pushed the Dead Sea Scrolls to the back pages. This one relegated King Tut to the dustbin of history. *Time* would plaster her face on the cover. Larry King would interview her. The president would call to offer congratulations. She simply couldn't let this chance slip through her fingers.

Her whole life had prepared her for this—her Ph.D. at Hebrew University in Jerusalem; her untiring work at isolated digs all over the world. She knew what people said about her, how they resented her quick climb up the professional ladder, how they tried to explain her success by pointing to her sparkling green eyes, her quickness with a sound bite, and her history as a teenage cover girl. But, even worse for those who disliked her for her advantages that had nothing to do with archeology, she had gained the spotlight for her expertise as well.

On her very first dig she had uncovered a small piece of readable papyrus at a site outside of Jericho in Israel. That discovery put her on the front cover of *Archeological Digest*. With that feather in her cap, she quickly became the head of her own archeological team. An expert with modern technology, she had made a specialty out of using sophisticated tools to reexamine excavation sites that others had previously explored. Particularly, she had focused on digs finished just after World War II. More than once she had found significant artifacts undiscovered by her predecessors.

It didn't take long for the rich to tab her as their "archeologist du jour." Old men who wanted to share a magazine cover with the amazing Dr. Martha Hinton doled out huge sums of money to sponsor her work, and universities far and wide clamored for her to grace their lectureships with her stunning presence. Everyone loved her.

Everyone, that is, except those who labored with her in the trenches. Her success made them jealous. But she couldn't worry about that now. Right now, she had a more significant concern. If she didn't find McAuley, everything she had ever achieved would crumble. The people in her crew reported to her. McAuley had no right to steal this prize! To do so violated every tenet of the archeological community.

She would make him pay, Hinton decided, crushing her cigarette butt into the ground beneath her boot. She would track him to the ends of the earth if necessary, take the scroll from him, and make it her own. Then, as systematically as a blender crunching walnuts, she would grind Hugh McAuley and his naked ambition into tiny bits of dust.

As she faced Ridings again, a realization suddenly came to her. At least one other person, maybe two, might know of McAuley's disappearance. "I want you back at the airport just in case," she told Ridings, hurriedly. "Though I don't think you'll find him there."

"Where you headed?"

"Don't worry about me. I have some calls to make."

Thirty minutes later, Hinton dropped Ridings at the airport terminal and headed her jeep toward the Izmir International Hotel. She had some calls to make, but she didn't want to place them on a cell phone.

EIGHT

Hugh McAuley regained consciousness slowly, his mind clearing grudgingly from the fog that enshrouded it. His head pounded, and he desperately needed a drink of water. His tongue, always thick, felt as heavy as a cow's udder. Forcing his eyes open, he raised his head and looked around. He was lying facedown on a concrete floor. Rolling over, he sat up, pressed his back against the stone wall that surrounded him, and checked his watch. Monday, just after six P.M.

He licked his lips, then heard his stomach rumble. Apparently, he hadn't eaten in a while. The day was a blur, a blank page with no beginning and no end. Puzzled, he scanned the room blankly, trying to recall what had happened. The walls were bare and dull brown, with no windows. The room, no more than twice his body length in any direction, nonetheless had a high ceiling—at least ten feet—from which a panel of tubular lights buzzed loudly, making his head hurt even worse. To his right he spotted a lidless commode. A cot sat opposite the commode, a dingy white sheet tucked under its corners. To the right of the bed he saw a door, a black steel rectangle with no knob on the inside. A square window the size of a playing card centered the top third of the door, providing the only break in the otherwise claustrophobic cubicle. Was he in a basement of some kind? Or the inner room of a larger building?

He took a deep breath and licked his lips, wishing for a drink of water. But there wasn't a sink in the room, and he sure didn't plan to drink from the toilet—at least not yet.

Fighting his nerves, McAuley pushed up and tried to stand, but weakness gripped his legs, and he sagged back down. The taste of rust soured his mouth, and his headache worsened. Where was he? He leaned against the wall and tried to focus. Gradually, bits and pieces of the morning came back. He remembered a small thin man with tiny hands, the hands holding a . . . a weapon of some kind . . . a gun? Should he be dead?

His fingers moving quickly, he inspected the place on his side where the man had touched the weapon to his skin, searching for the bullet hole he expected to find there. But where was the blood? He checked his fingers but found none.

A dim memory boiled up. The weapon hadn't exploded into his flesh, as a bullet would have. Instead, it had shocked him, pouring a sizzle of hot current into his side. The electric shock had knocked him to the ground and sent him into convulsions. A stun gun?

McAuley touched his side again and winced as his fingers found the spot where the probe had jolted his skin. It had to be a stun gun, he decided. Nothing else made any sense.

He exhaled heavily and closed his eyes. Okay, a stun gun. But why? Why would anyone kidnap him?

Suddenly, as if jolted once again with the stun gun, McAuley heaved himself up from the floor and staggered over to the bed. Jerking off the mattress, he searched for the scroll he had just remembered, knowing all the while that the search was useless. Whoever abducted him had obviously taken the scroll and the jar that came with it. Why else would anyone kidnap Hugh McAuley, a man of no wealth and even less reputation, a man no one would ransom and few, if any, would even miss?

The mattress on the floor, McAuley fell to his knees to check beneath the bed. As he did, he heard the unmistakable creak of metal. The door! Using the bed as a crutch, he forced himself up and faced the front of the room. A man no taller than a broom handle and barely thicker stepped inside the door, motioning him back with a pistol both larger and darker than the weapon he had previously used. The man wore beige army fatigues and a black beret. The color of the beret matched that of his mustache—a thick oiled rope over his lip.

McAuley backed up against the wall, his fists clenched at his sides, his heart pumping at full speed. He felt woozy and wondered if he would faint. *What an imbecile*, he thought. What a weak-kneed, lily-livered coward he turned out to be! For once in his life he had found something worth noting, but then had lost it before a single day had passed. He deserved it if this pint-sized terrorist shot him on the spot!

"You are awake," said his kidnapper, his voice clipped and slightly British in accent. "Good, that's good. I was not sure of the dosage. You are a man full of size." He opened his arms as if to encompass an elephant. "I am glad I did not overdo the task."

"What did you do to me?" McAuley asked, surprised he could even speak.

"A taser, an electric stun weapon. Then a bit of sedative to make you unconscious."

McAuley let the notion sink in for a moment, then asked the obvious question. "Who are you?"

The man motioned toward the bed with his pistol. "Sit down Dr. McAuley, and I will perhaps answer a few of your questions."

Glad to get off his shaky legs, McAuley quickly obeyed.

His kidnapper stood over him, the gun at his hip, but still poised. "You can call me Yoseph," he said. "Though my name is not important."

"What do you want from me?"

"Such a tedious question for a man of your intellect. Surely, you know the answer."

"You took the scroll." Thinking of the discovery gave McAuley a shot of unfamiliar confidence. Any man who found something so valuable wasn't a total waste. Maybe he could get through this, talk Yoseph into letting him go. If not . . . well, Yoseph was alone and he was so small—

"Of course I took it."

"Where is it? You haven't—"

"It's safe, believe me. Well guarded."

"How did you find out about it?"

Yoseph chuckled and perched himself on the edge of the commode seat, his gun never wavering. "You ask many questions, Dr. McAuley. But I'm sure I should expect as much. A scientist such as yourself, you make a living asking questions."

"But you didn't answer me. How did—?"

Yoseph threw up his hands, palms outward. "A simple matter for one like me who pays attention to such things. You sent an e-mail. The right eyes, or the wrong ones based on your viewpoint, managed to see it. Through that one it came to me. I am—how do you say it?—'an entrepreneur.' I pay people to keep me informed of all the important news in my territory. As simple as that."

"Others know?"

Again, Yoseph chuckled. "I don't know how many, but yes, others surely know. Computer mail is so easy to steal. That's why I had to work quickly before someone else found you."

Stunned, McAuley rubbed his goatee for several seconds. If what Yoseph said was true, then any number of people might know about the scroll by now. Which meant someone should be looking for him, someone who could rescue him! But then another possibility dawned. If Yoseph wanted him for the wrong reasons, so might others.

What a mess! A bead of sweat rolled down the underside of his arms. Trying to control himself, he focused again on his kidnapper.

"Are you a collector?" he asked, his voice less steady now.

Yoseph laughed, his gun bouncing in his little hand. "Not exactly. Collectors don't usually kidnap to get what they want. That would be too . . . uncivilized. No, I don't collect anything, not to keep anyway. I'm more of a conduit, you might say, a pipeline for artifacts of all kinds: paintings, jewelry, antiques, anything that others want to buy or to sell. I bring these treasures into my possession, then sell them to the one who will pay the most. I am a businessman, nothing more, nothing less."

McAuley nodded, trying to figure a way out of his predicament. An idea came to him. Maybe Yoseph would respect courage, see it as a badge of honor. "But businessmen don't kidnap to obtain what they want," he said. "Not where I come from."

Yoseph tweaked his mustache. "This may be so, but we are not where you come from, now are we?"

McAuley's pulse rate notched up again as he realized he had no idea where he was. More than twelve hours had passed since his abduction. In twelve hours, a person could travel a long way. Who knew how far? He had been unconscious the whole time. "Then tell me where I am," he said.

Yoseph smiled. "No need to concern yourself with that. You are safe. That's all you need to know."

A drop of sweat fell onto McAuley's lips, and his stomach growled loudly. He didn't know if it was tension or hunger. Swallowing hard, he kept his eyes on Yoseph's gun. But then a comforting realization hit him, and he unclenched his fists and took a deep breath. If Yoseph planned to kill him, he would already have done so.

"Why didn't you kill me?" he asked, feeling slightly more confident.

Yoseph shrugged, stood again, and eased back against the door. "Like I said, I'm a businessman. I need you to help me determine the value of the scroll. If it is authentic, it is, of course, priceless. But I cannot tell such things."

"Neither can I without testing. For that I'll need special equipment."

Yoseph waved his hand. "Oh, I'll sell it before any of that happens. I've already sent out the word. By Sunday, a number of bidders will make their offers."

"But how will you know what is reasonable without testing?"

"Please, Dr. McAuley, think it through. I can't keep such an item long enough to do testing. Where would I get the necessary equipment? And how could I protect myself for such a long time? No, you see, I won't ask for what it would bring if it turns out to be authentic. My price will come from the *possibility* of its authenticity. And you will guide me as I set that price."

"What happens to me after you sell it?"

Yoseph played with his mustache for a second, then smiled. "Not to worry, Dr. McAuley. I will let you go when I have sold this treasure. I am not a harsh man. I avoid killing unless it becomes absolutely necessary."

"So you're a thief, but not a murderer."

Yoseph's eyes narrowed, and he moved away from the door and closer to McAuley. The gun, just slightly higher than McAuley's eye level, seemed huge, the size of a cannon about to explode. When Yoseph spoke, his voice lost its British civility and his words spewed from gritted teeth.

"Don't speak to me of thievery, Dr. Hugh McAuley!" he hissed. "You and others like you have been coming to my part of the world for decades, digging up our history, carting our past away in your jeeps and airplanes, keeping the treasures of Turkey and Egypt and Israel and everywhere else in your museums and galleries for your own pleasure!"

He lowered a tiny hand and gripped McAuley's throat, his anger seeming to rise with each word, his eyes narrower and narrower. "Such a man as you, a despoiler of the earth, a molester of ancient cultures and sacred burial grounds, should never call another a thief! Who owns the scroll you took from the cave? Who deserves to keep it, study it, decide its authenticity? You? Do you deserve it?"

McAuley pushed down into the bed. Yoseph touched the gun to McAuley's forehead, and the barrel pressed like a thick steel dart between his eyes. "Answer me, you thief!" screeched Yoseph. "Tell me who the robber is!"

McAuley started to shut his eyes but then decided against it. Amazingly, the courage that had surged through him off and on ever since he found the scroll boiled up once again, and he decided if Yoseph was going to shoot him, he should at least die with some measure of self-respect. Feeling buoyed by the strange sensation, he looked up into the eyes of his kidnapper. The gun seemed to move, and he thought he saw Yoseph's index finger twitch. A torrent of sweat flooded down between his shoulder blades, and he smelled the odor of his own body.

The surge of boldness suddenly abated, and he felt sick to his stomach. "I am the thief," he whispered, totally spent. "I am the robber."

Yoseph lowered the gun, stepped away, and shuddered like a man pulling himself back from the brink of an abyss. "Exactly," he said. "And this time you stole something that others might find most valuable."

His body quivering, McAuley stretched out flat on the bed, grateful he was still alive. As if from a distance, he heard Yoseph speaking, but he didn't reply. He stared at the ceiling and let his mind go blank. He was alive. For the moment, that was all that mattered.

NINE

Breakfast for Michael Del Rio consisted of a grapefruit without sugar, two slices of wheat toast sprinkled with cinnamon, a banana, and three glasses of liquid—one milk, one tomato juice, and the third cold water. He was eating in a small, but elegant dining room in one of the many small buildings located in Vatican City. White cloth covered each of the twenty tables in the room, and rich dark wood covered both the floor and the walls. As in practically every building in the Holy See, a variety of tasteful religious paintings dressed up the interior of the attractive space. In the center of the room a fire crackled—its soft glow and smoky smell making the place cozy and warm.

To Michael's left and right, a variety of Vatican officials and their guests took advantage of the quiet atmosphere. Though conversation flowed freely, no one spoke loudly. Like Michael, many of the men in the room were dressed in priestly garb—some in solid black, others in black garnished with red at the sash.

Cutting his grapefruit, Michael stared across the table at one of the men who sported red—his uncle Severiano Roca. A hint of sunshine filtered through a set of windows to his left and conspired with the fireplace to cast a glow on his uncle's face, making him appear almost surreal, as if burning from the inside out. A bowl of oatmeal sat before him, a cup of steaming coffee beside it. A newspaper lay by the coffee cup.

"His Holiness made it through another night," Roca said, stating in a quiet tone what everyone in the room already knew.

"But with no signs of improvement," Michael said, nibbling his toast. "Is the prognosis any better?"

Roca reached for his coffee, took a sip, then shook his head. "The doctors are saying nothing. We don't know."

"It's amazing how hush-hush all this is," Michael said, indicating the newspaper. "The paper called the pope's condition 'fatigue.' Too much travel. Said he had a 'fainting spell and will require a few days' rest.'"

Roca smiled slyly. "We're not in America, my nephew. The Holy See has dealt with matters like this for centuries. We know how to keep our mouths closed, quite unlike the people in your country. Until we decide it's serious, it's not serious—at least not so far as the public is concerned. No reason to upset the faithful until we know more."

"So you keep it a secret that the leader of the most powerful religious force in the world lingers between life and death?"

Roca tried his coffee again. "It seems so, at least for now. Who knows, he may regain his health within a week, and no one will ever know. Why create the panic until we get more information?"

Michael grunted and tried his tomato juice. "Look," he said. "I'm not versed in the fine points of medicine, but from what I know of strokes, the first forty-eight hours are critical. Often, a patient makes as much progress as they ever make within that time. What if His Holiness stays like he is, in this . . . this vegetative state? How long before someone has to step into the void, not as pontiff, of course, but in the day-to-day decision-making? How long can this—?"

Roca raised a hand. "Slow down a bit. Your American impatience is showing. No one will act too quickly here. The Church has endured worse moments than this and surely will do so again. All is in control. Secretary Randuhar will handle the daily administration of the Church, and all major decisions will be postponed until the circumstances unravel themselves a bit more. That should suffice for the time being."

"But what about—"

"What about our beloved Mary? What about the New Year's Eve Mass? Is that what you want to know?"

Michael faced the fireplace. Roca knew him too well. "Of course that's what I want to know," he said, picking up his banana and peeling it.

"You were in the meeting yesterday," Roca said confidently. "As long as His Holiness is incapacitated, plans for the Blessed Virgin remain on hold."

"But if the pontiff stays comatose for months? Will that decision hold indefinitely?" Michael asked, biting from the banana.

"That is my understanding." Roca reached over and took Michael's milk and poured almost a third of it onto his oatmeal. Then, as calmly as a cat with the canary already swallowed, he faced Michael.

Studying him, Michael suddenly felt a sense of unease. Roca's expression seemed too pleased, as if he knew something no one else knew, as if he had . . . But no, that wasn't possible! Roca had no control over the pontiff's health! No matter how deeply he opposed the Marian Decree, the pope's illness had nothing to do with any machinations on Roca's part. To think otherwise was ludicrous. Michael pushed away the notion and finished his banana.

"Others might not accept the status quo," he said. "Marchino might push for a more immediate decision."

"Marchino is not in control here." Roca set the milk back on the table beside Michael's toast.

"And you are?"

Roca smiled again. "As much as any one person can be."

For several moments, neither man spoke. The sunshine that had played so cheerfully on the room just moments before suddenly dipped and disappeared behind a bank of clouds. The fire, too, seemed to die down as if dampened by a spray of water. Michael stared toward the window.

"I might as well go back to Indiana," he said. "The pontiff could remain like this for months. I don't want to hang around here like a vulture waiting on him to die."

Roca rolled his cardinal's ring, then placed both elbows on the table and leaned toward Michael. "You cannot go yet, my nephew. You recall I said I might need you?"

Michael stared at his hands. They were chapped and needed lotion. But they were steady. "Sure, I remember," he said. "But I can't do anything here. I'm a nobody—no standing in the Vatican, no power in the Curia."

Roca shook his head. "I don't need you here in the Vatican."

Puzzled, Michael frowned. "Then what—?"

Removing his elbows from the table, Roca reached to his side and lifted a briefcase to the table. Opening it, he pulled out a manila folder and handed it to Michael. "Read the piece in the folder," he said.

His curiosity pricked, Michael opened the folder and pulled out the paper inside. The word "confidential," written in thick black letters, stared up from the top of the page. The date indicated the memo had been drafted that morning. "You sure I should read—?"

"Read it."

Michael studied the first sentence, then the second and third. He lifted the paper closer to his face, reread the first three sentences, then finished the page. Done, he cleared his throat and faced Roca.

"Where did you get this?" he asked.

Roca shrugged. "It came to the Holy See from friends in Jerusalem, the World Archeological Society. Once here . . . well, I have friends in every directorate of the Curia. Such news as this comes to those who need to see it."

"Who else in the Vatican has read it?"

"Randuhar, I'm sure. Who else, I don't know."

"Marchino?"

"I expect so. He has his spies as I do. That's why I have to act fast."

Michael started to question the ethics of such practices, then decided against it. Though idealistic, he wasn't naïve. Men like his uncle lived and worked in a political environment as surely as any elected official in the United States. Though piety permeated the Church, it did so right alongside pragmatic realities. Men of power earned their positions through the combination of both spirituality and pragmatism. Such was the way of the world—the Church being no exception. If Roca's desire to shape the Church to his liking drove him into competition with Marchino, so be it. Who was he to say which man's view was right? Which one represented the will of God? At least his uncle's perspective matched his own. He took a deep breath and laid the confidential memo beside his milk glass.

"You think this is possible?" he asked, his voice indicating skepticism about the information in the folder.

Roca fingered his ring. "Who's to say what is possible? Is it possible for a man to fly to the moon? For a black hole to suck in everything, including the light of the universe? For a virgin to conceive a child? For a man to come alive again from a grave? Miracles happen in strange places, my friend. You know that as well as I."

Michael grinned wryly. "So now you believe in miracles, my uncle?"

Roca shrugged. "Miracles are in the eye of the beholder, my nephew. One man's miracle is another man's coincidence. I keep an open mind about such things."

Michael opened his mouth as if to debate the issue, but then changed his mind. "The timing for such a thing to turn up is certainly strange."

"A coincidence, I'm sure," said Roca, lowering his eyes to accent the humor of his statement.

"But surely you don't believe it's real?" Michael asked, ignoring the wit. "A document written by John, recounting the life of Mary? Found now in Ephesus?"

"Tradition says the Blessed Virgin may have lived in Ephesus with John after the death of our Lord."

Michael nodded. He knew the story. Just before His death on the cross, Jesus had entrusted Mary to the one the Gospel of John called the "beloved disciple," a man most scholars believed to be named John, a man many accepted as the writer of the book. For centuries the Church had debated what happened next. Some said Mary died in Ephesus, where John made his home for a time. Others asserted Mary returned to Jerusalem before her death. No one knew for sure.

"If this scroll is authentic, it has the potential to rattle a lot of cages," he said, his voice more serious by the second. "It could shake the Church to its core."

"My feelings exactly."

Both men fell silent. Outside the window, the day grew even darker. Inside, the flames in the fireplace had dipped down to nothing. The coals remained, but they seemed weak and uninspired.

Michael suddenly felt cold, as if someone had just wiped his body with a cube of ice. He felt odd and out of place, as if his mind had drifted away from his body. He thought of his boyhood home in Rolla, Missouri, of his family—his dad a high school football coach, his mom a fifth grade teacher, his brother two years younger than he—all now deceased. When they died his senior year in high school, his whole world had crashed, ripped apart at the seams. And now, here today, the same sensation of utter shock and helplessness swept through him again, and he felt completely out of his depth. The feeling scared him for reasons he didn't like to think about, reasons that conjured up hurtful images from his past, images that . . . He bit his lip and suppressed his thoughts. He wouldn't think of the past. To do so just messed him up and accomplished nothing positive. He thought of the scroll again, this supposedly ancient fragment of parchment from Ephesus.

"The Church has to find this scroll!" he said, his mind reeling with the significance of such a document. "We've got to study it, determine if it's authentic. If it is, then what it says about Jesus is crucial! It could fill in so many gaps, so much of the history of our Lord, His childhood, the years of His development before His public life began! Mary will tell us so many things no one else ever saw! It could revolutionize what we know—"

Roca threw up a hand, stopping him in mid-sentence. "It might reveal more than a mother's musings about her son," he said. "It should also tell us much about the mother."

Michael blanched, then grabbed his water, tilting it to his lips as he considered Roca's meaning. Of course! His initial thoughts had centered on Jesus. But any writing from Mary would also reveal the life of the author. Did she have children other than Jesus? Was she a virgin forever? What happened to Joseph? This discovery could make or break the entire Catholic system of belief about the Holy Mother! It could destroy or legitimize the idea of naming her Co-Redemptrix! Remarkable that it had turned up now, so close to the time when the pope might make such a declaration. Was it a hoax someone had created to confuse that issue, to postpone, explode, or support the possibility? Or was it a miracle of God, provided for just this moment to either stop the decree or affirm it as the right step for the Church?

Michael finished his water in one gulp and set the glass down. "This document could destroy the Church," he mumbled, more to himself than to Roca, his eyes lost in the dying fire.

"Or reform it."

Michael raised his head, then sighed. "One or the other."

Roca once again placed his hand on Michael's. "We have to find it," he said, the emphasis on the first word of his statement.

Michael jumped slightly. "What do you mean 'we'?" He pointed to the report. "It says the document has disappeared along with the man who found it. That's police work."

"The police will not know what to do with what they find. In the wrong hands, the message of the scroll could get misinterpreted, mistranslated. At worst, the media could get it, then God help us all. No way around it, we have to get it first."

"And how do you propose to do that?"

Roca rolled his ring as if considering the question. When he spoke, though, Michael knew his uncle had already mapped out a plan for what should happen next.

"You need to leave the Vatican," he said. "I am already in contact with Arthur Bremer, the American ambassador to the Holy

See. The good ambassador is in agreement with me that such a document as this has explosive potential, potential that is best controlled by people who know how to handle such things." He paused, as if giving Michael time to respond. When Michael remained silent, Roca pressed ahead.

"I, of course, cannot go anywhere, not with His Holiness in such dire straits. So, I need you to make a trip for me."

"To Turkey?" asked Michael, catching his uncle's direction.

"So perceptive you are."

"Why me? You have a number of assistants more suited to this than I am."

Roca shrugged. "Perhaps not. To send anyone from the Vatican now will automatically create suspicion. Marchino and others will want to know why I would send anyone from the pope's side at such a crucial time. No, that will not do. You're the only one I can trust to leave Rome without arousing suspicion. Play it correctly, and they'll think you're headed back to America."

"You expect me to find this document?"

"Not by yourself, of course. The ambassador has assigned someone to go with you, someone who will make sure you get proper support from the U.S. and Turkish governments. That's another advantage of your going—you're an American. You'll have some clout in Turkey."

Michael stared out the window. The room swirled around and around and he had the feeling of parachuting from an airplane, something he had done once while in college. The rush of fear— zipping through space like a rocket reentering the atmosphere, then popping a chute and floating to the ground as serenely as a hawk riding the upper currents—had energized him like nothing before or since. The danger scared him and thrilled him all in the same moment.

"What standing will I have?" he asked, warming to the idea.

"You will be an official representative of the Vatican. I have prepared all the necessary paperwork. The authority of the Church goes with you."

Michael started to ask how Roca had managed to get him such a portfolio, but then realized the question would be an insult. If Cardinal Roca said he had the necessary papers, then it was so.

"Who's going with me from the embassy?" he asked.

Roca produced a second folder from his briefcase and handed it to Michael. "Her name is Valerie Miller," he said. "She's assigned to the ambassador's office from the State Department, media relations. A standout, from what Bremer says. Languages, computers. She's religious too, though it is of the Protestant variety, a Baptist it seems. Bremer says she's the best young talent he's ever seen in the diplomatic corps, quite eager to make an impression. You're to meet with her as soon as possible to work out the details. Just remember, you have to act fast."

"She's young?" Michael glanced up from the paper.

"If you call twenty-nine young."

Michael opened the file and studied it quickly. Valerie Miller. Born in Columbia, South Carolina. Private religious schools until college. Numerous awards—academics, piano performance, student government. Attended Duke at the age of sixteen, a major in language studies with an emphasis in Italian, but also capable in Spanish and Turkish. Earned a Ph.D. at Georgetown in International Studies at twenty-five. Signed on with the State Department the same year. Short assignments since then in London and Israel. Connected to the Vatican for the last sixteen months.

"Impressive," he said, placing the file on the table.

"Bremer thinks so. He wouldn't give her this much responsibility if he didn't."

"But why her for this?"

Roca rolled his ring. "I asked the same question. Bremer pointed to the skill in the languages and the religious training. Thought she would grasp the importance of the hunt."

"I'm sure she will. But she's a Baptist. Will that cause any problems?"

Roca shrugged. "Not for me it won't. Look, you're searching for a document, not debating the Reformation. Doctrine doesn't even have to come up."

"She's in media relations?"

"It's fairly standard for career diplomats to take a turn in such a position. They learn how to handle themselves under the scrutiny of the print and electronic media."

Michael nodded. It made sense. He took a sip of his tomato juice. "Wonder what she looks like?" he asked.

"She's still single at twenty-nine. With all her other talents, you'd think some man would have claimed her by now, unless—"

"Unless she looks like the north end of a southbound mule."

A smile crossed Roca's face. "You have such a way of putting things, my nephew, even if they're not politically correct. For your sake, I hope what you say is true. A beautiful woman might be a distraction to you."

Michael waved his hands, dismissing the thought. "That dog won't hunt anymore," he said. "At my age, I'm past that particular temptation."

Roca continued to smile. "Don't get too confident, my friend. I saw you watching that woman at your gym."

Michael shrugged. "I *saw* her, but I didn't watch her," he said. "There's a big difference, you know what I mean?"

Roca laughed outright. "I think I can remember. But you need to remember something too, something many of us tend to forget. Temptations don't always stay dead; they have a way of resurrecting themselves when we least expect them."

Uncomfortable with the direction of the conversation, Michael changed the subject. "When do I leave?"

Roca produced an envelope from his briefcase and handed it to Michael. "Ticketed for Thursday," he said. "Figured you would need today and tomorrow to get things in order. Take all your belongings when you pack. It needs to look as if you're leaving for good."

Michael looked once more at the fire. A bit of flame had reappeared at the bottom and now flared up again, its glow bouncing in his eyes. A sense of yearning welled up in him, an emotion that felt awfully close to loneliness. "You think it's possible?" he asked, his voice barely a whisper, his hesitation about the task disappearing as he considered the ramifications of such a document for the Church.

Roca rolled his ring. "Go find the scroll," he said. "Then we'll see."

"I hope it is possible."

"I don't know what I hope," said Roca. "Just go and find it, for me and for the Church."

"I'll do all I can."

"The future of the Church may depend on it."

Michael stood from the table and faced his uncle. "Then may God help the Church."

TEN

A short distance away from where Severiano Roca and Michael Del Rio sat, a cleaning man named Benito Cellini wiped his watery eyes and walked into the papal apartment to begin his daily work. The last two days had been excruciating for Benito and the rest of the staff that served in the Vatican. These people—the cooks, the maintenance staff, the secretaries, and those like himself who cleaned the rooms—did their jobs as quietly as mice. But that didn't mean they didn't take their work seriously. To Benito, cleaning the papal quarters was a holy calling. So, in spite of the rumors that his beloved pope lay near death in Gemelli Hospital and his whole world felt shaky, Benito pressed ahead.

According to the stories, a stroke had felled the pontiff, but the doctors had kept his condition uncommonly secret, and no one truly seemed to know exactly what had happened. A few people even suggested in hushed tones that the police suspected some kind of foul play.

Benito knew nothing one way or the other. All he knew was that he found it quite difficult to do his job under such adverse conditions. Yet, out of his love for the pontiff, he would do his work, and he would do it to the best of his humble ability.

His jaw set in determination, Benito moved across the papal chambers to do what he had done nearly every day of his life since he turned eighteen. He began to clean the stately rooms. Even though the pope remained at the precipice between life and death, no one had instructed him to stop his daily cleaning, so he continued as always.

First, he scrubbed the bathroom, his eyes attentive to every detail. He cleaned the mirror before which the pope shaved each day. Next, he washed the sink where the pontiff brushed his holy teeth. Even the toilet demanded Benito's utmost effort.

Vacuuming the floor, he noticed a piece of paper in the corner by the sink, and he recoiled in horror. How had he missed such an obvious bit of clutter? Chosen for this work precisely because of his compulsion for cleanliness, such a violation upset every sensibility Benito held dear.

His eyes watering again, he backed up against the wall, his hand over his mouth. A sense of failure washed over him. Obviously, his distraught condition had caused him to miss what he normally would have spotted in a second. For several moments, he considered what he should do. Resign from his post? Let someone more qualified handle the holy chore?

Benito began to sob at the notion. No, there had to be another choice, some way he could hold on to the work that gave his life meaning. He pushed his fist into his mouth as his tears threatened to overwhelm him. Under his sobs, he uttered a brief prayer, asking for divine help for his predicament.

He straightened up from the wall as an idea came to him, an idea so simple yet so pure. He could keep his job only if he swore to God that he would never again make such a terrible mistake, only if he redoubled his efforts to make the papal chambers the most immaculate living quarters in the known world. A man so gracious as the pontiff deserved no less.

His heart gladdened and his resolve set, Benito left the bathroom and stalked into the bedroom. Though he had changed the unused bedclothes every day since the pope's sudden illness, that didn't matter. He would change them again. When the pontiff returned, he would find his bed fresh and crisp with new sheets.

Benito yanked away the covers of the bed. Then, with even more care than usual, he took fresh linens from the cart in the hallway outside, laid them across the papal mattress, and began to tuck them under the corners. Right foot corner, left foot corner. Right top corner, left top corner. Smooth and tuck. Smooth and tuck.

Finishing with the sheets, he gave the same attention to the top cover, a magnificent white comforter with a hand-embossed image of a shepherd stitched onto it. Bottom to top, smooth and tuck, every corner in place, every wrinkle pressed out.

Eager to place the pope's pillow exactly in the middle of the bed's headboard, Benito leaned over the top of the bed. Then, just as he set the pillow in place, his gaze dipped to the small slit of space between the headboard and the mattress. There, wedged firmly in place, was a book that he immediately recognized as the pope's personal journal. He had often seen it lying atop the pontiff's bedside table.

His heart racing, Benito knew immediately that he should call someone with more authority to come and take charge of the journal. But whom should he call? Cardinal Randuhar, the Secretary of the Curia? Yes, that made sense.

He started to move, but then another thought hit him, a disturbing one. Everyone knew that Randuhar would not succeed to the Holy Seat of Christ. If he gave the journal to Randuhar, then what reward would come his way? Benito knew he shouldn't think about himself in such a time as this. Yet, if he took the book to Randuhar, and someone other than the Secretary became pontiff, as he and everyone else expected, then he might no longer keep his job as cleaner of the papal quarters. Such a possibility gave him pause. If not to Randuhar, then to whom should he go with the journal?

Only two possibilities came to mind—Cardinal Marchino or Cardinal Roca. One of the two would most likely become the next pontiff. If not them, then almost assuredly someone picked by one of them. As Benito well knew, the two men were already locked in a grim match to see who would gain the upper hand in the pope's absence. The Curia reeked with daily rumors of which one had lined up the most support, which one had made the most progress. Though he personally disliked such palace intrigue and didn't know either man too well, Benito nonetheless did know the basic philosophy each of them held.

Marchino's supporters saw him, unlike the pope, as a true progressive on many issues, a rightful descendant of Vatican II and its desires to modernize the Church and make it relevant to culture. Yet, just like the pontiff, he practiced a most stringent devotion to the Beloved Mother of Jesus and supported the notion of Mary as Co-Redemptrix.

Roca, on the other hand, remained conservative on everything—social issues like abortion and euthanasia, women's ordination and the Marian Decree. To him, a further elevation of Mary smacked of a sellout to feminism, liberalism, and modernism, and he wanted none of any of that.

Standing by the bed, Benito recognized that his job depended on the choice he now made. To which man should he go with word of the pope's journal?

A disturbing notion rocked Benito, and he stepped away from the bed and shook his head as if to protest the idea. But then it came back to him, and it made all the sense in the world. Only by reading the journal could he know the man to whom to give the book. Without question, the pope's writings would point him in the proper direction, give him some clue about the pontiff's feelings about the two men. Even if His Holiness didn't mention them by name, his inner thoughts would show which man's philosophy he supported.

As if reaching for a cobra, Benito leaned down and touched the pope's journal. Then, pulling it from its resting place, he clutched it to his chest and ran across the room. His heart pounding, he pulled a chair from beside the desk. Then, his ears pricked to hear the smallest sound of anyone approaching, he did what in normal circumstances he would never have even considered. He opened the pages of the pope's journal and began to read.

At first he found it difficult to decipher the pope's tiny scrawling. But then, after a few minutes, he caught the rhythm of the letters. This journal began on October 15, and ended the day of the pontiff's stroke almost two months later. Reading hurriedly, Benito soaked up the holy words. Though he felt like crying a couple of times, he pushed back his tears and pressed ahead.

Almost an hour later, he finished the journal and laid it on his lap. For a couple of minutes more, he stayed still as a stone contemplating what to do. But then an intriguing notion came to him, a notion so bizarre, so beyond his capabilities to consider that he had no doubt that he could not have thought of it himself. Only God could have given him an idea like this.

Standing, Benito once again clutched the book to his chest. What he now planned to do guaranteed that if His Holiness died, the next pope, whoever it turned out to be, would surely feel beholden to him. In fact, what he now planned to do with the journal guaranteed that the next pope would no doubt give him credit for handing him the power he needed to ascend to the Holy See.

A rush of tears ran again into Benito's eyes, and this time he didn't hold them back. For some reason the Lord Almighty had seen fit to place him in this situation. And, with the help of that same Lord, he would do the right thing. He only hoped as he did so that the man who became the next Vicar of Christ would remember him when he ascended to the papacy and allow his loyal cleaning man the privilege of remaining in his present vocation.

ELEVEN

CAIRO, EGYPT

The wheels of the private jet touched down in Cairo at just past five o'clock local time. Sitting near the front, her blond hair pulled demurely behind her ears and pinned against her head, Dr. Martha Hinton unfastened her seat belt a hundred feet from the gate and hustled off the plane the instant the doors opened. Her clothes—a navy skirt that covered her legs to her calves and a white cotton blouse buttoned to the neck—were conservative in deference to her host. Though nervous, she kept her breath even as her eyes, glazed from a night with little sleep, swept over the terminal as she entered it. Though dying for a cigarette, she fought off the urge. A woman smoking in public in an Arab country just wouldn't do. Thankfully, it didn't take her long to spot the man she had come to meet.

From her left, a beast the size of a compact car approached, the knuckles of his hands practically dragging the ground, his legs swishing with the sound of his pants rubbing together at the thighs. Barely visible behind the behemoth walked a second man, this one more normal in size and no more than fifty years old, wearing an off-white three-buttoned suit, a stunningly blue shirt, and a tie the color of a fresh ear of corn. His face was dominated by two characteristics—a heavy black beard and a set of full, sensuous lips.

Having worked through his lieutenants, she had never met Addam Azziz in person. But she immediately recognized him from pictures she had seen in a variety of magazines and newspapers. An oil tycoon with enough money to challenge God to a poker game, as the saying went, Azziz popped up in places not usually associated with devout Muslims, though that was what he reportedly was. He attended charity benefits in London for the world's homeless children, dinners in Los Angeles to raise money for AIDS research, and parties in Paris to solicit funds for endangered species of wildlife. *People* magazine had labeled him one of the world's ten most charitable people.

Azziz stepped from behind his bodyguard and bowed at the waist as he reached Hinton. Careful of the protocol, Hinton bowed also, keeping her eyes discreetly downcast. Neither of them offered to shake hands.

"Dr. Hinton, so good to finally meet you," Azziz smiled at her as he spoke, his perfectly capped teeth white and straight, his English equally as precise. "I trust your flight was a pleasant one."

"Wonderful," she exuded. "Thank you for sending the jet."

"A small matter given the importance of your call."

"I've looked forward to the opportunity to meet you," she said.

"And I you. You are more beautiful than your pictures indicate. I must reprimand my subordinates for their failure to tell me this."

Hinton locked her eyes briefly onto his, boldly accepting his flattery. "Thank you for your compliments," she said. "But I would prefer to be known for my professional accomplishments."

"Can a woman not be known for both beauty and competence?"

Hinton tried not to smile too broadly. "Perhaps you have a point."

Azziz shrugged and his smile suddenly disappeared. "Too bad our meeting is not under better circumstances. Your message disturbed me most deeply."

Hinton swallowed and glanced at her feet. "Perhaps we should talk somewhere else," she suggested.

Without a word, Azziz pivoted and walked away. From points east and west, two other men—both dressed head to toe in black and only a touch smaller than the massive bodyguard leading Azziz—joined the three of them as they left the terminal.

Hinton followed quietly, her heart skipping, frantic for a smoke. Azziz had funded her last three digs, including the current one in Ephesus. Generous to a fault when it came to her requests, he never questioned how she spent the funds he sent and never denied her what she said she needed to do her work. The checks he wrote arrived precisely on the fifteenth of each month, and his only demand was a simple one—he received the

right of first refusal to keep anything she found. A collector of
many things beautiful, Azziz required this agreement in writing. Any significant find came to him first. What he wanted he
kept, no questions asked.

Hinton knew better than to break that agreement. Though
known as a generous man, Azziz was also known as a serious
man. He followed his code of honor to the letter and expected
others to do the same. Ever the pragmatic businessman though,
Azziz didn't leave such an expectation to the honor system. Hinton knew for a fact that someone from his staff monitored all e-
mail, all phone calls, and all reports posted from her digs. That's
why she had called him the morning after she discovered Mc-
Auley missing. To do otherwise jeopardized everything. As a result of that call, Azziz had demanded that she fly instantly to
Cairo.

Up to now, the strings that were attached to Azziz's gener-
osity seemed manageable—a small price to pay for his funding.
But now that McAuley had found the document at Ephesus and
disappeared with it? Would Azziz think she had something to do
with McAuley's treachery? That she had somehow conspired
with him? She didn't know.

Outside the terminal, Azziz stepped to a black limousine
parked at the curb. The windows of the car were completely
black, and Hinton could see nothing inside. The crew of bodyguards circled the vehicle, the biggest one leading the way and
climbing behind the wheel. A second took the passenger seat beside him, and the third disappeared, obviously to a following car.
Azziz opened a rear door and motioned for Hinton to enter, and
she quickly complied. Azziz circled the car and took the seat opposite her. Hinton glanced out the window, but the view was
murky, as if staring through dirty water.

"Drive," Azziz called to the driver. The car pulled away and
took its place in the torrent of midafternoon traffic.

Azziz faced Hinton. "Would you like a drink?" He gestured
toward the compact bar before him.

Hinton licked her lips, a bit surprised that Azziz would have
alcohol in his car. Not that she was tempted. What she wanted
was a cigarette. But she knew Azziz didn't smoke, and in the
Arab world, the notion of a woman smoking in front of a devout
Muslim was considered blasphemy. "Water, perhaps?" she
asked.

Azziz smiled, took a beautifully cut crystal glass from the bar,
filled it from a clear decanter, and handed her the water. Her

hands shaking slightly, she took it and drank a quick swallow. Azziz leaned back and rubbed his palms together.

"Let us move to the matters at hand," he said. "I have read Dr. McAuley's e-mail transmission. So I don't need a rehash of that. What I do need is your opinion, as an archeologist. Tell me whether or not you believe this . . . this Mary document to be genuine."

Hinton took a deep breath and laced both hands around her water glass. "I've been asking myself that question since Sunday," she started. "Theoretically, it's certainly possible that it's genuine. I don't know how much you know about Biblical tradition—"

"I am a Muslim, as you know, but I read widely. I am not illiterate when it comes to these matters."

"I didn't mean to insinuate—"

"No offense taken. Now, tell me the possibilities. If I need clarification, I will most assuredly ask for it."

Hinton started again. "Okay, let me describe this the best I can. Though I'm no Biblical expert, I did a lot of study in preparation for the work we're doing in Ephesus. I know, for example, that many scholars believe a man named John wrote the fourth book—it's called a 'gospel'—in the New Testament. In that book, there's a character called 'the beloved disciple.' Many scholars identify that man as this same John.

"In John's gospel, as in the others, a great deal of attention is given to the death of the man named Jesus. He was crucified by Roman soldiers in league with the leadership of the Jewish religious authorities."

She sipped from her water.

"Continue please," said Azziz.

"As Jesus was crucified, He told this 'beloved disciple' to take care of His mother. So, if this disciple is the same man as John, and if John wrote the book by his name, it shows that this John was literate and that he was also the one to whom Jesus entrusted His mother. Therefore—"

"Therefore, if Mary lived with John for a while, told him of her life with Jesus, then it's highly possible this John recorded her story."

"Exactly. Add to that the fact that Christian tradition says Mary lived with John in Ephesus, maybe even died there, and you have a real chance for this scroll to be authentic."

"How did it come to be in the cave?"

Hinton paused and took a long drink. "It's fairly simple,

really. We know that Christians suffered persecution off and on for the first three hundred years of their existence. At one point, John himself suffered exile on Patmos, an island off the coast of Turkey. During that time, Christians living in and around Ephesus took refuge in the caves above the city to escape the hand of oppression. If there is such a document from Mary, we would expect to find it in exactly this kind of place."

Azziz perched on the edge of his seat and rubbed his hands together again. "You make a strong case," he said. "But what about the other possibility? The chance of a hoax? Why would anyone want to fake this?"

Hinton studied her water glass for several moments. "I've been trying to answer that too," she started. "But that becomes more problematic. Why does anyone lie? Or cheat? Pretend to be something they're not? Do things that are dishonest?"

Azziz chuckled softly as the car took a hard turn to the left. "Ah, Dr. Hinton, you and I both know the answers to those questions. The usual motivations—money, fame, the thrill of it all, self-aggrandizement. We don't have to look far to know the answer to the question 'why?' If it's a hoax, then it is so because someone thinks they can gain something from it, something precious to them."

"But what that is, we cannot yet know."

"Then the question becomes 'who?' A forger of such a document would have to be highly skilled, am I right?"

"It's according to when it was done."

For the first time, Azziz seemed puzzled. He stroked his beard. "Explain yourself," he said.

"If it's fake, you know, was it forged in the first century? The fourth? Or six months ago? That makes a huge difference in the motivation and the skill level needed to do such a thing."

Azziz nodded, catching on as she continued her explanation.

"I mean, if someone wrote this in the first century, they did so for reasons totally different than if they did it a year ago or a decade ago. And if it's an ancient forgery, then the material on which it's written and the ink used to do it will be authentic. We won't be able to detect a forgery from the materials. We'll have to turn to the message within the document, the use of the language by the writer, try to determine if it matches with the way John wrote, the terminology he used in other writings in the Bible."

"But if it's recent, the materials used to produce it will reflect that."

Hinton sipped her water. She liked the feeling of teaching the esteemed Azziz. "Perhaps, but then again maybe not. You see, it's possible that even if it's a recent forgery, the person used ancient materials to do it. That would make a determination of its authenticity even more difficult."

"In what way?"

"Well, chances are, with modern Biblical scholarship being what it is, the person would know how to imitate John's writings, what words, patterns, images to use to make it seem real."

"So the parchment and ink would be ancient and the writing would seem authentic."

"That's right, which would make it a tough job to find out if it's authentic or not."

Azziz rubbed his beard, then asked, "But how could anyone get their hands on ancient materials?"

"Well, that would be difficult, to be sure. But inks and papyrus materials from the first century are available, even if rare."

Azziz stroked his beard again, his face blank. Hinton watched him, her own emotions an odd mixture of fascination and fear. She knew Azziz only professionally, not in circumstances like this. Public word said kind things about him—a man of charity, a man of broad interest, a man of intellect and civility. But she knew, too, of conversations whispered late at night after a few rounds of drinks in which some claimed that Azziz spent lavishly on charity in an effort to uproot a reputation gained in earlier years, a reputation reportedly earned by utter ruthlessness. Some even claimed that he had come to his wealth by murdering a wealthy cousin who owned land rich in oil. Seeing Azziz up close and personal, Hinton didn't know what to believe.

Azziz spoke, his clipped words breaking her thoughts. "Do you know of anyone else who might know of this discovery?" he asked. "Anyone else who might have found out?"

Martha dropped her eyes and took a deep breath. She knew she couldn't lie to Azziz.

"I'm not sure," she said. "But the World Archeological Society gets copies of my e-mail, they—

"And why would that be?" hissed Azziz.

Martha shrugged. "They paid me fifty thousand dollars for the right to study how modern digs use technology. It's a grant. They offered it, I took it. I never dreamed anything like this could happen."

Azziz cleared his throat and changed the subject. "Tell me where I can find your man McAuley," he ordered, his tone leaving no doubt he expected a definitive answer. "The only way to make a determination about this manuscript is to find it. And your McAuley is the key to that task."

Hinton sucked on her water and tried to stay calm. "I don't know," she started. "Like I said when I called you, he made reservations for New York, but didn't—"

"I know all of that," interrupted Azziz, a bit of temper in his voice. "Tell me what I don't know!"

Hinton clenched her water glass with both hands. "I have people looking for him all over Izmir. He must be close by. He didn't leave by plane. He—"

"He could have driven out of Izmir!" said Azziz, his mouth set in a grim frown. "No need to fly! I want to know where he is and I want to know it now!"

Martha Hinton studied her hands, her heart skipping in fear. "I'll find him for you," she promised. "I'll find him—"

"I have no doubt you will find him," interrupted Azziz. "I only hope you do so before it is too late."

When Hugh McAuley didn't show up on Monday as his e-mail had promised, Sarah Stanley Suggs wrote it off at first to the uncertainties of air travel from such a distant and exotic location. Equipment failures, weather problems, a hundred things could cause a delay from that far away. But then, when Tuesday came and he still didn't arrive, she became a bit more concerned.

She knew from long experience with him that Hugh McAuley didn't promise things he didn't plan to fulfill. Though they didn't talk that often anymore—Hugh not being the talkative type and her being married and all—the two and a half years they had spent together in college had bonded them in ways no one but they would ever understand. Neither of them had been attractive people—she had battled a bit of a weight problem herself— and they had found solace in each other. Both keenly intelligent but lonely, they had come together at the height of youth to explore the mysteries of love.

She knew McAuley had a lot of faults. Unlike her, who had finally found a diet program that worked, Hugh had never done anything about his weight. In fact, after their breakup, he ballooned even more. In addition, he developed an even stronger tendency toward isolation, spending far too much time in caves.

Maybe worst of all, Hugh cared nothing for the social niceties that might have helped him to get ahead in his profession.

In spite of those quirks, though, the man had always been punctual. If he promised to arrive on Monday, then he arrived on Monday unless providentially hindered. And though she didn't believe in Providence too much, she did believe in Hugh McAuley. In spite of the fact that she had married Terence Suggs, heir to a fortune big enough to stuff an airplane hangar, she trusted McAuley more than any man on earth. Which made her doubly concerned—not only about his whereabouts but also about the whereabouts of the document he said he had found.

Standing by an arched window in a plush executive office overlooking Central Park, Sarah Stanley Suggs placed her hands on her hips and wondered what to do. She wanted that document!

Sarah knew what people said about her—that she owed her job to her husband's bulging bank account and not to her own private abilities. Such whispers ticked her off more than she cared to admit, and if she had anything to say about it, she would eventually do something significant enough to prove all the gossips wrong.

Since the day her third and last son left home for college, she had felt useless, a middle-aged gray-headed woman slowly going to seed with nothing to show for her life but a make-work job and an overused charge card—both provided by her wealthy husband. Until now, she had seen no way to change any of that. But now she had read the e-mail from Hugh McAuley.

Leaving the window, Sarah moved to her desk and picked up the phone. Punching in a number, she snuggled down into her sumptuous black leather desk chair. At long last a chance to prove her worth had come, a chance to demonstrate to her overbearing husband that she had some talent he should respect. Fingering a string of pearls on her neck, a string bought at Tiffany's for her birthday last May, she leaned back and propped her feet on the desk. She would find that scroll. With Terence's money and her connections in the world of arts, archeology, and antiquities, she would find it and she would bring it home. Whatever it took, she wanted this document and she wanted it for herself.

TWELVE

Her eyes glazed from too little sleep and too much caffeine, Dr. Cindy Brown, private physician for media mogul Willard Madden, turned from her computer screen and stared out the window at a bird the color of dirty water perched on the edge of a bird bath, fluttering its feathers.

Standing, Brown walked from her desk and opened the window. A whiff of a Los Angeles breeze caught her hair and pushed it back from her face. A sun bright enough to blind bounced down and warmed her head. The bird chirped twice, then hopped to a feeder a couple of feet away from the bath. Cindy almost smiled, but not quite. Unable to sleep, she had been up since four A.M., searching and reading and studying—hoping to find something of value to the man who paid her salary. So far her search had proved useless.

For a brief second, Brown wished she had never left her position as chief medical officer for cancer research at West Shore Hospital in San Francisco. But when a man like Madden wanted something, he almost inevitably got it. A net worth of just over three billion dollars tended to make his every desire someone else's command.

Madden had approached her at a medical conference just over a year ago. Not knowing who he was or what he wanted, she had treated him politely but without much fuss—just like she treated everyone else who came to shake her hand at the conclusion of her presentation. Two days later, as she stepped out of the shower, the phone in her hotel suite rang.

"Willard Madden here," said the caller, as if she should know the name. "I checked up on you. You're the best in your field. I need your expertise." His words came fast, like some super secretary tapping them out on a computer keyboard.

Standing in a bathrobe with her hair dripping, Cindy rubbed her forehead, trying to recall the name.

"Excuse me?" she said.

"Oh, you don't remember. I met you after your speech on Tuesday. I'm late fifties, five ten, gray hair, the best tan an electric bed can buy. I'm in town visiting my family. Got a granddaughter here."

She remembered the tan. "Sure, now I recall. What can I do for you?"

"You can become my doctor," he said quickly. "I've got bone cancer. Have had it for almost a year and a half. I need the best cancer specialist money can buy. I can afford to pay for it. I'll pay you five hundred thousand dollars a year if you'll become my private physician. Every year I live past sixty, I'll give you a bonus of one million more. You'll have unlimited funds to find a cure for what ails me. What do you say?"

Brown sat down on the bed. Water from her head trickled down her chin. "But . . . I have a job," she said.

"Yeah, and you're getting tired of it. I checked, talked to people close to you. You're at the top, but it's too much paper pushing. I hear you're feeling detached from patients. Don't like it."

Brown wiped water from her neck and sighed heavily. Madden had obviously done his homework. Everything he said was true.

"Check me out," he spouted, not giving her a chance to say no. "I've got money, lots of it. I own GlobalCam, a media group. Maybe you've heard of it."

"Yes, I know the company."

"Good, let me take you to lunch, talk about the offer."

More than a bit intrigued, Brown accepted the invitation and, within a day, had also accepted the job—but not primarily because of the money. Having grown up the daughter of a navy family in San Diego, she was already making more money than she could ever imagine. Truth be told, she took the job because at fifty-two, she was, as Madden suggested, weary of the unending and often uninspiring nature of her work—far too many meetings to endure and red tape to cut and manuals to read. With less and less contact with patients, she wondered at times if her work made any difference at all in the lives of real people. The notion of becoming a private physician for one individual fascinated her. With Madden she would get firsthand feedback one way or the other. If he lived, she could celebrate to her heart's content. If not . . . well, she would cry like a baby, but at least it would come from real emotion, something she seldom felt anymore.

Finding the offer a challenge she couldn't resist, she moved lock, stock, and barrel from San Francisco to Los Angeles, taking up residence in a guest house on the grounds of Madden's Beverly Hills estate and giving him her undivided attention.

Now, thirteen months had passed, and she had learned that Madden expected a lot for what he paid her. Like a cure for his cancer. She, of course, couldn't guarantee him anything of the sort. But he didn't seem to understand her limitations.

"I don't like excuses!" He shouted at her time and time again, his sentences always fired in short bursts. "Excuses don't get the job done! I hired you because you're the best. Respected all over the world."

"But I can't do the undoable!" she countered. "You've taken all the standard treatments—chemotherapy, bone marrow transplant, radiation. That's as far as medical science can take it. After that—"

"Then explore the alternatives!" he shouted, his face turning red under his tan. "If standard medicine doesn't work, forget the standards. What about alternative medicines? All this herbal stuff I hear about? Pollen from South American flowers? Synthetic chemicals? Meditation and diet control? Does any of that work?"

For weeks they had shouted at each other, each one becoming more and more desperate as Madden lost more and more weight. Now Cindy felt out of options. She had checked every avenue, every road, every track, but they kept leading to dead ends.

Running a hand through her hair, Brown slumped away from the window and back to her desk. Wedged again in her seat, she clicked the computer mouse and opened yet another link on the Internet. For the last two months she had spent hour after hour trying to satisfy Madden's suggestion about alternative medicine. She had searched through medical journal after medical journal, talked with colleagues for hours on the phone, and explored the Internet link by loony link—hoping against hope to find something in the bizarre world beyond accepted science that might prove helpful. So far, though, nothing had come of it.

That wasn't surprising. All the talk of alternative medicine seemed like hocus-pocus to her; old-time snake oil dressed up in glittery containers and good publicity. Though she, like many doctors, accepted the possibility that healing sometimes took place beyond what science could explain, she hadn't seen much of it in her years of practice. From what her research had shown, if standard treatments didn't heal Madden, he wouldn't get healed. Which gave him somewhere between six and ten months of quality life before the ravages of the disease ate him up for good.

The computer screen stared back at her, but she found it difficult to focus. After all her work, Madden would still die—his body chewed up like a house with termites.

Brown's eyes moistened, and she pulled a tissue from a box on the desk and rubbed away her pent-up tears. For the first time in her life she had failed at something she really wanted to do. But that wasn't the only reason for her grief. As much as she detested it when Madden raged at her, she had come to admire other parts of his character—his drive for perfection, his insistence on total commitment to a task, and his obvious love for his family. A widower for over ten years, Madden doted on his daughter, his son-in-law, and the granddaughter he was visiting when he came to the conference where she met him. Having grown up in a military family where discipline often outweighed any overt displays of love, Brown especially appreciated the way Madden communicated his feelings for his kin.

Time and time again in her months as his physician, Madden had shown how far he would go for the people he loved. Once, a couple of months after she moved, he had received a phone call in the middle of the night from Katie, his seven-year-old granddaughter in San Francisco. Katie had a stomachache, and her mom and dad were out of town.

Without hesitation, Madden sprang into action, ordering Katie's nanny to take her to a doctor. Hanging up the phone, he called his pilot and told him to get the jet ready. In less than thirty minutes, he left for San Francisco. Two days later, he came back.

Brown met him at the airport. Madden looked like a blown-out tire, deflated and worn, much weaker than when he left, his skin sagging around his throat, his eyes deep in the sockets.

"You okay?" Brown asked, grabbing his luggage.

Madden shook his head, his brown eyes dull and lifeless. "When my baby hurts, I hurt," he said. Since then, Brown had found it easy to forgive him the worst of his tirades. A man who loved a child that much obviously had something worthwhile inside.

Dabbing at her eyes again, Brown admitted to herself that she had come to feel a deep affection for Willard Madden. But unless a miracle happened, neither she nor Katie would have him around much longer. Too bad.

Brown started to turn off the computer. She knew of nothing else to do—nowhere else to look. But then she stopped. Wait a minute! One thing she hadn't tried yet. She touched the mouse and the screen blinked. She typed "Miracle healing" in the search field, then clicked on the "search" icon. A couple of seconds later, a list of links appeared on screen.

She keyed up the first link, and the home page of a preacher from Texas popped up. She read through the page quickly, noting the demand for a forty-nine-dollar donation in exchange for "daily power-filled prayers." She clicked on the "back" button, then selected the second link in the list.

A list of dates stared back at her. Brown rocked forward in her swivel chair. The dates recorded miracles that had supposedly taken place across the world in the last three months. She clicked on the first item. "Bald man grows hair."

Stifling a laugh, Brown read the account of a thirty-four-year-old Atlanta man who claimed to have grown hair after ten years of total baldness.

"Teenager cured of scoliosis," claimed the next item. According to the account, a fifteen-year-old girl with a bad spinal curve had attended her church on Sunday evening, received prayer for her condition, then went home and fell asleep. The next morning, her affliction had disappeared. Her spine was as straight as a door edge. She took off her brace, marched to school with her head high, and used her miracle as a means to tell everyone about Jesus. Doctors couldn't explain the cure, according to the report.

Her curiosity stirred, Brown moved on to a third reported healing, this one originating in southern Mexico and dated December 8. She shook her head—amazing how quickly stories like this circulated in the instant-access world of cyberspace. She sucked in her breath and ran her hand through her hair again. A woman on the way to Mass had seen a vision of Mary, carrying what looked like a scroll in her hand. Mary cured the woman of a cancerous tumor, the report claimed.

Brown rocked back and touched the tissue to her lips. Was it possible? Did miracles like this really happen? She closed her eyes and considered the possibility.

Her experience told her to be skeptical. But she knew her experience wasn't the sum total of everything possible. Though it had never happened to her, she knew colleagues who claimed to have seen such things—tumors that disappeared, people in wheelchairs who walked, clogged hearts that opened up. Who was she to say what was or wasn't possible?

Brown opened her eyes and clicked the "print" icon on the computer screen. She didn't know whether to believe in the healing or not. But she did know that Madden needed to see it. Show him the file, she decided. Show it to him, then let him decide what to do with it. It sure couldn't hurt to do that. And if the miraculous did happen, maybe Katie would get to keep the old man a little longer after all. Maybe Cindy would, too.

THIRTEEN

Stepping through the front entrance of the elegant nineteenth-century home that housed the U.S. embassy to the Vatican, Michael Del Rio checked his watch and ran through a mental list of chores he still needed to finish before leaving Rome. It was almost six P.M. He traveled light—with only a few clothes and a couple of boxes of books brought from America—yet it still had taken all day Tuesday and half a day Wednesday to get everything in order. Pack and ship one stack of stuff back to South Bend, Indiana; prepare a suitcase for about three days; find and reserve accommodations in Istanbul; say good-bye to his friends in the Vatican. Though it took a bit of doing, he managed to complete his farewells without telling any direct lies.

As he headed to the stairway of the two-story building, Michael fingered his clerical collar and squeezed the handle of the briefcase he carried in his right hand. Being deceitful made him nervous. Though he had his faults like everyone else, he was acutely aware of them and suffered from guilt because of that awareness. At times he thought a tendency toward guilt was what made people like him different than most others. From what he could see, a majority of people recognized their failures but didn't seem to suffer as much from them as he did.

At the foot of the stairs, he took a deep breath. He hadn't told his friends any specific lies, but he had held back at least part of the truth—a little "misdirection," in football jargon. He wasn't headed back to America as his actions indicated. Instead, he was headed to Turkey on an assignment that could only be described as surreptitious. Sure, he could place the blame for the subterfuge on his uncle. Yet, the truth was he had accepted the task with very little argument.

What did that make him? If the pope regained his health and discovered his actions later, what would he think? Would he approve of his complicity with Roca? Even more to the point perhaps, what if his superiors at Notre Dame knew of his clandestine work? Would they applaud him for it?

His face flushed, Michael came to the second floor. For a second, he paused to gather his bearings. A pair of efficient-looking men passed him on their way down the stairs, each of them wearing a gray suit, white shirt, and striped tie. Michael thought of his own attire—black pants, shirt, coat, and white collar. Apparently, priests weren't the only ones with a dress code. His cell phone rang.

Setting down his briefcase, Michael leaned against the wall and cupped the receiver to his right ear. He immediately recognized the caller's voice.

"Michael my boy, are you all packed?"

"Just about everything."

"Meeting Miller?"

Michael switched the phone to his left ear, wondering why Roca had called.

"Yeah, in a couple of minutes. But I'm sure that's not why you called."

Roca grunted, but it sounded friendly. "Your American impatience, Michael, such a fault. But yes, you are right. That's not why I called. I have a bit of news for you, an interesting development."

"I'm all ears."

Roca chuckled. "You have such wonderful expressions. I can't wait to hear what you have to say about this."

Michael listened intently for the next five minutes as Roca continued to speak. The words sounded unreal to him, like a plot from some Hollywood movie. His collar seemed to tighten around his neck. If this was true—!!

"Now, Michael," Roca said, finishing his briefing. "What do you have to say to this that I have told you?"

"I think you need someone else for this job."

"Nonsense, it's a simple matter. Delicate, to be sure, but you have every necessary quality to negotiate for me. Here, write this down."

Michael almost started to protest again, to tell Roca of his misgivings, but he knew it wouldn't work. Roca rarely changed his mind once he had decided something. If the cardinal thought him fit to do this job, then he should trust his judgment. Plus, he admitted to himself, the notion of stopping this quest before he ever actually started it disgusted him. In spite of the fact that this venture had forced him to compromise the truth a bit and carried certain professional dangers with it, he wanted to see it through to the end. If he let this new development scare him off, and someone else stepped in and found the scroll, and it proved authentic, he would hate himself for the rest of his life. For better or for worse, he was in this up to his eyebrows and he couldn't turn back.

He took a pad and pen from his briefcase and began to jot down the information Roca dictated.

"Now remember, you're the only one I can trust," Roca said, finishing the conversation. "You're family."

"Just one thing," Michael said. "How do you know all this?"

Roca chuckled. "The Church has her ways, my boy, the Church has her ways. Keep an eye on Ms. Miller. I hear she is quite the ambitious one."

"You should know ambition when you see it."

Roca laughed once more. "Just stay alert, Michael." He hung up.

Michael stuck the pad back into his briefcase, pocketed his phone, and moved to Miller's office. Number 207, on the left, probably a former bedroom renovated in the 1980s after the Reagan administration bought the house and initiated official relations with the Holy See.

Michael stuck his head into an outer reception area but saw no one. An unoccupied desk sat five steps inside the door. He stepped forward a couple more steps, then spotted an open door to his left. Attached to the wall beside the door, a nameplate announced the occupant of the office inside—Ms. Valerie Miller. Knocking on the wall by the nameplate, Michael peered into the office.

Across the room, he saw a woman busy at a computer keyboard. She glanced at him for a split second, then held up a hand, palm outward.

"Hang on a jiff," she said, tapping the computer mouse.

Shrugging, Michael studied the woman's face for a second. She had cheekbones like round flat stones sitting just below her eyes, lips made for Revlon commercials, and thick auburn hair cut just to the top of her ears. A pair of tiny gold earrings cut in the shape of a cross sparkled in her earlobes, and her neck was long and slender. Her only flaw, if one could call it that, came from a nose that bore an angled similarity to that of the actress Michelle Pfeiffer. If one had to have a flaw . . .

Suddenly remembering his uncle's warnings about temptation, Michael smiled inwardly. Valerie Miller definitely did not resemble the north end of a southbound mule. Her hands, one fingering the computer mouse, the other drumming a steady beat on her desk, were exquisite—double advertisements for the benefits of good manicures. She wore an off-white blouse and a navy skirt. The clothes were well tailored and classy.

His inspection complete, Michael leaned against the wall, fingered his collar, and cleared his throat. But Miller continued to work, seemingly ignoring him. A bit perturbed, Michael stepped to the center of the room and stood over her.

Miller's hands suddenly became still and she glanced up at him, her eyes nervously darting out and back between his face and the computer screen. The eyes were green, like a cat's, arched upward at the corners.

"Yeah, okay," Miller said, her voice unsteady. "Sorry about this." She indicated the computer.

"I'm Michael Del Rio," Michael said, forcing a smile. "I'm a representative of Cardinal Severiano Roca from the Vatican. Ambassador Bremer and he have been in conversation."

Miller returned his smile, but somehow it didn't seem too friendly. "Yes, so they have." She glanced back at her computer screen, then looked once more to Michael. "I've met Cardinal Roca, just briefly, though I'm sure he wouldn't remember it."

Michael leaned across her desk. Her face was now no more than five feet away from his. "You want me to stay here, or should I sit over there?" He indicated a soft wing chair by the window.

Miller's eyes darted to the chair then back at him. "The chair's fine," she said, waving her hand at it. "Wherever you want."

Michael eased into the chair. Miller glanced at her watch, then began to tap her fingers again. "What can I do for you Father Del Rio?" she asked, leaning forward slightly.

"Cardinal Roca sent me," he said.

"Yes, I know that."

"He and Ambassador Bremer have—"

"I know, they've been in conversation."

Michael bit his tongue, unsure how to proceed. Miller seemed so defensive. Had he done something to offend her? Or was she just unsure about his involvement, hesitant to get mixed up with a stranger? He took a deep breath and tried again.

"You've seen the information regarding the document in Ephesus?"

"Yes, I read it. Pretty amazing, don't you think?"

"Can I assume you understand the magnitude of this—?"

Miller smiled slightly, the first sign of warmth from her since he entered the room. "Oh yes," she said. "I understand the magnitude." She rose from her seat and perched on the edge of the desk nearest him. "I'm a Baptist. I'm sure you know that. I've got the books of the Bible branded in my brain, the words of a hundred hymns hanging on the tip of my tongue, including the third stanzas that no one ever sings." Her green eyes bored into him like twin laser beams about to do surgery, and her voice inched higher as she spoke. "If this scroll is authentic, it's the most important thing to happen to the church since . . . well, since Jesus!"

"You obviously take this quite seriously," Michael said, trying to make the encounter more personal, hoping to take the edge off the tension in the room.

Valerie shrugged and stood again. "Some would say that," she said, her voice calmer again as she moved gracefully to the window opposite the wall from where Michael sat. "I grew up in the church, practically wore the varnish off a pew with my mom and dad." She stared out the window, one of her fingers rubbing a spot below her right ear.

As if mesmerized, Michael studied her angular frame. She was at least five feet seven inches tall, maybe a bit taller. Slender, but not skinny. Was she an athlete?

She turned back to Michael. "I'm one of those 'born again' folks, you know? 'Trusted Jesus as my Savior,' as we Baptists like to say, at the age of nine. My faith is crucial to me, sort of like breathing. You know what I mean?"

Michael nodded but didn't speak. Truth was, he wasn't real comfortable with such direct talk about God. To him, faith was more private than that. And though he had heard scores of people describe their faith in terms of "Jesus as personal Savior," he had no personal understanding of what that meant. In his mostly academic circles, it was fairly alien terminology.

Miller smiled slightly, then took up her perch on the corner of her desk again. "About this scroll . . ." she said.

"The consequences could be staggering," Michael said.

"It might fill in a lot of blank spaces about Mary and Jesus."

"Spaces we might not want filled."

Miller nodded. "If it says that Mary had other children . . ."

"Then it topples the Catholic apple cart big time."

"Not good for your side," she said, a bit of a smile again on her lips.

"But if the opposite happens . . ."

"Then my team takes it on the chin."

Michael thought he saw a twinkle in her eyes. "Not to mention what it might say about Jesus," he continued.

"Yeah, don't mention that. Not necessarily good for either of us."

The room fell silent for a moment as both of them considered the monumental consequences the scroll might unleash. The Christian world, Protestant *and* Catholic—or Orthodox, for that matter—had a lot at stake.

"How is the pope?" Valerie asked, suddenly changing the subject.

"I'm not the one to ask," Michael said. "Vatican spokesmen say he's tired, worn out from—"

"I know what 'Vatican spokesmen' say," interrupted Valerie. "I've spent hours at the hospital getting the 'official reports.' Thought you might be more forthcoming."

"That's not my job," Michael said, his gaze tight on her face. "I'm here to talk with you about the document from Ephesus. You and I are supposed to find it."

Miller took a deep breath and left the desk corner, taking her seat in front of her computer again. "Yeah, well . . . I'm supposed to find it, that's true. Ambassador Bremer and I agree I'm better off in Turkey looking for this scroll than I am here in Rome waiting for someone from the Vatican to tell us what's really going on with the pope's illness." She stared at the computer screen, her right hand moving as if by automatic pilot to the mouse beside it.

"Izmir seems a logical place to start," Michael said.

"I can't think of anywhere else," Miller said. "That's the last place anyone saw this—" She clicked the mouse and stared at the monitor for a moment. "—This Dr. McAuley."

"You think he's still there?"

"Where else would he be?"

Michael shrugged. "Oh, I don't know. Istanbul maybe."

Miller looked up from the computer, an expression of curiosity written across her face. Her arched eyebrows became more pronounced as she puzzled over Michael's suggestion. Her fingers moved to the spot below her right ear again, and Michael thought he saw a small indentation there, almost as if a scar or something had been covered up with makeup.

"What makes you think he's in Istanbul?" Miller asked.

Michael smiled. "I'm surprised you don't know. Surely you have the information somewhere in your computer files." He indicated the monitor.

Miller chewed on her lower lip. "You're teasing me, aren't you?" she asked.

"I'm a priest," he deadpanned. "We're not known for our teasing."

For a couple of moments, both of them stayed quiet. But then Miller rocked forward. "Look, Father—"

"Call me Michael."

"Okay, Michael. I'm Valerie, and I'm sorry if I seemed preoccupied when you first came in. I was rude and I apologize. But I don't feel comfortable about this whole arrangement. Ambassador Bremer has asked me to do a job, and I plan to do it and do it well. But I don't know you, and you don't know me, and it's a little out of my comfort zone to go flying off to Turkey with a man I've never seen before today."

"Good Baptist girls don't do things of that sort."

"Yeah, you got it. Makes me nervous, you know. The appearance of evil and all that. I'd rather go alone. Less complicated that way, maybe easier. So, I'd rather not have company . . . you know, especially male company. That's where I am right now. Any problem?"

"No problem with anything except the 'go alone' part," he said. "Since I've been asked to work with you, that gives me some heartburn."

"Ambassador Bremer gave me this job."

"And Cardinal Roca gave me this job."

"Your cardinal and the ambassador are close?"

"I think so, yes. They think we can help each other out, you know, the 'two heads are better than one' theory."

"I suppose. You seriously think we can help each other?"

Michael had her right where he wanted her. "I know I can keep you from running off to Izmir when McAuley—or at least the manuscript—is probably in Istanbul."

"Yeah, you mentioned that. Go ahead, tell me what you know."

"Well, just a few minutes ago—right before I came in here— Cardinal Roca called me. Seems a black market dealer in Istanbul has put out the word that he has a document of extraordinary potential he wants to auction to the highest bidder."

Valerie paused, obviously stunned. But she recovered quickly. "How do you know it's your document?"

"The profiteer gave a couple of clues. He called it the 'Ephesus Fragment' and gave us the birthday of Hugh McAuley. The birthday has been checked and it's correct."

"That's all he said?"

"I think it's enough to make us suspicious. Don't you?"

"Who's the dealer?"

"That's not exactly information he'd make public."

Valerie drummed her fingers on the desk. "In Istanbul you say. When is the auction?"

"Sealed bids are due by this Sunday at six P.M. To be delivered to the Istanbul International Hotel security office."

"How much will it take to buy it?"

"I have no clue."

"How did you get the information?"

"Roca didn't tell me, but I can imagine the process. When a black market dealer gets his hands on something like this, he has to communicate it in the right places. I expect this information has been given to a few select people in London, New York, Paris, Berlin, Rome—every city where a potential buyer can be found."

"So you're liable to have a ton of people interested in this?"

"Perhaps, but perhaps not. Only a few will know what the Ephesus Fragment is. And fewer still will have enough money to bid on it. I can't imagine the market for this kind of thing is too large."

"But will the Church bid on the document without seeing it?"

"Oh, we'll see it, I hope."

"But how—?"

Michael smiled. "We're going to visit with the dealer before the bidding on Sunday and make our pitch early."

"You know where he is?"

"I think so, the Church has—"

"Her ways, I know the line." She paused for a moment. "So you'll try to buy this before anyone else gets a chance to top your bid. And all without the approval of the pontiff, who's still unconscious."

"I don't know about all that. A lot is still up in the air. But Cardinal Roca has told me to go to Istanbul, meet with this dealer, make an offer. After that, whether he says yes or no, I'll wait for instructions."

"And you're inviting me to go with you?"

"Cardinal Roca has asked me to work with you. So yes, I'm inviting you to go with me."

"Even after the way I acted when you came in?"

Michael laughed. "You were a bit insensitive for a good Baptist girl, but yes in spite of that."

Valerie picked up a pen and stuck it in her mouth. "When do we leave?"

"Tomorrow morning, flight's at ten-fifty."

Valerie shook her head. "Can't go until Friday," she said. "Too many details to clear up."

Michael did a quick calculation. Roca wouldn't like this delay, but he couldn't help it. "I suppose I can wait another day," he said. "Though that'll push us to get this done before the other bidders make their offers."

"I'm a go for Friday," she repeated. "But not until."

"Then I'll change my ticket," Michael said.

"And I'll get a reservation," Valerie said, standing from her seat.

Michael stood too and shook the hand Valerie extended. "See you at the airport," she said, signaling the end of the conversation.

"I'll look forward to it."

Leaving Valerie Miller's office, Michael realized that in spite of her initial rudeness, his last statement was truer than he cared to admit to anyone else.

––––––––

An hour after Michael Del Rio met Valerie Miller, Cardinal Nelson Randuhar found himself sitting in a high-backed chair inside his private quarters in the Vatican. His elbows were propped on the arms of the chair, and his fingers were steepled together in front of his mouth. But the cardinal wasn't praying. Instead, he was wondering what to do with the transcript of the phone conversation that lay in his lap. The transcript, a word-by-word statement from Cardinal Severiano Roca to his nephew Father Michael Del Rio detailed some interesting possibilities.

Randuhar, of course, knew of the discovery of the so-called Ephesus Fragment. A devout Catholic who worked in the offices of the World Archeological Society had contacted the Vatican late on Monday with the word. Now everyone of importance in the Vatican knew of it. Few though, including him, had given much thought to it. With the pope's critical illness on his mind, who had the time to worry over such an unlikely possibility?

But then, quite unexpectedly, an audio technician from the pontiff's security office had brought the telephone transcript to him. Unaware of the taping device—indeed the technician said only the pope himself knew of it—Randuhar had at first felt betrayed. Roca should know better than to get involved in anything of this sort.

Yet, the more he considered the situation, the more he realized that Roca's actions made a certain kind of sense. Why shouldn't he investigate this document? To do otherwise seemed illogical, perhaps even foolhardy. In one way, Roca was simply doing what *he* might have done if the heavy affairs of the Vatican hadn't weighed so oppressively upon him.

True, Roca should have checked with him about it before he acted. But even that could be explained. Perhaps Roca didn't want to bother him with the issue until he knew more of the facts, or didn't want to burden him with unnecessary complications while he had so many other issues on his mind. All that was possible. No reason necessarily to read sinister motives into anything just yet.

For almost thirty minutes, Randuhar sat in the same place and in the same position, trying to determine what, if anything, he should do. Instinctively patient, he decided he should not act rashly. In fact, by the end of his thirty minutes of stillness, he had decided he would not act at all, or at least in any public manner. But behind the scenes? Well, though most people thought him quite timid, he knew better. Behind the scenes he could act as decisively as the most aggressive of men.

FOURTEEN

At 11:05 A.M. Washington, D.C., time, Roger Attles brushed his towel through his sparse brown hair one final time, tossed the towel onto the kitchen table, and sat down for a bite of breakfast. Not a tall man, his bare feet dangled off the chair but didn't reach the floor. As usual, a copy of the *Washington Times*, the *Washington Post*, the *New York Times*, and the *Wall Street Journal* lay beside his coffee cup. A radio played in the background, the words of a political talk show host adding a steady stream of pretty much useless, but nonetheless compelling, commentary to his coffee. To his left a television picture blinked at him, the sound muted but with the closed caption feature on. His ears were cocked toward the radio like twin satellite dishes as he picked up the *Post* with one hand and the coffee with the other.

His eyes darting from the paper to the television set, he finished the front page and the editorial columns in three gulps of coffee, black, no sugar, and always lukewarm. With no interest in sports or comics, Attles covered the business section next, then turned to "World Events."

To his right, his phone rang. Though his chief assistant Roland Carter called him every morning between ten-forty-five and eleven-fifteen, he still checked the caller identification number. Satisfied, he hurriedly picked up the phone.

"Morning, Roland," he said. "How was the dinner at the Capitol last night?" He continued to read the paper and watch the television as he spoke.

"The usual. A lot of politicians making promises they don't expect to keep to a bunch of donors jumping at the chance to pay top dollar for the privilege of hearing them do it."

"The president show up?" Attles finished one article and started another.

"Yeah, just in time for dessert as always."

"If his waistline gets any bigger, we'll have to hire the Coast Guard to protect him from whale hunters." Attles sucked in his own thin waistline and pulled his black robe tighter to his throat. "You get a chance to say anything to him about the prayer bill?"

"Not directly, but I did talk to the Speaker for a good twenty minutes. He's on board. Plans to bring it up again in the spring session."

"Good, keep me posted on that. Anything else of note?"

"Nothing worth mentioning."

"Then I'll see you at noon." Attles punched off the phone and continued reading the paper. The television was on a commercial, and the radio host was arguing with an irate caller. Attles, the head of the National Values Coalition, a six-million-member body committed to maintaining traditional religious values in government, sipped his coffee and kept his ears pricked. His job demanded that he stay in the loop on just about everything, and if a job was ever created for one specific person, this one was created for him.

Attles loved minutia, the bits and pieces of information that seemed to float in the Washington air like leaves falling from oak trees in the fall. He loved knowing the who, what, when, and where of everything that happened in and around his world. In fact, he craved such information so much that on the few occasions when he actually took a few days of vacation, he inevitably found himself calling into the office, logging onto the Internet, having his newspapers forwarded to him. As addicted to knowledge as an alcoholic to cold beer, Attles made it a point to know everything that happened in Washington.

Taking another sip of coffee, Attle's gray eyes narrowed as he read the article on the bottom right side of the newspaper. Interesting, really interesting! His pulse quickening, he finished the story, but then read it a second time to make sure he had digested its implications. Unbelievable!

He took another drink of coffee, then picked up the phone and dialed a number known to no more than a hundred people in the country. The number connected him directly to the president's secretary just outside the Oval Office of the White House. As one of the chief architects of the president's last campaign and a policy specialist both admired and hated for his money-raising and vote-delivering capabilities, Attles received intimate access to the president. Four rings later, the president's secretary answered.

"Roger Attles here, Lucia. Our man got a minute?"

"He's about to finish with a group of third graders from Minnesota. Hold on a second. I'll see if he can speak to you."

"I won't take long."

Attles read the article again while he waited, the radio show and television momentarily forgotten. The headline was low-key: "Words of Mary Found?"

The story, though told in a soft tone, raised fascinating questions.

"On Sunday, December 8, archeologist Hugh McAuley, working on a dig near the ancient city of Ephesus . . ."

Finishing the article for the third time, Attles laid down the paper and scratched his nose. He knew, of course, that the pope was rumored to be considering a new decree about Mary. As chief political strategist for the coalition, he made it his business to keep up with religious news from every conceivable denomination. If the Catholics burped or the Baptists coughed or the Lutherans scratched their chins, he inevitably heard about it. Right at ten percent of his sixty-nine-million-dollar budget went into the pockets of a score of operatives who did nothing but monitor current events and track hot personalities and keep him apprised of what they saw and heard. The data this army of informants had transmitted to him over the past six years had once filled a row of filing cabinets the width of a basketball court. Now, of course, he had the information stored on computers.

He took a sip of coffee and considered the uproar this new story might bring. Combined with the pope's continuing incapacity, the discovery of a document about Mary could shake up a whole lot of the names on his Rolodex. Leaders of the conservative wing of American religion, especially, would want immediate information about such a find.

"Roger, you still there?"

Attles set down his coffee cup and folded his feet under his chair. "Yes, Mr. President, right here. Hope you're having a good day."

The president laughed. "I never again have to run for office, and Congress is firmly controlled by my party. That's about as good as it gets. What's up?"

Attles cleared his throat. "Don't know if it's anything. But there's a story in the *Post* about an archeological find in Turkey."

"A scroll about Mary."

"You know about it?"

"Sure I do. Ambassador Bremer sent a brief to the State Department Monday afternoon. As you can imagine, the Catholic Church is quite concerned. Bremer says the pope's illness and the word of this archeological discovery have the Vatican folks as nervous as a bunch of elephants on ice. I gave State the go-ahead to nose around a bit. I think Bremer's on top of it."

Attles paused a moment, dredging up in his mind what he knew about Bremer. A man born with a silver spoon in his mouth, a former congressman from Maine, and a heavy contributor to both the president's campaigns. A Catholic certainly, as his post demanded, but Attles knew little about Bremer's true religious convictions.

"You confident Bremer can handle this?" he asked, hoping his misgivings weren't too obvious.

"No reason to think otherwise. It's a simple enough job. Assign someone to investigate. Help the Catholic Church if it requests it."

"What does he do if he finds out the document is authentic?"

"Don't know about that. Leave it to the Vatican, I suppose."

Attles weighed his words carefully. "Do you think that's the best course?"

"You're suggesting something else?"

"Well, let me put it this way. If this piece of parchment is legitimate, it might be helpful if the right people get it first."

"And by the right people you mean your people instead of the Catholic Church."

"I wouldn't say it quite that directly. I represent more than just Protestant clients. I also have a number of allies in the Catholic community."

"You never say anything that directly. You let others say it for you."

"But you do get my point."

"I do, but I don't know if I should do anything about it. I won't override the State Department on this without a compelling reason. And, to be honest, I don't think they'll think it appropriate if I intervene to make sure that a document like this ends up in the hands of the most conservative wing of my party."

"But that conservative wing largely put you in power. Don't you think you owe—?"

"I owe you, Roger, no doubt about it. Your people played a large part in putting me in office. But I'm not owned by you.

There's a difference there I'm not sure you grasp."

Attles bit his tongue and told himself to stay calm. Well aware of the president's infamous temper, he knew he didn't want to push this any further. If the president wouldn't help him, he would just have to handle matters himself.

"I appreciate your candor, Mr. President," he said, choosing his most soothing voice. "And I admit I sometimes press too hard. But I believe in what I do. If that makes me too aggressive for some people, I'll try to do better. And if you'll forgive me, I'll work to make amends at some future occasion."

The president's tone notched down to its normal level. "No problem, Roger, I know how you are. Don't sweat it. I'm with you, remember that. My faith is important to me too. I don't want this to go sour on any of us. So look, here's what I'll do. I'll keep you in the loop on what happens at State. Will that help a little?"

"That'll be wonderful, Mr. President. I appreciate that."

"Great, I'll keep in touch." The president hung up.

Attles hung up too and picked up his coffee. Sipping it quickly, he came to three quick conclusions. One, a slew of people would want to get their hands on this scroll. Two, though he'd like to think differently, he didn't really believe he could trust Bremer to do the right thing even if his people found it first. Three, if he wanted the outcome to please his constituents, then he had to get one of his men to handle the task.

Attles picked up the phone again and dialed Roland's number.

"Yeah, Roland," he said. "Check your files. I need a guy with some international expertise. Someone who can work discreetly, but quickly."

"What's the job?"

"I need to find a document."

"What kind of document?"

"Just get me a man. The rest is on a need-to-know basis."

"I'll call you back."

Attles hung up and grabbed his coffee. Two sips later, he dialed another number. If he wanted this document, and he did, then he needed to hurry.

———

Standing by an open window on the fourth floor of the Hyatt Hotel in Cairo, Egypt, Dr. Martha Hinton sucked deeply on a cigarette, then exhaled a long breath of smoke and satisfaction. Below her, the great city of the Nile stretched out in all its squalor and splendor. Night had fallen over the streets, and a million lights now cast a dull glow over the domes of all the mosques that dotted the city.

Hinton had always loved Cairo. Every time she came here, she found herself enchanted by its sights and sounds and smells. The place charmed her like a troubadour singing to a love-struck princess. Smiling contentedly to herself, she brushed a wisp of hair off her face and turned and faced the room. On the opposite side from the window Addam Azziz sat in a stuffed wing-back chair, his black tasseled loafers propped on an ottoman and two body guards standing as sentinels beside each shoulder.

"I've got good news," she said, her voice strong. "The manuscript is in Istanbul."

Azziz tilted his head and his black eyes sparkled. "You're sure of this?"

She nodded. Fortunately for her, years of work in the Middle East had given her good connections with the right people. A day's worth of phone calls to a list of wealthy patrons and a few promises that had nothing to do with archeology, and her network had given her the information she needed.

"I'm sure," she said. "It seems that an antiquities dealer somehow came onto it and now wants to auction it to the highest bidder."

Azziz licked his lips. "What about your man McAuley? What happened to him?"

Hinton shrugged. "No word. I hope he's okay, but I have no way of knowing."

"This dealer then, what do you know of him?"

She took a step closer to Azziz and pulled another drag from her cigarette. "Nothing except he's apparently well known for his work. He's a speculator, a fence for stolen goods, a master of the black market."

Azziz paused for a couple of moments. His bodyguards stayed still. Hinton wondered how they could stay so rigid, like ceramic Dobermans waiting on someone's front porch. When Azziz spoke, his voice took on a tone of steel.

"This dealer expects me to pay for this manuscript, this document found on a dig I sponsored—a dig I paid for with my own money?"

She paused, her cigarette frozen in her finger. She hadn't considered the possibility that Azziz might not want to pay. "I suppose," she stammered. "I guess we'll have to pay."

"We?"

"Well . . . you. I've done what you asked me to do. I found the manuscript. I'm an archeologist, not a financier. I'm not poor, but I cannot afford what the dealer will surely ask."

"But you're the one who lost the document!" Azziz pounced from the chair and jumped across the room at her. Grabbing her forearms, he squeezed her flesh as if trying to crush a coconut. Smoke curled up and surrounded his beard.

"You know the deal!" he shouted. "What you find, you owe to me first. That's the agreement. So you will get this document, and you will deliver it to me, and I will not pay for it! Do you understand?"

Her forearms turning purple, Hinton pressed back against the wall and fought to keep her composure. Tears washed into her eyes, but she pushed them back. "What difference does one scroll make to you?" she moaned. "You've got everything. Why do you even care about this stupid—"

Azziz pushed her harder into the wall. His beard brushed against her forehead as he stared down at her. His eyes were wild and his breath hot. "You idiot!" he spewed. "You who think you know so much. Don't you realize what this document might do? Used correctly in my hands it might split your so-called 'Western civilization.' If it casts doubt on your precious Jesus, imagine the chaos in the churches, the very backbone of your culture, your politics. If not that, then perhaps it'll create a schism between your Catholics and Protestants. Either way, the true faith, the faith of the Great Allah will gain advantage, an advantage that will enable us to propagandize your people, make inroads into your masses, all to the good of Islam. Who knows? Perhaps the Great Allah will pick up the pieces of your devastated society and create a new religious and political order! Don't you see the possibilities? Don't you see?"

Hinton stayed silent, her body shaking. She deserved better than this. It wasn't her fault that McAuley turned out to be a traitor. If he wasn't already dead, she might just do the job herself if she ever found him.

Fueled by her hatred of McAuley, Hinton stayed calm as she answered Azziz. "I understand," she said between gritted teeth. "I understand and I will get the document for you."

Azziz released her arms and stepped back. "You're a strong woman," he said, the fury in his voice completely gone. "I like that. You found out about the dealer. I wondered if you would. His name is Yoseph; no one knows his last name. He's been around for almost ten years, a lifetime for one in such a hazardous occupation."

"You know about him?"

Azziz smiled as if comforting a child. "Of course I know," he said. "Remember who I am!"

Hinton nodded, slowly understanding. Little in this part of the world escaped the attention of the great Azziz.

"Then you can get the scroll," she said, relaxing just a touch. "It'll be easy for you."

Azziz shook his head. "Don't tell me what I must do," he said. "You lost it, you are responsible for it."

"And if I can't?"

"Then of course I will step in at the appropriate moment and deal with it myself. But I hope for your sake that such a thing will not happen."

"Is that a threat?"

"Who is to say what it is?" he whispered. "Just get me the document." He turned and motioned to his bodyguards. Together the three men headed toward the door. But then Azziz paused and twisted back to her. "Dr. Hinton?"

"Yes?"

"Don't ever smoke in my presence again. Is that clear?"

She nodded limply and Azziz walked out, his two hulking protectors on either side.

Alone again, Hinton turned and walked back to the window. Below, the lights of Cairo's traffic curled in and out, a blinking stream of color as alive as a snake searching for food. But the people living among those lights were oblivious to her and her fears. For the first time ever, Cairo had become something other than an enchanting place. Now she saw the distress in the streets, the dirt and the danger.

Taking a last pull from her cigarette, Hinton hugged herself and started to cry, slowly at first but then harder and harder. She had no money to pay for the manuscript, and without money she knew she would have to resort to something else. Sadly, she realized that it had always been that way. When push came to shove, she always returned to what worked best for her, as painful as that was.

FIFTEEN

Cindy Brown found Willard Madden standing behind a simple mahogany desk in his office on the second floor of his sprawling, Spanish-style home. Behind the desk, an expansive window opened up to a backyard that resembled an English garden. Neatly clipped hedges bordered a curving, cobblestone walkway, and palm trees the height of telephone poles stretched serenely toward the sunny sky. Roses of innumerable colors graced a flowerbed the size of a basketball court, and a pond filled with exotic fish anchored the back left portion of the contemplative space.

Madden was dictating to a secretary as Brown entered, his hands in his pockets. Three other men sat in high-backed chairs to his right, and a row of computers bordered the wall to his left.

"Mr. Madden?"

Madden pivoted at her voice, and Brown noted the dark circles under his eyes and the sagging skin beneath his chin. Though an expensive tan suit, white silk shirt, and hand-painted tie covered his body, she knew how frail he had become. His five-feet, ten-inch frame now carried no more than a hundred and thirty pounds. Her heart sank. If she didn't find something soon, he wouldn't live more than another few months or so.

"Yes, Cindy?" Madden asked, his eyes registering surprise at her interruption.

She hesitated, unsure whether to tell him about the so-called miracle healings or not. Somehow the notion seemed silly now, stunted by the reality of his emaciated body. Was she giving him false hope, something no doctor should ever do?

"Speak up, Doctor," he pressed, continuing to stare at her.

"Speak up or move along. I've got things to do and not much time to do them."

"Well . . . I've . . . you see, I think I need to show you something."

"Over here," he said, pointing to a seat to his left. "Save me a few steps."

Hurriedly, Brown crossed the room. Taking the seat, she opened the folder in her hand and handed the sheet inside to Madden. Still standing, he scanned the paper.

Watching his dark brown eyes, still clear in spite of his illness, read through the report, Brown came to a startling conclusion. She, a woman too busy with medical school and the career that followed to fall in love, had done just that—fallen in love with a man about to die. Good heavens!

She thought of her own appearance—brown hair graying at the temples, a body built a bit like a snowmobile, wider in the back than in the front, a face unremarkable except for deep blue eyes and eyebrows that would make a movie star envious. Of all her qualities, she knew her eyes were her best. But did Willard Madden care? Had he noticed her eyes at all?

Madden looked up from the paper and spoke to his assistants. "Leave us," he said, dismissing them with a wave. "I'll call you when I'm finished." He took a seat at his desk and faced Cindy as the four disappeared.

"What's your opinion of this?" he asked, placing his feet up on the desk.

Cindy shrugged, not sure how to answer.

"A shrug won't do it," said Madden. "The money I pay buys more than that. What's your assessment of this report? Not exactly what I expected from you. But I'm open-minded. Spit it out."

Cindy cleared her throat and sought to put her honest conclusions into words. "Well, it's obvious that I'm skeptical. But, at the same time, I can't dismiss the notion out of hand. As a scientist, I have to write it off as bunk, religious fraud. Even if I do accept the possibility of mysterious healing, which I do, I have to conclude that such things happen because of the power of the mind over the body, the . . . I don't know . . . the power of the psyche to do things we don't understand yet."

"So you don't believe in the miraculous. The 'power of God' as the fanatics put it." He said it without inflection, not indicating his views about the possibility. Cindy ran her hands through her hair, considering the question.

"There have been some reputable studies," she offered, though without conviction. "Studies in San Francisco in fact, a Dr. Randolph Byrd, and at Dartmouth Hitchcock Medical Center. The studies said prayer was a factor in helping people overcome heart problems. And a Dr. Larry Dossey has written a book, *Healing Words*, that validates, according to his definitions, some remarkable experiences."

"You buy these studies?"

"I don't know. I guess I'm like everyone else. Maybe such things are possible; I just haven't seen them. If miracles of this sort happen"—she indicated the sheet in Madden's hands— "they're beyond my experience."

Madden dropped his feet to the floor, twisted to the right, and pulled a newspaper from the table next to his desk. Opening it, he flipped a few pages and folded it back. "Read this," he said, sliding the paper over the desk and pointing to a story on the right side, two columns from the left. "See if this makes any difference."

Confused, but wanting to please him, Cindy dropped her gaze and read the headline, "Mary Scroll Found in Ephesus." Not sure what it had to do with the subject at hand, she looked up at Madden.

"Read the story!" he commanded.

She turned back to the page. The article didn't take long to read. An American correspondent in Istanbul had received a report that an archeologist had uncovered an ancient manuscript in a cave outside of Ephesus. Though the archeologist wasn't available for comment, the manuscript was supposedly written by St. John, detailing the life of Mary, the mother of Jesus. A number of experts in the field of Biblical studies and archeology had disputed the possibility, but no one could say for sure whether it was authentic or not. Until the manuscript was found and tests were run, speculation did no one any good.

Interested, but unsure of the relevance, Cindy laid the paper on the desk and faced Madden. He raised his eyebrows but stayed quiet. She said nothing.

"Well?" he said. "What's your opinion now?"

"I don't see how this changes anything."

Madden grabbed the paper, stared at it for a second, then crumpled it and threw it to the floor. "Then you're just dense," he sputtered, standing and walking to the window. "Don't you see? The scroll and the vision happened on the same day. A woman in Mexico sees a vision of Mary holding a scroll. She reports a healing to her priest, who reports it to her bishop. Half-way across the world an archeologist finds a scroll, one suppos-edly telling the story of Mary with her son Jesus. Just a coincidence? I don't think so!"

"But what difference does that make?" pressed Cindy. "Even if I accepted both situations as factual accounts, which I don't, what's the point?"

Madden stared out the window at his garden. For several sec-onds, he remained silent. When he spoke, his voice was slower than she had ever heard it, a decided change from the rapid-fire rhythm he usually used.

"I'm not sure there is a point," he started. "But I'm not a man who takes coincidence lightly. You don't know this, but thirty-five years ago I was in Vietnam, a second lieutenant with a pla-toon operating near Que San. The third month I was there, we were beating the bush with several other platoons late one af-ternoon. We thought we were pretty safe, miles from any hot zone.

"While we were walking, our chaplain eased up beside me and slipped off his helmet to wipe his face. The guy behind him grabbed his helmet and shoved it on my head. I never wore a helmet—it chafed my ears. I jerked the thing off and tossed it back to the chaplain. 'No cross on my head,' I said.

"A couple of the guys started ragging me, telling me to put the helmet back on, I could use a little religion. I started cussing, one word after another, the vilest things a man can say. They kept at me, at least five of them, hooting and screaming for me to wear the helmet. I know it sounds loony, but war is crazy. Any-way, I had finally heard enough. To shut up the racket, I jerked the helmet from the chaplain, popped it on, and started dancing around like a kid at a sock hop.

"There I was, dancing the shag when it happened—a shot out of nowhere. Seems a sniper about fifty yards away wasn't enjoy-ing the floor show. The bullet hit the helmet just behind my left ear, ripped a hole right through it, tore out a piece of my skull, then lodged dead still where it was. See this?" he tilted his head toward her, indicating a spot right behind his ear.

"The bullet is still there. I've got the helmet in my closet." He paused to let Cindy soak in the story.

"Two weeks later the army sent me home. Three months after that our hometown newspaper went on the auction block. With one loan from my old man and another from the bank, I bought a fifty-one percent share. The rest, as they say, is history."

Finished, Madden turned, walked over to Cindy, and rested his hands on the desk.

"Most people would see all that as sheer good fortune, luck, *bon chance*. I see it as a whole line of sheer good fortunes, too many for all of them to occur without a reason. All my life, things like that have happened. One thing after another, a twist here, a turn there—how do you think I made so much money? Hard work and brains? Sure, those helped, but tons of people have more brains than me and work just as hard. It's more than that; it's a whole series of breaks, coincidences if you will. No one like me, no matter how smart, succeeds this much."

"But you're not even religious," Cindy said, trying to figure him out.

Madden shrugged. "Not in the traditional sense, you're right. But that doesn't mean I don't think something is going on out there"—he waved in the general direction of the ceiling—"that I don't understand. I do. But It's bigger than I am, and all I can do is try to play the hand when It, whatever It is, deals the cards."

"Seems you keep getting great hands . . . except for the cancer, of course."

"Yeah, well, this morning, I read the paper like I always do, cover to cover. Didn't pay much attention to this story at first. But then you come in here and hand me information about a miracle by Mary in Mexico. And Mary is holding a scroll. So I remember the newspaper article: Mary's story on a scroll? Coincidence? You better believe it!"

He straightened, stuffed his hands into his pockets, and stomped back to the window.

"But neither account has been verified," Cindy countered, trying to stay objective but feeling overpowered by Madden's sense of fate. "Stories, that's all they are, stories. We don't know if either of them is true, if either will stand up to the tests of science, if they have any connection to each other, if—"

"Forget your science!" shouted Madden, facing her again, his face turning red. "People like me are dying, and your science is as useless as hair spray at a bald man's convention! We've trusted science to find a cure, but so far we've found nothing but pain and more pain, medicine and more medicine. Don't you think it's time we tried something else—anything else? Don't you think something like this is at least possible? Possible when nothing else is?"

Again, Cindy hesitated. She didn't want to give Madden any

illusions, to lift his aspirations beyond what she or anyone else could deliver. "I just don't know," she whispered. "I just don't know. It's so far-fetched. A woman in Mexico, a scroll in Turkey. What's the connection?"

Madden shook his head and took a deep breath, then crossed the room and placed his hands on the chair behind her head. "Cindy, Cindy," he said, his voice seeming to slow down even more. "I don't know the connection yet, don't know that I'll find one. But visions of Mary often seem to bring claims of healing with them. All over the world you see it, and it's been that way for years. Lourdes, Guadeloupe. Mary shows up and miracles happen. In the last couple of years, I've read about more and more of them."

She twisted to face him. "But you can't create a vision of Mary. How—?"

"I know that," soothed Madden, leaning over her. "But maybe . . . maybe I can find this scroll. Somehow that seems the key to it all, the one thing that ties the vision to the discovery in Ephesus. I don't know, but that seems the right thing to do . . . find the scroll. Maybe it holds the secret to all this, a formula of some kind for healing. Do you think that's possible?"

Cindy hesitated, but her heart went out to Madden, and she wanted to lift her face toward his, her lips . . .

"Tell me what you think, Cindy," Madden continued. "Don't worry about your professionalism at this point. Things are too far gone for that. For once, just this once, act like something other than my doctor." He placed his hands on her shoulders, and she felt the warmth of his fingers through the fabric of her blouse.

"Be my friend," he said, his voice registering a tenderness she had heard in him only once, the day he returned from the visit with his granddaughter. "Tell me what you think. I'm down to my last hope here. Put aside what your mind tells you. I need to know what your heart says."

Cindy closed her eyes. More than anything else, she wanted to comfort Willard Madden. No matter what her medical training told her, she couldn't refuse to offer hope to the man she had come to love. Even if she was wrong and he died before the New Year, she didn't see how it could do any harm to give him the encouragement he so obviously sought.

She felt him remove his hands and move around the chair. She opened her eyes and found him staring straight into her face. "I think it's possible," she said. "Though everything I've ever learned tells me otherwise, something in me tells me to open up to this. So, yes, miracles can happen. I . . . I'm sure they can. If this scroll is from the mouth of Mary, then it might contain some secret message, some insight that only she can give to the world."

Madden nodded quickly, then stepped away from her, his systems on go again, full speed ahead. He touched a button on the phone on his desk and barked an order into the air. "Get Red Cashion on the phone!" he shouted. "He's in the data base!"

He turned again to Cindy. "Red Cashion is a cynical, pot-bellied son of a dog who drinks too much and cares too little. But he's also the best private investigator I've ever known. He's retired somewhere up in Wyoming and won't like me bothering him. But he hasn't liked anything since a horse threw his wife and put her in a wheelchair a few years ago. He'll come for me, though. He's always come for me. We got history, you see. He's the guy who put the chaplain's helmet on my head over in Nam. And I introduced him to his wife, one fine woman if I ever met one. He'll find this scroll for us."

SIXTEEN

At just past five-thirty A.M. Rome time, Cardinal Antonio Marchino respectfully lowered his eyes and stepped forward into the chambers of Cardinal Nelson Randuhar. Knowing the Secretary's habit of rising early, he had discreetly asked for and received this audience before the majority of those within the Vatican began to stir.

Randuhar, fully dressed, greeted him warmly as he entered, leading him to a small study area to the left of the main bedroom. The study contained few furnishings. A simple desk sat in the middle. A chair with an extra-tall back to accommodate Randuhar's height sat behind it. Two winged chairs, obviously well used, framed the two sides of a circular burgundy rug in front of the desk, and a coffee table centered the rug. The only thing unusual about the room was a ring of photographs that encircled the entire space, each showing a scene from some tribal setting from Africa. The photographs, though, weren't pleasant pictures of smiling "natives." Instead, they showed image after image of human suffering—emaciated bodies, burning huts, and teeming crowds reaching for food handed down from a relief truck.

Randuhar motioned for him to sit and Marchino did, taking one of the winged chairs. Randuhar hesitated for a moment, and Marchino thought he was going to sit behind his desk. Instead, the tall African man took the other chair. So it was to be informal. Good.

Marchino knew he took some risk by asking for the meeting. If word leaked that he had come to lobby Randuhar for any specific purpose, his fellow cardinals might see it as desperate, and he would immediately lose standing. So, this meeting had to stay secret if at all possible. If word of it did come out, he would have to spin it as a meeting of two equals concerned about the health of the pope and the Church.

"The pictures are intriguing," he began, indicating the walls.

Randuhar sighed and nodded. "Scenes from my homeland," he said, his characteristic elongation of words evident even this early in the morning. "Every one of them."

"Your history means much to you."

Randuhar stood and walked to the wall behind his chair. "We are a violent people," he said. "Tribal conflicts centuries old. My father died in such a war, my mother from starvation in the aftermath of it. These on this wall are scenes from that war." He pointed to four different photos, each of them stark in their portrayal of reality.

"I keep the photos to remind me who I am," he said. "To remind me that no matter what happens to me, I have to do all I can for my people. If we are to survive, someone has to pull us out of our cycle, show us a better way."

He quickly turned from the wall, and Marchino knew by his body language that he would talk no more of it.

"Coffee?" Randuhar asked.

"Please," Marchino said. "Black is fine."

Randuhar stepped to a side table and poured two cups. Back in his chair he handed one to Marchino and dropped a spoonful of sugar into his own.

"What is the word on His Holiness this morning?" Marchino asked, adjusting his glasses.

"His doctor lets no one see him," Randuhar said. "But according to his report, he's about the same. He says he could remain so for many days." He sipped his coffee.

Marchino dropped his eyes. "These are anxious days for the Church," he said. "The people wonder what will happen."

"Only God knows the future," countered Randuhar. "The people will have to go on wondering."

"How long can you fool the press?"

"I will let the press fool themselves. We say nothing. They make up their own truth."

Surprised by the hint of sarcasm in Randuhar's voice, Marchino paused, trying to decide how to proceed. Should he come out aggressively and say what he wanted to say? Or should he hint at the edges and depend on Randuhar to read between the lines? He touched his coffee cup to his lips.

"Perhaps we could help the people with some of their questions," he said, choosing to play it safe for the moment. "Perhaps we could give them more up-to-date information on the pontiff. The media is doing as you suggest, and speculation is rampant. Some say," and here Marchino paused for effect. "Some say the pontiff did not faint but is actually dead, and a conspiracy is afoot to keep it a secret."

Randuhar's expression never wavered, and Marchino found himself admiring the Secretary. So far as he knew, no such rumor existed, but he had suggested it to see how Randuhar reacted. But the man was inscrutable. Which made him perhaps more dangerous than he had expected.

"Rumors," Randuhar said, dismissing them with a wave. "Rumors say all kinds of things. One even suggests that you want to be pope."

Marchino chuckled. So, Randuhar had a sense of humor! "As you say, rumors say all kinds of things."

Both men tipped coffee cups to their lips. Marchino decided to stop dancing around the issue.

"One thing is surely not rumor," he said. "The people want to know what we plan to do about the Marian Decree. Will we move ahead with the pontiff's plans to name her Co-Redemptrix? The New Year's Eve Mass arrives in less than three weeks, and we cannot wait much longer before deciding."

Randuhar smiled demurely. "So, my friend, we finally come to the point of your visit. I wondered if you would speak directly. I'm glad you did."

"Then you agree we should make a decision about Mary?"

Randuhar placed his coffee cup on the table between them. "No, I didn't say that. I said only that I'm glad you raised the subject. Such a decision can come only from His Holiness. And, as we well know, he cannot tell us his wishes. So we cannot act, one way or the other."

Marchino paused for a moment, then cleared his throat. "But we do know what he wants," he said, his voice forceful. "His writings indicate—"

"The pontiff's writings," interrupted Randuhar, "indicate he loves our Blessed Mother and that he has considered the possibility of naming her Co-Redemptrix with Jesus. But never, in any official document that I've seen, has His Holiness unequivocally stated his position. If we had anything definitive, then yes, we could move ahead, but I know of no such public statement. Do you?"

Marchino took a deep breath and started to speak, but then

stopped and again drank from his coffee.

"Tell me about yourself," Randuhar said, changing the sub-ject. "Why such devotion to the Holy Mother? Such a drive to press this announcement?"

Marchino tilted his head and stared curiously at the Secre-tary. "Few ask so directly," he said. "But it's simple, really. At the age of ten, polio beset my body. Everyone thought I would die. The priest came to perform the last rites. But my mother, God rest her soul, refused to give up. She said the Holy Mother would protect me. She sat by my bed for days, never leaving, holding the rosary, praying to the Virgin. I drifted near to death. My mother stayed beside me, holding my hand with one hand, the rosary with the other. Sometime near the end of it all, I awoke in the dark of the night. I looked at my mother. But I did not see her. I saw the Virgin instead, sitting by my bed. She touched my head with her hands, then smiled at me. The most beautiful smile one could ever see. I thought I had died and she had come to meet me. But I had not died, as you can see." He smiled at Randuhar and waved his hand over his diminutive body. "I awoke the next morning and my recovery began. I pledged myself to the Holy Mother that day, and believe she de-serves every elevation the Holy Church can offer to her."

"A moving story," Randuhar said, though not visibly touched. "An illuminating one."

Marchino nodded. "It is what it is," he said. "It made me who I am."

Randuhar nodded, then steepled his long fingers.

"What do you think of this document found in Turkey?" Mar-chino asked, moving away from the personal issues. "I assume you have noticed the communications concerning it?"

"You assume correctly," Randuhar said. "And it gives me an-other reason for caution concerning our beloved Mary. Though I suspect forgery at worst and bad archeology at best, it behooves the Church to know more before moving ahead with any new declarations about the Virgin."

"I understand the man who found it has now disappeared."

"From the news reports, it seems so."

"There are rumors that foul play may have occurred."

"So I've heard, but we both know about rumors." Both men smiled slightly as Randuhar continued. "What isn't a rumor is that both the archeologist and the document seem to have dis-appeared."

"Is the Church making inquiries?"

Randuhar reached for his coffee again and took several seconds with it before he spoke again. When he did, he looked straight into Marchino's face. "I can assure you," he said, "the Church is taking all appropriate measures to locate the scroll. In fact," and here he paused for two sips of coffee, "I even hear that some within the Vatican are working independently to find it."

Marchino arched his eyebrows and pretended innocence. "Is that so? Our brother Roca by any chance?"

Randuhar smiled discretely. "Ah, rumors once more. I dare not repeat them. Perhaps Roca, perhaps another or two. Perhaps even yourself?"

"Will there be recriminations if such rumors prove true?"

Randuhar shrugged. "That all depends. Surely, the Church frowns on such independent action. But if the document is a hoax, what's the harm?"

"But if testing shows the scroll as authentic . . ."

"Then the man holding it will wield great power."

"Power that could elevate him to the papal throne if His Holiness should—"

"You go too far," interrupted Randuhar. "We will not speak of such a possibility."

Marchino touched a napkin to his lips, considering whether to play his last card. Deciding to wait, he placed his coffee cup down and shifted to the edge of his chair. "I keep you too long," he said. "I know you have important duties. I pray for you as you lead the Church in this difficult hour."

"I covet your prayers," Randuhar said, standing to end the meeting. "And I appreciate your continued guidance and advice. The Church depends on men like you."

Marchino nodded, then stood as well and turned to leave. By the door, he faced Randuhar one final time. "The decision concerning Mary has to be made before too long," he said. "The Mass is—"

Randuhar held up a hand. "I know the date," he said. "Believe me, when the time comes, I will act as I believe I should."

"Please know that I will assist you in any way I can," Marchino said.

"I have no doubt of it, and I shall call on you when the time is right."

"I am glad to hear this," Marchino said, staring up at Randuhar, wanting to make his point clear. "A partnership between the two of us might be helpful to all concerned."

Randuhar steepled his fingers. "Perhaps it will happen, my friend. God willing, of course. Let's talk again . . . soon."

"Of course." Marchino bowed just a touch, then walked from the room. Stepping down the marble hallway, he clenched his teeth and decided two things: one, he had best not underestimate the mysterious Secretary Randuhar, and two, if he wanted the scroll, he had better move even more quickly than he had previously planned.

Watching Marchino leave his chambers, Cardinal Randuhar grunted, then walked quickly to his desk. Sliding open a drawer, he ran his fingers over the black leather journal that lay facedown on the bottom. Inside the journal, the pope's unmistakable handwriting told him exactly what His Holiness wanted to do about the Marian Decree.

Taking a deep breath, Randuhar closed his eyes and assured himself once more that he was doing the right thing. Knowing the will of a comatose pope on such an important issue but not acting immediately in accordance with it weighed heavily on his soul. But before he took any precipitous action on the issue of Mother Mary, he needed, if possible, one more piece of the puzzle. Before moving any further, he had to find the scroll that supposedly told her story. Without assurances about the contents and authenticity of that book, acting on the pope's words made no sense, no sense at all.

PART THREE

Come now, you who say, "Today or tomorrow we will go to such and such a city . . ." Instead, you ought to say, "If the Lord wills, we shall live and do this or that."

St. James 4:13, 15

Plans get you into things but you got to work your way out.

Will Rogers

SEVENTEEN

Rubbing sleep from his eyes, Michael Del Rio awoke slowly on Saturday morning, his mind sluggish and requiring several moments to remember where he was and how he got there. But then, as he sat up and stared around the room, it all came back to him. The Grand Hyatt Hotel in Istanbul, Turkey. He checked the clock—7:20. He had perhaps the most important appointment of his life at nine A.M.

Instantly excited, he threw his feet onto the floor and shifted into gear, showering quickly. Out of the shower, he slipped into his underwear, then snapped off a five-minute stretching routine, followed by fifty push-ups. His blood pumping vigorously now, he finished dressing, choosing khaki slacks and a plain white shirt instead of his normal clerical black.

The flight yesterday had passed in a hurry. The only thing memorable about it was the unexpected and somewhat unsettling discovery that though he and Valerie Miller had booked their flights independently, his seat assignment put him right next to her. Which would have been fine except for the fact that the attitude she had displayed in her office seemed to have undergone a complete metamorphosis. Instead of treating him like an unwelcome cousin, she communicated nothing but warmth and good humor.

Brandishing a book entitled *Key Turkish Cities* like a conductor wielding a baton, she regaled him with a litany of facts about Istanbul. By the time the plane landed at just past noon, he knew far more about their destination than he had ever expected to learn. Even more, his attitude about Valerie Miller had become completely confused. Having predetermined that the two of them would tolerate each other only long enough to do the job they had been assigned, he now found himself actually liking her.

Slipping on his shoes, a pair of black lightweight walking boots, Michael pondered her new attitude. Had Valerie decided that since she had to deal with him whether she liked it or not, she might as well make the most of it? Or had her earlier demeanor been a false front that she peeled off once absent from her professional setting?

Forcing himself to concentrate on more immediate matters, Michael stepped to a mirror to brush his hair. For several seconds, he studied the image that stared back at him. If all went well, the Ephesus document might be in his hands within a few hours. Would that change him any? Certainly not if the book proved to be a hoax. But what if tests proved it authentic? Would he end up on television? The author of a best-selling book? A celebrity?

Michael picked up his hairbrush. Though he felt a bit guilty for it, the idea of fame pleased him. Who among his colleagues, even the most devout, wouldn't like that if it came his way? He knew, of course, that success often led to pride, and pride often led to downfall—had seen it happen to far too many people not to know its tragedies. But if it happened, it happened.

He brushed his hair a couple of strokes and noted the streaks of gray at the temples. Was it his imagination or did the streaks get more prominent every morning? Michael smiled ruefully. Encroaching gray was a sure sign of the ravages of age, the one thing that made all pride so silly. In time, nothing of which he or anyone else was so proud would survive.

Michael laid down the brush, then stepped out of the bathroom and over to a table by the bed. From the table, he pulled a manila folder from his briefcase. Opening the folder, he once again studied the information Roca had given him before he left.

A man known only as Yoseph, a dealer in all kinds of legal and illegal commodities, currently held the manuscript. Known for his network of informants and an uncanny ability to find rare treasures, Yoseph, according to all indications, was not a particularly violent man. He had the document for sale and invited all interested parties to make their best offer.

Michael shoved the paper back into the folder and stuck both into the briefcase. Roca had empowered him to offer Yoseph up to a half million dollars for the document, sight unseen, and had given him the number of a bank account in Istanbul into which the money had already been deposited. Though a bit disturbed that such a huge amount of money could be raised in the Church without the benefit of official channels, Michael shrugged it off. He didn't know the inner workings of the Vatican. Perhaps Randuhar had approved the funding. Or one of the innumerable committees within the Church's ruling Curia had such funds at its disposal for its own peculiar purposes. Who was he to hesitate when a man so respected and trusted as his uncle directed him to act?

Roca had instructed him to start out at two hundred thousand, then offer more if Yoseph balked. Though without a clue as to what another bidder might offer, neither he nor Roca could imagine anyone going much higher than half a million for something so untested. Anxious to get his offer to Yoseph before anyone else, Roca had personally contacted the profiteer and set up the meeting. Now it was Michael's job to go to the man and make the preemptive offer.

His jaw set, Michael shut his briefcase and called Valerie on the phone.

"You ready?" he asked.

"You in a rush?" she teased him, her voice perky.

"Like a man climbing into a lifeboat on the Titanic. I want to get this thing moving." He thought back to the afternoon and evening they had just spent together. Walking the intoxicating streets of Istanbul's Grand Bazaar, the largest covered market in the world. Examining the incredible array of embroidered rugs and tapestries, hand-shaped silver and gold jewelry, copper and brassware. From Valerie's book he had learned that the bazaar held almost forty-five hundred shops and that it had started in 1452, the year the Muslims captured the city. Though fire had consumed it several times over the centuries, the bazaar had somehow survived—a testament to the power of commerce and community—a swirling, dizzying array of humanity.

People by the thousands choked the narrow passageways that served as streets. Wiry men carried carpets on their heads and women, wrapped in the Turkish "purdah," stared from behind black "yashmaks," with only their eyes visible. Gypsies begged from the tourists, and people from every nation haggled with the Turkish shopkeepers. The smell of apple tea and strong black Turkish coffee and spices of every imaginable fragrance had tickled his nose and tantalized his appetite. Once or twice he thought they were lost in the maze created by the end-on-end array of shops, but Valerie had smiled and, using the Turkish language, asked a shopkeeper for directions, and they quickly found their way again.

Forgoing the most adventuresome possibilities for food, they had eaten at the hotel, swallowing a combination of Turkish delights that had surprisingly agreed with both his palate and his stomach. For her part, Valerie wolfed down her food, barely chewing it, as if she were a young pup too hurried to eat properly. They talked about everything and nothing, their words as easy as breathing and as natural as an ocean pouring in and out on a shore. For the most part, however, they ignored any discussion about the document that had brought about their unlikely pairing.

Though trying to keep his thoughts about Valerie as professional as possible, Michael found it more and more difficult as the evening progressed. Her irrepressible enthusiasm, her energetic humor, and her eye-catching good looks caused his mind to wander into areas he had long since considered tucked away. Completely unbidden, an unprecedented notion came to his mind, and a sense of yearning he'd never before experienced rushed through him—a sense that he had missed something vital in choosing to become a priest.

By force of will, he tamped down the feeling and enjoyed the rest of the evening. Retiring to his room after the meal, Michael spent almost an hour in private devotions, then another thirty minutes doing calisthenics, hoping by doing so to clear his head of Valerie Miller. For the most part, he succeeded. Yet, even as he prepared for bed and fell asleep, he knew that something was amiss and that at some not-too-distant point in the future he would have to deal with the unsettling emotions Ms. Miller stirred in him.

"What are you wearing?" The sound of her voice jolted him back to the present.

"What kind of question is that for a lady?" he asked, trying to get a grip on his own thoughts.

"Perhaps not one a priest would understand."

He smiled, then decided to leave well enough alone. "I'm ditching my clerical garb, if that's what you're asking. Khakis, white shirt, a jacket. That okay?"

"Sure, I'll do something similar. You plan to eat anything?"

"Don't tell me you're hungry again—not after the way you stuffed yourself last night."

"I've got a busy metabolism. You eating or not?"

"Yeah, a quick bite, I guess."

"See you in five minutes in the restaurant."

"I'll meet you there."

"If you beat me down, order me some fruit, a couple of pieces of toast, oatmeal and a . . . let's see . . . a yogurt, orange juice, and water."

"No coffee?"

"Nope, coffee makes my heart flutter."

Hanging up, Michael bit his tongue. His heart was fluttering too, but it wasn't from coffee.

———

Just over seven miles away, in the back bedroom of a three-room hotel suite, Yoseph rolled over into a sitting position and twiddled his fingers through his mustache. Then, stiff from the night's sleep, he stepped out of bed, stretched, and headed for the bathroom. At the sink, he washed his face, the cold water jogging him to full consciousness. Toweling off his face, he opened his mouth and began to brush his teeth. Bending to spit, he failed to see the reflection of the square-bodied man that suddenly appeared in the mirror before him. Only when the man spoke did Yoseph look up and notice his presence. The man had a face as flat as a book cover, and he held a gun that Yoseph recognized as a Mauser Bolo, seven millimeter, a weapon much in style in situations such as this.

"The scroll," said the man in Yoseph's native Turkish. "I'm here for the scroll."

Yoseph washed out his mouth with water, dried his lips, and placed his towel on the rack before speaking. When he did, his voice stayed steady, his nerves calm from ten years of dealing with similar circumstances. "I don't have it anymore," he said.

"Move," said the man, motioning with the Mauser.

Slowly, Yoseph obeyed, leaving the bathroom and entering the bedroom again. There he saw another man, this one taller but thinner, waiting by the door. The man with the Mauser motioned him closer, and the second man stepped to Yoseph's side, his hand also holding a menacing pistol. His eyes darting over the room, Yoseph wondered what had happened to his own security team, then spotted two bodies stacked neatly in the corner by the door that exited from the bedroom into the center of the suite. A splotch of red the size of a tire spread out from the bodies. Not a good sign.

Stiffening his spine, Yoseph faced his abductors again and waited for instructions. If he kept his head, he could perhaps survive this, even if his bodyguards had not. Scars from three bullet wounds, one in the upper stomach and two in his lower back, constantly reminded him that terrible moments could be endured if he kept his wits about him.

"Sit on the bed," said the flat-faced man.

"May I put on my pants?"

"As you wish."

As deliberately as he thought acceptable, Yoseph slipped on his trousers, an undershirt, and a pair of black boots, the delay giving him a few more seconds to think. All his experience taught him one sure thing. Money often soothed even the most adversarial of relationships, and he had plenty of money. Dressed, he eased to the edge of the bed and sat down, turning sideways to offer as small a target as possible.

"You want the scroll," he said matter-of-factly.

"This is true."

"But, as I said, I don't have it anymore."

"Then who does?"

"A man, I don't know who he is. An American from what I could tell, though it's possible he was something else. He came to me last night. Offered me a price I couldn't refuse."

"How did this man find you?"

Yoseph played with his mustache. "As you no doubt know, I invited certain parties to submit bids here in Istanbul. A smart man could begin with that, as you so obviously did. With that information and a bit of money, finding me would not be particularly difficult. You managed."

"But you asked for bids by Sunday."

"You are right. But money in hand is far better than money yet to be received. And he offered me far more than I thought the document would command."

"How much did he pay?"

"Two million in American dollars, secured in the usual Swiss account."

"A handsome sum."

Yoseph smiled. "I thought so."

"But too bad for you that you took it."

"And why is that, my friend?"

"Because I came for the scroll, and now you say you don't have it, and you don't know the identity of the man who does."

"I will gladly pay you for your troubles. Two million splits well."

"I didn't come for money."

"No, but you can leave with it. Not a bad substitute."

The hand holding the Mauser dropped for a second as the flat-faced man considered the offer. But then he raised the weapon and stepped closer to Yoseph. "If it were my choice, perhaps we could make a deal. But, too bad for you, it's not my choice."

"With a million dollars a man can afford to make choices for himself."

"If he's willing to risk his life."

Yoseph shrugged. "Yes, this is so."

The flat-faced man reached into his pocket and pulled out a pair of pliers. "I will need to see one of your fingers," he said. "Just to make sure you're telling me the truth about the scroll and the man who took it."

"That's a bit crude in this modern age, wouldn't you say?"

The man shrugged and his flat face wrinkled up like a blanket. "I'm a simple man. I like the old ways better. Give me a finger."

"Just one?"

"One is a start," said the man. "After that, we will see."

Yoseph extended his hand to the intruder. Though he knew the pain would hurt like burns from a desert sun, he also knew that a finger or two was a small price to pay if having them crushed gave him a few more minutes to think about a way to escape with his life.

———

The taxi ride took less than thirty minutes, and Michael, sitting in the front seat, said little as he drew nearer and nearer to his meeting with the mysterious Yoseph. Concentrating on what he would say to the profiteer, he gave no notice to the sights and sounds of the passing streets. To his relief, he even managed to push aside his thoughts of Valerie Miller sitting in the back—no easy task, considering the way she looked when she came down for breakfast.

Her khakis fit her like a glove, and her black blouse gave evidence of a femininity that he had long since believed he had stopped noticing. Mumbling through his grapefruit and cereal, he had tried to get a grip on himself. But breakfast had been a struggle as he chewed on his emotions more than his food.

Now, though, he forced himself to think of other matters. Like how did Roca know the location of Yoseph the profiteer? Where did he get the money to make the offer for the scroll?

What would he do with the scroll once he got it, especially if it said something about Mary and Jesus he didn't want it to say? Michael had no answers to such questions and knew that none might ever come to him.

Keep the conversation with Yoseph simple, he told himself as the taxi stopped in front of the hotel. *Do as Roca instructed. Make the offer, get the scroll, and get out.*

Not accustomed to such cloak-and-dagger work, the whole task made Michael extremely uneasy, and he decided the sooner he finished with it the better. Paying the driver, he stepped quickly into the hotel, Valerie right beside him.

"You ready for this?" he asked her, his breath quick.

She nodded and Michael noted her tightly drawn lips. This woman was intense, no doubt about it. She had her mind on her job, her concentration focused.

In the elevator, he punched the button for the twentieth floor, then stared straight ahead. His hands gripped his briefcase, the number of a bank account holding half a million dollars printed on a sheet of white paper in a folder marked "Ephesus Document" inside.

"I can't believe this is happening," Valerie said, her eyes glued to the numbers on the elevator panel. "It seems too easy."

Michael shrugged, trying to appear nonchalant. "Don't know why it shouldn't be easy. We offer the money, the man says yes or no, we take it from there."

"And you're sure he's here?" A bit of disbelief sounded in her voice.

"Cardinal Roca said he was, or at least he was when we left yesterday. But even if he's not, we haven't lost anything. We can still make the offer as Yoseph requested it, before Sunday."

The elevator stopped and Michael faced Valerie. She rubbed her hands together. A splotch of red colored her neck where the collar of her blouse met her throat. Just above the splotch, Michael saw the scar he had first noticed in her office at the embassy.

"You okay?" he asked, surprised to see such obvious signs of anxiety in her.

"Sure, just nervous. I get this way, skittish. You should have seen me the day I interviewed for my first job with the State Department. My neck turned as red as a lobster. It doesn't mean anything, just the way I react. I know this is important and I want it to go well, quick and safe, you know? You don't have to worry about me. I'll do my job, no problem."

Michael grinned slightly, then stepped back as Valerie eased from the elevator. In the hallway, he quickly looked both ways but saw no one. Moving to the side of the hall, he stopped for a second and leaned against the wall. Valerie faced him.

"Look," he said. "I'm nervous too. But I don't see anything dangerous about this. This Yoseph character is just a salesman, a guy with a product, and he wants to get as much as possible for it. It's capitalism at its best. We're potential buyers, simple as that. So, it makes no sense for him to harm us. Just remember what we came to get—a scroll that could revolutionize the religious landscape as we know it. Keep the scroll in mind. That's why we're here. Okay?"

Nodding, Valerie closed her eyes for a second, and Michael found himself wanting to wrap his arms around her, to protect her from any possible harm. Without thinking, he started to reach for her hand, but she suddenly shifted and crossed her arms over her chest. Hoping she hadn't noticed, he jerked his hand back and stuck it in his pocket. He stepped back and turned away, his eyes darting down the hallway.

To his right and three rooms down, a man no taller than a big screen television and just about as wide slipped a key into a door. The instant the door opened, the man disappeared inside. The man, a blond with a crew cut and a set of eyebrows thicker than a caterpillar and as white as beach sand, looked distinctly out of place in a land populated primarily by swarthy, bearded Middle Easterners.

Startled, Michael quickly checked the door number just to his right. 2004. Yoseph was in 2010. If the numbers held up, that would make it the third door down, the door through which the blond man had just passed. Though not exactly sure why, Michael shuddered, then faced Valerie again. Her eyes were wide open, staring in the direction of 2010.

"Did you see what I saw?" he asked.

"The same."

Without another word, he tiptoed down the hallway, hoping the numbers would somehow change, but they didn't. Within seconds, he stood before 2010. Pausing, he turned to Valerie. "What do you think?" he asked.

"Maybe your man Yoseph has checked out."

"You think the guy we just saw is a new occupant of the room?"

"No way to know except knock and find out."

Michael nodded. Then acting before he lost his courage, he

knocked on the door. To his surprise, no one answered. He waited half a minute, then knocked again. But no one responded. He looked at Valerie.

"He did go into this room, didn't he?"

"I'm sure he did."

"Then he has to be in there." He knocked a third time but again received no answer.

"We can't leave without finding out," said Valerie, her voice insistent. "We've got to know what's going on."

Michael stepped back a pace, considering his next move. "We should check with Roca and Bremer first," he said cautiously. "They might know something about this we don't. Maybe Yoseph has already left for some reason. Roca found him once—he can find him again."

"You told me to keep my mind on the scroll," countered Valerie. "You said it could revolutionize the religious world. Now you're telling me you want to leave here without finding out if it's just a few feet away in a hotel room? Is that what you're saying, that we should give up our one chance to get our hands on what may be the most important archeological find of this century?"

Michael fingered his shirt collar and suddenly felt naked without his clerical band. A proper priest didn't act without authorization in such matters as this, no matter how much he wanted to do so. A "Lone Ranger" mentality worked poorly in a system like the Catholic Church, and he automatically rejected it as the wrong approach.

"We need to wait," he said, gritting his teeth. "Let me call Roca."

Valerie didn't speak. But then, before he could stop her, she pushed by him, grabbed the door handle, and twisted. To his surprise it opened, and she stepped through it and into suite 2010. Though momentarily stunned, it didn't take but a second for Michael to react and follow. Inside the room, he hurriedly shut the door and stepped to Valerie's side. His heart thumping, he scanned the suite.

To his left he saw a small kitchenette—an eating table, a wall of cabinets, a refrigerator, a coffeepot, and a two-burner stove. To his right was a sitting area complete with a leather sofa, two soft chairs, and a television set. Just past the sitting area, he saw a door to the left and another to the right. Obviously, those doors led into two bedrooms. A light burned from the bedroom on the right.

"Hello!" yelled Valerie. "Anybody here?"

No one answered. Valerie stepped toward the lighted bedroom, but Michael grabbed her arm. "We've gone far enough," he said. "This isn't right."

"But where did the man go?" she asked, her eyes determined. "He's got to be in here!"

"Maybe there's an exit from one of the bedrooms."

"Maybe so, but I say we find out." She jerked out of his arm. "If you want to leave, go ahead. But you don't dangle a diamond in front of me and then tell me I can't see if it's real." Her head down, she headed toward the lighted bedroom.

Knowing he couldn't leave without her, Michael gritted his teeth and stalked after Valerie. She disappeared into the bedroom, him one step behind. As he entered the bedroom, he heard a sharp intake of breath, a catch in Valerie's throat as if she had choked on a marble. Instinctively, he ducked and jumped to the right. As he did, he heard a click. Though not well versed in the use of weapons, it sounded like someone pulling back a trigger release.

As if punched in the face, Valerie suddenly stumbled backward and he caught her as she fell, her shoulders in his arms, her weight light but firm. Holding her against his chest, he looked up just in time to see the man with the blond eyebrows point a black-barreled pistol directly into his forehead.

EIGHTEEN

On the tenth floor of the Gemelli Hospital in Rome, a short, slender man, his arms covered with thick black hair, stepped off the elevator and began to slowly but confidently stride down the corridor. Dressed in the pale blue uniform of the maintenance staff, the man pushed a cart laden with a mop, an assortment of cleaning fluids, and a metal squeeze bucket filled with water. On his feet, he wore a pair of cloth shoes the same color as his uniform. A name tag on his shirt pocket read, Henriqo Baldas.

Keeping his eyes lowered, he eased down the hallway toward the suite of rooms on the right side of the hall, the suite to which the Vatican medical staff had taken the pontiff after they stabilized him on Sunday. Fifty feet from the room, one of the six security guards who stood sentry over the floor held up a hand, palm outward, indicating he should stop.

Henriqo immediately obeyed, one hairy hand on each side of the cart. Turning slightly sideways, he pushed his chest out, displaying for the guard the hospital identification tag that hung off his shirt pocket.

"Are you new?" asked the guard, his suspicions obvious in his crisp Italian.

Henriqo knew all about the security detail and realized he needed to take care with them. They were part of the Swiss Guard—just over a hundred men born in the quiet little country that gave them their name. Actually trained in the military of Switzerland, these men served as the official "army" of the Vatican. As part of their duty, they acted as protectors of the pope. Though they cooperated in this task at the hospital with the local police, the Guard had ultimate authority over papal security. Well acquainted with small arms weaponry, each member was also extremely proficient in the martial arts.

"Yes, I am filling in the shift for a sick man," Henriqo said, a story that was completely true. "He had a bit too much wine at dinner, from what I understand." He chuckled at the man's indiscretion, and all of the guards laughed with him.

"How is His Holiness?" he asked, tilting his head toward the pope's rooms.

"No one tells us," said the lead guard. "But we gather nothing much has changed."

Henriqo sighed and shook his head. "All the world loves our pope," he said. "May the Holy Mother see fit to make him whole again."

The guards nodded gravely, obviously feeling the same concern he displayed. The one who had stopped him stared at his identification tag for another moment. Henriqo knew this was the crucial point of the operation. Someone in his position came by every eight hours or so—no surprise in that. But to have a new man come unexpectedly created a bit of a dilemma.

He decided to take the initiative. "I have only just started to work on this shift," he said. "But, as you can see"—he fingered his identification badge—"I have the proper credentials." He paused again. No need to oversell himself. That would seem too anxious. All was in order even if the guard called personnel to check on him. He stayed still and easy, knowing any sign of tension would doom him.

The guard shrugged, then waved him through the checkpoint. The other five men did likewise. Forcing himself to remain calm, Henriqo pushed his cart past the guards, every step taking him closer and closer to the pontiff's room.

Quietly opening the door, he stepped inside and took a deep breath. *Excellent. Excellent.* The guards were competent men, but it had been years since anyone threatened a pope in any serious way, long enough for even the most diligent security force to become somewhat lax. Certainly, no one suspected any danger here, under such conditions as this. *Excellent.*

Scanning the room, he saw a single small window dead ahead and another set of double doors off to his left. Right below the window was a bed, and in the middle of the bed lay a sheet-draped figure. Henriqo swallowed hard.

The back of the pontiff pointed in his direction, the almost hairless head visible above the white sheets that covered the rest of his body. A host of monitoring devices stood vigil around the still form, a lineup of medical sentinels, each of them keeping track of some key physical function. Several tubes snaked from beneath the covers, obviously connected to the body underneath. Though not certain, Henriqo suspected that one tube came from the pontiff's nose, another from a forearm, and a third perhaps from the groin area. His Holiness was indeed near death. What he was about to do was merciful, the simple act of a compassionate subject who wanted the pontiff's suffering to end. He nodded slightly, his conscience salved by his rationalization, then focused again on his task.

Without looking, Henriqo knew that a camera mounted over the door eyed him from behind. The security guards outside used the camera to keep second-by-second vigil over the pope. Right now, he had no doubt that one of the six guards was watching every move he made. If not, then they were more lax than he suspected.

But he had planned for any unusual contingency. If anything happened that he had not anticipated and he saw that he could not finish his assignment without apprehension, then he would simply scrub the floor and leave quietly, no one the wiser. But if not, then . . . well, he knew what then.

Henriqo lifted the mop from the squeeze bucket and gently placed it on the floor. Swish, swish, swish, he pushed the mop. A streak of soapy water appeared on the floor. Swish, swish, swish. The soapy water washed away several drops of blood and a spot of shoe residue that had been rubbed into the floor. Swish, swish, swish, he moved the mop nearer to the bed, his back to the camera over the door, his head low and moving with the mop. Swish, swish, swish.

With his right hand pushing the mop, he slipped his left hand to the waistband of his blue cloth pants and pulled loose a syringe that he had taped to his hairy stomach. With a dexterity that would have surprised the guards outside, he pulled a plastic cap off the needle with his left hand, positioned it precisely between his fingers, and moved even nearer the sleeping pontiff.

Careful to keep his body between the needle and the camera, he quickly but smoothly took the final step to the bed, lifted the white sheet, and aimed the syringe toward the pope's buttocks. One quick injection and the potassium chloride in the needle would penetrate the skin and set off a devastating chain reaction in the man's body. Throwing off the electrical impulses of the brain, the drug would cause what the medical examiner would surely see as a heart attack. In a pope already ravaged by stroke and age, chances are no one would even ask for an autopsy.

Advancing the syringe toward the pope, Henriqo allowed himself a tiny smile as he saw the skin exposed by the gap in the back of the hospital gown. The pontiff was near death anyway, he told himself once more. Why not speed the inevitable process and earn the payment that he so desperately needed? In a sense he was an angel of God, a heavenly pawn in the hand of the Almighty.

He gripped the syringe more tightly. Another split second and he could insert the needle, step away from the pope, collect his payment and—

As if seeing an apparition, Henriqo watched in startled horror as the "pope" suddenly rolled over and faced him, his eyes wide with energy. A hand with the grip of a robotic arm grabbed his wrist and turned it back toward his elbow. The needle he had pointed at the pope was now aimed directly back at him. The grip squeezed harder, and Henriqo squealed loudly and dropped the syringe. As if in a dream, he watched it as it clattered to the floor and bounced under the bed, its deadly juice spilling onto the tile.

The pope, who was not the pope, rose up from the bed, his feet hitting the freshly mopped floor, his grip pushing the would-be assassin to the ground. The man had legs as bowed as a rubber band, forearms as thick as a blacksmith, and a birthmark the shape of Italy running down the left side of his nose.

Standing over the imposter, the man in the hospital gown gritted his teeth and grabbed the assailant by the neck, his thumb digging into his Adam's apple like a drill bit into concrete.

"You have many questions, I am sure," he hissed. "But your questions will have to wait until I am finished with mine. Are we agreed?"

The would-be assassin squealed and nodded his approval as his neck bent grotesquely backward in a direction it was never meant to go.

NINETEEN

Standing rigidly in the corner of the hotel room beside Valerie Miller, Michael Del Rio gritted his teeth and kept his eyes on the weapon in the blond man's hand. Valerie, equally stiff, leaned close to him as if seeking comfort in a storm. Though her shoulders hunched around her neck as if she wanted to make herself smaller, a bit of red colored her cheeks, and Michael saw the color as a sign of anger. *Good*, he thought. They may need that kind of emotion to get out of this mess.

On the floor about a car length away, two bodies lay in a heap. Beside them lay a third man, not yet dead but not far from it. His fingers were grotesquely swollen and bent at odd angles, and a pool of blood spread out from behind his head.

Though keeping the gun trained on them, the blond man squatted and bent close to the lips of the man with the broken fingers. "Yoseph," he whispered. "Yoseph, I need to know about McAuley."

Yoseph's eyelids fluttered, then opened. "Mr. Cashion," he muttered weakly. "You returned? Is everything not in . . . not in order?"

"Everything is fine," Cashion said. "Everything is okay, except one thing. I need to find McAuley."

He waited for Yoseph to reply but he didn't.

"He needs a doctor," Michael said, daring to interject.

Cashion flashed him a warning glance. "It's too late for that."

"My fingers," Yoseph moaned. He held up his hands, and Michael saw they were tiny, but well manicured, the hands of a delicate man with soft sensibilities.

"Do they know where to find McAuley?" Cashion asked. "The men who hurt your fingers?"

Yoseph stirred momentarily and what seemed like a question mark came to his face. "I can't remember," he said, his eyes closing again. "I can't remember what I told them. They broke my . . ." his voice trailed off and his head lolled to the side.

"Yoseph, talk to me!" urged Cashion, cupping the man's chin in his hands. "Tell me about McAuley! Where is he?" He shook Yoseph's shoulders, bouncing the man's head side to side.

"Leave him alone!" Michael shouted, stepping from the corner. "He's dying, can't you see that?" He grabbed Cashion's wrist, his fingers digging into his flesh. Cashion twisted around and pointed the gun at his face again.

"Back away!" he hissed. "Let me do my job!"

"Is it your job—"

They heard a groan and both simultaneously turned back to Yoseph. His broken fingers touched Cashion on the leg. "McAuley is in a . . . in a hotel," he whispered.

"Where?" pleaded Cashion. "Which hotel?"

"The hotel—" He sagged to the side and his fingers dropped to the floor. Michael knew he would never speak again. Cashion grabbed Yoseph's wrist to search for a pulse, but after a few seconds, he sighed and gave it up.

No one spoke for several moments. Michael studied Cashion, wondering if he was a policeman of some kind. Or an agent of the U.S. government. Maybe a mercenary hired by some unknown employer to find McAuley and the scroll. Or did he want the document for himself?

Cashion looked older up close than when Michael first saw him in the hall. A ridge of fat at the belt line of his black turtleneck and plain brown slacks somewhat negated the imposing width of his shoulders. The skin around his thick eyebrows showed definite signs of heavy wear and tear. He had a thick face, with a square chin. He looked to be in his mid-fifties at least and maybe older.

Cashion stood and motioned Michael and Valerie toward the bed. "Sit down a minute," he said. "We need to untangle a couple of things."

"Is this the place for it?" Michael asked, not moving. "What if the guys who did that decide to come back?" He indicated the three dead men.

Cashion shook his head. "No, they're done here," he said. "They got all they could. We're safe." He motioned to the bed

again. "So shut up and sit down. The faster we talk, the faster
we leave."

His blood boiling but his options limited, Michael obeyed,
and Valerie joined him on the bed. Cashion took a seat in a side
chair, his gun steady, his eyes calm. He slouched slightly, as if
somewhat bored with the circumstances. Obviously, he had
faced danger more than once.

"Now, who are you two?" Cashion asked. "How are you involved in all this?"

"We're wondering the same thing about you," Valerie said,
joining the conversation for the first time, a challenge in her
tone.

"But I'm the one holding hardware," Cashion said, waving
his weapon. "So you go first—I insist."

Valerie turned to Michael. "I'm Michael Del Rio," he started,
"A priest—"

"A priest?" interrupted Cashion.

"Yes, a professor of New Testament at Notre Dame actually,
sent here by Cardinal Severiano Roca, a member of the Curia.
Maybe you've heard of him."

Cashion grunted and shook his head "I think not," he said.
"I pay about as much attention to that kind of thing as I do World
Wide Wrestling." He turned to Valerie. "So what's your story?"

"I'm a representative of the U.S. embassy to the Vatican," she
offered.

"Great," Cashion said sarcastically. "A busy-body holy man
and a female bureaucrat. It's worse than I thought." He shifted
positions. "So how did you get here?"

Swallowing hard, Michael and Valerie told their story, from
the moment they first heard of the document from Ephesus to
the moment they arrived in the hotel room. Cashion listened
carefully as they spoke, showing little emotion. As their account
progressed, the pistol gradually dropped lower and lower in his
hand. By the time they finished the account, the gun, though
still aimed in their general direction, rested on Cashion's knee,
a great deal less menacing than a few minutes earlier.

Confident that Cashion had no plans to shoot them on the
spot, Michael shifted the conversation.

"Now what about you?" he asked.

"None of your business," Cashion said, rising as if to leave.

"Look," Michael said. "Three men are dead, and whoever
killed them can't be far away. It seems to me the more we know
about each other, the better off we are. For all we know, you

might be mixed up in all this." He motioned toward the three bodies. "Maybe you set the whole thing up, then came back to make sure your men did the job right."

Cashion snorted a quick laugh. "That's an idiotic idea," he said. "Wrong from the get-go. My name is Red Cashion. I just made a purchase for a client—that's all. A man named Willard Madden, maybe you've heard of him. He called me on Wednesday morning, offered me a job. I told him to take a hike. But he kept after me, as insistent as a con man. Told me he needed my expertise to find a document for him."

"So you're some kind of private investigator?" Michael asked.

"Yeah, used to be. I've pretty much given up this line of work, but nobody I know can refuse Willard Madden, least of all me. He and I did time together in Vietnam in 1971. He saved my backside more than once."

"I've heard of Madden. A reclusive media mogul," Valerie said, sitting up straighter.

"Yeah, not exactly Ted Turner. Anyway, Madden tells me he wants me to find this manuscript."

"Why does he want it?" asked Michael.

Cashion grunted. "Stupid question, even for a priest."

Michael started to protest the aspersion, but then decided to let it go.

"How did you find out about Yoseph?" Valerie asked.

"That was easy enough. The word has been out since Monday that he had this document for sale. I was already on the way to Turkey when Madden got wind of the auction and called me. His research guys had been busy, gave me the information I needed to contact Yoseph. Last night I made him an offer he couldn't refuse. I paid him and took the scroll with me. Easy as that."

"You have the scroll?" Valerie asked.

"Yeah, snug as a bug in a rug. I'll get it to Madden just like I promised."

"Did you look at it?" Michael asked, anxious at the thought.

"No way. That's not my job. I just bought it, made sure I had it well secured."

"Then why did you come back?" Valerie asked, clearly puzzled. "If you had the scroll, why return?"

Cashion shrugged. "It's simple, really. I called Madden after I bought the document—told him I was headed home. He asked me about McAuley, the guy who found this thing."

A sinking feeling hit Michael in the pit of the stomach. So that was why Cashion was so anxious to get information from the dying Yoseph. He hadn't really thought about McAuley. Given Yoseph's condition, the archeologist might be dead too.

"I suppose Madden wants McAuley to translate the manuscript."

"It seems so. Guess I'm a little rusty, but I didn't even think about him until Madden brought him up. Anyway, I called Yoseph again last night after talking to Madden but couldn't reach him. Then I couldn't get Madden back on the line either. I stewed all night, then called Yoseph again this morning. No answer. So I came to check things firsthand."

"And you found this." Michael motioned to the bodies.

Cashion dropped his eyes. "Yeah, guess I should have come last night."

"You think McAuley's in danger?" Valerie asked.

Cashion grunted. "Did Elvis have sideburns? If Yoseph told them what he just told me, then he's definitely in trouble. They'll want to check him out one way or the other—whether he knows anything or not. If McAuley's not already worm food, it'll surprise me."

"But how would they know about him?" Michael asked.

"Same way we did. From what I understand, his name is all the buzz in archeological circles, and several newspapers have picked up the story."

"And the ones who did this," Valerie grimaced, indicating the bodies, "will go after him if they think he can lead them to the scroll."

"You're so smart," Cashion said sarcastically. "They'll go after anyone they think knows anything about this stupid document."

"That means they'll go after you too," Michael said.

"I'm no rookie," Cashion chuckled. "I've been in the crosshairs more than once."

"But we haven't," Michael said.

"No, but you might be now."

Michael and Valerie glanced at each other. "Why would anyone bother with us?" Michael asked, shocked at the notion.

"The jerks who did this will come after anyone who shows an interest in the scroll. They don't know who knows what. When you're looking for treasure, you dig a lot of empty holes if necessary in order to find the one with the gold in it. The bad guys will want a conversation with you two if they have any inkling you know something."

"But how will they know we've been here?"

Cashion smiled, revealing a row of straight but brownish teeth. "Simple," he said. "Word gets out easy when money greases the conversation. I have no doubt that a number of people know exactly who's in Istanbul for this auction. Fact is, if I had a week and a generous budget, I could give you the hat and shoe size of every bidder who came to make a play for the scroll. I might not know who wants it enough to do this . . ." He motioned toward the dead men. "But I could tell you where to start."

"Then what now?" Valerie asked, a slight tremor in her voice. "Are we safe to go back to Rome?"

Cashion waved his pistol. "Maybe, though I'd keep my eyes open. It might be wise for you to spend a few nights in the embassy until things settle out."

Michael stood and shook his head. "I can't go back until I see the scroll. It means too much to the Church for me to leave now."

"I can't let you do that," Cashion said. "I'm taking it back to Madden like I promised."

Michael paused and considered his options. There was only one thing left to do. "I'll need to find McAuley then," he said. "If he's read the document, he can describe it to me, tell me what's in it."

"That's also a negative," Cashion said. "Too dangerous. You're an amateur. You start snooping around for McAuley, and trouble will fall on you like January snow in Buffalo."

"Unless you're going to use that"—Valerie pointed to Cashion's pistol—"you have no way to stop us." The splotch of red Michael had noticed earlier was once again evident above her collar.

For several moments, no one spoke. Michael, marveling at Valerie's courage, waited for Cashion to respond. The woman had brass. And he liked it.

Cashion grunted, then stood and motioned Valerie to do the same. "I'm the one who needs to find McAuley," he said. "And I don't want more dead people on my conscience, what there is left of it. So you two will stay with me for a while. Any arguments?"

Knowing that staying with Cashion gave him his best chance to see the scroll, Michael agreed instantly. So did Valerie.

"What do we do with them?" Michael asked, nodding toward the bodies.

"We make an anonymous call," Cashion said, motioning for them to move. "The local police will take care of it."

A moment later, the three of them stepped furtively into the hotel hallway. Humming softly, Cashion shoved his weapon into the waistband of his slacks, pulled a bag of tobacco from his pocket, and stuffed a chew into his cheek. Moving quickly down the hall, he began to work the tobacco. His humming became a bit louder. Though not sure, Michael thought he could make out snatches of "Love Me Tender," the old Elvis tune. His ears perked, Michael followed as Cashion led them to the back stairs, down the twenty flights of steps, and out into the human congestion of Istanbul. In the full glare of the sunshine, Michael felt naked, as if everyone around him knew what lay on the floor in the hotel just above. For a second, his knees wobbled and he felt like collapsing. How had everything turned so violent so fast? And what was going to happen next? Was he safe? Was Valerie?

Trailing Valerie and Cashion across the street, he suddenly noticed three men approaching, one from the right, one from the left, and one directly ahead. Each of the men wore gray slacks, white shirts, navy blazers, red-and-blue ties, and black shoes and looked like models for a Mormon missionary magazine. But Michael instinctively knew better. Unless he missed his guess, each of the men was armed.

The men silently formed a triangle around Cashion, a human phalanx of protection. At the corner, the man on Cashion's right touched him on the shoulder, steering him to a left turn. Five steps later, Cashion stopped, motioned to Michael and Valerie, and stepped up into a tan-colored van that sat by the curb. Two of the men dropped back to a second vehicle, and Michael and Valerie followed Cashion and the lead bodyguard into the first. The bodyguard slipped behind the wheel, and Cashion, still humming and chewing, took the passenger side.

Pulling away from the curb, Michael took a quick look over his shoulder, half expecting someone to come rushing out of the shadows to take a shot at them. No one did.

But that didn't mean that no one stood in the shadows. Several people did, including one man whose face was flat enough to fry eggs on, if he could only have warmed it up enough.

TWENTY

It took Red Cashion until almost midnight to find McAuley. With Valerie and Michael and his bodyguards at his side, Red Cashion systematically visited twenty-one hotels known to cater to Westerners. Humming and chewing tobacco all the while, he sought out the supervisors of three groups of people at each of the hotels—the maids who cleaned the rooms, the deliverers of room service, and the bellboys. To each one he made the same offer: twenty-five thousand American dollars for the person who found the good Doctor Hugh McAuley and twenty-five thousand for the supervisor of the person who found him. But it had to be kept quiet, Cashion told them. No need to get anyone else involved, including the police. Leaving each supervisor a phone number, he moved to the next hotel.

His emotions doing flip-flops, Michael quietly followed Cashion as he made his rounds. In one minute, he could feel his stomach rolling over and over with fear. But in the next, his heart thumped with sheer excitement. From time to time he glanced at Valerie, wishing he could talk to her, wanting to ask how she was dealing with all this, but he had no opportunity. She stayed silent too but showed no outward signs of anxiety except the redness that now appeared on her throat as permanently as the paint on a fire engine.

Finished with the hotels, Cashion piled the whole crew into the vans once again and directed the driver to the Swissôtel, one of the finest establishments in the city. For the rest of the day, the entire group took refuge in a four-room suite on the top floor.

Michael and Valerie each made one phone call—Michael to Roca in the Vatican, and Valerie to Arthur Bremer in the U.S.

embassy in Rome—and then compared notes. Though both Roca
and Bremer expressed concern at the turn of events, they agreed
with the decisions Michael and Valerie had made. Stay with the
scroll, both men said, but not if it gets too dangerous. Use good
judgment and get out if necessary. Call immediately if you need
help.

Cashion also worked the phone. In fact, he stayed on it all
afternoon, apparently reporting to Madden, or trying to locate
McAuley, or making plans for the security of the scroll. As he
talked, Cashion kept a steady flow of smelly brown saliva shooting from his cheeks into a small silver cup he produced from
some unknown source.

From time to time Cashion broke into his humming again.
Each time Michael tried to identify the song, but he couldn't. The
humming wasn't very loud for one thing, and Cashion constantly
switched his tunes, never staying on one song long enough for
Michael to get a fix on it. For some reason, though, the singing
made Michael feel more at ease. In fact, as the day wore on and
he watched Cashion work, he found himself feeling a strange
sense of security. Though he knew little or nothing about the
man, a sense of comfort not unlike the one he once found in the
presence of his own father somehow settled over him. Curious—
especially so, since Cashion had shown an obvious disdain for
the Church that Michael loved so completely.

As the afternoon passed into early evening, Michael thought
more and more about the scroll. The desire to read it became an
ache in his gut, a drive stronger than almost anything he had
ever felt. In spite of the ache, though, he knew not to ask to see
it. Though Cashion obviously planned him and Valerie no harm,
he just as obviously disliked the annoyance of having to baby-
sit a priest and a diplomat. He might as well poke a stick at a
surly dog as to ask to see the document. Maybe later, after they
found McAuley and everything had settled down, maybe then he
could convince Cashion to let him read the document before he
gave it to Madden. Regardless of Madden's plans for it, surely
Cashion would see the value of letting someone from the Church
study the manuscript first.

At about nine o'clock, Cashion's men mysteriously disappeared from the hotel suite as Cashion continued to work.
Watching them leave, Michael realized they almost never spoke,
and only then if Cashion spoke to them first. They lowered their
eyes when he or Valerie approached, and they seemed ghostlike,
faceless men. If someone had asked him to identify any of them

in a lineup, he suspected he wouldn't be able to do it.

For the most part, he and Valerie said little also, even to each other, choosing to stay within their own thoughts for the time being. Yet, though they had enough rooms in the suite for them to separate and have some privacy, neither did. Instead, they stayed in the central area of the suite—ignoring the television and only rarely glancing out the arched window that overlooked the city. As the hours ticked away, they kept their own counsel and sat and waited.

Though he didn't pry, it seemed to Michael that Valerie was in shock—no surprise given the events in Yoseph's hotel room. Two dead men in a corner and another speaking his last words in her presence gave her good cause to fall into such a state. Michael wanted to speak to her, to tell her that having experience with death didn't make it any easier, but an appropriate moment never quite seemed to come. So the evening passed quietly—silence settling on the room like dust from a ploughed field.

Michael was sitting in a lounge chair when the phone rang, staring out the window but seeing nothing. Valerie was resting on the bed, and Cashion sat in a chair beside her.

Grabbing the phone, Cashion twisted away from Michael and Valerie, standing with his back to them. Though they both stood and moved closer, Cashion practically swallowed the telephone, making it impossible to hear the conversation. After a couple of minutes, Cashion hung up the phone and moved immediately toward the door, indicating that they should follow him.

"A supervisor of the cleanup crew at the Ceylan Hotel," he said, leading them from the room and into the hotel hallway. "Says a night maid there remembered a big, red-headed man who came into the hotel a couple of days ago. Three Turkish types came with him, one on each side and one in front."

They were in the elevator now, Cashion punching the button for the lobby. "The supervisor checked it out. Says he thinks he has our man. We'll see."

As the elevator reached the bottom floor, Cashion barged out into the lobby, his stout legs moving like pistons, his humming getting a bit louder the faster he walked. His bodyguards appeared from nowhere again and formed their human wedge around him. Michael pushed himself to keep up, and Valerie tagged quickly behind.

"Is McAuley okay?" Michael asked.

Cashion shook his head but didn't slow down. They were outside the hotel in the dark now, headed to the vans. "Not sure yet," puffed Cashion. "The guy said he's all tied up."

"But he's alive?"

Michael turned quickly as Valerie spoke. Her voice sounded an octave higher than normal, and a look of horror squeezed onto her face.

Cashion spit a wad of tobacco onto the pavement at his feet. "We'll see."

The night felt cool, but not harsh as the group reached the vans. Cashion and his driver jumped into the first vehicle. Michael and Valerie climbed into the back.

"Are they getting a doctor for him?" Michael asked.

"Nope, no time for that. I told the hotel guy to hold him there exactly as he is and tell no one. I don't want the authorities mixed up in this. I'll get a doctor if he needs one."

The van lurched ahead, dodging a taxi as it accelerated. A bit of traffic moved on the street, but not enough to slow them down.

"Who do you think. . . ?"

"Don't know that either." Cashion turned to Valerie as he interrupted her. "Maybe Yoseph messed McAuley up, or maybe the clowns who snuffed Yoseph hurt him. Maybe some player we haven't met yet is responsible. Only one thing is for sure. We aren't the only ones who want this document, and the word will spread pretty fast that it's gone."

"You think McAuley can travel?" Michael asked, his mind clicking ahead.

"Don't keep asking me what I don't know!" Cashion growled, facing the road again.

Valerie turned to Michael. He held up a hand, palm outward, and exhaled heavily. At this point, he didn't know any more than she did.

———

Near the end of the hallway on the fifteenth floor of the Ceylan Intercontinental, three men, one of them with a face flat enough to roll pennies on, stepped furtively through the door that led from the hall to the stairwell. Motioning silently to his accomplices to lead, the flat-faced man waited patiently as they sprinted down the hall before him.

Yoseph the profiteer had proven more difficult to break than most men the flat-faced one had encountered. Only after the loss of eight fingers, six more than the average, had he begun to talk. Amazingly, even then his words came grudgingly. But come they did, one by one, one by one. As he talked, Yoseph had revealed the location of a man named Hugh McAuley, but not the location of the document itself. In addition, he had finally handed over a crinkled sheet of yellow paper that listed the names of the parties he had invited to make a bid on the scroll. If finding the archeologist McAuley didn't lead to the new owner of the document—and chances were good it wouldn't—then the list would surely do it. At least it would lead to the operatives sent to procure it.

Unsure of his next move, the flat-faced man had spent the balance of the day tracking down his employer, seeking the necessary authorization to move on McAuley. To end the life of a Turkish black marketer was one thing, but to harm an American archeologist was quite another, and he refused to act without proper clearance.

Once the approval came, he had waited a few more hours, giving the people of the city the opportunity to settle into the quiet of the night. No matter how lawless a place like Istanbul seemed to outsiders, its police had their own brand of justice, and he didn't want to run afoul of it. With Turkey and America on such amenable terms, one never knew how Turkish officials would respond if the archeologist came to some harm, and he, a practical man in a necessary yet dangerous business, received the blame for it. So he had waited until his chances to get in and out cleanly were better.

The flat-faced one shrugged and tensed his thighs. Then, keeping his black eyes alert, he slithered across the carpeted floor behind his companions. Beneath the black leather jacket he wore year-round, regardless of temperature, an Uzi nine-millimeter Parabellum hung ready on a strap around his neck.

McAuley was in a two-room suite, the second door on the right from the stairwell, and he reached it within seconds. His men waited at the door for him, their weapons also poised, black snakes of hot poison ready to strike.

For one more moment, Flat Face glanced up and down the hallway, his black eyes busy, watching for motion. But nothing moved. Apparently, all the guests in the hotel had either stepped out to enjoy Istanbul's vibrant nightlife, or they had tucked themselves into bed for the evening. Good. If gunfire erupted, it would take several minutes for any authorities to respond.

Flat Face grinned to the best of his meager ability and nodded to his associates. The moment had come. Sliding his Uzi from his chest to his back, he pulled a knife the length of a pencil and the width of a ruler from his waistband, situated it tightly in his right hand, then threw a heavy shoulder into the door. The door popped backward into the room, and Flat Face pounced inside. Before him, a slightly built, older gentleman in a beige hotel uniform fell back from the door, his legs deserting him as he tumbled.

In an instant, Flat Face was on the hapless man, pinning him to the floor with his knees, slipping his knife through the polyester of the beige suit and into the man's chest as calmly as if inserting a key into a car ignition. The hotel employee never raised a hand or uttered a whimper as his life ebbed out with his blood onto the carpet.

Wiping his knife clean on his victim's uniform, Flat Face signaled his men. Within seconds, one of his accomplices entered the second room in the suite, then stepped back out, indicating it was safe. Now all three men entered the bedroom, Flat Face in the lead. He spotted McAuley to his left, a large, red-haired man, lying wedged on the floor in the corner, his body slumped to the right but his eyes wide open.

McAuley wore simple khaki slacks that appeared too big for him and a pullover sweater the color of cedar boughs. His feet were hidden under the bed, his hands were tied behind his back, and a white towel had been shoved into his mouth and taped solid behind his head. A look of sheer joy broke out in the big man's eyes, and Flat Face realized that McAuley thought him a friend, even a rescuer. Squeezing up a grin, he decided to play along.

He stepped to McAuley and bent to one knee. With a sharp rip, he jerked the tape from the man's head and pulled the towel from his mouth. Then he motioned for McAuley to turn so he could undo the bindings on his wrists. As McAuley obliged, the killer wrinkled his nose and made a small joke.

"You need a bath, my friend," he said.

"Get me loose," McAuley whispered, his voice raspy. "And I'll do that first thing—even before I eat!"

The assassin slipped his knife through the bindings and cut them in two. Then, helping McAuley up and onto the bed, he smiled one final time.

"Are you Dr. Hugh McAuley?" he asked, as pleasantly as possible.

McAuley nodded eagerly, rubbing his wrists and flexing his fingers. "Yeah, a guy named Yoseph kidnapped me . . . robbed me . . . kept me tied up here. I don't know what happened to him, he—"

"Here, let me see those," interrupted Flat Face, feigning concern as he gently took McAuley's hands in his. "I know these must be quite stiff." For a couple of moments, he caressed McAuley's hands and wrists, his fingers light and compassionate.

"Thank you," McAuley said. "That helps a lot." He started to pull his hands away.

Not letting go, Flat Face squeezed a bit harder. McAuley grimaced and tried to free his hands, but Flat Face held firm.

"I need to hold your hands," said the assassin. "Or should I say one of your hands."

McAuley's brow furrowed. Flat Face dropped McAuley's left wrist but put a vice grip on his right one. Flat Face's accomplices took up positions on either side of McAuley, standing over him like a pair of attack dogs.

"Who are you?" McAuley asked, finally sensing the danger.

"I'll ask the questions here," growled Flat Face. "And the first question is a simple one. Where is the document? Who took it from you and the man named Yoseph?" He gripped McAuley's index finger as he spoke, his fingers pushing it back toward McAuley's wrist.

"I . . . I don't know," McAuley said, gritting his teeth against the pain. "Yoseph took it from me. I haven't seen it since."

"Are you telling me the truth, Dr. McAuley?" He bent the finger even further. McAuley's face turned red, and sweat began to pour into his eyes.

"Yes!" he shouted. "It's the truth!"

"I'll need to make sure of that," Flat Face said. "A couple of fingers usually guarantee me the certainty I need."

———

His heart racing, Michael hustled to keep up with Red Cashion as he stepped through a back entrance to the Ceylan Hotel and darted toward the stairwell. With Valerie and three bodyguards in hot pursuit, Michael and Cashion bounded up the concrete steps two at a time. The stairs, nine to a landing, then a turn and nine more to the next floor, smelled like new paint and still glowed with the fresh luster that came after a major redecoration. Surprisingly, Valerie kept pace, her breathing measured but not stressed. Still farther back, Cashion's bodyguards moved cautiously, the last one backing up the stairs, his eyes focused on the way they had just come.

Michael kept his eyes peeled too. On the way to the hotel,

Cashion had cautioned everyone to stay alert—Yoseph might have told the men who tortured and killed him where to find McAuley. And even though Cashion suspected that anyone who knew McAuley's whereabouts should have already found him, he couldn't necessarily count on that.

At the top of the stairs at the fifteenth floor, Cashion stopped briefly and glanced at his watch. "Thirty-two minutes," he whispered to no one in particular.

"Since the phone call?" Michael asked.

Cashion nodded once, then pulled his pistol from the waistband of his slacks and held it straight down at his side. Two of his men stepped up from behind, each of them carrying identical weapons. Michael studied the guns.

"Glocks," Cashion said quickly, noting his interest. "Ten millimeter. Guys in my fraternity have a preference for them."

"I hope you won't need it," Valerie said.

Cashion nodded. "Maybe we won't. Everything seems pretty quiet. Maybe we can secure McAuley and get out of here before anyone sniffs us out. At least that's what I'm hoping."

He pivoted and stepped to the door leading from the stairwell to the hallway. For a couple of seconds he stared through a book-sized windowpane that centered the top half of the door. Then he turned and faced Michael and Valerie again.

"We're going right down there," he said, pointing through the glass. "Second door on the right, about forty feet away. You two stay right here and stay quiet. I'll be back in less than ten minutes."

"You're not leaving us here," Michael said, his voice calm but firm.

Cashion spat onto the concrete floor, and his face turned mean. "Oh yes I am. I wanted to leave you at the Hyatt, but that seemed too risky. Someone looking for me might have found you. And that could get messy. So, here you are, but this is it, as far as you go and I don't have time to debate the point!"

Michael glanced at Valerie and started to protest again, but then realized he didn't have much of an argument. Cashion was right. If he and his men did run into trouble, he didn't want Valerie anywhere near it. At the same time, though, he couldn't leave her all by herself either. Michael relented.

"You got a watch?" Cashion asked.

Michael nodded and held up his wrist.

"Don't move from this spot for five minutes," commanded Cashion. "Pretend you're a couple of fire hydrants. But if we're not back after that, get out of here as fast as you can."

Michael stared at Valerie. She glanced at her watch, then nodded.

"Five minutes," repeated Cashion. "Then you're greyhounds, I mean gone!" With that he and his three silent partners slipped through the door and crept down the hallway.

————

His Glock poised, Red Cashion began to hum. Then, a couple of steps later, he did what he always did during situations like this one—he began to sing. Not loudly, but to himself, choosing an old James Taylor tune this time. "I've seen fire and I've seen rain, I've seen sunny days that I thought would never end . . ."

He jabbed a thumb into the air, indicating to his lead man that he should take one side of the door. The man positioned himself like a pro, his body crouched on the opposite side of the door from Cashion.

"I've seen lonely times when I could not find a friend . . ."

A second later, Cashion jerked his head quickly to the right, and his man lifted a foot, kicked it out, and pounded his weight into the door. A crack like a bolt of lightning sounded in the hallway, and the lock on the door gave way. As the door fell open, the lead man bounded through it.

Cashion and his other men followed instantly, each of them scattering like soldiers storming onto a beach, their heads low and their weapons drawn. With the practiced eye of a man who had done this more times than he had shopped for groceries, Cashion systematically surveyed the room. A four-foot high bar with liquor bottles on the wall behind it sat to his right. Beside the bar was a door to a second room. An unoccupied, king-sized bed waited straight ahead, about ten feet away. Standard hotel furniture surrounded the bed—nightstands, lamps, a winged chair. A bathroom opened off to Cashion's immediate left. A television perched in a wooden cabinet also on the left wall, just past the bathroom. But no sign of Hugh McAuley.

Scanning the floor, Cashion spotted a scarlet stain in the carpet about seven feet from the television cabinet in the left corner of the room.

"On the deck!" he barked, rolling onto the floor, and behind the cover of the bed. From his new position, he saw the door to a second room open, revealing a man with the flattest face Cashion had ever seen—eyes as black as coal sitting like buttons on the surface of his skin, gleaming in feverish excitement.

The man brandished an Uzi, and he slammed it into action, its firepower spitting indiscriminately in Cashion's direction. A lamp on a table beside Cashion's head splattered against the wall. Singing under his breath now, Cashion ducked, rolled to his left, and fired under the bed. The bullets from his Glock crawled along the floor and caught Flat Face in the right foot. Though the man crumbled, the Uzi in his hands kept spitting, its bullets raking the wall to Cashion's left.

"Nobody knows the trouble I've seen . . ." Cashion sang to himself, his blood surging. In his head he calculated the time the firing had started.

Two more men piled out of the second bedroom, and Cashion jerked himself along the carpet, his elbows digging into the floor. More Uzis erupted now, and the room exploded with the roar of small arms fire. Behind him, Cashion heard a grunt, then a cry of pain, and he realized one of his men had been hit.

His anger overcoming his judgment, he stopped singing and rolled up from his crawl into a crouch and squeezed off a series of rounds in the direction of the wet bar where the two men behind Flat Face had positioned themselves. A row of liquor bottles shattered, and Cashion darted to his left into the bathroom. As he reloaded, he saw one of his men behind the television cabinet, his weapon busy, his face contorted with rage. Another of his men jumped from behind the winged chair and charged the wet bar, but his charge fell short when a quick exhalation of Uzi fire cut him down.

Cashion began to sing again, his voice little more than a whisper. "Oh, Lord, won't you buy me a Mercedes Benz . . ." Nearly a minute had passed since the first machine gun erupted.

Before he reached the end of the stanza, Red stormed out of the bathroom just as the two men behind the bar rose up and charged toward him. He dropped the first one with a single shot that caught him in the throat, but the second one slammed into him before he could take aim again. The man's shoulder barreled into his chest, knocking him back into the television cabinet. His head banged into the corner of the cabinet, and for an instant, the room swam in black swirls as he fought to stay conscious. Shots fired over his head. He looked up just in time to see the last of his men come charging from behind the cabinet, his Glock aimed at Flat Face, still on the floor behind the bed. One of his bullets hit its mark. A splash of red suddenly appeared beneath the man's left ear, and his flat face became a mask of contorted pain.

Ignoring the throb that flared from the base of his skull, Cashion willed himself off the floor. The man who knocked him down had fled the room, and Cashion knew he wouldn't take the elevator.

"Check the next room!" he shouted. "Find McAuley!" About two minutes had passed. Probably no more than two more before someone from hotel security came rushing from the elevator.

"Worked hard all my lifetime, no help from my friends, oh, Lord, won't you buy me a Mercedes . . ." Singing softly again, Cashion stumbled to the door, his weapon ready. At the door, he turned left, just in time to see the fleeing killer aim his Uzi toward the two faces that stared at him through the glass partition that centered the upper middle of the stairwell door.

Michael and Valerie spotted the man with the Uzi the instant he exited the bedroom. Though Cashion and his men had been gone less than three minutes and the shooting had lasted only a portion of that, the time seemed like an eternity. Not knowing whether to run toward Cashion, stay put, or go for help, the two of them had momentarily frozen in confused indecision.

But now a bearded man with an Uzi brought the battle to them, his face a mask of sweat and thick black hair. Watching him come, everything seemed to slow down for Michael. A few seconds felt like forever.

Without conscious thought, Michael grabbed Valerie, pushing her to his right, up against the stairwell wall and away from the door. From the hallway, he heard gunfire, then realized the bearded man was shooting at him. The zing, zing, zing of ordnance snapping into the door shocked him. Ducking into a crouch behind the partition, he felt Valerie fighting to get loose, but he had her pinned against the wall, out of harm's way at least for the moment.

More shots popped into the door, and Michael jerked his head up and saw the bearded man no more than four feet away, his gun angrily spewing bullets like a geyser spraying water. The man's eyes were frantic, seeing but not seeing, focused but glassy.

Still crouched, Michael grabbed the door handle with his loose arm and tensed himself for the collision. Then, with all the power in his well-muscled arms, he twisted the handle and shoved the door out into the hallway. The door's edge popped into the bearded man's face with stunning speed, and he staggered backward.

The impact jarred Michael too as the man's weight boomeranged the door in the opposite direction and back into him. His eyes watering from the reverberation, Michael pounced out of the stairwell and grabbed for the man's weapon, his hands locking onto the barrel of the Uzi and twisting it toward the ceiling. Near his feet, he felt a whoosh of air and realized too late that the bearded man was kicking at him. As the man's foot connected, Michael's right knee collapsed, sending him to the ground.

His back on the floor but his hands still fighting for the gun, Michael thrust his legs up, jammed his feet into the man's stomach, and pulled the gun toward him. Thrusting his knees skyward, he propelled the man and his gun against the wall.

As his head hit the wall with a heavy thud, the bearded man released his grip on his weapon, and it tumbled to the floor. Michael regained his feet and pounced at the man, lowering his right shoulder. With a sound reminiscent of a punter kicking a football, Michael slammed into the man's chest, knocking him down.

The man stumbled to his knees and grabbed for his Uzi not more than five feet away. Michael dove toward it too, though he knew instantly he was too late. The bearded man's fingers opened to grab the gun. But he never reached it.

From the left, Valerie suddenly appeared and scooped the weapon off the floor. Using the Uzi like a bat, she cracked the man across the forehead. He fell like a stone.

His fists clenched and his chest heaving with exertion, Michael stood over the bearded man, ready to pounce on him again if necessary.

"Move it," he hissed.

Behind Valerie, Cashion suddenly reappeared. "We've got to get out of here!"

Michael looked up, confused for a second. But then he understood. Cashion didn't want Turkish authorities involved. No telling where that would lead—a trial for whatever mayhem had occurred in the hotel room—a possible claim on the scroll by the Turkish authorities. Who knew what else?

"Shoot him if he twitches," Cashion barked, facing Valerie and nodding toward the unconscious man.

Valerie looked shaken but nodded and aimed the Uzi in her hands toward its former owner.

Cashion darted down the corridor to Michael's right and raised his weapon. He punched the button for the elevator, then stepped inside the door as it opened and fired point blank into the electric panel of the elevator car. A plume of black smoke rolled out of the elevator as Cashion returned.

"It's been four minutes," barked Cashion. "Michael, come with me."

Michael limped hurriedly down the hall and followed Cashion into the suite. The sight of blood staggered him momentarily, but Cashion didn't give him a chance to get squeamish.

"Get Rick!" Cashion ordered, pointing to one of his bodyguards, who lay on the floor beside the television cabinet. To Michael's relief, Rick was still breathing. Cashion lifted a second man off the bed and hoisted him over his back. Out of the second room, the third of his men appeared with a large, redheaded stranger leaning heavily on his shoulder. Michael knew instantly the redhead was McAuley. The archeologist didn't look too good—his face was bruised in several places, blood had caked under his nose, and his khaki pants hung loosely over his hips. But at least his legs were functioning.

Before exiting the room, Cashion paused for a split second and stared down at one of the men who had attacked him. The man had a face almost perfectly flat—practically no nose at all. Blood seeped from a wound in his neck, but he appeared to be breathing.

His eyes hard, Cashion quickly but calmly lifted a boot and kicked the man in the rib cage. The man groaned and opened his eyes, the black orbs scanning the room. For a second the man's gaze landed on Michael, and the rage in his eyes became a palpable force in spite of his weakened condition. Michael looked at Cashion again, who stepped over the man and into the hall.

A door opened and a head popped out five rooms down.

Cashion jerked toward the sound, his Glock aimed. The head disappeared back inside.

"Move it!" he growled to the others. "Our time here is up."

Leaving the unconscious bearded man sprawled in the hallway, he led his troop down the stairs and into the vans outside the hotel.

———

The Christmas reception in the East Room of the White House was in full swing at nine P.M. when Roger Attles walked in unescorted. A live band played "I'm Dreaming of a White

Christmas" in the background, and a row of white lights hanging on the green garlands that draped off the crown molding bounced a steady twinkle of glare onto his thinning hair. The room smelled like a combination of expensive perfumes, colognes, and Christmas pine.

Attles, attired in the requisite black tie and tuxedo, felt completely at ease in the mix and mingle demanded by such ostentatious events. Taking a glass of Sprite from the bar—no alcohol for him—he patted the inside pocket of his tux jacket and moved into the crowd.

Almost everyone in the room knew him, and one by one most of them noted his presence as he passed from one group to another. A slight bow here, a thumbs up there, a wave of the hand, a series of nods—in their own way each person caught his eye and acknowledged his power.

Attles moved slowly, smiling as if on parade. With a succession of winks and nods, he shook hands with the men, offered largely insincere compliments to the women, and passed along the latest political jokes he had heard to whoever seemed inclined to hear them. Gradually, handshake by handshake and plastered smile by plastered smile, he made his way across the room toward the thirty-foot-high Douglas fir in the back left corner. The tree, blanketed with white lights and gold ribbons and surrounded by a score of gifts in red boxes and green bows that would go to the poor children of Washington on Christmas Eve, was the source of the pine smell that dominated the room. The president and his ever smiling wife stood in front of the tree at the end of what seemed like an endless receiving line.

It took Attles almost forty-five minutes, but he finally made it to the tree. Only two other people—the ambassador from Finland, whom he recognized but couldn't name, and his wife—separated him from the president and first lady. Sipping from his Sprite, Attles tried to appear nonchalant. But inside his stomach his nerves were doing back flips. He patted the pocket of his tux again.

The ambassador bowed slightly and moved away from the president, but his slightly inebriated wife stopped for one final word. Trying to stay calm, Attles stepped forward and took the first lady's hand.

"You're radiant tonight," he said. "The combination of this dress"—he indicated the green gown she wore—"and your big brown eyes, and you're prettier than any light on the tree."

"And you're a charmer," beamed the first lady. "But you always have been, so it's no surprise. How's Beatrice?"

Attles blanched at the mention of his wife. A shy country girl from Walhalla, South Carolina, she didn't like the social demands his job put on her. "She's at home, as usual. You know she's too righteous for all these sharks." He waved his hand over the room.

"But we're not?"

Attles laughed. "We're the worst of them," he said, "The absolute worst."

To his left, the Finnish ambassador finally managed to pull his wife away from the president, and Attles stepped from the first lady to her husband. Another guest took the spot he had just vacated.

Too hurried for small talk, Attles immediately grasped the president's hand and leaned in close. "You got one minute?" he asked, his voice conspiratorial.

The president winced and dropped his hand. "It's not the time," he said. "We've got guests everywhere."

"It'll only take a second, I promise."

Sighing, the president nodded, then stepped away from the receiving line and behind the Christmas tree. A couple of Secret Service men shifted too, taking up spots not far away, their eyes concentrated on Attles and the president.

"Make it quick," said the president, his face serious.

Attles swallowed hard, then launched ahead. "The document I called you about a few days ago. It's disappeared."

The president shrugged. "I know that. Bremer's keeping me updated."

"I think this document is critical," Attles said, his teeth almost clenched. "Someone who knows how to handle things like this needs to find it before anyone else."

"What more do you want me to do?" asked the president, glancing at his watch. "I'm working through the State Department. Bremer says they're on top of it."

"I'm not too sure about Bremer." Attles shook his head slowly. "I'm not confident he's enough in this situation. I understand some people have been hurt and the archeologist has disappeared—as well as the scroll."

The president fingered a cuff link on his shirt. Attles couldn't tell how much he knew. "Can Bremer's representative handle it if things get tough?" he asked.

The president shrugged. "Who knows? I guess we have to trust his judgment."

"But if he blows it and this document falls into the wrong hands?"

"How's that my problem?"

Attles grunted, appalled at the insensitivity of the man. "You may not have another election to face, but your party does," he said, straining to keep the anger from his voice. "And you know as well as I do that my people hold the key to that election. I'm concerned about this document, concerned that it could split the coalition I've built between the Catholics and the Protestants. What do you think that will do to your party, the party built on the theme of bringing genuine values back to America. It'll kill it, you know that. Do you want that to happen? Even if you don't care about your party, you should at least care about your legacy. What may be the most significant archeological discovery of the century could fall into the hands of those who may use it against what you believe! Is that what you want?"

The president took a deep breath and fingered a cuff link again. "Look, Roger, so far I've been going through channels on this one, but if you think it will help, I'll check a little closer first thing in the morning. I'll make it more personal, encourage Bremer to get more aggressive."

Attles bowed slightly, immediately backing off his aggressive tone. He knew when to charge ahead and when to step back. "Thank you, Mr. President, I think that's a wise course."

The president took a step away from him, but then turned quickly back and eased up closer, cheek almost to cheek. "I take it you've got someone involved as well?" he whispered.

Attles nodded, then held his breath, hoping the president would take the inquiry one step further.

"Good," said the president. "I applaud your efforts. It might be best if your people get to it before Bremer does—less complicated that way. Let me know what happens."

Attles smiled as the president stepped back to his wife. Then walking away from them he reached into the inside breast pocket of his tuxedo and switched off the thumb-sized tape recorder he had secreted within it.

———

At four-fifteen A.M. Istanbul time, Michael sagged into a sofa-sized seat beside Valerie Miller as the jet on which they were passengers prepared for takeoff. Directly behind them sat Red Cashion, a phone to his ear, a chew of tobacco in his mouth.

"Just sit back and relax," Cashion said, pausing for a moment from the phone. "We've got a long flight ahead of us."

"How far is it?" Michael asked.

Cashion grinned slightly. "Don't know exactly, six or seven thousand air miles. But this baby zips along at five to six hundred miles an hour. You do the math."

Michael stared around the cabin for a moment. Though he didn't know much about aircraft, the size of this one told him it had to be a 737 or 747, whichever was bigger. The thing looked like Air Force One. It had two levels, several bedrooms, a full kitchen, the flight deck, and the room in which he, Valerie, and Red Cashion sat, a room that looked more like a family den than an airplane compartment.

Exhaling for what felt like the first time since morning, Michael told himself to follow Cashion's instructions and relax. His mind felt like mush, and his body, alive with energy through the crisis of the day, now sagged like a piece of soggy bread. Turning to Valerie, he started to pat her hand, but then knew he didn't dare. He settled for a weak smile instead.

"You hanging in there?" he asked.

She nodded. "Yeah, I think so, just stunned I guess. I've never . . . never been involved in anything like this, you know . . . seeing bodies like that . . . up close and all. It's just hard to believe what's happened in the last twenty-four hours."

"Hard to believe we're on the way to Costa Rica," agreed Michael. "Never thought Cardinal Roca would go for it. But he didn't even hesitate when I called. Told me again to stay with the scroll."

"Bremer said about the same thing. The White House had called the State Department and told them to do whatever was necessary to find out if the document is authentic."

"So now we're headed halfway across the world with a man we hardly know."

"And he's taking the scroll to a reclusive billionaire who wants it for some mysterious purpose he won't reveal."

"That's a normal Saturday for me."

Both of them laughed gently. Without thinking, Michael placed his hand on Valerie's forearm. Her skin felt warm to his touch, and a delightful but disconcerting thrill ran through him when she didn't pull away. She looked squarely at him, a gentle light in her eyes.

"Look, Michael," she started. "I know I didn't respond too well when I first met you. But I'm pretty careful about appearances. My background, you know how that is—single man, single woman, strange place, all alone. Easy for someone to get the wrong idea."

Michael grinned at her. "But I'm a priest."

She arched her eyebrows. "So? Does that mean you're immune?"

He shrugged.

"And that's not all of it," continued Valerie. Maybe not even the most important part. I . . . well, I'm something of a loner. As the only child of a very wealthy family I've traveled all over the world, lived in several places, never built a lot of close relationships except with my mom and dad. I just split up with a fiancé too, about six months ago. Everything felt like it was closing in on me. I've never worked real closely with anyone else, depended on myself most of the time. So I didn't think we'd do too well together. Can you understand that?"

"Sure," he said, moving his hand and staring out the window into the darkness. "I've got no problem with that. And I think I know what you're talking about. I've been alone too—since I was seventeen, since my family was killed in a car accident."

"That must have been awful."

"You don't know the half of it."

"You want to talk about it?"

"You want to talk about breaking up with your fiancé?" he asked, facing her again.

"Touché," she laughed.

Michael took a deep breath. "Maybe someday, when this is all over, I'll tell you about my family, and you can tell me about your fiancé. That a deal?"

"A deal," she said, leaning back.

For several seconds, neither of them spoke. Michael closed his eyes and tried to think of something other than the woman at his side. But he couldn't. A number of disturbing "what ifs" flitted through his head like scrap pieces of paper pushed by the wind. What if he hadn't become a priest? What if the Catholic Church allowed its priests to marry? What if he fell in love?

For the life of him, he couldn't figure out why Valerie Miller affected him the way she did. He had known beautiful women all his life, and more than a couple had made their availability known. But he had found them all easy to refuse. So why was Valerie Miller so enticing? What about her did he find so compelling? Was it his approaching fortieth birthday, a midlife crisis of some kind? Or the more basic reaction of a normal male thrust into close proximity with an attractive woman at the same time he faced the most intoxicating adventure of his life? Had he unwittingly transferred some of the emotional energy created by the search for the document onto his feelings about Valerie Miller?

Valerie interrupted his thoughts. "We did pretty well together back at the hotel, didn't we?"

"I thought so. I knock 'em down, you knock 'em out, as easy as that."

Valerie smiled. "So I guess we're stuck with each other for a while."

"Seems that way. Surviving a gun battle tends to bond people—right up there with sharing a covered dish dinner."

"Do Catholics do those too?"

"More often than you'd think."

"I'm glad," she said. "It's strange though."

"What's that?"

"Oh, you know . . . a Catholic priest and a Baptist girl all hooked up in this mess."

"Yeah, we carry the notion of ecumenism to a whole new level. Religious détente run amok, I—"

"I suggest you two pipe down and get some rest," Cashion growled at them, lowering his phone again to interrupt. "You've had a full day."

Michael took a deep breath. "How's McAuley?" he asked Cashion.

Cashion spit tobacco juice into his silver cup. "He's beaten up pretty badly. Three fingers are a mess, no doubt broken, plus he probably has a concussion. He's drifting in and out. We'll know more as soon as a doctor can see him, but he's still alive. Looks like a survivor to me. Now pipe down."

Michael nodded at Cashion. "You saved our lives back there," he said.

Cashion shrugged. "Don't think so. You were fine."

"Maybe so, but thanks anyway. You're obviously not new to this kind of work."

Cashion spat again. "I was a homicide cop in Seattle for almost ten years, then a private detective for twenty more. I know how to handle myself. Now do what I tell you—shut up and sleep. Even if you don't want some quiet, I do."

Though he didn't think sleep was possible, Michael nonetheless closed his eyes and told himself to rest. By his side, he felt Valerie Miller's head nestle down on his shoulder. Ignoring the alarms that bonged inside his brain, he made no attempt to move away, content for the moment to listen to his heart.

PART FOUR

For now we see in a mirror, dimly, but then face to face. Now I know in part, but then I shall know just as I am also known.

St. Paul, 1 Corinthians 13:12

At no time are people so sedulously careful to keep their trifling appointments, attend to their ordinary occupations, and thus put a commonplace aspect on life, as when conscious of some secret that if suspected would make them look monstrous.

Nathaniel Hawthorne

TWENTY-ONE

A single slice of midafternoon sunshine slipped through the window of the beachfront warehouse as Hans Walter, a forty-four-year-old mercenary of German birth, pulled himself to his full six feet and six inches of height and motioned for his special operations team to gather around for their last briefing before takeoff. Though his original assignment had called for him to go to Istanbul, buy an artifact, and deliver it to his employer, that task had fallen by the wayside. Misfortune had occurred and men had died. Now everyone who wanted the document had to start over again. Not the way he liked to do business, but things happened. The American mercenaries with whom he occasionally worked called it Murphy's law—the belief that what one expected to happen usually didn't, and that if something had even the least possibility of going wrong, it usually did. So be it.

Rubbing the sides of his shaved head, Walter proudly surveyed the group of six men he had rounded up for this particular job. These men represented the toughest of their kind—an international team of true soldiers untraceable to any particular government and committed to no ideology but that of the warrior—a true priestly caste of no religion but adventure and fortune.

"I have a job for us to do," he began, his voice heavily accented with the thick brogue of his birth. "The document we were hired to procure has quite unexpectedly disappeared. I have been most busy the last two days seeking information regarding its whereabouts."

He locked his hands behind his back, flexed his well-formed biceps so all could see his strength, and began to pace across the concrete floor of the warehouse. "As you all know, the man called Yoseph, who held the scroll, is dead along with two of his companions. The newspapers have reported this widely."

Walter's men nodded. Men died in such a business as Yoseph's. He had met his end Saturday morning.

"Other information I received came before any official news agency picked it up for broadcast. According to my sources, including one police officer who gladly accepted a small bribe for his cooperation, some serious activity took place at the Ceylan Intercontinental Hotel Saturday night. Guests on the fifteenth floor reported a short but intense armed skirmish at just past midnight. The authorities found one man dead, and blood trails suggest a number of others were wounded."

Walter stopped pacing and propped his chin in his right hand. "Most important of all, the police officer said that an occupant of a nearby room stuck her head out into the hall just long enough to see the back of a stout blond man as he disappeared through the stairwell door. In addition, a number of hotel employees say that a man of identical description had that very afternoon offered a major finder's fee for a Dr. Hugh McAuley, discoverer of the document that we've been hired to recover."

Stepping deliberately to a man at least six inches shorter than he, Walter grabbed the man's hands and held them firmly at his belt buckle. "What does the blond hair tell us, Alfred?"

Alfred lowered his eyes and studied his feet. "I'm not sure," he said. "Hadn't thought about it."

Walter wanted to scream but didn't. One did not embarrass one's brother in such a way, even if the brother was excruciatingly inattentive to such matters, matters he knew were crucial to the operation. For several seconds, Walter studied his brother, wondering what in the world he should do with him. If not for his promise to his mother to look after him, he would long since have cast his underachieving sibling aside. But one did not break promises to one's mother. And Walter wouldn't if he could possibly help it.

Twisting away from Alfred, Walter answered his own question. "The blond hair tells us the job at the Ceylan was the work of a foreigner," he said. "Someone other than a Turk now has the document, and he will no doubt take it out of the country."

His square jaw working his gum, Walter started to pace again. "Working on this assumption, I paid a handsome sum of money to a well-placed but terribly underpaid computer technician at the Ataturk International Airport. Since Sunday morning the technician has been hard at work sorting through the flight plans of every international flight that has left the country since Sunday at one A.M. His reports have given us the starting point necessary to find the new keeper of the document."

Walter paused and walked to the window of the warehouse. His men stayed at attention as he took a deep breath and stared out. They didn't need to know everything. Ignoring the group for a minute, he reexamined what he had done to narrow down the list of suspects from the flight plans. First, he had considered only the people who had entered the country since Wednesday, the earliest that anyone could have learned about the auction of the document and flown into Turkey. Second, he decided that anyone with enough money to bid on the document had probably traveled by private jet just as he had done. Though not completely ignoring the commercial airlines, he zeroed in on the manifests of noncommercial and nonfreight flights since Wednesday. There weren't that many between Wednesday and Friday—fifty-four in fact.

Of these, thirty-seven left before Saturday evening—the time of the fire fight at the Ceylan Hotel. Obviously, whoever had the document couldn't have left before then. That left seventeen possibilities.

Using the seventeen names registered as owners of these private jets, Walter had asked the computer man to cross-reference them with the airport data system. Within a couple of hours, he knew that fourteen weren't candidates. Ten were corporate jets carrying an assortment of common business people, two were filled with Italian doctors who had participated in a medical conference on Middle Eastern diseases, and one each held the head of a French university and the assistant prime minister of the Netherlands.

That left three possibilities, and Walter studied their flight information diligently. Each of these jets carried Americans— one a wealthy woman in town for a meeting of a charitable organization that provided food for the Kurdish population of Turkey, the second a radio personality gathering information on American-Turkish relations. The third jet grabbed his attention instantly for a couple of reasons: first, because four men with undetermined business flew in, and six men, plus a woman, and a body on a stretcher flew out; second, the jet left Istanbul at around four A.M. on Sunday. Just the kind of hurried flight one should expect from a man with a valuable commodity in his possession.

His suspicions aroused, Walter plied his informant with a bonus payment and discovered that the jet carrying the last group was listed as the property of a man named Willard Madden, an entrepreneur known worldwide for his wealth and his expensive tastes in many fields. Madden was just the kind of man who might want the document and who would have the money to pay for it.

In addition, though the airport official didn't know for sure, rumors suggested that the man on the stretcher was seriously injured and might not live. When Walter added that to what he knew about the events at the Ceylan Hotel, he became even more convinced that he had isolated the group that had the document.

Even more interesting, Madden's jet wasn't headed back to the United States from which it originated. Instead, according to the plans filed with Turkish airport officials, it was headed farther south, to Costa Rica. Walter liked that turn of events. Authorities in Costa Rica didn't have nearly the same sophistication as those in America when it came to law enforcement.

His chin rigid, Walter turned slowly and faced his men again. Then, stepping in a clockwise motion, he stared for a few seconds into the faces of each of his warriors.

"Listen well," he called. "We have a simple job to do."

He motioned to Alfred, and his brother stepped to the side and flipped a switch. The lights in the warehouse dimmed to a dull glow. A video screen the size of a refrigerator illuminated the relative darkness, and Walter pointed to it.

"Here is our target," he began, grateful that his employer had the means and the expertise to secure such information and images for him. "A home sitting on a tiny island off the northeast coast of Costa Rica, a private island, I might add, an island owned by a Mr. Willard Madden."

"I heard of him," interrupted Alfred. "A billionaire. His home in California was in some big magazine."

Walter nodded, pleased with his normally ill-informed brother. "Madden has at least three homes," he said. "Each of them extraordinary. The Internet has pictures of them all at his Web site. This particular house sits on a plateau on Madden's island. The island has cliffs on the east side, at the back of the house. Madden's security alarms surround the house on the front and on both sides. But the cliffs side is unprotected."

"What about bodyguards?" Alfred asked, his tone a bit fearful.

Walter flicked a wrist to dismiss the worry. "Four to six men of grade B training," he said. "We can handle them if we're careful."

"They won't expect anyone to come up the cliffs!" declared an Asian man to Walter's left.

Turning to him, Walter motioned to Alfred again, and he flicked the lights on full again. For several seconds, he studied the man who had spoken—the only one with whom he had not worked in the past. He was even shorter than Alfred, but as broad in the shoulders as Walter himself, as broad as a bookcase. His eyes were black, and his nose lay slightly to the left, as if someone had pushed it that way more than once. A ponytail as dark as his eyes hung in a single braid down his back. Highly recommended, the man came from South Korea, a former intelligence officer with the government there, a man known for his skill with a variety of sharp-bladed weapons.

"That's true, Sonji," responded Walter, not particularly happy with the interruption. "Normally, no one would dare such an intrusion. But, as you know, we are not normal men."

The men smiled at him and nodded appreciatively. They knew who they were and what they could do. Gathered in Cyprus as they were, they could be airborne in their own plane at a moment's notice and on the ground in Costa Rica before anyone knew they were coming. The small nation didn't even require passports. After landing, they would do a final debriefing at a hotel near the airport outside of San José. Then, in the wee hours of the morning, they would take a helicopter to Madden's island. The helicopter would drop them into the surf just off the small beach on the east side. They would re-group on shore, make the climb up the cliffs, and enter the house within a couple of hours after landing.

"What is the task?" shouted Sonji. "A kidnapping?"

Walter smiled and rubbed his head with both hands, but mentally he made a note to keep an eye on Sonji. "No, my friends, not a kidnapping."

"An assassination then?" Again Sonji asked what they all wondered.

This time, Walter didn't smile when he answered. Instead his granitelike face became even stonier than usual. His eyes, closer to gray than anything else, became dead still. His voice thundered when he spoke. "No, not an assassination! In fact, we want no one dead. No one! We want a clean operation. Do you understand? Unless absolutely necessary and unless I order it, I want no one harmed, no one to die! Do you all understand this simple command?

He raked his eyes over the group, and each of them nodded in obedience. Sonji, his head down, nodded with the rest.

"Good," Walter said, his voice amazingly calm again. "We're after a document," Walter continued, "as simple as that. An archeological find of some magnitude. An important person wants this document, and this person has entrusted us with the task of retrieving it. Are we up to that task?"

He surveyed the group again, going in a counterclockwise motion this time. "Can we get in, get this document, and get out without harming anyone and without getting hurt ourselves? Can we do that?"

In succession, each of the men noted the question and accepted the challenge. "We want a clean operation. Do you understand? Unless absolutely necessary and unless I order it, I want no one harmed, no one to die! Do you all understand this simple command?" Alfred saluted him. Two men winked. Two more mouthed the word "yes."

Deliberately, calmly, Walter stepped within inches of Sonji's face. "Do you understand, Sonji?"

Sonji smiled from the left side of his face. "Yes, I understand, sir."

Without another word, Walter leaned down and embraced his companion. As he did so, he whispered into Sonji's ear. "You disobey me even one time, and you will find one of your own knives buried forever in your South Korean spleen."

The room in which Henriqo Baldas sat contained no windows at all. A single tube of overhead light illuminated the room instead, and the hum from that light had gradually seemed to get louder and louder as his captivity became longer and longer. At this moment it sounded more like a loud horn than a light to him, a horn that he wished someone would shut off!

Squirming in his seat, he tried to move his hands over his ears but couldn't. Handcuffs shackled his hands, and these were attached about six feet off the ground to a steel rod that protruded from the concrete wall behind his head. Not the most comfortable of positions, but at least he was sitting now—unlike most of the last two days when his captor had forced him to stand. His legs ached, but not nearly so much as his arms. They felt like someone had stretched them between two horses going in opposite directions.

He had cried long and often since his capture, and his eyes felt as puffy as small biscuits. His captor had fed him nothing and had allowed him no sleep. And he had not turned off the horn! The noise from the lights pounded through his brain, a blasting torment that threatened the last measure of his sanity.

Henriqo tried to drop his head, to bury at least one ear in a shoulder, but the man in front of him would not allow it.

"I will ask you still again," said the man who had pretended to be the pope. "Who sent you? That's all I want to know. Tell me that and your sufferings will end. I'll give you some food and water. You would like that, would you not? A glass of wine? A giant plate of pasta? Tell me who hired you, that's all I need to know."

The pretender knelt before him, a big hand on Henriqo's knee, his tone soothing, comforting.

"I wish I knew," Henriqo said, tears welling up in his eyes once more as the humming from the light blared into his brain. "But I cannot tell you. A man came to me on Friday morning just as I finished my night shift at the hospital, a man I had never seen. He was small, like a mouse, with little hair and crooked teeth. He knew much about me, my recent difficulties in finding work, my need for money to care for my aged mother, to—"

"And he offered you five years wages to do this 'simple thing,' as he called it, this thing he said someone needed to do for the good of the Church, for the good of the pontiff himself. Yes, yes, you've told me all this! Your name is Henriqo Baldas. You work at the hospital. You pondered the man's proposition all day, then accepted late in the afternoon! He paid you half the money on acceptance, promised the rest when you did your merciful deed! You plied your friend with drink Friday night, then volunteered to take his place the next morning. The man with the bad teeth provided you with the drug and needle with which you planned to kill the pope. That's all you know . . ."

The interrogator jerked up from his squatting position, kicked the chair from under Henriqo's bottom, and stomped his feet as if trying to put out a fire. His massive forearms bulged, and a vein the color of lead pulsed from his elbow to his wrist.

"I will not hear this again!" he shouted. "No one does what you tried to do without more information than you claim to possess. You know who hired you for this, now tell me . . ." He drew back his hand, and Henriqo ducked back against the wall. But the handcuffs kept him from dropping far, and he hung there like a bug stuck to a piece of cardboard. His eyes closed, he hunched his shoulders in preparation for the blow he knew would now come, the blow that surely signaled the beginning of even worse treatment than he had received so far. But the blow didn't fall.

Henriqo opened his eyes. His captor stood frozen, his face a mass of wrinkled rage, his hand a thick club about to fall. But then the hand dropped and fell to the man's side. Henriqo sagged as low as possible, but his arms were on fire and the horn in the lights was blaring again.

"What have you done with His Holiness?" begged Henriqo. "Did you get to him before me? Are you the one who will earn the money?"

The pretender smiled crookedly. "I have taken care of the pope," he said. "You will not need to bother yourself anymore with him."

"Then what about me?" Henriqo asked. "Can't you let me go?"

"You will stand some more," said the captor. "And you will starve some more. I am a forgiving man, but my patience is wearing most thin. I will know the truth—and soon. You can be sure of that."

Watching the bowlegged man stalk from the room, Henriqo hung his head. The horn in the lights screamed down at him, and his arms burned like a welder's torch. Closing his eyes, he wailed against the wall and wished for death. *O Mother of Jesus, what have I done? What have I done?*

TWENTY-TWO

Michael woke up at just past eleven A.M. Costa Rica time, his body wiped out from the emotional exhaustion of the shoot-out at the Ceylan Hotel and the overnight flight across the Atlantic Ocean. Showering and shaving quickly, he slipped into some white slacks, a golf shirt, and a pair of deck shoes provided by one of Red Cashion's bodyguards, and walked to the top of the stairs that led down from the third floor of Willard Madden's home. For several seconds, he stopped and surveyed the incredible house.

Situated on the atoll of an island that Cashion said stretched almost a mile wide and two miles long, the estate dwarfed anything Michael had ever seen. Not only was the home spacious—three stories and at least fifteen thousand square feet, he suspected—but it also contained the absolute latest in electronic and computer gadgetry. The bedrooms, at least six on the third floor from what he could count, were connected to sensors that turned lights on and off as a person entered or exited. Individual computers in the rooms responded to voice commands for the thermostat, television, and other electrical appliances. In addition, the bedrooms contained king-sized beds, exquisitely made contemporary furniture, high-powered computers, fax machines, and printers. The ocean side of each room was nothing but glass. French doors led through the glass and onto balconies overlooking the water below the cliffs on the back side of the home.

The sweeping staircase below where he stood would have made the creator of "Gone With the Wind" proud. On the main floor, a great room large enough in which to toss a football dominated the structure. As in the bedrooms, glass dominated the back wall. Most amazingly, Madden had built a huge stone fireplace in the room and, according to Cashion, sometimes turned the air conditioner down so low that he actually needed it.

Rubbing his eyes, Michael walked down the stairs and into the kitchen area near the back of the house. At the refrigerator he ran into Red Cashion.

"You hungry?" Red asked, opening the refrigerator door so he could see inside.

"Like a wolf," Michael said, peering in. "Some good stuff here?"

"Everything you could want."

Behind them, Michael heard someone coming, and he turned to see Valerie headed his way. Dressed in black sandals with socks, a pair of girlish blue jeans, and a white sleeveless top, she looked like a magazine cover girl.

Involuntarily, Michael sucked in his stomach, but then caught himself and inwardly shook his head. He was a priest, end of story, end of discussion.

"What's to eat?" Valerie asked, her eyes sparkling.

"You name it," Red said. "One of the perks of working for a rich man. Enough food to feed an army."

"Let's do a picnic," Valerie said. "It's such a gorgeous day."

"When's Madden getting here?" Michael asked, forcing his eyes from Valerie to Red.

Red shrugged, pulled a handful of cold cuts from the refrigerator, and sat down at the dining table in the center of the room. "Not till tomorrow. A couple of things came up there, and we've got a few more things to get ready here too."

Michael started to protest, but then decided against it. No rush, not really. He faced Valerie again.

"I'm good for a picnic," he said. "No reason not to take advantage of the surroundings."

"What about you, Mr. Cashion?" Valerie turned to the detective.

"It's Red, and thanks, but I'm okay here." He held up a loaf of bread. "My sandwich is already made, and I'm too hungry to wait. You two go ahead."

Valerie faced Michael. "You're game?"

"Sure, why not?"

An hour later, toting a basketful of assorted sandwiches, fruits, soft drinks, and cookies, the two hiked down to the beach below Madden's home. A lush display of tropical splendor surrounded them as they walked—huge trees, thick ferns, and shrubs that Michael couldn't identify, from the ground to the sky.

At the beach, Michael stretched out a blanket, arranged the food on one corner, stuck an umbrella the size of a bedsheet into the ground, plopped down, and beckoned Valerie to join him. Demurely taking a spot in the center of the blanket, she lifted a sandwich from the basket and began to munch. From the left, the sun slanted past the umbrella and landed on her face. Michael pulled a banana from the food stash and leaned back on his elbows. The air smelled like the ocean, a touch of sand and salt and wet surf all rolled and mixed together. Though intensely aware of Valerie's presence beside him, Michael forced himself to keep his eyes focused on the ocean lapping onshore less than fifty feet away. It wasn't easy.

For a long time, they didn't say anything. But then, as they ate, they gradually began to talk. At first the conversation centered on the events of Saturday—all the fear they'd felt, the awful danger, the death. As if pulling marbles from a bag, they hauled out their emotions one at a time and rolled them out for mutual inspection. Reviewing every moment of the fateful day, they talked about every single event, every sight and sound, every nuance of the frightening experiences they had shared. As if drawn together by an invisible magnet, they inched closer and closer to each other as they talked. Michael found himself mesmerized by the inflections of Valerie's voice, the sultry but still girl-like tones in her enunciation. A light breeze came off the ocean, blowing Valerie's hair into her eyes, and he found it almost impossible not to push it away for her.

After a couple of hours, they ran out of words to say about Saturday and once again stared silently at the ocean for a while. The waves continued to lap at them, and a handful of squawking birds fluttered overhead. Michael pulled a cookie from the basket, handed it to Valerie, and took another one for himself.

"Tell me about yourself," he said, gathering his courage. "Tell me where you come from, what you like, dislike. You know, just generally spill your guts."

Valerie took the cookie, munched a bite from it. "Not a lot to say," she said. "My parents live in Charlotte, North Carolina, now. My dad is the CEO of PrimeAmerica, the country's fifth largest banking chain. He's a great dad, even if he is gone a lot. Supported me all my life in everything I ever wanted to do."

"And your mom?"

"She's fabulous too. Taught art in a community college when

she and Dad first married, but once I came along, she willingly gave it up to stay with me. No need to work, anyway, since Dad makes a ton of money. Mom takes care of the house and spends hours and hours serving the church. She gives out food to the homeless, goes on missions trips, teaches English to the Hispanic population in Charlotte. Plus she's still busy with art—paints, and leads the board of a local museum. You name a good deed and my mom does it."

"And what do you do when you're not climbing the career ladder of the U.S. State Department?"

Valerie smiled. "I read a lot, love biographies, literary fiction. And I play the piano."

"I saw that in the biographical sketch Roca furnished me. You're pretty good, I take it."

Valerie shrugged. "Used to be, but I don't play as much now. I've always loved it, you know, the precision of it all, the rhythm. It's so incredible when you play something well, so . . . I don't know . . . so perfect."

"Sounds like your life," Michael said. "Perfect family, perfect career, perfect from every angle."

"Close to it. A regular Norman Rockwell painting, only more money."

They both laughed and continued munching their cookies. The breeze toyed with Valerie's hair again.

"I've never really had anything bad happen to me," she said.

"What about the broken engagement?"

She brushed back her hair. "Oh, well . . . that wasn't good, but it wasn't bad either, not really. I dated the guy for about three years. But we didn't see each other that much. He's a doctor in Raleigh. And I've lived everywhere the last few years. It just didn't work out, not his fault. Not my fault, not anyone's fault, really."

"You make that choice?"

"Yeah. He took it okay. I mean, what could he say? We both knew it wasn't going to work, two people going in different directions. I've moped some, but it's livable. Looking back, I think I agreed to the engagement because it seemed appropriate, time to do it, know what I mean? The pressure to get married squeezes pretty hard when you get my age."

Michael laughed. "Yeah, you're definitely getting close to being over the hill."

"Almost thirty."

"But other than that, you've had it easy."

"As easy as pie. Even with the broken engagement, I don't really know what it feels like to suffer. My whole life has pretty much been a fairy tale." She raised her knees to her chin and wrapped her arms around them.

Michael shifted on the blanket. "Don't be embarrassed about your good fortune," he said. "Be grateful for it. Not many have experienced what you've had."

"I know," she said. "I guess that's why I feel guilty, like I'm stealing or something, taking something I don't deserve."

Michael tossed a chunk of his cookie at a fist-sized bird that had landed near him. "Some people get more than their share of suffering," he offered. "And they don't deserve that either. Maybe that's how it all balances out in the big scheme of things. Some get more suffering than they deserve, some get less."

"You sound like you know about that," Valerie said, her tone inviting him to go deeper.

"Oh yeah, I know something about suffering. You could say I'm an expert, a regular specialist."

The bird beside Michael pecked at the cookie, broke it, grabbed a chunk in its beak, and darted back into the air.

"You going to tell me about it?" Valerie asked.

Michael looked at the ocean for several seconds, then shook his head. "No, not the details anyway, don't deal with the details. Suffice it to say, I'm a pro with life's pains and got the share you missed."

Valerie shrugged but didn't press him. "That's not fair, is it?"

"No one said life would be fair."

The bird dropped back to the ground beside Michael. He studied it for a second, noted the slightly reddish plumage on the back of its head, and wondered what kind of bird it was. The flora and fauna of Costa Rica weren't his area of expertise. He tossed another piece of cookie at the bird.

"Those men in the hotel," Valerie said. "Yoseph's men. Wonder what they deserved?"

The bird darted away with a huge bite of cookie in its beak.

"Don't know," Michael said. "Maybe they were violent men themselves, maybe not."

"I don't understand all that," Valerie said. "Don't know how to deal with it."

"Violence isn't part of your equation."

"No blood on a Norman Rockwell painting."

"But Norman Rockwell isn't real life," Michael said.

"I'm discovering that, but it's hard for me. Hard for my faith, you know. It's all been so simple to this point, so easy. Just be good, pray, go to church on Sunday, help others, read your Bible. One, two, three. You, God, and me."

"Then a couple of strangers die in a hotel room and you're sitting in a front-row seat to see the aftermath of it all."

"Yeah, where does that fit with my fairy tale faith?"

"It doesn't."

"I know."

"But that doesn't mean your faith isn't real. Just that you have to find a place for it in the midst of what is real, the tragic as well as the perfect. That's what true faith is anyway, it seems to me, the ability to believe . . . to trust in God in the midst of suffering, not in the absence of it."

Valerie nodded and took a deep breath. "I'm just having to adjust to that, that's all. When this is over, I think I'll go home for a few days, take some vacation, see if I can sort it all out."

Michael wanted to take her hand and hold it. He wanted to tell her that maybe she wouldn't ever adjust to the suffering, that things might get more complicated now that tragedy had come into her life, that some long shadows would now seep into the sunny faith she had long accepted. But he knew he didn't dare. She was no more prepared to hear all that than he was to take her hand and hold it. So he said nothing.

In lieu of speaking, he just stared at the water for a long time. His bird friend flittered in and out several more times, but Michael threw him no more cookie. The shadows of the afternoon grew longer, but he and Valerie stayed pretty quiet now, their silence a soothing thing, as if they both realized they were comfortable in the absence of words. The sun dropped lower and lower in the sky, and eventually they packed up their blanket and basket and made the trek back up the road to Madden's home.

Not long afterward, night fell on Madden's island and Michael said good-night to Valerie and walked to his bedroom, and sat on his balcony for a long time and stared out at the ocean beyond the cliffs. Then he buried his head in his hands and wondered to himself what he would do when all this ended and he had to face the conflicts Valerie Miller had stirred up deep in the crevices of his soul.

TWENTY-THREE

Day Ten—Tuesday

His thin gray hair blowing wildly, Willard Madden stepped out of the helicopter before the blades stopped beating and hustled toward the circle of people waiting for him on the veranda outside his house. The veranda, made of a fine black-and-white marble, was split in two by a pool over a hundred feet long and shaped like a peanut. At least two dozen solid wood lounge chairs surrounded the pool, and a fully equipped bar sat on the north end. A bathhouse big enough to hold most American families bordered the pool on the south, and a television half the size of a cinematic movie screen sat beside it. The television wasn't on.

Forty feet on the far side of the pool, a rim of wild green underbrush marked the boundary between the civilized and the untamed. Past that underbrush, a cliff dropped down almost two hundred feet into a foamy surf. Past the surf the ocean stretched out almost two miles until it reached the mainland of Costa Rica.

Sitting between Valerie Miller and Red Cashion in a cluster of chairs near the bar, Michael Del Rio watched Madden approach from the heliport. Dressed in simple tan slacks and a teal sports shirt, the billionaire looked like a man on a long fast. His skin, though tanned almost to the point of seeming unnatural, hung loose at his neck, and his hair, a tired flat gray, made him appear like little more than a cadaver. Michael recognized instantly that the man was seriously ill. Yet even with the obvious sickness, he still carried himself with dignity, his gait that of a man once strong and athletic.

"Sorry I wasn't here to greet you when you arrived yesterday morning," Madden called in a hoarse but rapid voice as he stepped around the pool. "But I had a couple of stops to make in

San Francisco, had to see my granddaughter before I left."

Red Cashion stood to greet him, his thick hand extended. Michael and Valerie stood too, and Madden shook hands with them as well. "Please sit back down," he said, indicating their chairs. "Looks like you were enjoying the sun."

Michael eased back down with the rest of the group. Madden also took a seat.

"You okay, Mad?" Cashion asked Madden, placing himself like a palace sentry at Madden's left elbow.

Madden held his hands out, palms up. "Good as you can expect," he said.

From behind Madden, a woman approached, her hair mussed by the helicopter, her blue eyes bright in the sun. Neither Madden nor Cashion introduced her as she sat down, and Michael, though curious, didn't ask.

"You've found the accommodations sufficient?" Madden asked, his eyes bouncing from one person to the next.

Michael almost laughed.

"The place is lovely," Valerie said. "Fantastic, really."

"You slept well? Rested up some while you so patiently waited on me?"

Three heads nodded yes. Michael glanced at Valerie and decided she looked as if she had slept well every night of her life. In blue jeans again, a bright peach top, and the same sandals from yesterday, she looked gorgeous. He felt like a teenage boy with a crush on the head cheerleader. Though he kept trying to ignore it, the truth was that he had never met a woman like her. Add to that the intense emotions generated by the danger they had faced together, and it was no wonder she had his head spinning.

As if in a fog, he heard Willard Madden talking again. "I'm pleased you're comfortable here," Madden said. "Really pleased. This is an incredible place to rest. That's why I bought it. No disturbances here."

Incredible about summed up the past few days, thought Michael. Incredible that his uncle had sent him on this mission. Incredible that he had met a woman who made him feel in ways he knew he shouldn't. Incredible that Hugh McAuley was still alive and that Red Cashion had rushed them to this palatial Caribbean hideaway owned by one of the twenty richest men in the world. Incredible that somewhere on this property, a manuscript that had already cost at least three people their lives waited for inspection, just out of his reach. He took a deep breath and listened as Madden suddenly moved past the chitchat.

"Look," Madden continued. "I'm glad you like the place. But I know you didn't come here to spend time at Club Med. You've got other things on your mind. I understand you ran into some unpleasantness in Istanbul." He faced Cashion for confirmation.

"Yeah, Mad, like I told you on the phone. But we're all okay now, safe and sound."

"Your knee okay?" Madden looked at Michael.

Michael sat up straighter, surprised that Madden knew or cared enough to ask about the injury at the hotel. "No problem," he said. "A little sore, some stiffness, but nothing serious."

"And McAuley, how's he?" Madden turned to Cashion again.

Cashion shrugged. "He floats in and out, but we've had a local doctor over from the mainland to check him out. If I know anything at all, he's going to make it. Just needs some more time, that's all."

Madden touched Cashion's hand, and Michael noticed the billionaire's fingers were thin, little more than skeletons. Whatever this man had was pretty far advanced.

"You're the best, Red," Madden said.

"For a slow-footed old dog who wants to get back home, I do okay," agreed Cashion.

Madden patted Red's hand once more, then turned back to Michael and Valerie. "I'm sorry you got mixed up in all this. But since you did, I'm glad Red was there to get you through it. Now I'm sure you're wondering why I wanted the document. What I plan to do with it. Am I right?" He stared at both of them, his eyes stronger than Michael would have thought.

Thinking of the manuscript, Michael's pulse zipped up at least four notches, and he found it difficult to swallow.

"We both went to Istanbul to get the document," Valerie said. "So yes, we have more than a little interest in knowing your plans for it."

"It belongs with the Church," Michael said, his tone determined. "Where it can be handled professionally."

Madden stared at him for a second, but without any discernible animosity. Cashion squirmed in his seat but stayed quiet. Madden did a half turn and faced the woman who hadn't been introduced. "This is Cindy Brown," he said. "She's my personal physician. As you might guess by looking at me"—he indicated his body—"I'm not well. Cancer—it's all inside me, liver and lungs. I've tried everything, even a liver transplant two years ago. But now that liver is shot too, and I refuse to try another one. So I'm down to the experimental, the offbeat. That's where the scroll comes in. I've got to do something before I die. Cindy, explain to our guests what's happening."

Madden leaned back in his chair, and Michael noted that the short speech had tired him so much that his breath, though he tried to mask it, came in short gasps. Beside him, Cindy Brown stood up. She placed a hand on Madden's shoulder as she talked, and Michael thought he saw something more than a doctor's compassion for a patient in the gesture. Studying her, Michael decided her eyes were her best features—wide and bright blue with eyebrows that arched clear and dark, giving her face a mysterious quality. For a moment, he wondered if Madden and his doctor had a thing going.

"I don't know how to start," Cindy began. "Except to tell it like it happened. I've been trying for months to find some new avenue to explore. In the process, I've found all kinds of alternative medicines, have tried several of them on Willard. But nothing seems to work. It's all been a dead end. So I've continued to look, trying anything and everything even remotely possible."

She paused and pushed her hair from her eyes. "Last week, on Tuesday, I ran across an Internet link that described a number of so-called miracles. Found one originating in Mexico. According to the description, a woman had a 'Mary sighting,' then a healing of a tumor in her stomach. You know how those things are—someone sees the Virgin, then declares she healed them of something awful. Well, that's what happened here. A peasant woman apparently saw or thought she saw . . ."

As she continued the story, Michael gradually came to understand where it was all headed, and his hands began to ball up into tight fists. Madden wanted the manuscript because he thought it could heal him! Talk about incredible! How could one person act so selfishly as to purchase the most important archeological discovery of the century for his own personal needs?

For a second, Michael wanted to shout at Madden, tell him in no uncertain terms that no one person deserved such special attention, no one man deserved such a unique gift. But then another possibility came to him. What if the scroll did cure Madden? What if he touched it or read from it, and his health suddenly improved? What if his cancer shifted into remission? Would that prove the authenticity of the document? Or would it matter either way?

Michael knew that unexplained healings sometimes happened. But how much God had to do with it, he didn't know. To be honest, he had always supposed such things could be traced to other factors—the power of the psyche, improved diet and exercise, the simple fact of chance.

Wanting to interrupt Brown but not sure exactly how to do it, he pushed back in his seat and gritted his teeth. Within a couple of minutes, she drew to the end of her story.

"So we sent Mr. Cashion to Istanbul, and he brought the scroll back to us. That's where we are. We have the scroll, and it's time to see what's in it."

Michael couldn't hold it in any longer. "But you can't do that!" he exploded. "The conditions aren't right! We don't know how brittle the scroll might be. I don't know a lot about this kind of thing, but you don't just take a piece of ancient parchment, a discovery of this magnitude, and lay it down on a table to read like a newspaper! That might destroy it completely!"

Cashion leaned forward in his chair, but Madden touched his shoulder and he stayed in place. Facing Michael, Madden nodded as if understanding. This time when he spoke, his voice slowed just a little. "I'm well aware of the dangers here, Father Michael, and I can assure you I've already thought about this. You may not have noticed, but I have a vault in the basement of this house—a good sized one. Over the last couple of days, my guys have been making some adjustments to it, sealing it off from any outside air. I've also had some tools brought in, tools that will enable us to handle the document without actually touching it. Believe me, we're going to take every available precaution."

Madden stood and towered over Michael as he continued. "Having said that, though, you need to know I do plan on having this document read—and soon."

"For your own healing?" Valerie interrupted. "Don't you think that a bit presumptuous?"

Madden shrugged and eased onto the edge of the table by the chairs. "I'm one of the wealthiest men in the world," he said. "I bought the scroll fair and square. If I want to use it as a rag to clean toilets, I have that right."

"But what about the Church?" Michael asked, his tone fierce. "The Church should get the chance to—"

"Forget the Church!" It was Cashion who interrupted.

"You're angry at the Church, aren't you?" Michael asked, noting the detective's flushed face.

"Not any church in particular, but the notion of it all, the idea that there's some kind of God out there who actually gives a rip about what happens to somebody as insignificant as you and me. I had a grandma who believed all that stuff, but when the doctors started chopping off bits and pieces of her toes and feet as her diabetes got worse, I didn't see any evidence of your so-called God. And out there on the streets"—he waved his hand as if to encompass the whole world—"out there where people live, where cops do their jobs, where . . . well, out there your God is about as absent as trees in the Sahara Desert. So don't—!"

"Just calm down, Red," interrupted Madden, touching his friend's shoulder. "I'm sure we could all enjoy a late night conversation regarding the merits—or lack of such—of religion. But that's not our purpose here."

"No, our purpose is to make sure that you misuse a historical artifact for your own selfish purposes!" Michael said, not willing to back off the confrontation.

Madden sighed heavily. "Judgment, judgment, judgment," he whispered. "Everyone is so quick to judgment, even those from the Church."

As though wearied beyond rest, he suddenly dropped his head and exhaled heavily. "Look, if you must know, I didn't bring the scroll here for my own personal use. Whether I live or die at this point is not especially important to me except for one thing. I have someone I deeply care about who needs what I hope the document can—"

Cindy Brown grabbed Madden's arm, stopping him in midsentence. "It's not for you?" she asked.

"No, Cindy, it's not for me, never has been," he said. "It's for my granddaughter, Katie. She's got leukemia. Remember a few months back when she called me complaining of a stomachache?"

Cindy pressed her fist against her mouth as Madden continued. "Without some kind of miracle, Katie might not live as long as I do. That's why I want the scroll read—why I need to act immediately. If there's anything in it that will help her, I want to know it as soon as possible."

"But why didn't you tell me?" Cindy asked, her eyes registering her hurt. "I'm a doctor, remember, I might have helped her."

Madden patted Cindy's hand. "I'm sorry, Cindy, but . . . well . . . her mom and dad know the doctors in San Francisco, trust them. I suggested you, but they wouldn't hear of it. Said you had enough on your mind taking care of me."

For several seconds, no one spoke. The breeze off the ocean pushed across his face, and Michael turned to Valerie. She was staring off toward the water, her face a blank, her shoulders sagging. Apparently, the notion of a little girl struck with deadly leukemia had hit her with decided force, a force that, when combined with the death she had just seen in Istanbul, was more than she could accept.

Watching her, Michael ached to comfort her, but he had no idea how, or even if she would allow such a thing. Worse still, he personally wanted to feel the presence of God in the face of such tragedy, but God remained silent to him as always, an absent deity whose face he had never seen and whose touch he had never felt.

"So that's where we are," Madden said, breaking the silence. "An unbelievable mess, don't you think?"

"So what next?" Cashion asked.

"Someone has to read the document," Valerie said. "That's obvious enough."

Madden nodded and turned to Cashion. "Do you think McAuley is up to it?"

Cashion shook his head. "No way, at least for a while yet. Like I said, I think he'll make it, but it's going to take some time."

"Then who?" Valerie asked. "Who'll read it?"

"Only one man here can read it, so far as I know," Madden said. "Only one New Testament scholar in this group."

It took Michael a moment to realize what he meant. But then, as everyone turned toward him, he began to shake his head. "I won't do it," he said as calmly as he knew how. "The motivation isn't right. Besides, I could damage it."

Valerie placed her hand on his. "But you have to read it, Michael, regardless of the motivation. Just think of it—one way or the other, you can do something no one else has ever done. You can—"

"I know the implications," he said, cutting her off. "But it's not right, it's not my place."

"A child is going to die," Cashion said. "If something in that document can save that child, don't you think your God would want you to read it? I don't know much about this stuff, but my Lutheran grandma told me once that Jesus blessed little children. Isn't saving a child a good motivation, maybe even a holy one?"

"But you don't understand," Michael insisted, feeling his argument losing steam with the group. "I serve the Church, and the Church makes these kinds of decisions, not individual priests like me, not a professor out on his own, making up the rules as he goes along. That's not the way the Church works."

"Even to save a child?" Cashion asked.

"Even to save a child," Michael said, his breath slowing, a sense of dread rising in his chest. "Even to save a child."

"Something is wrong with that kind of church," Cashion spat. "And you ask me if I'm angry."

Again the group became silent. Michael felt Valerie's warm hand on his. More than anything else he wanted to explain himself, to explain how he had given himself to the Church and how it dwarfed individuals, kept them subservient to the whole, how any other process than that destroyed what it had taken centuries to build. One did what was best for the Church, not what was best for the individual, no matter how important the particular person. But he knew his arguments sounded ridiculous to anyone on the outside, anyone beyond the circle of the priesthood. For that matter, they even sounded ridiculous to him at the moment, and he had grown up with them, had used them to justify so much that he couldn't understand.

Madden broke the silence again. "Here's what we're going to do," he said. "We're going to put Father Michael in the vault with the document. Then we're going to leave him there all alone. We'll allow him to decide what to do—read the manuscript and tell me what's in it or refuse to read it and leave this place and the document tomorrow. As simple as that."

"There's a third choice," Valerie said. "He can read the document, then refuse to tell us what's in it."

Madden nodded. "Yes, he can do that, but I don't think he will."

"Why won't he?" It was Cashion who asked the question.

"First, no one who loves what he loves can turn down the opportunity to be the first person to read this manuscript. Think what that would mean. No man in his right mind can say no to the possibility of making history. So he'll read it, no doubt in my mind."

"But will he tell you what's in it?" Cashion countered.

Madden rolled his tongue across the front of his teeth. "He is a man of God, isn't he?" The question sounded just a touch sarcastic. "He knows I have a granddaughter who may be no more than a few weeks away from the grave. I don't think he'll leave me in the dark about the contents of the scroll. No true man of God would do that. One way or the other, he'll tell me if this document contains anything that can help my Katie. Am I right, Father Michael?"

All eyes turned to Michael. Without a word, he closed his eyes and nodded. Madden had read him correctly. He would read the scroll. And, one way or the other, he would tell Madden what the manuscript revealed to him.

TWENTY-FOUR

At just past three o'clock Michael left everyone else upstairs with the sunshine and the ocean and descended eighteen steps into the basement of Willard Madden's magnificent home. Closing the door behind him, he stepped through a room that contained a pool table, an aquarium filled with exotic fish, and four rows of theater seats in front of another gigantic television. Just past that room, he made a short right turn and found himself at the doorway to the vaultlike space that Madden had told him he would find. The room looked to be about sixteen by sixteen, and Madden had told him it was encased in solid steel.

His legs wobbly, Michael stepped into the vault. Though it had no windows, light seemed to pour from every direction, and for a moment, Michael was blinded by the bright glare. But then his eyes adjusted, and he carefully examined the entire space. A safe the size of a refrigerator sat in the left corner. A file cabinet just as tall but half as thick centered the back wall. A single white vase sat on top of the cabinet, but it didn't contain any flowers.

Michael's inspection moved to the middle of the room, and there, sitting on a metal table similar to those found in an industrial-sized kitchen, he saw a tubular steel canister and a black zip-up bag as a doctor might carry. Ignoring the bag, he focused on the metal canister. About the length of a child's baseball bat and the diameter of a family-sized jar of peanut butter, the canister was a pewter color and sitting on its end. Surrounding the canister lay a number of instruments and accessories— the items Madden had procured to handle the manuscript— plastic gloves, rubber tipped tweezers and tongs, a surgeon's mask, a couple of clean cotton cloths, a magnifying glass, and a camera without a flash.

Working to control his breathing, Michael slowly approached the table. Five feet away he stopped and almost turned around. Whether authentic or not, the notion of reading the scroll gave him the shakes. He stared around the eerily quiet space, noted again its shocking illumination. Nothing hung on the slate gray walls—nothing. But, strangely, instead of making the room look dead and dull, the bleakness made it seem alive. The overhead lights bounced off the walls, giving them a pulsating quality. The hair on the back of his neck stood on edge, and a tingle ran through his legs. The air felt dry and he remembered that Madden had equipped the room with a dehumidifier to suck all the moisture out.

The notion of saying a prayer came to him and he almost knelt, but then he felt foolish and stood up straight once again, dismissing the notion. Swallowing hard, he told himself to settle down. There was nothing here to stir him up so much. Though he believed in God, he had never known God to work in any way he couldn't explain. When a sick person recovered from an illness, doctors received the credit. When a jobless person found work, perseverance and effort took the bows. When the opposite happened and tragedy struck . . . well, chance did operate in the universe, and people brought much of the evil on themselves. Though he had never actually put it into words, Michael suddenly realized that he didn't believe that God directly intervened in human life one way or the other! Yes, God created the world, but then God left the world to its own devices. In a sense, the Church existed to do the work of God in the human arena. With the Church at work, who needed God's intervention anyway?

Standing in the barren vault, the realization overwhelmed Michael, a revelation as bright as the lights overhead. He had felt this way about God since his seventeenth birthday, had built his entire adult life on just this notion. To give it up now would destroy everything he had come to trust. The Church was the center of his faith in God, not any kind of personal connection or relationship.

To Michael's surprise the recognition of this submerged truth acted as a sedative to his nerves. If nothing divine ever intervened, then nothing specifically good or evil existed in this room. So the scroll contained no special power, one way or the other. It was probably a poor forgery, nothing more and nothing less.

Fortified, Michael took a step closer to the table, and the walls of the room seemed to close in around him. Though he knew that several people waited on him upstairs, he felt totally alone, more alone than ever, even more alone than on the day his family had died, the day he turned seventeen, that horrible day he . . .

Shutting his eyes, he forced himself to concentrate on the scroll. Reliving that day made no sense at all at a time like this, a time when what he was about to discover might change his life forever. But then he realized why he was remembering his seventeenth birthday. That day had changed his life forever too, though it had been for the worse. If this day changed his life that way . . .

Pushing away the thought, he took one final step and reached the table where the scroll lay. Not wanting his breath to moisturize the document, he picked up the surgeon's mask and slipped it over his mouth and chin. Then, his hands shaking, he pushed his fingers into the paper-thin gloves Madden had procured for just this purpose. Next, as carefully as a doctor about to operate, he picked up the canister. It weighed almost nothing and felt quite normal. The metal was smooth and cool to the touch.

He rolled the canister around in his hands several times. Surely, there was nothing extraordinary about the document inside, just the jottings of some ancient forger. Even if the apostle John did write it, and even if it did contain the words of Mary, so what? She was just a poor Jewish woman who happened to give birth to an unusual son, a son who became the most marvelous teacher and spiritual leader the world had ever known.

Michael squeezed the canister, and his body began to shake. Though he had spent his entire adulthood hiding it, he couldn't deny the truth any longer. If God never intervened in the world, then his faith made absolutely no sense. If rational thought explained everything, then no miracles ever happened, nothing supernatural ever took place. God never healed a child of cancer or created forgiveness in the hearts of a divorced couple or touched a miser and made him generous.

If this view was right, then faith had no meaning at all. How could he call himself a man of faith when he believed he could explain everything that existed, when he removed all mystery from life? No wonder he had failed to pray as he approached the scroll. Why pray if God never responded—if the world was a closed system of cause and effect?

Holding back the tears that had watered up in his eyes, Michael came to a startling conclusion. If nothing supernatural ever happened, then he needed to resign from the priesthood! A man without faith shouldn't serve in a Church that said it lived on the basis of such a commodity!

For several seconds, he remained still, dealing with the stark truth. His heart pounded like a jackhammer, and his face flushed with a sudden sense of embarrassment. He had been found out—a priest with no faith! Like an emperor with no clothes.

Turning the notion over and over in his head, a strange calm suddenly hit Michael. As quickly as it had appeared, the embarrassment ended, and a sense of freedom replaced it as he realized he had just confessed a dark secret. Calmed by the admission, his hands became steadier with the canister. Why worry about something that contained no ultimate truth, no genuine power? Why get so agitated about a piece of parchment with a few ancient jottings on it?

Moving quickly now, Michael twisted the top off the canister, picked up the rubber-tipped tongs, and caught the end of the wooden stick that stuck out from the ends of the document. Still using the tongs, he carefully but firmly slid the manuscript out of the container and laid it on the table. Underneath his feet, the floor seemed to shiver, and his fingers seemed to heat up where they had touched the document. He heard a low rumble, almost like the sound of a baseball-sized metal ball rolling across a hardwood floor. The hair on his neck jumped to attention again. For a moment, he thought he was imagining things, but then he noticed that the canister sitting by the manuscript was actually shaking. But then it stopped and everything became quiet and still again.

Michael stared at the document for another few seconds. Did Costa Rica have earthquakes? Light tremors? He'd have to ask. Or did the document have some kind of—? No, he rejected the idea immediately—it was too preposterous to consider. Costa Rica, a land created by volcanic activity, almost certainly had earthquakes, even if minor ones.

Sweating profusely in spite of the dry air, he wiped his forehead with one of the cotton towels and took another breath. Then, as calmly as possible, he focused again on the work he had entered the vault to accomplish. Though his hands had started to shake again and still felt strangely warm, he gently took the tweezers, and with his right hand at the top, he slowly began to unroll the scroll.

It was ragged at the top, with the left edge lower than the right and the papyrus in between frayed and jagged as if someone had ripped the material with their bare hands. For a second, Michael wondered if another piece of document waited to be found somewhere else in Ephesus, but then he dismissed the notion. Nothing he could do about it anyway, at least for the time being. The fragment he had was problem enough for one day.

Touching the scroll lightly, he noted the crinkled and brownish edges that marked the papyrus for about a half-inch on the top and each side. The edges looked as though someone had toasted the document slightly, then crumpled it up, then unrolled it and patted it back into place. Though not an archeologist, Michael knew enough to expect these signs of aging. No document sat in a cave for nineteen centuries without suffering some kind of deterioration, no matter how dry the environment. If this was a forgery, it was a good one.

He caught his breath as he saw the first words appear. Squinting slightly against the glare of the lights, he began to read, slowly at first, not pausing even for a second to reconsider his actions. The words were good New Testament Greek, and he translated them easily, instantly forgetting the tremor that had so unnerved him just moments ago.

In the last days of this temporal life, I, John, a follower of the Lord Jesus and witness to many signs and wonders that He did . . .

Finished with the opening, Michael unrolled more of the scroll and began to read the next section. Though he knew little about forgeries and couldn't tell whether he held one or not, he did know the New Testament, and it didn't take him long to conclude that whoever wrote the document used the Greek language well. Even more remarkable were the similarities to the Biblical writings attributed to the apostle John.

As he read, Michael found himself strangely calm. A hurricane could have been blowing overhead, but he wouldn't have known it. He had entered his own private world, a world populated by Roman soldiers and Jewish religious leaders and wandering messiahs and poor common folk trying to survive in a cruel and primitive society.

According to the document, this book was Mary's story, Mary's account of the life of Jesus. And, Michael had to admit, aspects of the writings reflected a woman's touch. The story of her pregnancy took on a feminine tone. The account of Jesus' early life contained details never before described.

Directed by the Spirit of God, Jesus and Mary and Joseph settled in Nazareth after their sojourn in the land of Egypt. And in his twelfth year, Jesus' father Joseph became ill unto death and Jesus mourned with great tears and sorrows. On the day of the death of Joseph, Jesus said to Mary, his mother: "Death is a great darkness, but God the Father is the author of light. In the Father's house are many lighted rooms." Mary was comforted by such words and kept them close in her heart . . .

For the second time since he entered the vault, Michael felt tears nudging the corners of his eyes. How well he knew death as the great darkness. But what he didn't know was whether or not the Father's house contained many lighted rooms. Only by dying could he test the truth of these words. But oh, how he admitted to himself, oh, how he hoped to find them true.

Wiping his eyes to keep the tears from falling on the scroll, Michael continued to read, and the words on the parchment astonished him. Numerous stories untold by the other gospel writers flowed from the pen of the one who identified himself as John. Insights only a mother could offer came from the account. Details that, if true, might reshape the Church jumped off the page.

Michael's emotions did catapults as he read—leaping from sheer joy in one moment to sheer terror in the next. In one second, he hoped for the authenticity of the document, but in the next he prayed for it to be a hoax. One thing he knew for sure. If authentic, this book would turn Christianity on its head. For that matter, the world as he knew it would never be the same either.

The scroll unfolded turn by turn, and the writing on the parchment ran out long before he wanted it to conclude. The story of Mary and Jesus came to an end. Brushing his eyes once more, Michael checked his watch. About two hours had passed since he had entered the vault. He stretched for a moment. Then hesitant to leave, he reread the last section one more time, mouthing the conclusion to himself. The words caught in his throat, but he forced himself to finish them.

On the day before his return to the Father after his resurrection, Jesus appeared to his mother Mary, who had taken up her lodging in my house.

"Fear not," Jesus said. "I am the resurrection, and death cannot hold the life. Forever you are my mother, and forever I am

*your son. I go from you now, but in the days to come you too shall
be raised, and the sorrows of this life shall pass away. Be of good
cheer, for I have accomplished the work the Father gave to me. I
have taken away the sins of the world."*

*Then Jesus ascended to the Father, and Mary told all that she
had seen and heard to those who loved her and cared for her from
that day until now. I, John, bear witness to her words.*

Exhaling quietly, Michael rerolled the scroll, slid it back into
the canister, twisted the canister shut, and laid it back on the
table. For just over a minute, he stood dead still, trying to decide
how to communicate what he had just read to the people upstairs. Though no good way came to him, he knew he had to try.
He had to leave the document, climb the stairs, and tell Madden
and everyone else the truth. That's why he had entered the
vault.

Resigned to the task, Michael trudged out of the vault and
up the stairs. In the great room again, he spotted Valerie and
Red Cashion sitting on the sectional sofa that stretched out in
front of the fireplace. Both of them stood instantly, expectation
written on their faces.

Michael stumbled toward them, his legs weak.

"Well?" Valerie asked. "What does it say?"

"Let me get Madden first," Cashion said, then darted out of
the room. He returned a moment later with Madden and Cindy
Brown in tow. Everyone but Michael took a seat around a square
crystal table in the center of the room. Michael stood by the
stone fireplace and turned from one to the other. His face felt
warm and his hands tingled.

"Well, speak up!" commanded Madden. "Everyone's here.
What does the document say?"

Michael cleared his throat and opened his mouth to answer.
Nothing to do but say it straight out. His lips opened and shut,
but no sound came from them. He tried again, mouth open, lips
moving. But still he heard nothing. He grinned sheepishly, feeling like a bad actor in a silent movie.

Grunting and clearing his throat again, he tried a third time
to squeeze out a word. But no luck. He rubbed his throat from
top to bottom, up and down, and licked his lips and pressed his
vocal chords with his fingers. But no sound came out. Not a
squeak, not a squawk. To his great horror, Michael Del Rio discovered he was mute.

TWENTY-FIVE

A wad of blue silk sheets tangled between her knees, Valerie Miller sighed for at least the ninety-ninth time, rolled onto her back, and stared upward into the skylight over her king-sized bed. Counting off another fifty stars, she told herself to relax and go to sleep. For several more minutes, she closed her eyes, hugged her pillow to her chest, and listened to the sounds of the ocean that filtered up from below the cliffs and through the windows that covered the left side of the room. But unable to shut down the emotions that kept surging through her head, she still didn't fall asleep. She thought again and again of Michael Del Rio and his inability to speak. How strange, how utterly strange! Frustrated, she glanced at the clock again—3:29 A.M.

For another five minutes she waited on the bed, hoping that the pounding ocean would lull her to sleep. But her eyes stayed open, her stomach tight.

Giving up, she sat on the edge of the bed, her feet resting on the floor. She liked Michael, she admitted as she rubbed her eyes and stretched. She liked his looks, his obvious intelligence, and his gravity. She liked everything about him but the obvious—he was a Catholic priest! Not that she had anything against Catholics, but wouldn't you know it—the most fascinating man she had met in years, including her former fiancé, and he turns out to be a priest! No future in that! Though she knew some Baptists who had married Catholics and lived happily ever after—no small feat in and of itself—she couldn't expect Michael to throw away his calling for even the possibility of a relationship with her. That wouldn't be fair to either of them.

Frustrated, Valerie stepped to the French doors that separated her bedroom from its balcony. Pushing back the doors, she pulled down the black nightshirt that Madden's guards had provided for pajamas and walked outside. Yawning, she threw her arms behind her head and took a huge whiff of ocean air. A light breeze feathered through her hair and tickled her neck.

Why couldn't Michael talk? All evening, she and everyone else had encouraged him to speak, but to no avail. A number of different liquids had been tried—bottled water, Coke, lemon tea, wine—but none made any difference. Time and time again he opened his mouth and tried to speak, but nothing but froglike groans and grunts came out.

At first Cashion accused him of faking and suggested that a certain kind of encouragement could loosen his tongue. "Let me have him for an hour," Cashion urged Madden. "Then we'll really see a miracle."

But no one took Cashion seriously. One look at Michael's tortured efforts to communicate, and no doubt remained. He simply couldn't talk. Even Madden, as desperate as he was, could see the agony etched in Michael's eyes. Something had happened to him in the vault, something had grabbed his throat and squeezed it shut.

Valerie placed her elbows on top of the wooden rail on the edge of the balcony and stared into the dark. A floodlight on each end of the house illuminated Madden's yard, the fingers of light creating alternate rows of shadow and visibility. A row of clipped hedges about four feet tall bordered the yard, and natural underbrush ran out beyond the hedges. Jagged rocks fell off behind the underbrush, and the ocean rolled in and out below the rocks. Palm trees almost as tall as the house danced in the light breeze, and a half moon hung overhead, bright and clear for the moment as a bank of clouds drifted to its left. A canopy of stars accompanied the moon, and a shimmer of light washed in and out over the pool. Valerie took another deep breath, trying to inhale the enchanting scene, hoping the gentle quiet would lull her toward sleep. But then she thought again of Michael. . . .

Willard Madden had produced a legal pad and pen and asked him to write down what he had read in the scroll. Michael took the writing materials and sat down to try. But, incredibly, when he lifted the pen, his hand began to shake as if he had an advanced case of Parkinson's disease. A look of panic came to his face, and his eyes pleaded for everyone to understand—something beyond comprehension had taken control of him.

"It's a psychosomatic reaction," Madden said. "I've seen it

happen more than once. A guy ordered into combat in Vietnam suddenly can't walk. A cop facing a criminal can't get his pistol out of his holster. The body goes where the mind takes it—if you disrupt a person's emotions, the physical will follow."

No one argued with him, and the rest of the day and night passed without any change in Michael's status. Finally, at about eleven o'clock, Madden suggested they go to bed and try again in the morning. Seeing no other option, everyone followed his advice. But Valerie had found it impossible to sleep.

She had found a novel on some shelves beside her bed, but the plot failed to grab her interest, and she gave it up after a few minutes. After that, she had e-mailed her mom and dad, telling them where she was but nothing about the events at the Ceylan Hotel. No reason to worry them. Finished with that, she played a couple of computer games for an hour or so, but that too petered out pretty fast, so she went back to bed and tried to sleep. But again, nothing happened. What a night!

Valerie stood up from the balcony and wondered about the scroll. Did it really possess some kind of strange power, a power that had silenced Michael so he couldn't reveal its secrets? Or was Madden right? Was Michael's reaction simply a case of runaway nerves? She certainly didn't know.

Her own faith, as strong as it was, provided few answers on a matter like this. How could it? She'd never faced anything even remotely similar. A cloud drifted over the moon, and Valerie pushed her hair out of her eyes. She didn't have a frame of reference for anything that had happened since Saturday morning—the death, the mystery. To this point, her life had unfolded as routinely and sweetly as a morning glory that never faded—all bloom and bright color.

Her parents, Dad the banker and Mom the community leader and volunteer, had supported her in everything she ever tried. School had come easy, and her career was on a fast track to major achievements. Nothing tragic had ever happened. But now? Well, now she had seen death up close and personal, and she didn't know how to deal with it. She wasn't sure what her faith, untested as it was, had to say in circumstances like these.

Valerie closed her eyes, hoping to think of more pleasant matters. Ocean waves lapped in the distance, and the sound caused her shoulders to relax. She rolled her neck side to side, and her breathing slowed. She decided to go back to bed and try once more to sleep. If nothing happened with Michael in the morning, she would fly back to Rome and see what Ambassador Bremer wanted to do next.

Opening her eyes, Valerie took one final look at the pool, then the cliffs past the finely edged hedges. Something moved in the undergrowth. She squinted into the darkness. A shadowy figure darted out of the hedges and rushed toward the pool, stopping when it reached the bathhouse to her left. In the moonlight, the figure looked like a man, but she couldn't make it out for sure.

Valerie pressed onto her tiptoes, then noticed a second movement—this one to the right. The figure copied the rhythm of the first one—several quick steps, then a sharp stop. She recognized now that the figure was a human being, dressed completely in black. Whoever it was now squatted by the edge of the bar past the pool.

For a couple of seconds, Valerie remained rigid, her imagination working feverishly. Was this a security exercise of some kind? Were Madden's bodyguards running a drill, a practice maneuver?

Before she could decide what to do, four more black-clad figures slithered out of the hedges, darted into the yard, and took up positions in and around the back of the house. As the last man took his place, a finger of moonlight dipped to the ground, and Valerie saw that the man wore goggles and held a weapon similar to the one she had seen in the Ceylan Hotel in Istanbul.

She screamed at the top of her lungs, and the lights around the perimeter of the house flickered and died.

———

Though sprinting toward Willard Madden's palatial home, Hans Walter glanced toward the upstairs balcony the instant the screaming began. Through his infrared goggles, he spotted a feminine form outlined in the moonlight. He pointed his weapon, an AK-47, in her direction, the red beam from its sight line playing on her forehead. But he didn't fire. To his left and right, his men also held their weapons in check. Though the screaming might have panicked less accomplished men, it failed to have the same effect on his troops. They stayed steady, professional to the core.

Reaching a set of double glass doors, Walter pivoted left and flipped a "thumbs up" sign to his companions. Though he had hoped to neutralize the security system, subdue the occupants of the house, and secure the document without a fight, the screaming had surely destroyed that possibility. Such was the

way of his work. The law of Murphy again. Okay, deal with it—
move to contingency plans.

His hands steady, Walter pointed his machine gun and fired
point blank at the two knobs in the center of the back entrance
to the house. Glass splattered at his feet, and the door collapsed
and fell inward. Knowing that Madden's security forces would
respond soon, Walter jumped through the door, his men following rapidly.

"Bedrooms on the third floor!" he shouted, glancing at the
stopwatch on his wrist. "Secure them first! Find Madden and
hold him! His men will not fire if we have him hostage! But hurt
no one!"

Bounding through the kitchen, Walter rushed toward the
stairs he knew he would find on the other side. At the stairs, he
paused for a split second to listen for movement. But nothing
stirred. Perhaps Lady Luck rode his shoulder tonight, he
thought. Perhaps Madden's security agents had gotten lax.

With a jerk of his head, he led his men up the stairs—one
flight, two, then onto the third floor. Surprisingly, they met no
resistance. On the landing at the top of the stairs, Walter paused
for a split second. Where were Madden's bodyguards? Did they
not keep vigil on the same floor as their billionaire employer? Or
did Madden think himself beyond such intimate protection?

A negative thought occurred to Walter. Did Madden sleep
somewhere other than on the third floor? His information told
him all the bedrooms were here. Was his information wrong?

His troops darted like black ghosts down the hallway, and
Walter pushed away his questions and took up a position outside
the first door on his right. Normally, he would have taken the
time to find out who slept in which room. Unfortunately, this job
had given him no opportunity for such detailed preparations.

Twisting open the door, he pounced into the room, his knees
flexed into a squat and his back to the wall. He saw a bed
straight ahead. A large man lay in the bed, a white bandage
wrapped around his head. Stepping closer, Walter flashed a light
into the man's face. Bruises covered his cheeks and a goatee decorated his chin. The man snored as serenely as a newborn. Walter smiled. Lady Luck did ride his shoulder tonight. If everyone
slept as soundly as this man did, his forces might yet secure the
document without bloodshed.

As the invaders smashed through the back door, Valerie

Miller scrambled out of her bedroom, her nightshirt billowing. With the house completely dark, she stumbled to the door next to hers and pounded furiously on it, yelling at the top of her lungs for Michael to wake up. When he didn't respond immediately, she dispensed with protocol and shoved the door open, still screaming for all she was worth.

Twenty feet away, Michael jerked up in bed, his eyes wide and frantic in the moonlight from the skylight overhead.

"Someone is here!" Valerie yelled. "Downstairs! They have guns!"

Instantly awake, Michael jumped out of bed—a pair of long gym shorts his only clothing. Valerie felt her face flush, but then she heard footsteps in the hallway. She yelled again, and Michael rushed toward her and took her hand, and the two of them sprinted to the door.

But at the door a man clothed in black and smeared with facial grease flashed a bright flashlight into their eyes and shoved an automatic weapon toward their faces. Her hand clutching Michael's, Valerie stood frozen in the light, shaking with fear.

With the ease of one accustomed to such tasks, Walter took only seconds to secure his prisoner. A pair of handcuffs that Houdini couldn't unlock, a double strip of duct tape, and a piece of nylon cord did the trick quite well—hands, mouth, and ankles were incapacitated. Though the man glared at him with enough anger to melt steel, Walter kept his cool. His orders were to hurt no one, and he tried to follow orders whenever possible. Yes, he accepted violence when it came his way, but he didn't seek it out. Whatever the employer wanted suited him just fine. And, given the fact that the conditions of this contract promised a double fee if he completed the work without harming any one, he had extra incentive to treat his captives well.

Leaving the big prisoner behind, Walter hustled into the hallway again, still surprised at the lack of response from Madden's security. But he suspected he knew why. With the electricity cut off and everything so confused, the bodyguards had to proceed cautiously. Though they had surely heard the screaming and the gunfire that followed, they had no real clue what was actually happening. No doubt they needed a few moments to collect themselves, to formulate a plan to address the unknown conditions. To do anything else would be foolhardy.

Walter checked the stopwatch on his wrist. Less than four

minutes had passed since his forces had entered the house. Good progress so far. Lady Luck instead of Murphy's law.

From downstairs, Walter heard heavy footsteps, then saw a floodlight whisk across the ceiling. His weapon ready, he ran to the top of the spiral stairwell and blocked the path from below. If Madden's forces were all downstairs and his team had Madden trapped upstairs, then he held all the high cards. The trump was making sure he had Madden.

Still facing the downstairs, he yelled into the darkness. "I need a status check!"

The light from below crisscrossed his position, then twisted quickly and came back to rest on his face. He stayed as still as a statue, deliberately giving the man with the light a good view. Let the enemy see his clothing, his expensive weaponry. Let him know he faced a pro. That would slow him down a notch.

Overhead, the lights suddenly flickered, then pulsed and burned again, casting everything in the house in a fresh bath of illumination. But Walter remained steady. He had expected this. A house as expensive as this one inevitably had a generator geared to kick in after a few minutes without power. No problem.

Walter stared down the stairs. A barefooted, bare-chested man in gray sweatpants and a blond crew cut glared up at him. The man held a Glock in his right hand and a floodlight in his left. Behind that man, two others also stood, wearing navy suits, white shirts, and holding small machine guns.

"Drop the weapon!" yelled the blond man, his voice firm. "There's three of us and only one of you."

Walter grinned hugely. "I don't think so," he said, nonchalantly holding his weapon by his side. "Yes, it seems for the moment you have me outnumbered. But appearances, you know . . . they often do deceive. Even more importantly," and here he paused for effect, "I have your Mr. Madden."

The blond man quickly leaned to the left as if to look past him, perhaps trying to determine if the words were a bluff.

Perfect, thought Walter, seeing the concerned look on the blonde's face. So the billionaire did sleep on the third floor. Hopefully his men had him in custody by now . . .

"All clear, Walter!"

Walter heard the words to his rear but didn't turn around. Within seconds, four of his men had called out their status, each one clear and safe. The only one who hadn't checked in was Sonji.

Feet shuffled behind him, and Walter knew the prisoners

were being herded into the hallway. Though a bit perturbed at the South Korean for his failure to report, he didn't show it.

"Show me Madden!" demanded the blond man. "Show me he's okay!"

"Gladly," Walter said, holding up a hand, palm out. "Just stay calm and all will be well."

He twisted and motioned to Alfred, indicating he should replace him at the top of the stairs. As the two exchanged places, Walter surveyed the prisoners, two women—the one from the balcony in a long T-shirt, the second in standard pajamas—and three men. One of the men wore gym shorts, while the other two were dressed in identical black sweats and white T-shirts. One of the men in the sweats had a cast on his right leg, and the other carried his left arm in a sling. Walter studied the injured men for another second, then realized they were part of Madden's security group, probably hurt in the process of obtaining the scroll. With these two out of commission, Madden's security was shorthanded! Lady Luck indeed!

"We need to see Madden," the blonde shouted testily.

"A second, please," called Walter. "Impatience is a dangerous emotion in such circumstances as these, remember that!"

A sense of dread crept over him. Willard Madden wasn't with the prisoners. And Sonji hadn't reported.

"One minute!" he yelled again, stepping down the hallway, his weapon poised. "We're giving Mr. Madden an opportunity to dress himself!"

Moving past the woman in the nightshirt, Walter grabbed her by the elbow and pushed her down the hall before him. If Madden had somehow managed to get past Sonji, he wanted a shield to protect himself against any unpleasant surprises.

———

Willard Madden woke up the instant Valerie Miller first screamed, but he didn't immediately react. Having survived almost eighteen months in the jungles in Vietnam, he knew that sometimes the best move in a dire situation was no move at all. For the next ten seconds, he stayed flat on his back, his nose twitching, his ears cocked toward the back of his house.

Within those seconds, several things happened. One, someone shut off the electrical current and killed the lights. Second, he heard gunfire, then the splatter of glass, then the sounds of four to eight people, almost certainly men, blasting through his back door. Third, he realized that his own security team, caught off guard by what must have been an up-the-cliffs attack, wasn't yet prepared to respond.

The sound of footsteps on the stairs prodded Madden to action. Moving rapidly, he pulled on a pair of jeans and a navy T-shirt. Grabbing a Browning, thirty-eight caliber semiautomatic pistol from the nightstand by his bed, he headed toward the deck outside his bedroom. The deck, twice as large as the simpler balconies that led off all the other bedrooms, was surrounded on three sides by the steep inclines of the roof of the house. Only the back side of the balcony opened to the back yard.

On the deck, Madden took a quick look at the roof. Given his weakened condition, he knew this route was dicey. But what choice did he have? Behind him, he heard his bedroom door pop open. Twisting around, he saw a beam of light rake over the bed where he had just been sleeping. Throwing a leg over the deck railing, he hoisted himself onto the roof.

Like a rat escaping a snake, he scurried toward a chimney about forty feet away. His senses supercharged with adrenaline, he heard a door click and knew his pursuers were about to step onto his deck.

Madden reached the chimney and threw himself behind it, his thin frame crouching sideways to make himself as small as possible. To his right, a trail of light probed across the roof. But the light didn't find him.

Madden allowed himself a small grin. People had kidded him for years about his fireplaces in the tropics, about the way he sometimes chilled his house to fifty degrees so he could burn real wood and enjoy the smell. Who was laughing now?

The light washed across the roof again, stopping here and there like a dog sniffing to pick up the scent of its prey. Holding his ragged breath, Madden pressed against the chimney, his Browning ready. Out of nowhere, a strange sense of freedom came over him. What was the worst thing anyone could do to him? Shoot him? But how bad could that be? He was three-quarters dead already from the cancer. Getting shot might be a relief—a quick, clean way to check out. Much better than letting the cancer chew him up over the next few months!

The light shifted back toward the chimney, its bright glow searching the roof. Madden tilted his head, suddenly intrigued by the notion of getting shot and ending his misery. Why not?

Before he could stop himself, Madden stepped out from his hiding place and stared straight ahead at his pursuer. The man turned slightly but didn't see Madden at first. Madden studied his profile in the moonlight. The man was short and stocky and dressed in black. A braided ponytail fell over his right shoulder. His facial features looked Asian, Korean maybe.

For a split second, Madden wondered what the man wanted. Money? Was this an old-fashioned hostage for ransom deal? But then he decided not. The coincidence of this attack at this particular time was too great for anything else. This man and his companions had come for the scroll, no doubt about it.

Madden pointed his Browning at the intruder, but he didn't squeeze the trigger. "Let him see me," he thought. "Let him see me and let him kill me and let me cheat this cancer—!"

The Asian turned another half body to the left and spotted Madden. His slanted eyes grew round with surprise and then, with a shocking swiftness, he flashed his light across the roof and drew his weapon to hip height.

As Madden braced for the bullet to come, a strange calm hit him, and he found it fascinating that he felt no fear. More than anything else he felt receptive, open to the mystery of death. He opened the palm of his empty hand and stretched out his arms to embrace the moment, to accept the bullets that would now rip into his body. But nothing happened.

The Asian didn't move. His weapon remained cocked but unused. Frustrated by the man's unexpected behavior, Madden pulled himself to his full height, braced his Browning in both hands, and aimed it at the man. The man had to shoot him now, he thought, shoot him or die himself.

Madden thought of Katie one last time, her bright smile, her green eyes as bright as a firefly. His desire to die disappeared as instantly as it had come.

A split second before the Asian squeezed off his weapon, Madden jumped to the side and ducked behind the chimney again. A hail of bullets splashed into the brick behind his head, spraying bits and pieces of mortar in all directions. One of the pieces of debris hit him and a slice of pain cut into the left side of his back, just under his shoulder blade. Radiating outward, the burning sensation surged through his body and into his chest.

Madden slumped down, his breath jagged and hot in his throat. He heard a thump and knew that his assailant had jumped the balcony and was on the roof, headed his way. His chest pounding, Madden pushed away from the chimney and began to skid down the roofline. Blood poured down his left arm and into the palm of his hand. But he kept moving, his body sliding down, his hands steering him as best they could toward a vine-covered trellis that he knew snaked from roof to ground on the back side of his home.

————

Pushing Valerie down the hall, Hans Walter heard a spray of gunfire and cursed under his breath.

"Take her!" he yelled to his men, releasing Valerie and sprinting through the door from which the gunfire had sounded. In the bedroom, he glanced hurriedly side to side but saw no one. Straight ahead a set of arched doors stood open. He ran to the doors. A second round of bullets erupted from the roof.

On the deck, Walter quickly scanned the area. Several potted trees sat in the corners. A small fountain gurgled to his left, and patio furniture—a table, chairs, and a barbecue grill—rested by the fountain. To his right, another round of small arms fire popped. Staring toward the gunfire, he saw Sonji on the roof sliding down the back of the house.

"Is it Madden?" Walter yelled.

"It is!" called Sonji. "And I hit him, I know I did!" He disappeared into the shadows.

"Take all necessary measures!" shouted Walter. "But keep him alive!"

Sonji didn't answer, and Walter spun on his heels and ran back into the house. Two seconds later, he appeared at the head of the stairs again, pushing Alfred to the side so he could speak to the blond guard. More than anything else he wanted to keep the man from deserting his post to search for Willard Madden, as he would surely do if he suspected that Madden had escaped. If that happened, chaos would reign, and he might lose control of the situation. Such chaos spelled trouble, trouble he could ill afford.

Staring down the stairs, Walter almost groaned. The two men in the navy suits had replaced the blonde. The suits held their weapons ready and aimed his way.

"Where is the other man?" Walter shouted, a scowl prominent on his brow.

The suits shrugged. "He went to get dressed," said one. "He asked us to keep you company until he came back."

Walter gritted his teeth. Matters were escalating and he didn't like it. A round of gunfire sounded from the rear of the house. He recognized the weaponry—Sonji's Heckler and Koch HK53. Hearing the shots, Walter took a sharp deep breath and reconsidered his situation. Unless he missed his guess, Murphy's law had prevailed over Lady Luck, and someone would surely die tonight. Chances were, Madden was already dead. If so, that meant he had already lost one half of his contract payment, a half he desperately needed to cover some major debts to a gambling casino in Rio de Janeiro. Without that money, he knew a whole legion of South American financiers who would take great pleasure in hiring a hit man or two to "punch his ticket," as the Americans liked to say. Not a pleasant prospect!

Walter stepped back a pace and considered his options. Go ahead with the plan, deliver the scroll, collect the payment as promised, pay off part of his debt, and plead for more time to collect the rest? Or . . . or what? Or renege on his contract, take the document for himself, and sell it to the highest bidder. He rolled the idea around for a moment. Such an action wasn't unprecedented in his trade. Other professionals like himself had moved beyond their station as hired hands and become chieftains in the ranks. Why shouldn't he? Who knew how much he could get for the scroll, especially if it proved authentic? Perhaps enough to pay off his debts and settle down in Argentina somewhere.

"The hostages!" he called, his decision made. "Front and center with the hostages!"

Alfred reacted instantly, pushing the cluster of frightened people to the top of the stairs. Now they stood between Walter's forces and the two security men below.

His gray eyes fierce, Walter rubbed his head, then cradled the stock of his machine gun to his chest. Taking a deep breath, he nodded to Alfred, took dead aim down the stairs at Madden's bodyguards, and opened fire.

When Red Cashion heard the first round of gunfire popping from the roof, he knew instantly what it meant—someone had slipped onto one of the balconies in an attempt to escape. Though he didn't know who it was, that didn't matter. He had to act.

Without a word, he turned and sprinted away from the stairwell, leaving Madden's regular security to deal with the mercenary at the top of the stairs. Within seconds, Red had darted out of the house, his bare feet running full speed toward the back, his right hand holding his flashlight, his left hand clutching his weapon.

As he ran, he began to hum slightly, his voice keeping rhythm with his fast-moving feet. As he hummed, he made several rapid calculations. One, six men had invaded the house—the bald-headed leader, the man guarding the stairwell, the one doing the shooting, and three others who had responded when the bald guy demanded a status check. Two, it was a pro team, major league all the way. No one else could have scaled the cliffs behind Madden's place. Three, they wanted one of two things: Madden for ransom or the scroll.

Turning the corner at the back of the house, Cashion dropped to his knees and scanned the area. Though a set of floodlights bathed the yard, their yellowish glare did little to illuminate the spaces just past the manicured lawn, and a bank of clouds covered the moon.

Cashion's humming grew louder. To his left and from behind the pool, he heard someone running. Coming out of his crouch, Cashion spotted a man sprinting horizontally to the yard through a thick stand of trees. But he couldn't see well enough to identify the runner. Running after the sprinter, he heard gunfire erupt from the house, and he knew the situation was deteriorating rapidly. He began to sing under his breath. "Celebrate, celebrate . . ."

For a split-second, he considered going back to the house, but then knew that made no sense. Someone out here needed him—maybe Madden, maybe not, but that made no difference. Every life was valuable, and the one in the woods deserved his help as much as anyone in the house.

His Glock set and his feet pounding past the pool toward the cliffs, Cashion pointed his light into the darkness. But still unable to identify the runner, he didn't shoot. The hesitation cost him.

The moon peeked around the clouds. Cashion saw a man with a black ponytail drop to his knees and take dead aim, but he couldn't see the man's target. Before he could react, the man squeezed off a hail of semi-automatic fire.

"Celebrate, celebrate, dance to the music. . . !" Red charged across the yard, his music keeping rhythm with his pumping knees.

His own weapon spat now, a stream of pistol fire nicking and clacking through the trees, splintering leaves and branches. In the beams of his light, he saw now that his target was a thickly muscled Asian. Within two seconds, Red reached the pool. Another three carried him past the yard and into the brush toward the intruder. But the pony-tailed man didn't stay still. Instead, he moved away, his chunky body moving faster than Red thought any man could move. In one second, Red had the man's head in his sights; in the next, the head disappeared.

Cashion sprinted after him, pushing himself faster and faster, his calves beginning to burn, his bare feet taking the punishment of the uneven, rocky surface. Too many years of relative inactivity had slowed him considerably. A fist seemed to grab and squeeze at his heart and lungs. But his anger kept him going. He reached the spot where the intruder had been. Pausing to catch a breath, he flashed his light along the ground. Not more than twenty feet away, he spotted a small splotch of blood on a low shrub. Moving to the spot, Red knelt and touched it. The gunman had wounded someone but hadn't killed him.

Moving through the brush again, Red began to sing once more. "Ain't nothin' but a hound dog . . ." The singing seemed to energize his legs, and from somewhere deep within, he found a new burst of speed.

Lunging into the underbrush, he caught a glimpse of the gunman fifty feet away, his ponytail streaming out and down his back like a horse's mane. Cashion urged his legs to move faster, and they responded with still another gear of speed. Up ahead, the Asian suddenly stopped, but this time he didn't lift his weapon. Instead, he squatted to his knees, slung his machine gun over his shoulder, and reached for something on the ground.

Cashion instinctively knew what was happening. The person being chased had fallen. The hunter had reached his downed prey.

With a scream as loud as that of any wild animal, Cashion covered the remaining distance between himself and his enemy. Not more than ten feet away now, he raised his Glock to fire.

The gunman saw him coming now, but he didn't panic. As if handling a rag doll, he lifted a body off the ground, tossed it over his thick neck, and stood quickly and faced Cashion as he came at him.

Red's finger itched to pull the trigger.

The intruder's black eyes were stern but not afraid. He held a ten-inch, serrated knife in his right hand, and the knife was poised directly under the throat of the body on his shoulders.

Red lunged to a stop, his breath coming in mammoth gasps, his chest bursting. But he didn't shoot. He didn't shoot because the man on the intruder's shoulders was Willard Madden, and Red didn't know if he was dead or alive.

Inside the great room in Willard Madden's house, the smell of gunfire hung in the air. Spatters of blood decorated a section of the wall just to the right and almost at the bottom of the spiral staircase leading into the large space. One of Madden's security team lay crumpled and moaning on the third stair up from the first floor, but other than that, all was quiet. At least half the people were too scared to speak, the other half too preoccupied.

As if preparing to direct an orchestra, Hans Walter stepped onto the upraised hearth of the stone fireplace in the center of the room and called everyone to attention. Following his direction, Alfred and Sonji prodded six of the prisoners to the base of the hearth. The other three—Madden, the woman in pajamas, and the man with the goatee Walter had found sleeping—sagged into a leather sofa that sat across from the fireplace. Each of these three was wounded—Madden and the woman from the skirmish just finished.

Walter stared down into the faces of the six people standing before him: the three remaining security guards, the blonde with the crew cut, the dark-haired man in blue gym shorts, and the woman in the nightshirt who had screamed from the balcony. Walter rubbed his head from front to back, then exhaled heavily. Perspiration ran down his neck and into the space between his shoulder blades. Circumstances had overtaken his best-laid plans. Madden's security team had proven more difficult than he had imagined. Though his initial fire had taken down one of the men at the bottom of the stairs, the second one had dropped to the floor and disappeared. Within seconds, a counterattack began with two more men joining the unwounded one.

Using the prisoners as shields, Walter had hoped to avoid casualties among his own team. But again, Madden's men surprised him. Two of his comrades fell under their withering counterattack. One took a round in the head and died instantly while a second fell to a bloody but inconsequential flesh wound to the upper left bicep. But that was, as the Americans liked to say, "water under the bridge." Time to move ahead.

Walter cleared his throat. "Allow me to introduce myself," he began. "My name is Hans Walter, and I am sorry that our operation led to bloodshed. That was not my desire." He waited as if he expected them to answer. No one did.

"But we don't always have control of the situation, am I right? Yes, well, I know I am right." He paced across the fireplace hearth. "So now we have to do the best we can with what we have. And what we have is this—I came with one object in mind, and that has not changed. I came to retrieve an archeological discovery, a scroll stolen from a cave in Ephesus. I am sure you know of this scroll, am I right?" He paused, but again no one answered.

Walter's face flushed. "You think your silence accomplishes something?" he asked. "What a silliness this is. I have two of my men searching for the scroll even as I speak. But this is a big house with many places to hide such a thing. A search might take hours. I don't want that." He paced back in the opposite direction. "So I need your help. Who will help me?"

His machine gun in hand, he jumped down from the hearth and towered over the woman in pajamas. A bullet had clipped into her calf, and a thick tourniquet wrapped her right thigh. "What is your name?" he asked the woman.

"Cindy Brown."

"Will you help me, Cindy Brown?" he asked, poking his Uzi under her chin.

"I'm a doctor," she said weakly. "I don't know . . . what . . . what you're talking about."

Walter grinned, but there was nothing friendly about it. Then, the grin never leaving his face, he fired his Uzi. The explosion of bullets blasted to Cindy's right, and she grabbed her head against the sound, but the bullets didn't hit her.

"That was the last warning," Walter said, calmly stepping from Cindy to the woman in the nightshirt. "In five minutes I think I will have better aim. Am I right?" He touched the woman's chin, running a finger up the side of her face. "And your name, pretty woman?"

She hesitated for a second. Walter pinched her cheek and a red welt appeared.

"My name is Valerie Miller," she said, her teeth clenched. "I'm a representative of the United States gov—"

"I don't care who you represent!" Walter shouted, grabbing Valerie by the hair. I need someone to help me find the scroll. Who will help—?"

From his left, Walter heard a growl, and he turned just in time to see the dark-headed man barreling toward him, his face contorted in rage. With a quick pivot, Walter danced out of the way, chopped down with his weapon and caught the man in the back of the head. He crumpled to the floor, his eyes rolling back and disappearing.

"Michael!" The scream came from Valerie Miller, and Walter grinned again as the woman ran to her injured friend.

"Three and a half minutes," Walter said. "My aim will be better this time." With a swift kick, he popped Michael in the ribs, then climbed the hearth of the fireplace once more. Another thirty seconds passed. Walter glanced at his watch. "Three—"

"We found a vault!" The yell cut Walter off.

From his left, one of his troops sprinted into the room. "In the basement," the mercenary shouted. "We found a vault!"

"Alfred, hold them!" Walter shouted. "Sonji, come with me."

———

As Walter disappeared from the room, Red Cashion nodded to Alfred, then motioned his head at Michael and Valerie.

"They're hurt," Red said. "Let me check on them."

For a moment, Alfred hesitated.

"You got the hardware," Red said, leaning a shoulder toward Alfred's weapon. "And I'm no fool."

"Okay," Alfred said, his face a grim mask. "But move slowly."

Cashion stepped to Michael and Valerie and dropped to his knees. Valerie had Michael's head cradled in her lap. He was out cold. Cashion ran his hand over Michael's skull. A lump the size of a marble swelled out behind his right ear, but his breathing seemed steady. Cashion checked his pulse. It was solid and rhythmic.

"He'll have a headache in the morning," Cashion told Valerie, "but I think he's okay." She nodded but didn't speak.

After checking with Alfred again, Cashion moved to the sofa. Though squatting in front of Madden, he directed his question to Cindy Brown. "You hanging in there?" he asked.

"Not bad," she said, her face the color of flour. "But I'm worried about him." She indicated Madden. "He's lost too much blood. And he's already weak. I'm . . . I'm . . ." She broke down and began to sob, her tears washing into her mouth.

"Shush," Cashion said. "He's tough, he'll surprise us yet, just you watch and—"

"Hey! Hey!" yelled Walter, suddenly reappearing, a silver-colored canister held high over his head. "I think I found what I came to find. How fortunate for all of us! Am I right? Am I?"

"Don't open that canister!" Cashion shouted, standing quickly and darting toward Walter. "You'll ruin it if you get humidity on it!"

Alfred blocked his path before he reached his brother, his Uzi at Red's chest.

"I'm aware of the danger," Walter said, lowering the canister. "I opened it briefly in the vault, but only long enough to verify that the scroll is actually inside. It will not be opened again except to test its authenticity."

"And how do you plan to do that?" Cashion smirked. "Not exactly your area of expertise, if I'm guessing right."

———————

His eyes steady on Cashion, Walter stuck the canister under his arm and rubbed his head. His original orders called for him to deliver the scroll, not get it tested. But now he had jettisoned the original plan, and that meant that testing would be necessary. Unfortunately, he had no clue where to turn to get such a thing accomplished. The matter called for some creative thinking.

Stepping to the hearth, he slowly surveyed the prisoners once more. Madden had brought these people here. But why? What brought them to this place? What capabilities did they possess that Madden wanted to use? How did they connect to the scroll?

As he paced across the stone hearth, it came to him. Madden had brought these people and the instruments he had seen in the vault to this island because he planned to have someone give the scroll an initial reading. And from what he had seen in the vault, someone had already done just that. But who? Which one of the prisoners possessed such training?

Cindy Brown was apparently Madden's doctor. The blonde with the crew cut was a security man of some kind, the procurer of the scroll. Four of the men—the one down on the stairs and the other three in the room—also served in security. That left the woman in the nightshirt, her overprotective friend, and the big man with the goatee. For several seconds, Walter considered the redhead. Without doubt, he was the archeologist McAuley, the one hauled out of Istanbul on a stretcher. When he left the island, he would take McAuley with him. If and when the big man came to his senses, his expertise would be invaluable, exactly what he needed to get a first opinion of the scroll. For now, though, he looked terribly useless. Which meant he needed someone else in case McAuley never recovered. But who?

Walter paced the hearth again, noting that Michael had regained consciousness and now leaned against Valerie Miller's shoulder.

"One of you two will come with me!" he snapped at the pair. "And *you* get to tell me which one it will be!"

"Leave them alone," Cashion growled. "Take me if you need a hostage. I'll go easy, no trouble at all."

Walter sneered at him. "You're a soldier like me," he said. "You know nothing about the scroll."

"Neither do they," countered Cashion. "She's a U.S. diplomat. You don't want that headache. And he's a priest—totally worthless."

"Whoever they are, one of them has read the scroll. I saw the mask in the vault. But which one has the expertise to do such a thing? That's what I need to know."

No one spoke.

A smirk tickling his lips, Walter stepped down from the hearth and kicked Michael in the ribs again.

"Leave him alone!" Valerie screamed. "He can't speak, he can't help you!"

"Are you the one then?" Walter asked. Valerie didn't answer.

Walter kicked Michael once more, this time in the face, and Cashion heard the snap of a cracking bone.

"Leave him alone!" Valerie wailed, her arms now cradling Michael's head in her lap. "You're going to kill him, leave him alone. . . ."

"Then you will come with me!" Walter shouted. "Are you the one who can read the scroll? That's all I need. I will leave the rest of you here in peace if you will give me the one who can read the document!"

Sobbing, Valerie shook her head. At her side, Michael groaned, rolled over, and then pushed up from the floor. Clutching his side, he tottered to his feet, his hands grabbing the sofa for support. Blood dripped from his nose and mouth, and his right eye was beginning to shut. He opened his mouth and tried to speak but nothing happened.

Valerie held him by the elbow. Placing a hand on her shoulder, Michael took a deep breath and tried again to talk. Nothing came out.

Walter grabbed Valerie by the hair and jerked her away from Michael. But then, as mysteriously as his speech had disappeared, it suddenly returned to him.

"I'll go . . ." Michael mumbled through swollen lips. "I'm the one who can read the scroll."

PART FIVE

Greater love has no one than this, than to lay down one's life for his friends.

Jesus, St. John 15:13

By associating with good and evil persons, a man acquires the virtues and vices that they possess, even as the wind blowing over different places takes along both good and bad odors.

Franklin Edgerton

TWENTY-SIX

At just past two P.M. Rome time, Cardinal Severiano Roca opened the door to his personal quarters and stepped back to allow Secretary Nelson Randuhar to enter. Though it was most usual for such meetings to occur in one's private chambers, Roca had readily agreed to the request of the Secretary to do so. How could he do anything else? Matters in the Vatican remained chaotic, and any chance to visit privately with the Secretary, a man given more power each day the pope remained incapacitated, was welcome. Who knew what might come of such a conversation?

"Come have a seat," suggested Roca, pointing Randuhar toward a pair of simple wooden chairs that sat on opposite ends of a round burgundy rug in the center of the room. "I know you have had a long day already."

Randuhar nodded and followed him across the hardwood floor to the chairs.

"Tea?" Roca asked, indicating the silver tray on the table sitting in the middle of the rug.

Randuhar declined. "Our meeting will be short," he said, dropping his angular frame into one of the chairs. "I can perhaps do without the tea." The words were clipped, not elongated as usual.

Wondering about the discrepancy in Randuhar's normal speech patterns, Roca took the other seat and cleared his throat. "Do you mind if I have a cup?"

"Help yourself if you wish."

Roca poured the tea, his mind busy trying to size up his fellow cardinal. Randuhar's lips were jammed together as if glued, and his shoulders were straight and square—the posture of a man being squeezed by intense pressures.

Randuhar lowered his head into his long hands, then looked up. Roca held his breath.

"I am aware of your efforts with Father Del Rio to find the Ephesus document," Randuhar said, his voice flat.

Roca sipped his tea, trying to hide the fluttering in his stomach. "I thought it a prudent course," he said. "As head of the Congregation for the Doctrine of the Faith, it is my duty to stay abreast of such matters."

Randuhar shrugged. "Did you not think it appropriate to keep me informed of your actions?"

Roca fingered his teacup and tried to discern Randuhar's emotions. Was the Secretary angry? Envious? And how much did he know of Michael's situation? Though he and Bremer had agreed to keep their collaboration as quiet as possible, had the ambassador seen fit to talk with Randuhar about their joint efforts to find the scroll? Did Randuhar know that Michael had been abducted and that the scroll had disappeared? Or only that he had sent Michael to Turkey? Unsure, Roca decided to stay patient and hope the Secretary revealed his hand.

"You had weightier issues on your mind," he stroked the Secretary. "I saw no need to bother you until I knew more. Why disturb your concentration with something that might turn out to be nothing more than an amateurish hoax?"

Randuhar nodded slightly, and Roca knew his arguments sounded reasonable. A man as rational as the Secretary would no doubt see that.

Changing his mind about the tea, Randuhar leaned forward, poured a cup of the hot liquid, then sat back again. For a couple of seconds, the two men faced each other, their tea steaming, their eyes locked. Randuhar spoke first, his eyes still unblinking.

"So what has Father Del Rio discovered?" he asked.

Roca's heart flipped. Randuhar's question put him in a tough position. Having received a phone call from Valerie Miller only that afternoon, he knew the awful circumstances of Michael's disappearance and had started an immediate effort to track down his nephew's whereabouts. Unfortunately, that work was greatly hampered by the fact that he couldn't tell anyone the whole story. To admit, even in private conversations, that he had sent a personal aide on a surreptitious mission made him seem devious if not downright dishonest, and no man in the Curia who had ambitions could afford that label. To this point, he knew nothing more about Michael's predicament than what Ms. Miller had told him. But did he dare tell the Secretary all this? Or did the Secretary already know? He set his tea cup back on the silver tray.

"Michael found the document," he said.

Randuhar stayed still, not revealing anything.

Roca continued. "But it's not in his possession."

"Do you know who has it? Where it is?"

"I was given a name by the young woman from the U.S. embassy who traveled to Turkey with Father Del Rio. A man named Hans Walter took it. Ms. Miller didn't know if Walter worked for someone else or for himself."

"What have you learned about this Walter?" Randuhar asked, his eyes intense.

"Nothing as of yet, but I'm working on it."

"And Father Del Rio?"

Roca dropped his head, then rolled his ring around his finger. He felt a flush come to his face, and he couldn't disguise the tremor in his voice when he spoke.

"He's my nephew, you know . . . I'm his only living relative. I've mentored him for years, loved him as the son such men as you and I can never have. . . ." He stared into the gold pattern that swirled through the rug at his feet.

"Ambassador Bremer tells me he is missing," Randuhar said.

Roca sighed. "Yes, the man Walter abducted him."

"And the archeologist McAuley as well."

Roca raised his eyes and stared again at Randuhar. The Secretary knew everything. Had Bremer told him?

"I worry for Michael's safety," Roca said, unable to conceal his grief.

"I am assured by Ambassador Bremer that the U.S. State Department is bringing its full power to bear in his behalf," Randuhar said.

"He has said the same to me."

"I will pray for Father Michael and Dr. McAuley," Randuhar said.

"I am grateful for your prayers."

Silence again came to the room. An unfamiliar rush came to Roca's eyes, and he recognized it as the nudge of tears. For a moment he just sat there, letting the sensation take hold. It felt so strange, this sadness, this overwhelming sense of regret that came because he had put someone he cared about in danger. He knew that his ambition had driven him to it, an ambition that clouded his judgment and caused him to use others for his own purposes. But if his desire for the papal chair caused something bad to happen to Michael, then none of that power for which men such as he inevitably grasped meant anything. If his petty self-ishness caused any hurt to even one hair on Michael's head, then . . .

Pushing away the thought, Roca brushed back his tears and reached for his tea again. The meeting seemed to be over, yet Randuhar remained seated. Roca focused on the Secretary again. Did the man have another reason for this meeting other than to see what he knew about the location of the scroll? But what else could Randuhar want? Then it came to him! Of course the Secretary had another reason for the visit! He didn't know everything! He didn't know if Michael had read the scroll! Or if he had, what it had revealed to him! The Secretary had re-quested this visit in an effort to put the final piece in the puzzle as he weighed his decision about the Marian Decree. Without knowing the contents of the scroll, he could make a terrible mis-take either way.

Roca sipped from his cup and realized that if his reasoning was correct—and he had no cause to suspect otherwise—he now held incredible leverage in the palm of his hand. The Secretary needed him more than he had ever dared to hope. He decided to take the offensive.

"His Holiness remains critical from what I hear," he started. "And the media clamors more and more each day to know what will happen as we approach the New Year's Eve Mass. Will the pope be well enough to make his position concerning Mary known? If not, will you seek to speak for him? A difficult position for you, I am sure."

"You know I have stayed publicly neutral on the matter of the Marian Decree."

"And you know I am staunchly against such a declaration."

"What if I told you I knew the pope's desire on this issue?" Both men moved almost imperceptibly to the edge of their seats, and the air in the room seemed to get thinner.

"That would surprise me greatly," Roca said.

"I have his journal." Randuhar said it as simply as if telling his secretary to get him a file.

"His personal journal?" Roca's voice caught in his throat.

"None other. It came to me late last Tuesday, two days after our pope's unfortunate stroke."

"And you've read it?" Roca asked, his hands squeezing his cup.

Randuhar dropped his eyes. "Not at first, that seemed too . . . too invasive. But then, when His Holiness remained incapacitated . . . I thought it, well, sensible to do so. Who knows how long His Holiness will remain unable to communicate?"

"So what does it tell you?"

A slight smile came to Randuhar's lips. "It tells me far more than I ever expected."

"About the Marian Decree?"

"About many things."

Roca stayed still, afraid to move lest he reveal his nervousness. "So what will you do with what you know?" he asked, his voice almost a whisper.

Randuhar grunted. "I had hoped to have this Mary scroll in my possession before I did anything. But now . . ." He looked expectantly at Roca.

Roca pretended to sip his tea, giving himself time to consider his response. What should he say . . . or should he speak at all? No one expected Randuhar to become the next pope, and the new pontiff—whoever that ended up being—would surely replace him as Secretary after a short season of necessary transition. So Roca didn't need to reveal anything more than what he had already said. But then again, why not tell all he knew? Randuhar would find his candor admirable. Later, if the pope didn't survive, such honesty might lead the Secretary to support him when the cardinals gathered in the holy conclave to choose their new leader.

"I am told that Michael read the scroll," he said matter-of-factly.

Randuhar leaned forward but kept his feelings well hidden. Roca marveled at the man's emotional control. Had Valerie Miller reported all this to Bremer? Had Bremer told all this to Randuhar?

"The billionaire Madden forced him to do it," Roca continued.

Randuhar's breathing came quicker.

"An amazing thing happened." Roca paused to stretch out the suspense. "When Michael tried to tell the others what he had read in the scroll, he found that he could not speak."

Randuhar seemed to have stopped breathing.

"So I don't know what's in the scroll," Roca said, placing his teacup on the table and leaning back. "No one but Michael does."

Randuhar sighed, rolled his shoulders, and leaned back. "An

interesting turn of events, Father Del Rio's inability to talk."

"Yes, amazing, really."

"Do you think he faked his muteness?"

Roca considered the possibility, then shook his head. "Not likely. Michael is . . . how shall I say it? . . . not good at deception. He has a very active conscience about such things."

Randuhar steepled his fingers, then stuck the steeple under his chin. "Then I am still hesitant to act on the words of the pope," he said. "Do you have any counsel for me?"

Roca paused. Should he tell all that he knew—reveal everything that had come to his awareness? He took another sip of his tea, then decided against it. He needed to keep at least a couple of cards close to his chest.

"Act on your best instincts," he offered. "Act on what you believe is right."

"Wise words," Randuhar said, placing his cup on the table and standing to leave. "Wise, wise words. I will pray to discern what the right is and then for the courage to act on it."

"Then you cannot go wrong," Roca said, following him to the door.

"Blessings be upon you," Randuhar said.

"And upon you," Roca said.

Roca closed the door and turned back to his quarters. Stepping from the receiving room into his bedroom, he opened the drawer of a night table beside his bed and pulled out a handful of folded eight-by-eleven sheets of paper. Then, sitting on the edge of the bed, he flipped the pages almost to the last one. Reading near the bottom of the page, he once again saw the tiny scratchings of the most powerful man in Christendom. Nearly five minutes passed as Roca read for at least the tenth time the most intimate thoughts of his beloved pope, thoughts that had come to him in this copied form, also late last Tuesday.

Laying the papers back in the nightstand, Roca stood and walked to the circular window that bordered his bed on the left side. Staring out the window at the cascade of heavy rain that had been falling all night, he took a deep breath and bowed his head. Then, as sincerely as he knew how, he offered a two-fold prayer. First, he prayed for Michael, his beloved nephew. Finished with that, he prayed also for himself, asking the God in whom he believed to show him what he should do with the words he had just read.

TWENTY-SEVEN

A cutting pain jabbed through his ribs, and Michael Del Rio leaned to his left, trying to take some of the pressure off his right side. For what seemed like the thousandth time, he yanked against the steel beam behind his head, a beam that ran from the floor to the ceiling. His hands, bound behind his back by a rubberized cord, were attached to the beam, and he couldn't turn around. His feet, also bound, were bare, and the back of his left heel was raw and tender—a scrape he'd received as Walter's men threw him into the boat they had used to make their escape from Madden's island to the mainland of Costa Rica.

Though he had drifted in and out of consciousness over the last number of hours, Michael's eyes felt as if someone had paved them with loose sand. The right one, swollen almost shut, throbbed from cheek to eyebrow.

He sat flat on a cold concrete floor, and a numbing chill seeped through the khaki slacks and short-sleeved sports shirt Walter had allowed him to slip on before leaving Madden's place. The floor ran at least a hundred feet to his left and right and fifty or more straight ahead, broken only by a row of rounded steel columns that ran from floor to ceiling every twelve to fourteen feet. A dilapidated conveyor belt ran the length of the wall before him, but nothing moved on it. A set of double windows, about six feet off the ground, ran down the wall behind the conveyor, and a row of plain round light bulbs marked the otherwise unadorned ceiling. The windows were open to the weather outside, and the black sky told Michael it was evening. The smell of old oil hung in the air like a dead ghost, and an abundant assortment of spider webs decorated the corners under the windows.

From all appearances, the place was an old warehouse of some kind and, hearing the sound of a ship's horn, Michael guessed he was near some water—either an ocean or a huge lake.

Sitting up as straight as possible, Michael tried to ignore the pain that seemed to penetrate every muscle of his body. He didn't have a watch, so he had no idea how long it had been since Walter had unceremoniously dumped him there after what seemed like an unending flight from Costa Rica. Blindfolded and gagged, he had been thrown into a boat, rolled into a plane, flown for hours and hours, then tossed into a truck, and finally dropped onto this concrete floor. He felt like a sack of potatoes, only with more bruises.

Michael tugged once more at his wrists, but again he felt no give in the bindings. Same with his ankles. But the movement did warm him a bit. His stomach growled, reminding him that he hadn't eaten since his abduction. He stared toward the windows and wondered what lay on the other side. Where had Walter taken him?

From behind, he heard movement and involuntarily hunched his shoulders against the imagined threat. But nothing happened. He tried to twist around but couldn't. He heard someone groan. What in the world? Could it be McAuley? Had Walter left him here too? Had the big redhead been asleep all this time? Was he finally conscious?

"That you, Dr. McAuley?" he asked, hoping he was right.

He heard another groan, then a series of heavy coughs.

"I'm Michael Del Rio. Are you okay?"

"Yeah," the man sputtered, his voice scratchy. "I'm Hugh McAuley. I've been better."

"Haven't we both?"

Another cough. Then, "Any idea where we are?"

"No clue. We were in Costa Rica, left there early Wednesday morning. It's late Wednesday now, maybe Thursday morning."

"Costa Rica? Last thing I remember was being in Istanbul. A man named Yoseph . . ." McAuley stopped for a moment, then coughed several more times.

"Yoseph is dead," Michael said, his voice flat.

"Dead?"

"Yes, and you were close to it when we found you."

"You found me?"

"Well, a man named Red Cashion did. But I was there, me and a woman named Valerie Miller . . ."

Resting against the beam, Michael filled in the details for

McAuley—the assignment from Cardinal Roca, his trip to Yoseph's to buy the Ephesus fragment, the meeting with Red Cashion, the discovery of Yoseph's body, the search for McAuley, the gun battle at the hotel, the flight to Costa Rica, and the attack and abduction by Hans Walter. He left out nothing except the fact that he had read the scroll.

"So Walter expects you and me to make some determination about the authenticity of this document. That's why he brought us here."

"He's got no . . . no idea what it takes to . . . to do something like that," offered McAuley. "Just look at the Shroud of Turin. Years and years of study, and we still don't know for sure if it's authentic or not."

Michael nodded. "You don't have to convince me. But I don't think this man Walter will listen to your objections. He wants us to tell him whether we think this thing is real, and I have a feeling our lives depend on our cooperation."

For several moments, McAuley stayed quiet. A spider the size of a quarter and the color of a chocolate bar crawled by Michael's left foot, and he watched it pass.

"Have you seen the document?" McAuley asked, an almost reverential tone in his voice.

Michael held his breath. "Yes."

"What did you think of it?"

Michael pushed his toes into the cold floor. "I don't really know. It's not easy to figure."

"Did you . . . did you read any of it?" McAuley whispered.

Michael hesitated.

"You did, didn't you?"

"Yes."

"And what did you think?" McAuley gushed, the scratch disappearing from his voice as he questioned Michael. "Is the Greek as it should be? Johnanine? Gnostic? What's your guess? Is it genuine? Is it?"

Michael felt a surge of heat in his feet in spite of the cold floor. The pain in his ribs, head, and ankle subsided momentarily. Every bone in his body cried out for the answer to McAuley's question, and one part of him wanted to scream, *Yes, yes it's genuine!* But another part refused to accept such a conclusion, refused to acknowledge that such a mystery could exist, that such an incomprehensible, unimaginable possibility could become a reality.

"I'm not ready to say," he said weakly.

McAuley sighed. "That's what I expected, though I've got to tell you I had hoped for more."

For an instant, both men stayed quiet. Michael took a deep breath and let his emotions subside.

"It'll take a good bit of testing if we're going to do anything but guess," McAuley said.

"That's your department, not mine," Michael said. "I don't know anything about parchment, ink, lettering, those kinds of things. I can read it, but not much more."

Silence came to the room again. The huge spider inched toward Michael's feet and stopped. Michael wiggled his toes and the spider darted away.

"Does Walter know how tough it is to date something like this?" McAuley asked.

"I don't know what he knows. I haven't seen him since he dumped us a few hours ago."

"He's got to be smart enough to realize we can't tell him anything definite by just looking at the thing. You need a full lab for that, a whole battery of tests—carbon 14 dating on the parchment, ceramic petrology on the pottery, studies of the chemicals in the ink. Any sane person would understand that."

"The equipment for that kind of thing is pretty rare, isn't it? Not sold in your neighborhood Wal-Mart."

McAuley grunted. "The Israel Museum in Jerusalem might have it or the Sadat Center for Ancient Studies in Cairo, I'm not sure. London and Johannesburg, South Africa, have labs, but not many other places. But even if you have the lab available, it takes a while. No way to do carbon 14 dating in less than ten days or so, and that's under the best of circumstances."

"So what do we tell Walter?" Michael asked. "He's not going to respond too well to what you just said."

McAuley didn't answer right away. Michael tugged at his wrist bindings again but got no result. His spider friend passed by going in the opposite direction, some kind of white, gummy-looking substance in his front pincers.

"I can make a guess without equipment," McAuley said finally.

"How so?"

"Well, you know, take the jar that contained the scroll. The shape of it, the form and design, etc., tell us a lot. Does it fit what we know about pottery made in the era we're considering? Is the clay the right color? Does the jar have the right kind of handles, the right markings, that kind of thing? It's called morphology—

the science of shapes and figures. I'm no expert, but I know enough to take a stab at it. And there's paleography too; some call it epigraphy, maybe the most important method of all. I'm a bit more sophisticated in that area—have done a good bit of study."

"How does that work?"

"Paleography is the study of ancient writing. It's based on the fact that people formed letters differently in different eras of time. For example, the Declaration of Independence refers to the Congress of the United States. The double 's' in the word 'Congress' look like a double 'f' with elongated tails, that sort of thing. An 'a' in one era looks somewhat different than an 'a' in another."

"So you study the shape of the letters to see if they fit the patterns of the time frame the document is supposedly from."

"You got it. Then you compare the spellings of words, the use of grammar—it all adds up, gives you enough to reach an initial conclusion or two."

"Do we tell Walter all this?"

"Do we have a choice?"

Before Michael could answer, he heard a door creak open to his right. He squirmed sideways, squinting into the shadows, and instinctively squeezed in closer to the steel column at his back, trying to make himself smaller. A man with a shaved head strode from the corner of the room, and Michael instantly recognized Hans Walter.

Walter clapped his palms together, then rubbed his head. "So, my friends, you are among the living again. Good, good, I am in need of your services."

"Where are we?" Michael grunted.

Walter squatted beside him and placed a hand on his shoulder. "Such an idiotic question," he said. "You are where I want you to be. That is enough for you to know."

"You really think you can do this?" Michael asked, his voice surprisingly calm. "Kidnap the two of us, steal the scroll, have us study it, then sell it and disappear?"

Walter smiled slyly, then rubbed his head again. "You make it sound so complicated," he said. "But I will keep the scroll only long enough to place a value upon it and make a transaction. I'm a mercenary, remember? A nobody in all of this. Once I rid myself of the document, few will bother themselves with me."

"What about us?" Michael asked.

Walter took a heavy breath. "That I have not yet decided. You do what I ask and you may live. If not . . ."

"And what do you want us to do?" McAuley asked, a tremor in his voice.

"Another idiotic question," Walter said, his voice rising. "Am I dealing with imbeciles? I have to place a value on this document! To do so, I need authentication! You will give me that—you and the holy man! That's what you will do!" Walter's face had turned red as he shouted, his hands clenched into fists, and the veins in his forehead bulging.

"I won't do it," McAuley said. "I won't help you."

Michael heard the sound of flesh smacking as Walter slapped McAuley. The archeologist grunted loudly but made no concessions.

"Stop it!" yelled Michael, fighting against his restraints. "He's helpless. Can't you see—"

Walter smacked McAuley again, his hands popping like a boat paddle into the archeologist's skull. Though unable to see him, Michael felt McAuley rock forward against the blow, his bindings the only thing that held him back, his body whipsawing forward, then back again. But the big man remained silent, and that surprised Michael. Though he didn't know McAuley at all, such stubbornness took a lot of courage, more than he expected he possessed.

Walter stepped sideways between Michael and McAuley and drew back a third time, but then stopped his fist in midair, his red face suddenly shifting into normal tones of color.

"You're a stubborn man, Dr. McAuley," he offerd, his breath jagged. "But I can appreciate the macho thing. So let's try a different approach here."

He took a step back toward Michael. Then, before Michael could duck, he gripped his palms together and slammed the meaty club into Michael's forehead. His head banging into the pole behind him, Michael's eyes blurred, and he almost passed out.

A low growl erupted from McAuley's throat, but Walter drew back his hands again. Michael closed his eyes and tensed for the blow.

"I'll do it!" McAuley yelled. "Just leave him alone. I'll do what you want . . ." His voice trailed off and sobs wracked his big body.

His eyes open again, Michael looked at Walter. His hands were still clasped, his face furious. For an instant, Michael thought he was about to strike him again, but he didn't. Like a snake retracting its fangs, he checked his anger, his fingers relaxed, and the color subsided in his cheeks.

"So we have an understanding?" Walter asked, kneeling by McAuley.

"I'll do it," McAuley moaned again. "I'll do what you want. Just leave us alone."

You are a smart man, Dr. McAuley, as I knew you would be."

"I'll need to . . . to see the scroll," the archeologist said, gaining control of his voice. "And any conclusion I reach will only be preliminary. Anything more than that will require . . . equipment and time that you don't have."

"A preliminary opinion will do fine for my purposes."

"You'll bring me the scroll . . . and the jar that held it when it was found?"

"You'll see them both."

"Both of us?"

"Both of you. And soon."

"And then? What will you do with us when we have finished?"

Walter smiled. "That question again? Let's face that when the time comes. No reason to rush such an important decision."

Michael stared hard at Walter. Unless something happened between now and the time they finished with the scroll, he and McAuley weren't long for this world.

———

At just past eleven P.M. Cairo time, Dr. Martha Hinton pulled a final drag from her filterless cigarette, pinched out the fire with her thumb and index finger, and tossed the butt into the trash can by the elevator in front of her. Then smoothing down her ponytail, she stepped onto the elevator and punched the lighted button for the top floor. Nothing had gone well over the last few days. In fact, she couldn't remember a worse spell of luck in her entire life. Everywhere she turned she hit dead ends. Yoseph the profiteer was dead, everyone knew that. Worse still, McAuley had disappeared, the scroll with him. And the man who had pledged to help her had turned out to be worthless.

The elevator bell dinged and Hinton slumped into the hallway. Two bodyguards, each of them dressed completely in black, instantly appeared. Hinton desperately craved another cigarette. The bodyguards ushered her down the hallway and into the living room area of a luxurious suite. She spotted Addam Azziz at the arched window on the opposite side of the room. Dressed in a tailored tan suit, immaculate white shirt, and multicolored tie, he faced the streets below, his back to her. She cleared her throat. Azziz slowly turned around, a glass of water in his hands. With a wave, he dismissed the bodyguards.

"I am glad you could meet with me again, Dr. Hinton," he began when the guards had gone. A bemused smile played on his face. "I know you have been busy."

"Glad to . . . glad to come," stammered Hinton. "You know I want to do what I can to—"

Without warning, Azziz threw his glass against the wall to his right, the liquid spilling onto the hardwood floor in a sudden spray as the glass shattered.

"You have done nothing!" he screamed, his face a rage. "You have not brought the Ephesus scroll to me! You are such a waste of a human being . . ." He stepped toward her now, his thick body approaching like a small tank, his anger clearly mounting. "You know our arrangement! What you find belongs to me!"

He stood nose to nose with her now, and she smelled a light touch of spearmint on his breath.

"You failed me!" he shouted. "You are a waste, a sorry excuse for an archeologist. You lost the most important find of your career. I reject you—"

Azziz pivoted away from her and stalked to a door on the right side of the room. "I reject you," he repeated, his voice slowing down, his tone diminishing. "You are a waste, worth nothing, a sorry excuse . . ."

He knocked on the door. "Tehraq!" he called. "Tehraq, enter now." Azziz eased away from the door and faced Hinton again. "You will do nothing more about this scroll," he stated. "You are out of it."

Hinton started to argue, but then knew Azziz wouldn't allow it. The door to the adjoining suite opened, and a bearded man, dressed in identical fashion as the bodyguards outside, lumbered through it. Seeing him, Martha involuntarily staggered backward. A sense of foreboding seeped off the man, a palatable aura of danger. He had a face as flat as a cutting board, and a white bandage the size of a small piece of toast covered a section of his neck beneath his left ear. He seemed to stoop just a bit as if he had some sort of problem with his chest.

"Meet Tehraq," Azziz said. "He's also searching for the scroll for me."

"But . . . but you told me to find—"

Azziz sneered at her and walked to a bar beside the window. Pouring a fresh glass of water, he shook his head and laughed. "You didn't think I would leave something this important to an

American, did you? And a woman? A most alluring one to be sure, but still a woman. Come, my dear, try to be serious."

"So he's been involved with this from the beginning?" she asked, indicating Tehraq, who had not moved since he entered the room.

Azziz sipped from his glass. "I'm a careful man," he said. "I like options—you gave me one, he gave me another. Who knows, perhaps I have arranged others."

A sudden realization came to Hinton, and she raised her shoulders and came to full height again. "But he didn't get the scroll either."

"No," agreed Azziz. "But he came close. A few hours too late, that is all."

"But still the same result as me, am I right?"

Azziz shrugged and left the bar. At her side again, he placed his glass on a table.

"You are right, Ms. Hinton. Though his methods were somewhat cruder, the results were the same, at least momentarily. But he didn't fail me completely, as you did. He brought me something else, something quite helpful."

Azziz slipped a hand into an inner pocket in his suit, pulled out a slip of paper, and flipped it open.

"What's that?" Hinton asked.

"It's a list, Martha Hinton, a list taken from Yoseph, a list of nineteen people."

"The people he had contacted to see if they wanted to make offers on the scroll?"

"Or they contacted him once they heard of its existence. An interesting group, to be sure."

"Do you recognize any of the names?" Hinton asked nervously.

"More than you would think. Art dealers of the highest rank, wealthy collectors, a king or two. Some run in my circles."

"And those you didn't recognize?"

"Research, of course. I've had over twenty people working on this around the clock. Computer data banks, international files on important personalities, contacts in governments all over the world."

"Did you find what you needed?"

"I now have a dossier on all of them, their likes, dislikes, contacts, financial status, even the type of toothpaste they use. You name it, I know it."

"Do you know who took it?"

Azziz studied the list as if seeing it for the first time.

"That was easy, an American according to Yoseph, an American working for the billionaire Willard Madden."

"I've heard of Madden."

"Haven't we all. But Madden's agent no longer has the document."

"He doesn't? What happened?"

"The details are sketchy. But it seems that he carried it to Costa Rica. Madden met him there. But then some kind of trouble erupted. Someone else wanted the scroll worse than he did."

"What kind of trouble?"

Azziz smiled. "Deathly trouble. Shooting and thievery. Madden's security faltered."

"And where is the scroll now?"

"I'm working on that. The list contains a number of people who might have gone to such lengths for such a document. I'm investigating them all, one by one, have narrowed it to just a couple who might have both the motive and the means to do such a thing." He eased a step closer, slipped an arm around Hinton's waist, and pulled her close. She didn't resist.

"And when you've discovered who has it?"

"Then I'll do whatever is necessary to take what is rightfully mine."

"Am I on the list?" she asked, trying to keep her voice even in spite of her nervousness. "Did you find my name with Yoseph?"

Azziz ran his fingers up her spine to the back of her neck. "Yes," he said. "You are listed."

"I wanted to get it for you," Martha whispered. "Since I lost it, I wanted to get it back."

"But you had no money to do such a thing."

His fingers intertwined themselves in her hair, and she felt the tension in his body notch higher. She fought to stay calm. "I have many friends. I would have found the money. I knew I had to get it for you."

"I have no doubt you would have found the money. Perhaps from a Mrs. Sarah Suggs, is that a possibility, that she would have given you the money to purchase the document for me? Is she that good a friend of yours that she would do such a thing?" His fingers grabbed her hair and pulled it backward, and his face turned to stone.

"Did you forget who I am?" he hissed. "The power I have at my disposal? I control a small army, own a satellite, give orders

to thousands! Every conversation you have, I know about it—
every phone call, e-mail, letter, fax! Before you move, I know
where you're going. Before you speak, I know what you will say.
You can't make a side deal against someone like me! Do you
think me such an imbecile?"

He turned to Tehraq and laughed heartily. "Tell her Tehraq,
tell her if I am an imbecile."

Tehraq's expression never changed. "Mr. Azziz is no imbecile," he said simply.

"I know that," protested Hinton. "But Suggs called me. I had
met her years ago. She sponsored a museum display that included some work of mine. She found out I was the chief of the
team at Ephesus. She asked me to make the contact with Yoseph
for her. But I promise you I would never have given her the
scroll! I wanted to use her money to get the document, then bring
it to you. That's what I planned the whole time, that's what I was
doing, you've got to believe me. . . ."

Azziz yanked her head farther back. For several seconds, she
teetered on the edge of her toes, almost falling backward. But
then he released her, and she stood straight again.

"I don't know whether to believe you or not," he cooed. "But
what you say makes good sense. And if it's not true . . . well, I
am greatly impressed that you came up with such a good lie
under such dire circumstances. You think well when you're in
danger. I like that."

Martha pushed her shoulders back and smoothed out her
hair. "I do the best I can with what I have at my disposal," she
said.

"I'm sure you do," Azziz said, his breath coming more quickly.
"In spite of your failure to bring me the scroll, I admire you. But
the question is, what are you willing to do to get what you want?"

Martha smiled slightly, her green eyes widening as she
grasped his meaning. A man with the money and power of
Addam Azziz could do much for her.

"I am willing to do whatever is necessary," she offered. "The
scroll means as much to me as it does to you."

Azziz snapped a finger at Tehraq. "Leave us," he said softly.
Without a word, the sphinxlike man disappeared, the expression
on his flat face still sour.

Azziz smiled at Martha Hinton. "A woman like you is rare,"
he said, stroking her neck. "So beautiful, yet so . . . so driven by
her ambitions."

"I am like you," cooed Martha, her eyes closed. "I want it all, everything . . . everything."

"Perhaps you can have it all," Azziz said. "With you and me and Tehraq all together, we can still find this scroll. We can . . ."

Martha kissed him then, covering the rest of his sentence with her lips, molding her slender body into his arms. Yet even as she kissed him with all the warmth at her disposal, she kept her mind aloof, her thoughts focused on the Ephesus fragment. Though she would not give up her own efforts through Sarah Suggs to find the scroll, she would gladly accept the help that a man like Azziz—properly handled of course—might offer to her.

TWENTY-EIGHT

Valerie Miller landed in Rome at just after four P.M., her spirits as black as the wet sky outside. Wrapped in a sweater and dressed in wrinkled blue jeans and a long-sleeved flannel shirt, she coughed over and over again as she climbed off the plane. Her head felt like someone had heated it with an iron, and the joints in her elbows and knees ached terribly.

Picking up her luggage, she quickly caught a cab and directed the driver to the U.S. embassy. A slick rain splattered onto the cab as it splashed through the streets. Valerie leaned her head against the tattered backseat and shivered from head to foot. The flight from Costa Rica had been a page right out of her worst imaginings of what hell must be like. True to his word, Hans Walter had left the rest of the group behind when he kidnapped Michael and Hugh McAuley. At that point, Red Cashion took charge. He reported Walter's attack to the Costa Rican police and hauled Madden, Cindy Brown, and the bodyguard to a hospital on the mainland for emergency treatment. Finished there, he loaded everyone into Madden's huge jet and directed the pilot to fly them to Miami.

From there, the group split up. Cashion, Cindy, Madden, and the guards headed to Los Angeles, and Valerie caught a flight to Paris and then on to Rome. Somewhere along the way, the fever attacked her with the ferocity of a starving hyena. Now her eyes felt like someone had sandpapered them with concrete blocks, and her head throbbed as if clubbed with a baseball bat.

The cab stopped for a pedestrian, and Valerie rubbed her throat as if she could rub off the soreness inside. She couldn't remember ever feeling this bad. As bad as her illness was, though, she felt even worse about everything else. Michael and McAuley were missing, the scroll was gone, and Madden, Cindy, and a guard had been seriously hurt. To make it all as ugly as possible, she now had to face Arthur Bremer and explain to him what had happened. Having to admit to Bremer that she had failed in the task he gave her made her sicker than any virus.

A favorite line of her father's flashed into Valerie's head. "Only failures fail." If he had said that once, he had said it a million times. She cleared her throat. Though she suspected Bremer would accept the situation with a certain amount of graciousness, she refused to allow herself to do anything of the sort. The high limbs of the tree had beckoned, but she had fallen out before she even reached the middle branches.

The cab twisted left, its tires sliding on the wet street. Valerie hugged her arms around her waist. Bremer, of course, already knew about the fiasco at Willard Madden's. A phone call had alerted him to the situation. As expected, he had ordered her back to Rome. With the deaths in Istanbul and the attack on Madden's house, he refused to leave her on her own any longer. Though she had argued vehemently, he refused to budge. She had eventually given up and accepted his demand to come back. What choice did she have?

Valerie shivered again and laid her chin in her hands. A hint of tears ran to the corners of her eyes, and she bit her lip. For all she knew, Michael and McAuley might already be dead. Though Walter had said he wanted them to advise him about the scroll, he might have changed his mind. What if he decided it was too risky to take the time to inspect the document? What if he decided to sell it on the spot as Yoseph had done? In that case, Michael and McAuley became worthless to him, threats instead of assets. He wouldn't keep them around long if that happened. Even more frightening, what if Michael or McAuley tried to escape but didn't make it? Walter would execute them without a second thought!

Valerie shook her head and forced herself to focus on the rain. No need to dwell on the negatives that might happen when so many negatives that had already happened were so readily available. She sighed and pulled her sweater closer.

At the embassy, she paid the driver and scooted through the rain to the front entrance. Passing through the security checkpoints, she trudged straight past her office and made a right turn into the suite of rooms reserved in the corner of the hallway for Arthur Bremer, U.S. ambassador to the Vatican. Her hair dripping, she pushed it back off her face and smoothed down her bedraggled jeans. She looked like an unmade bed, but Bremer had insisted that she come to his office the minute she landed.

Bremer's receptionist, Betty, a gray-headed matron of the diplomatic corps, looked up and spotted her as she entered the office. Popping up from her chair, the woman's maternal instincts kicked immediately into gear.

"Just look at you child," she sympathized. "Wet as an old mop." She wrapped her arms around Valerie and hugged her close. "Are you okay? Let me get you some tea."

Before Valerie could respond, Betty steered her to a seat and pushed her into it before rushing out of the room. Moments later the older woman reappeared, a cup of hot tea in her hands.

"We've all been so worried about you," she said as she handed the tea to Valerie. "It must have been awful! Are you okay?"

Valerie nodded and took a sip of the tea. Its warmth soothed her sore throat, and she relaxed for a moment in the chair, her fingers wrapped tightly to the cup. A series of shivers washed through her shoulders, and she found herself shaking almost uncontrollably. "Arthur told me to come straight here," she chattered. "I know . . . I know I look a wreck, but . . . but he . . . he insisted."

"He's waiting for you," Betty said. "Calls me every five minutes to see if you're here yet. You just sit there and drink your tea, warm up a second, and I'll ring him."

Too tired too argue, Valerie slumped back and closed her eyes, the tea momentarily helping her chills. As soon as Bremer let her go, she planned to collapse in her apartment and sleep for a week. If she made it to her apartment. She clutched the warm cup, its steam rising to her face.

From behind, she heard a door open. With a great effort she forced herself to open her eyes. Swiveling, she saw Ambassador Bremer step into the room. Dressed, as always, as if he had just stepped off the runway of a men's fashion show, Bremer rushed to her, his long fingers stretched out to take her by the arm. Valerie pushed up from the chair.

"Here," Bremer offered, steering her to his office. "Come on in here and sit back down." Turning to Betty, he ordered, "Find me a blanket. This poor woman is freezing to death."

Perching on the edge of the leather chair opposite Bremer's massive wooden desk, Valerie told herself to focus. There was no reason to upset Bremer any more than her foul-up must have already done. Betty suddenly entered the office, a waist length green coat in her hands.

"We don't have a blanket," she cooed. "But this old coat of mine ought to help."

Gratefully, Valerie took the coat and wrapped it around her shoulders. Betty left, closing the door behind her. Across from Valerie, Bremer took a seat, placed his elbows on his desk, and leaned forward, his face grave.

"I'm sorry about what happened," he said. "I should never have let you go by yourself. You could've been killed."

Valerie shook her head. "No, it's not your fault. I'm the one who should apologize. Nothing went like I planned."

Bremer sighed. "It is my fault that I sent a young woman on a dangerous assignment without proper backup."

"But you had no reason to expect any trouble, no way to foresee that."

Bremer stood, walked around his desk, and took a seat on the corner beside Valerie. "But I'm in charge," he said gravely. "I'm supposed to anticipate all the possibilities—all the potential scenarios. It's not too hard to imagine some danger in this type of operation. This document might attract all kinds of unsavory characters. You'll understand it yourself someday when you're sitting where I am or somewhere even more important. Leaders get paid to do things right, not to send innocent people into harm's way."

"But you didn't—"

"Oh yes, I did!" he interrupted, standing again, towering over her. "I blew it big time, bigger than you'll ever know. I sent an inexperienced envoy to find a document the whole world wants to find, a document perhaps more valuable than the Dead Sea Scrolls. People of bad intentions always get involved in things like this. But I didn't see it coming, I really didn't. And now the scroll is gone, and we might never get the chance again." He stopped talking, moved back to his seat, slumped into it, and buried his face in his hands.

For several seconds, neither of them spoke. Valerie sipped from her tea once again, thankful that it and the coat had warmed her enough to stop her shivering. She felt as though she needed to comfort Bremer, but somehow that didn't seem appropriate. The poor man looked so distraught. She hoped his heart was holding up.

"Don't give it up just yet," she offered gently. "Who knows what will happen? Hans Walter will have to surface somewhere.

He can't sell the document without telling someone where he is. We'll pick up the trail there."

Bremer didn't respond. Valerie waited for a second, then tried again. "I'm sure we can still work with the Vatican on this. Between their sources and ours, maybe we can get to him early, just like we tried with Yoseph, make our offer before anyone else, make it high enough to—"

Bremer threw up a hand, palm outward, stopping her in mid-sentence. "It's not going to happen," he said. "Not for you at least."

Valerie sat up, the coat dropping from her shoulders. "What do you mean, not for me?"

Bremer stared out a window to his right. The rain poured down in driving sheets. "I can't take the chance," he said. "You're out of it—too inexperienced."

Valerie sat her tea on the edge of the desk, using the silence to try to get a grip on her feelings. When she spoke, though, her voice trembled. She hoped Bremer didn't notice. Her life was deteriorating right in front of her eyes, and she couldn't do a thing to stop it.

"You're taking me off this assignment?" she asked.

Bremer nodded. "No way around it. You—"

"But you can't do this!" Valerie came halfway out of her seat.

Bremer threw up a hand. "It's already done," he said. "You had your shot. It didn't work out. Now we need someone else, someone with more background in this kind of work."

"Who's that going to be?" Valerie asked, thinking through a mental list of her co-workers at the Vatican. "Someone here?"

Bremer placed his face in his hands and shook his head. "No one here," he said.

"Then who—" A new idea suddenly dawned on Valerie, and she stopped in mid-sentence. "It's out of your hands, isn't it?" she asked. "Someone else is running the show now—someone higher up at State. Is that it?"

Bremer stared at his desk.

"Is it CIA?" she asked. "Or NSA?"

Bremer looked up at her, frowning. "I can't answer that," he said. "And it's not important, not really. The bottom line is, you're out of here, probably up for reassignment. Someone else from State will take your files and handle the search for the document from here on out."

"And I get no say in it, no chance to make my case?"

Bremer grunted, then stood. "Welcome to the real world, kid."

Utterly defeated, Valerie remained seated, her shoulders slumped. She felt as low as she could ever remember, her heart as broken as a piece of glass, her dreams shattered, her faith . . . well . . . her faith of little value and no perceptible help.

"I want some time off," she said glumly. "A few days to get a grip."

Bremer nodded. "Take as long as you want. Then call me. We'll talk."

Near tears, Valerie pulled herself from her seat, handed Bremer the coat Betty had loaned her, and headed to the door. Stumbling out of the embassy, she reached the curb and hailed a taxi. A blast of heavy rain soaked her hair and shoulders, but she hardly noticed. Inside her stomach a knot of desperation the size of a basketball bounced up and down. She wanted to cry again, but knew that wouldn't accomplish anything.

A taxi sped by but didn't stop. As it spun down the street, a gush of muddy water splashed from its tires onto her legs, soaking her jeans. For a couple of seconds, she just stood and lamented her awful condition—sick as a dog, worn out, and hungry. Christmas was less than a week away, and she had been relieved of her job. And now, here she stood, covered from the waist down with oily, nasty water. But instead of crying in frustration, she started to get angry. The feeling began in her wet feet and moved upward into her calves, stomach, and head. She shouted and shook her fist at the taxi driver as he disappeared around the corner. Sputtering her frustration, she began to stalk toward her apartment.

If Arthur Bremer thought he could shut her out as easily as a snap of the fingers, he was badly mistaken! No way could she give up now. No way could she step out of the picture and let someone else finish what she started! She wasn't built that way, and Bremer might as well get used to it.

A second taxi rolled to the curb beside her, and she climbed in. Her jaw firm, she gave him directions to her apartment, then laid her head back. Though soaked to the skin, she was too mad to shiver anymore. A tumble of ideas rolled through her head, ideas about what to do next, where to go, whom to ask for help.

Staring out the window, she wrapped her arms around her stomach. She didn't have many options. Her mom and dad could give her plenty of money but not much else in a matter like this. She had a number of friends in the State Department, but she knew that word of her dismissal would circulate fast in those circles, and she didn't want to jeopardize anyone else's career by asking for their help.

The cab came to her apartment and stopped. She paid the driver, then stepped back into the rain. For a couple of seconds, she just stood in place, her face to the sky. The rain had slowed a bit, and the drops felt like wet feathers splatting onto her cheeks and chin. She opened her mouth and several drops plopped onto her tongue, and the worst of her anger seeped slowly away.

But then, from what seemed like nowhere, a sense of freedom washed through her, and she knew in that second where she would go. Since the State Department had thrown her out, she would go beyond it. She would go to the one person she knew who had the brains and the brawn to do what needed to get done.

Lowering her head, she took a deep breath. She would be taking a big risk bypassing the State Department. Like those at any government agency, the authorities at State didn't take kindly to people who ignored orders. If Bremer found out she had stepped back in when he had told her to butt out, her whole career could go right down the toilet. But she saw no other choice. It wasn't just a matter of a career anymore. For that matter, it wasn't just a matter of a scroll anymore either, regardless of how important that document might be. For Valerie, it was about a person now, a person she had come to appreciate in a way she had never appreciated anyone in her life.

Valerie stepped toward her apartment. Though she knew she couldn't have a future with Michael Del Rio, at least not the future that her heart told her she wanted, that didn't matter. If nothing else, she wanted him safe.

Overhead, the clouds suddenly parted, and a shaft of late afternoon sunlight broke through, one single sliver of bright yellow. Seeing the light, Valerie smiled. What she did next might end her official career. But for the first time in years, her career took a backseat to her concern about a human being.

Back at the U.S. embassy, Arthur Bremer pushed his glasses up on his nose, and shuddered. Feeling guilty, he suddenly craved a respite from it all. Rocking out of his seat, he pressed his intercom button and told Betty to have his car brought around. Then he picked up the phone and dialed his apartment two miles away. His wife of forty-one years picked up, her voice sleepy.

"It's Arthur, honey," he said. "I'll be home in a few minutes."

"You okay, Artie?" she asked, her tone showing her surprise that he would come home so early in the day.

"I'm going to retire," he said. "At the end of the year. Enough is enough."

"What's wrong, Artie? What happened?"

Bremer hesitated. In all their years of marriage, he seldom carried his problems home. But like a riverbed getting too full of muddy water, he felt as though he was about to flood out.

"It's politics," he sighed. "Too much of it, too many years, too many good people put in untenable positions."

"Come on home, Artie," said his wife. "I'll fix us a big chocolate sundae. You can tell me all about it."

Bremer smiled. As always, Lucille was right there for him, a woman as solid as a rock and still good-looking at sixty-one. In fifteen minutes he would plop down in his leather recliner in his den, flip off his wingtips, and dig into some chocolate ice cream.

But one thing he wouldn't do—he wouldn't tell Lucille everything. He wouldn't tell her about his recent phone conversations with Roger Attles, a man whom he knew only from a distance, maybe a good man even, but still a man with far too much influence, in his humble opinion. To tell Lucille about the conversations with Attles would bring politics too deeply into his den.

TWENTY-NINE

Dressed in a goose down parka, flare-legged blue jeans, and a baseball cap with the logo of the Utah Jazz on the front that she had bought at the Salt Lake City airport, Valerie Miller stood on the front porch of a low slung, ranch-style home and knocked for the third time. Stomping her calf-high leather boots in the effort to keep her toes from freezing, she blew on her hands and hoped to heaven someone was home. A temperature hanging near ten degrees, a twenty-mile-an-hour wind, and a foot of crusted snow on the ground offered no comfort for a southern girl more accustomed to beach sand than frozen snow. Worse still, she hadn't really slept since the debacle at Willard Madden's estate, and she felt like one of the Grand Teton Mountains off to her right had fallen on her. The cough she had picked up on Wednesday had mutated into a full-blown case of fever, chills, and body aches. Her skin had turned as pale as white bread, her eyes had circles the size of small Frisbees under them, and her hair drooped so much it resembled a three-year-old mop.

Under normal circumstances, she would have visited the doctor, taken a shot of penicillin in the hip, and hit the sack to ride out the illness. But these were anything but normal circumstances.

Leaving Rome in a rush, she had stopped only long enough to pick up some aspirin, a box of tissues, a bottle of cough syrup, and a few necessary clothes. Cramming everything into a small carry-on bag, she had jetted from Rome to New York, from New York to Salt Lake City, and from Salt Lake City to Jackson Hole. Catching direct flights with almost no interconnecting time, she had landed in Jackson Hole at just before midnight on Thursday.

Though anxious to reach her final destination, she had tamped
down her eagerness long enough to take a room at a hotel and
wait until morning to make her pitch to the man she had come
to see.

Glancing at her watch, Valerie knocked again, but no one answered. Surely he was up by now, almost eight A.M. She coughed
raggedly, and her breath hung in the air like a cloud of frozen
steam. Setting her jaw, she squeezed off the cough, pulled a bottle of cough medicine from her jacket pocket, and poured a swig
down her throat. Repocketing the bottle, she stepped off the
porch and crunched around to the side of the house. She saw a
chimney, then noted a plume of gray smoke curling up from it.
By the chimney she saw a light pouring out of a room near the
back of the house. Sure looked like someone was home. But
where were they?

For several seconds, she stood still, wondering what to do
next. The logical thing was to give up, drive her rental car back
to her room in Jackson Hole, take medicine for a couple of days,
catch up on her sleep, and then try again. But given her general
state of panic, she felt anything but logical. Coughing into her
gloves, she stepped farther around the house.

At the back now, she quickly scanned the yard. A corral the
size of a small parking lot and a barn with two double doors sat
to her right. An unidentifiable piece of farm machinery squatted
to the left, its black tires and enclosed cab making it appear
alive, ready to pounce. A well-cut path through the snow, obviously shoveled out by an expert, led from the back of the house
to the corral and adjoining barn.

Beyond the barn, she saw nothing but snow. As white as a
dove's feathers, the icy landscape stretched out as far as the eye
could see. The only thing that broke the snow was the mountain
that loomed in the background, a craggy outcropping that
surged toward the sky off to the east. Behind the mountain, the
sun seemed to quiver as it climbed into the sky. Valerie shivered
in spite of the sun and hugged her arms around her waist. She
heard the neighing of horses coming from the barn.

Unwilling to give up just yet, she dug in her heels and
crunched toward the sound. At the barn door, she balled up a fist
and pounded it against the weathered wood. A horse snorted.
She pounded again.

She heard singing. "It's gonna be a blue Christmas without
you . . ."

Red Cashion!

She kicked the door with a boot.

"It's gonna be a blue Christmas . . ."

Valerie grabbed the door handle and pulled hard, and the door creaked open. She took a half step inside the barn. To her left, Red Cashion pushed back the brim of a black hat and nodded to her. He held a pitchfork, and his cheeks were swollen with a giant wad of tobacco. Six stalls, three of them filled with sturdy, shaggy horses, ran down the left side of the barn. Cashion spat into a head-high haystack to his left.

"Come on in and shut the door," he groused. "We already got enough air conditioning in here."

Valerie obeyed quickly, glad for the relative warmth of the barn. The door closed behind her and she faced Cashion.

"You're a long way from Rome," he said, jabbing the pitchfork into the hay.

"Thought I needed a break," she said, inching toward him like a cat sneaking up on a mouse. "Rome's not as much fun as it used to be."

"Wyoming in December ain't exactly what most people call a break." Cashion tossed the hay into one of the empty stalls.

"Can't argue that," she agreed, stomping her boots. "Cold enough to make a polar bear wear mittens."

"Some folks like it that way. Keeps outsiders from getting too comfortable. They come here to ski a little but don't stay long. That's best for everybody, them and us."

"You a native?"

Cashion spit a stream of brown into the dirt, then jabbed another load of hay onto his pitchfork.

"You didn't come all this way to find out about my origins," he said. "What's going on?" He tossed the hay into the stall, then jammed his pitchfork into the ground and leaned on the handle.

Valerie stepped closer and pointed to a hay bale. "Mind if I sit down? I'm not feeling so good."

"Sure, help yourself."

Seated, Valerie took a deep breath, then coughed. "Bremer reassigned me," she said. "When I got back to Rome. Just like that. Said I didn't have enough experience to deal with something as important as the scroll."

Cashion shrugged. "Sorry to hear it," he said. "That's tough. You think he's wrong . . . about the experience thing?"

A flush crept onto Valerie's face, but she didn't get angry. "Sure he's right. But that doesn't mean I couldn't do the job. It wasn't my inexperience that lost the document. You were there—you know that. There was nothing any of us could do."

Cashion lowered his eyes, then pulled off his gloves and took a seat on a stall rail by Valerie. "You're wrong about that," he said. "I could have stopped it. A better security plan, that's all we needed, more attention to the perimeter of Mad's house. But you're right about it not being your failure—the botch-up was mine, plain and simple. I blew it from the beginning, had my mind in the wrong places, too worried about . . . well . . . too distracted by other things. I didn't want to be there in the first place, and that got us in trouble . . ." His voice trailed off, and he stared at the ground, his eyes as vacant as the stall in front of him.

Valerie stood, walked over to Cashion, and climbed up on the rail beside him. "It's easy to place blame," she said, her voice tired. "Everybody does it. Blame somebody else, blame the environment, blame, well . . . blame God. But the truth seems different than that to me. Sometimes things just happen, and you can't blame anybody, not even yourself. Things happen that are totally out of our control, out of our hands. I knew a guy once whose mom died in a tornado. The twister hit her house smack in the middle of the night. But my friend ended up in a mental institution, then strung out on drugs because he couldn't convince himself that it wasn't his fault."

"That's just stupid," Cashion said.

"My point exactly. But we torture ourselves, at least I should say I always have, if something goes wrong. I see myself as a failure."

"My guess is you haven't failed at much."

Valerie blew out a puff of cold air. "It's all relative," she said. "One person's success is another person's failure. My bar has just always been higher, that's all. So I've felt the guilt, the self-blame. But this time, I don't know, it just seems that everything that happened was beyond what any of us could do. No reason for you to feel guilty about that."

"You taking your own medicine?" Cashion asked. "Listening to what you just told me?"

Valerie shrugged. "I'm working on it."

Cashion spat, then pulled off his hat and perched it on his knee. "You didn't come all the way out here just to make me feel better," he said.

"You know why I came," Valerie said. "I need your help. I want to find Michael, and I don't have a clue where to start. We know Walter is dangerous. He's already murdered Yoseph, and he almost killed—"

"He didn't kill Yoseph," interrupted Cashion.

"What?"

"Walter didn't kill Yoseph. Two different groups are at work here."

"How do you know that?"

"Think about it. The men at the Ceylan found McAuley because they tortured Yoseph. But they were all Middle Easterners. I'm guessing Walter was German or Swiss. His men were definitely mixed—Europeans, an Asian, a Hispanic. Two groups, no doubt about it." He spat into the hay.

For several seconds, Valerie remained quiet, digesting the information. It was so obvious now that she thought of it. Her breath gushed out in white puffs of cold. She really was an amateur in matters like this.

"This complicates the situation," she said. "Two different people wanting the scroll enough to kill for it."

"And those two might be just the tip of the iceberg."

Valerie sighed. "I can't do this without you. It's way over my head."

"That's true," agreed Cashion. "But I'm out of it now—gone. I'm past prime. A T-bone steak aged a day too long, a step slow, a thought behind, and a disaster waiting to happen. If I had any illusions about my skills anymore, the catastrophe in Costa Rica put them to bed once and for all. I almost got everybody killed, Madden included."

"How's he doing?"

"One foot in the grave, the other on a banana peel. And it's my fault."

"I don't believe that, not for a minute."

He stuck his hat back on and jumped off the railing. "You got no choice," he said. "True is true." He walked toward the barn door.

"You can leave it like this?" called Valerie, desperate for him to stop. "With Michael and McAuley missing? Your friend Madden almost dead? The scroll lost? What about finishing what you started?"

Cashion pivoted on his heel and faced her again, his face pinched, his jaw hard. "Nothing is as simple as that!" he growled. "It never is! But not everyone is so free as you . . . able to drop everything and fly across the world looking for . . . for what, I don't know. Adventure? Fame? Love, maybe? Some of us already found that, all of it, every last bit. But you know what? You know what?"

"What?"

"Somewhere in all the excitement of growing up . . . in all the adventure of the search, you end up with responsibilities, responsibilities you can't escape, don't want to escape. Things and people start to mean more to you than all the adventure in the world. Those responsibilities tie you down . . . tie you down to the point you have to leave some other things unfinished. Here, come here!"

He grabbed her by the elbow and pulled her out the barn door. "Look at that light!" he insisted, pointing toward the back of his home. "The light in the house. You see that light?"

"Sure, I see it."

"My wife is in there, my wife who can't walk. My wife who will never walk again because one of the horses—the black one you saw in the barn—threw her six years ago. He threw her, stomped on her, and paralyzed her from the waist down. You think I should leave her again and go traipsing off with you to find some blasted scroll—a scroll that just about got my only real friend other than my wife killed? Is that what you think I should do?"

For several seconds, Valerie stayed still, her heart as frozen as the snow under her feet. Things weren't supposed to work this way, she thought. Not for people like her, the blessed people. No one turned her down; she didn't meet dead ends, doors that wouldn't open. At least she never had before now. Up to this point, everything she touched turned to gold, everything she tried came up roses. Wasn't that the way it should happen? Wasn't that what God promised to those who followed Jesus? That's what she had always believed, at least until now. But now that didn't seem true at all. People had died and she had seen them, the frozen stares, the rigid limbs. She had failed and Michael had disappeared. And now the only man she knew who could help her had rejected her request for assistance. Not exactly what she had expected. But she saw no choice but to accept it.

Utterly beaten, Valerie shook her head. "I didn't know," she said to Cashion. "I'm sorry about your wife."

Cashion dropped her arm, the steam gone from his anger. "I want to go with you," he said, his voice pleading for her to understand his situation. "More than you can ever know. It chews at my gut like a buzzard on a dead rat to know that Michael and

McAuley are missing, that Madden is a step away from the grave and I can't lift a finger to find the dirt bags who caused all of that. But you know what?"

"What?"

"The responsibilities that tie you down sometimes make you whole too. It's like when you come to the end of a day when you've done a lot of work, maybe you've not done everything you planned, but you've stayed faithful to what you wanted to do. That's what satisfies, the knowledge that even when you don't finish some things, you know you've finished some others. So I'll leave Madden to the doctors. He's got the best that money can buy. And I'll leave Michael and McAuley to the authorities at State, the police, the people trained for that kind of thing. My first responsibility is right there." He pointed to the light in the house. "Her name is Margaret—Mags I call her—and she's my gal, the love of my life."

Valerie coughed, and took another swig of cough medicine. "I can't argue with that," she said.

Red tugged on his hat, his eyes studying the snow.

"I guess I need to get going," Valerie said. "Maybe I can catch a flight out of here before dark."

"I'd help if I could," Red mumbled.

"I know," Valerie said. "But you're right about your wife. She needs you here."

Red took off his hat and looked inside it for a second.

"If you change your mind, my dad's name is Tyrone Miller. He's head of PrimeAmerica, headquartered in Charlotte," Valerie said. "He'll know where to find me."

"That where you're going?"

She shrugged. "Not sure. Maybe I'll go to my folks, rest over the holidays, then go to Plan B."

"You got a Plan B?"

Valerie smiled weakly. "Not yet. But just give me a couple of days. I'll come up with something."

Cashion spat into the snow. "I got no doubt you will."

———

At just past ten P.M. Rome time, Cardinal Severiano Roca sat slumped in his seat, rubbing his tired eyes. His heart felt heavy, like a brick in his chest. He had heard nothing about Michael, and he feared more each hour that the news, when it came, would almost certainly be bad.

Forcing his thoughts away from such possibilities, he stared deliberately around the table at the six men gathered with him in a small conference room just off the hallway that led to St. Peter's Basilica. The room, sparse in decor and seldom used, seemed a strange place to call together such a mysterious meeting. A single chandelier hung overhead. No rugs covered the plain, hardwood floor. A fireplace with a marble mantel sat on the north end of the room, but no one had bothered to start a fire. Roca pushed his hands under his thighs to warm his fingers.

He knew each of the men in the room—Cardinal Marchino, Secretary Randuhar, himself, and four other cardinals—the most powerful men in the Catholic Church. Each represented a particular constituency in the Vatican, and each, except for Randuhar, had been mentioned as a possible successor to the pope.

Dressed in nightclothes, again except for Randuhar, the men didn't look happy. A low murmur drifted through the gathering, and Roca could feel the unrest bubbling up—a steam valve about to explode. Though feeling equally perturbed, he tamped down his emotion and forced himself to concentrate.

Secretary Randuhar had called the meeting, had pulled together these eminent leaders of the faith just as they were preparing for bed. But why such a sudden gathering? What was so urgent that it couldn't wait until morning? And why just these six men? Why not the entire Curia? These were undoubtedly the questions on everyone's mind. Had the pontiff taken a turn for the worse? Had he—forbid the thought—died? Was this the meeting to make that announcement to the inner circle?

Randuhar cleared his throat and everyone stopped mumbling. Roca glanced at Marchino, whose tiny head tilted to the left. Randuhar lifted his hand. Everyone froze in place, all breathing interrupted.

Randuhar spoke even more slowly than normal, his words stretched out like long rubber bands. Roca had no doubt now that the Secretary did this for effect, perhaps subconsciously, but perhaps not. In private conversation, he spoke normally, but not in grave public moments, moments like this one.

"Everything that I or any of you say in this meeting is of a confidential nature," Randuhar began. "We must keep it 'under the seal.' Can we agree on that before we begin?"

The men at the table glanced quickly at one another.

"Are we agreed?" Randuhar asked again, just a bit of anxiety evident in his tone.

Roca rolled his ring. These men took such pledges quite seriously. Cardinals had many failures, but the pledge of the seal was quite sacred to them. To Roca's surprise, Marchino nodded first and two others, men known as his allies, quickly followed.

Randuhar faced Roca, his eyes a cross between a challenge and a plea. For several seconds, Roca hesitated. Without knowing exactly why, he felt treachery in the air, a surprise of some kind coming. But he didn't know how to deny the Secretary's request, what excuse he could give for doing so. If he said no without cause, he risked the appearance of not cooperating at a time when everyone had to hold together. Unable to think of a reasonable rebuttal, he nodded slowly. To his left, the other two cardinals followed suit.

"Okay," said the Secretary, his relief almost palpable. "All are agreed." He cleared his throat again. "Let me get to the point quickly," he intoned. "No reason to keep everyone in suspense." He steepled his fingers and propped them under his chin. "I have reached a most important decision, one I wanted you to hear before I announced it to the public."

The cardinals let out a collective breath and glanced quickly at one another. This wasn't an announcement about the pontiff.

Randuhar continued. "At noon on Christmas Day, I will announce my decision to follow through on what I believe to be the desire of His Holiness. I will name Mary the Co-Redemptrix with Jesus Christ."

The room exploded with voices, each of the cardinals shouting for Randuhar's attention, each trying to make his point heard over the others.

"The Lord will bless you!" called Marchino. "His Holiness will thank you when he—"

"This is insane!" shouted the cardinal to Marchino's left. "To make this decision now makes no—"

Roca found himself yelling with all the others, his face flushed, his hands punching the air in agitation. How dare Randuhar do this now? How dare he make a pronouncement that affected the Church so completely? What made him think he could get away with it? And why choose this option? Why choose to name her Co-Redemptrix? That question was the toughest to answer. Randuhar had stayed publicly neutral in this matter up until now. What had changed his mind and brought him to this conclusion? What did he hope to gain?

Randuhar stood suddenly, his towering frame appearing even larger than normal in the small room. When he lifted his right hand above his head, he looked like a giant black tree, a powerful force that threatened to swallow every man in the room

in its shadow. The other cardinals fell silent in his presence, and
Roca realized that everyone, including himself, had underestimated the Secretary. The circumstances of the last few days had
called something heretofore unseen from him, a power and charisma latent but untapped until now. But was this new persona
a fresh expression of something good and decent? Or was it an
innate evil now unleashed—a combination of ambition, pride,
and greed loosed by the position he held and the position he
might hope to achieve? The answer to those questions Roca did
not yet know.

When Randuhar spoke, his voice thundered in a tone Roca
had never heard, a tone filled with authority and command. It
held none of the caution everyone had come to expect from him.

"I will make the announcement!" Randuhar shouted over the
commotion. "I believe it is the will of His Holiness! I believe it
is the will of God!"

Though Randuhar continued to roar, Roca no longer listened.
Instead, inside his head, he was listening to another voice, the
voice of His Holiness himself, the voice he had heard in the pages
of the pontiff's copied journal, the journal he knew Randuhar
also held in his possession. In that journal, the pope had spoken
concerning his plans for the Marian Decree. But, amazingly,
what the pope had written directly contradicted what Randuhar
had just announced.

THIRTY

His back aching, Michael Del Rio raised from his bent position and stretched, twisting side to side in the effort to loosen up his back. Beside him, Hugh McAuley also paused. Michael turned from McAuley and faced Alfred, one of the two men Hans Walter had left to guard them. Alfred sat in a cushioned chair several feet away, his weapon resting carelessly on his lap. Though much shorter than the enormous Walter, he had the same shaved head, identical gray eyes, and square Teutonic chin. Michael figured the two were relatives, maybe even brothers.

"We need a break," he told Alfred. "We've been at this for hours."

Alfred, his eyes droopy from lack of sleep, nodded, then held up ten fingers. Michael faced McAuley again and studied him for several seconds. The archeologist's pants drooped low on his hips, an obvious sign of a man losing weight, and the skin beneath his jaw line looked elastic, like someone had stretched it past its intended limit. On the right side of his face was a bruise the color of a Concord grape and the size of a small shoe. Worst of all his injuries, however, were the first three fingers on his left hand. They were badly disfigured, as gnarled and twisted as the roots of an old tree. But McAuley complained of no pain.

"You still okay?" Michael asked McAuley. The two had been working almost nonstop for thirty-six hours.

McAuley nodded. "Yeah, I feel fine, better than I have in a long time. It's strange. I've been beaten like a stepchild, I've lost so much weight I can see my toes again, I haven't slept since Wednesday evening, and I've eaten nothing but a piece of bread and an apple in two days. But I feel like I could run a marathon right now. I don't know . . . but this whole thing"—he indicated the table over which they had been bending—"has me . . . well, intoxicated, full of energy. Maybe I'm just too pumped up to feel any pain."

Michael smiled at his new friend. His pains had disappeared too—the throb in his head, the shooting jab in his ribs where Walter had kicked him. He thought back over the last two days. . . .

After keeping them tied to the pole in the warehouse all day Thursday, Hans Walter had blindfolded them, thrown them into the back of a truck, and hauled them for a couple of hours across a series of bumpy roads to a city Michael hadn't yet managed to identify. Once in the city, Walter took off their blindfolds, pushed them through the back entrance of a poorly lighted hotel, and ushered them up the stairs to a suite of rooms on the top floor.

Once inside the room, Walter produced a large brown carry-on bag, from which he pulled the canister that protected the scroll and the jar in which McAuley first found it. Placing both items on a card table he had covered with white paper, he then pulled out the tools Michael had used to read the document at Madden's house—the gloves, the cotton cloths, the tweezers and tongs, a couple of masks, and a magnifying glass.

Untying their wrists, Walter pointed to the table and told them to get to work. But McAuley shook his head.

"Too many people in the room," McAuley said, indicating Walter's troop of five. "The moisture from all the breathing will damage the document."

Walter clenched his jaw for a moment, but then relented. "Two of us will stay," he said, his tone allowing no more argument. "One in the room with you, another outside the door. The others will wait in the next room." He indicated the interior door to the adjacent suite. Everyone but Walter and the brooding man the others called Sonji filed out.

After once more reminding Walter that anything they decided would be tentative, Michael and McAuley began their inspection. With gentle care, Michael donned the gloves and mask, removed the scroll from the canister, and laid it out on the table. Beside it, he placed the ceramic jar.

With a quick glance at each other they began, Michael with the scroll, McAuley with its original container. Not wanting to touch the scroll any more than necessary, Michael laid it on the table, unrolled it as far as possible, and placed one of the white cloths on each corner to hold it in place. Then, his breathing a bit jerky, he began once more to read the document.

This time, however, he studied it much more deliberately than at Willard Madden's house. Doing his best to ignore the overall message, he concentrated on several specific aspects of the manuscript.

First, he considered the language itself, comparing it to the style found in the books traditionally attributed to the man named John in the New Testament. Though these writings—the Gospel of John, three brief epistles, and the book of Revelation—contained differences that caused some scholars to doubt their common authorship, Michael examined the document to see if he could find common language with any of them. Was the Greek parallel in any way? Did the writer use similar or identical words, key phrases, and expressions? Thursday night passed into Friday morning.

Finished with his study of the jar, McAuley joined Michael poring over the scroll, McAuley using the magnifying glass like a jeweler inspecting a diamond, his left hand at his side, his right hand holding the glass. Though sliding to the side to give McAuley some space at the table, Michael was so focused that he barely noticed the big man.

After studying the Greek, Michael began a consideration of the theology of the book. Did it agree with the view of the world, the cosmos, the realities of God and Jesus, the notions of life and death, light and darkness, evil and goodness that a reader found in the writings usually ascribed to John?

Though Michael paid it no heed, morning became afternoon and afternoon became evening. At eight he and McAuley lay down for about four hours to sleep, but it was fitful at best, and both of them renewed their deliberations again about midnight. Alfred replaced Walter as their in-room guard, handing them some bottled water and a couple of apples to eat.

After pausing just long enough to eat, Michael shifted his attention from theology to the overall historical tone of the fragment's writings. Did it reflect the "*sitz in leben*," of the New Testament world, the "life situation" of the people, the political context, the social structures, the religious background?

At about four A.M., Hans Walter returned, whispered something to Alfred, then left, leading his other men down the hallway away from the suite they occupied. Switching places with the remaining guard, Alfred stepped into the hallway, a cigarette in his hand.

Standing over the scroll, Michael watched the men come and go, but it all seemed unreal to him now, the activities of another world, a world past his comprehension or care. For all intents and purposes, Michael had cut himself off from time and space. He focused entirely on the document at hand, totally ignoring the implications of what he read to become the pure scholar—a man concerned with the technicalities of the material rather than the message itself.

Using hotel stationery, he jotted reminders to himself, questions the document raised, issues that needed more in-depth consideration. As he worked, he immersed himself in the story, more and more taken with it, caught up as one transported back in time. Without realizing it at first, the characters in the Mary book became more real to him than ever before, more real than he ever imagined. In fact, he finally admitted to himself, the characters took on a humanity he had never really quite grasped, never really quite felt. Jesus the boy became a flesh-and-blood person, a human being with all the struggles that came with that humanity.

Michael's heart broke as he read of the death of Mary's mother—a woman unknown to Church history—and how a young Jesus comforted her. As he read, Michael remembered his own mother and the day she died, the day he couldn't comfort her—the day no one comforted him. He wished he could have heard Jesus' words on that day, but he hadn't, not personally, not as if addressed to him. He had not heard them that day, and he had not heard them since that day either. True, he had the Church and all the comfort it offered, but somehow that seemed insufficient now, valuable in its own way but not quite enough, not nearly everything he needed.

As he studied the scroll through the night, Michael realized how truly impersonal his faith really was, how utterly thin and unsteady. Like a half-inch of ice on a pond, it appeared solid on the surface but was unable to hold any real weight. Though not knowing what, if anything, he could do about it, he now recognized that his faith—centered as it was in an institution—was simply too weak to deal with the vital matters of life . . .

As the sun rose outside, Michael gradually returned from the disembodied state into which he had lapsed overnight. The heat of a full sun filtered through the windows that bordered the card table.

Beside him, McAuley yawned, then whispered, "I've done all I can do without real equipment."

Michael stretched and nodded. "Same here, at least for now. Any conclusions?"

"The jar seems genuine," McAuley said quietly, rubbing his eyes. "Though—"

"I know, pending more elaborate tests."

"And you?"

"Whoever wrote this knew his Greek," whispered Michael. "I've got some questions about a number of key words, but for the most part, it's awfully close to what we know of Johannine language. The theology too. Hard to tell this from the biblical writings."

McAuley sighed and hitched up his pants. Michael glanced toward the guard. The man's eyes were almost closed, and his shoulders slouched into the chair.

"We can't let them keep this document!" breathed McAuley, his voice low but intense.

"We've got no choice."

"I say we do. Look at him! And Alfred is the only guard outside the door. If he's as sloppy as this one, we've got a chance. The others are gone. I heard Hans say something about needing to make some 'arrangements.' "

"But what about—?"

"No!" interrupted McAuley, his face flushing in spite of his quiet tones. "I've spent my whole life toiling and sweating and digging, but with zero for results. You think I'm going to give this scroll up without a whimper? I think this thing is real, and I'm not going to leave it in the hands of a bunch of thugs. It's now or never and—!"

The guard stirred slightly and McAuley shut up. Michael's mind raced ahead, trying to figure what, if anything, they could do. To go for the guard's weapon was risky, maybe suicidal. But if they waited, they might not get another chance. And Walter might kill them anyway now that they had done all they could with the document.

Before he could act one way or the other, McAuley took the decision away from him. The big man grabbed his chest and stumbled forward as if having a heart attack. He pretended to choke and his body, still heavy in spite of his lost weight, fell over toward the guard.

Jumping from his seat, the guard danced out of the way as McAuley fell, his eyes wide with wonder, his weapon at his side. Landing, McAuley rolled onto his back, his legs twitching.

The guard stood frozen in the middle of the room, his eyes

glued in disbelief at the spectacle of the distressed archeologist dying right in front of him. McAuley flopped like a fish, his heavy legs thumping against the cheap hotel carpet.

As mesmerized as their captor, Michael stayed motionless too, holding his breath. The guard darted over to McAuley, then knelt to the floor beside him. Michael knew he should do something, should take advantage of the diversion McAuley had given him, but he didn't know what he could do, how he could attack. So he remained still, immobilized by his uncertainty.

More quickly than Michael thought possible, McAuley suddenly opened his eyes and grabbed the guard's ankle and twisted it to the side. The man jerked his weapon up as he fell, his fingers reaching for the trigger.

Michael awakened from his trance the moment he saw the guard shift his Uzi. Another second and he would kill McAuley! Acting on instinct, Michael lunged to his left and grabbed a lamp from a table by the wall. McAuley jerked at the guard's Uzi, preventing him from firing it.

Taking two huge steps, Michael crushed the lamp into the man's head. The lamp broke with a soft crack, and as easily as that, the guard sagged to the floor, blood seeping from a cut in the back of his skull.

"Get the scroll," whispered McAuley, up from the floor and taking the guard's weapon.

"Is he still alive?" Michael asked, concerned for the man.

"Get the scroll," growled McAuley. "He's still breathing."

Michael obeyed without more protest, seizing the scroll, rolling it back up, and shoving it as carefully as possible into the canister.

"Alfred is in the hallway," he panted.

"Our luck has turned to the good," whispered McAuley, the guard's Uzi in one hand, a long thin knife in the other. "He didn't hear anything."

"Maybe he's asleep," Michael said.

"Perhaps, but either way, we can do this. I know we can."

Michael held up the canister. "Ready?"

McAuley nodded and brandished the gun.

"One second," Michael said. "The jar."

He pulled the jar from the table, his eyes searching the room for something to carry it. Behind the guard's chair, he spotted the carry-on bag Hans had used. Shoving the canister and jar into the leather bag, he took one last look at the unconscious guard, threw the bag over his shoulder, and faced McAuley once more.

"Okay," he said, his adrenaline thumping. "We got no choice. Let's do it."

His weapons ready, McAuley led the way. At the door, he took a deep breath, shoved the knife into the waistband of his slacks, and twisted the knob. Michael braced himself. The door swung open. Alfred waited on the other side, his chair leaning backward against the wall, his weapon at his side. For a split second, Michael thought they might actually get past him without having to fight.

McAuley kicked the front legs of the chair and Alfred tumbled over.

"Run!" McAuley shouted, the machine gun over his head ready to club Alfred.

But Michael didn't run. Unwilling to leave McAuley, he threw himself at Alfred's weapon and felt the hard steel pop into his hand. The mercenary scrambled to get up, his hands closing onto McAuley's pants leg, pulling the archeologist to his knees.

In an instant, everything seemed to shift into slow motion. Alfred grasped the knife from McAuley's waistband and rose to his feet with the knifepoint aimed toward McAuley's face.

Michael launched himself into the air, his fingers grabbing for Alfred's neck. But he moved too slowly. The knife ripped at McAuley, and its point plunged through the redhead's throat.

Without thinking, Michael pounced on Alfred from behind, his hands like talons clawing at his enemy's eyes. With a quick twist, Michael felt his forearms and fingers tense, then turn. He jerked Alfred's head sharply to the left, every ounce of his strength poured into the moment, every second he had ever spent in the weight room focused in the sheer fear and panic of the struggle to save McAuley's life. The mercenary's neck cracked, and his head tilted sideways, as loose as a rag doll's.

For a split second, Michael stared down at his hands as if they belonged to someone else. The taste of guilt rose up in his throat like a geyser of bile, and he felt his stomach go bitter. For the second time in his life, someone had died because of him. His mouth suddenly moistened, and he knew he was about to throw up. But then McAuley moaned.

Pushing down the sour taste of death, Michael fought off the urge to vomit and rolled Alfred off McAuley. Then, wiping his mouth, he dropped to a knee to check his friend. McAuley lay prone on the floor, his shirt blanketed in blood.

"Get out of here," McAuley sputtered. "Take the scroll, leave—"

"Shush," choked Michael. "You're . . . you're coming with me."

McAuley grinned slightly, then coughed up another mouthful of blood. "I weigh almost two fifty," he said. "Even with my latest diet. You can't do it. You've got to . . . to leave now. Walter will return . . . soon."

"But I can't leave you!" Michael protested, his raw feelings blanched by his concern for McAuley. "Not like this, you need a doctor."

McAuley closed his eyes. "Do it," he insisted, his voice weaker. "It's what I want. Get the scroll out of here. . . ."

Michael leaned closer and took the big man's right hand in his. Though he didn't know McAuley well, he felt bonded to him, a bonding forged in the fires of danger and common knowledge. He wanted to say something comforting, something to carry McAuley through the mysterious darkness that he now faced. But knotted up by the shackles of guilt, Michael found it impossible to speak.

"I think it's real," whispered McAuley, breaking the quiet. "The document—I think I did it . . . I think I found something the world will never forget . . . something wonder—"

As if suddenly losing electricity, McAuley's eyes closed in midsentence. Then his head lolled to the side and his breathing stopped.

Michael finished his sentence for him. "You found something wonderful, Hugh McAuley. Something truly worthy of awe."

McAuley didn't respond.

Michael took a deep breath, laid McAuley's hand across his stomach, then etched the sign of the cross on the big man's forehead. Though wanting to do more, he knew he couldn't. Time wouldn't allow it.

Standing, he quickly hauled McAuley and Alfred back into the hotel suite. As if on autopilot, his instincts took over and his mind clicked into high gear, calculating and careful. He grabbed one of the machine guns and the carry-on bag off the floor and pulled a black jacket from the chair where the still-unconscious guard had been sitting. Slipping into the jacket, he frantically checked the unconscious man's shoes but found them too big. He turned to Alfred—his boots looked about right.

Pushing down his revulsion, Michael ripped off Alfred's black boots and slipped them on. Quickly searching Alfred's pants pockets, he found a handful of change and a number of bills in a wallet. Pocketing the money, he touched McAuley's forehead one last time, pivoted, and headed for the back stairs of the hotel. At the stairs, he began to pray.

"May his soul and all the souls of the faithful departed rest in peace. And may the God of heaven protect those who now seek to fulfill the work that he sought to complete. Amen."

The prayer carried him down the four floors to the bottom of the stairs. Shoving the machine gun as fully as possible under the jacket, he hoisted the bag onto his shoulder and stepped into the sunlight. As if turned on by a switch, his eyes suddenly watered. Turning left, he stumbled down the street, his vision blurred by the grief that now gushed down his face like a runaway waterfall. For the first time since Tuesday morning, he was free. But a friend had just died in his arms, and he had just killed a man with his bare hands. He didn't know where he was, and he wasn't sure yet where he was going.

THIRTY-ONE

A sliced carrot, three radishes, a hunk of cheese the size of a bar of soap, and a peeled orange lay uneaten on a cream-colored salad plate. A glass of water, no ice, remained untouched. A wheat roll sat unbroken beside a butter dish. Sitting alone at a small wooden table in his office, His Eminence Cardinal Severiano Roca stared at his hands, rolled the ring on his finger, and ignored his lunch. He felt like a soccer ball that had been kicked by a multitude of feet at odd angles until it simply deflated.

Nelson Randuhar's premidnight announcement about his plans for the Marian Decree had left him totally confused. Trying to determine what, if anything, he might do to derail the decision, he had spent the entire evening in conversation with a couple of his closest advisors. But no one had any solutions. If Randuhar wanted to make this decision and had the support of a majority of the Curia, he could act—and no one could stop it. It was unusual for any kind of major decree to be made without a living pope's approval, but these were unprecedented circumstances, and normal protocol simply didn't apply to them.

Roca rubbed his black eyes. Though he knew he couldn't sleep even if he tried, his body, up since the night of Michael's disappearance, craved rest. He shook his head as if to clear cobwebs from its corners. Standing, he walked to the window a few feet away. He had underestimated Randuhar, a major mistake. The man had made a convincing case for his point of view last night.

After the uproar had settled a bit, the Secretary presented what he called "convincing evidence of the pope's wishes." Producing an impressive collection of papal quotes that spoke glowingly of the Holy Mother and favorably of a discussion of the issue of Mary as Co-Redemptrix, the Secretary had used them to support his conclusion. The pope wanted this, he assured everyone in the room. His own speeches and pronouncements demonstrated his desire for it to happen. How dare they stand in the way of the pontiff's expressed wishes?

Roca, of course, knew of the quotes. Everyone did. The pontiff had made no secret of his consideration of the idea, and the news media had chronicled it for years. But these writings didn't tell the whole story. The pope had made no final public decision on the matter, and he had written and spoken in other places— quotes conveniently left out of Randuhar's compilations—in ways that contradicted what Randuhar had declared. Knowing the problems such a decree would create within the larger Christian world, the pontiff had, on a number of occasions, suggested that perhaps such an elevation of Mary should not happen.

But that didn't matter now. Randuhar had cast the discussion in terms of the pope's wishes, "perhaps his final wishes," he suggested, and no one wanted to stand against such a decision as that. After all, if His Holiness did eventually recover and come out in favor of what Randuhar said he wanted, anyone who had argued against it would likely end up in trouble with a pope who prized loyalty as much as any other quality. On the other hand, if the pope recovered and disliked the choice Randuhar had made, then only the Secretary would suffer. To go along with Randuhar seemed the wiser course.

Roca stepped to his desk. Pulling out his copies of the pope's journal, he fingered through the pages once again. Obviously, though Randuhar had these same writings in his possession, the Secretary had not mentioned them to the group last night. And since they had fallen into his possession in a manner he didn't care to explain, Roca also stayed quiet. For a moment, he wondered who else had them—Marchino maybe. Had the chamberman Cellini been smart enough to cover his bases by making sure that each of the three most powerful men in the Curia received a copy? Perhaps so.

The papers in hand, he moved back to the table and sat down. One part of him wanted to use the papers now, to make them public, to go to the press if all else failed and reveal to the world what he knew. But to do so violated the oath he had sworn last night to keep the conversation of the enclave private. Again, he had made a mistake, agreeing to the condition before he knew the nature of the meeting. But this too came from the first and most basic error—the underestimation of the mysterious Secretary Randuhar.

Roca studied the most salient passage from the pope's journal once more, a passage written not in the pontifical plural first person "we" of the Vatican, but in the singular first person "I" of a simple, devout man.

No one can doubt my love for the Holy Mother, wrote the pontiff. *I have spent my life seeking to lead others to a similar love. The Virgin sustains me each day, gives me encouragement and inspiration. The Church worships at her feet, as do I. But is this reason enough to declare a new doctrine for the Church? Is this enough to create theological uncertainty in the Church universal? Is this enough to create schism within our own ranks, discord among the brothers and sisters I love and have given my life to unify? Is this enough to part ways with the larger religious community, divide the ecumenical movement that yields dividends for all of Christendom? These are hard questions, but I think the reasons for refraining are greater than the reasons for pressing ahead.*

I am old now. My days grow short. I have tried to stay faithful to our Blessed Lord. If the Declaration of Mary as the Co-Redemptrix is within God's Holy Will, then I leave it to my successor to do so. Let that be his legacy. I am content under God with mine as it is.

Roca laid the papers on the table. Beside him, his telephone rang. He ignored it, his mind sifting through options for the future. The phone rang again. Roca picked it up.

"Uncle?"

Roca squeezed the phone and stood. "Michael, is that you? Where are you? Are you—"

"Whoa, whoa, let me talk, I don't have . . . don't have long." Michael pushed his words out in a hurry, his breath ragged. "I'm okay for now, but I need help."

"What can I do? Tell me and I'll do it, anything, just tell me."

"Listen, just listen. I'm in Cyprus, a port city, Limassol, in the lobby of a small hotel. I'm not hurt, but I'm not safe either. I'm . . . on the run, not sure what to do, where to—"

"Come to Rome, come now, get on a plane!"

"I can't do that, no money. No passport either, no way to get out of here."

Roca tried to clear his head. Michael was safe. That was a start, a good one. A sudden question came to mind and, though it seemed a bit out of place at the moment, he couldn't resist asking it.

"Michael, do you have the scroll?"

"I do."

"Your assessment?"

"I don't know, but . . . well, I'm more positive than negative."

Roca wanted to ask more but restrained himself. Michael was safe—that was enough for now.

"Then you definitely can't come to Rome. Things are in such chaos here. Randuhar has . . . well, there is no time to talk of it. This is not the place for such a document just now. Go to the U.S. embassy in Cyprus. Tell them to call Ambassador Bremer here in Rome. He knows the circumstances and has people all over the world looking for you."

"I thought of that," Michael said. "But I can't do that either."

Roca paused, waiting for Michael to continue. But he didn't. Then Roca understood.

"You don't want to give up the scroll, do you?" he said.

"You got it. I'm not sure what to do with it yet, but one thing I do know—I don't want it falling into government hands. I've read it, and I can tell you it doesn't belong there."

Roca started to probe further but again held himself in check. "I'll send someone to you," he said. "I'll get you a passport, all in proper order. Can you stay out of sight until then? I'll get you out of there."

"I don't think I should stay here. The city's not that big, and I'm not that far from where I was being kept prisoner. As soon as Walter gets back . . . if he hasn't already . . . we, well, we killed one of his men . . . his brother—"

"You killed a man?"

"There was no way to avoid it. It was self-defense. McAuley is dead too."

Roca swallowed hard but stayed focused, wracking his mind for what he knew of Cyprus. He had been there once, almost five years ago. Bits and pieces of information rambled through his head. The island was divided between Turkish-occupied territory in the northern third and the Greek-Cypriots in the south. Capital city was Nicosia, but the government in the south had declared that a restricted access area because the Turks controlled it. He had flown into another city, what was it called? Paphos! That was it, not more than forty miles or so from where Michael was.

"Go to Paphos," Roca said. "To the airport there. The city is west of you, and it can't be more than an hour away."

"I can do that," Michael said. "But where from there?"

"I'll send a plane," Roca said. "Just get to the airport, and I'll send someone."

"But what next?" Michael repeated, his voice thin with panic.

"I don't know, we'll have to figure that out. You get to Paphos. I'll get someone moving. Call me from the airport, and we'll designate a meeting place."

"I'll do it . . . I need to go."

"Michael?"

"Yeah?"

"I wish I could come myself, but you know I can't."

"I know."

"God be with you. Take care of yourself."

"That's the plan."

Michael hung up and Roca laid the phone down. For several seconds, he stayed still, staring at it. Michael was safe and he had the scroll. But that might not last. Men with evil intent wanted him caught. Roca picked up the phone again. If he wanted to save Michael he needed to get busy.

———

Just less than thirty minutes after Cardinal Roca hung up the telephone, an electronics technician tapped on the door outside of Nelson Randuhar's private study. Responding quickly, Randuhar moved to the door, invited the man inside, then motioned for him to sit.

"You asked me to inform you when anything I thought significant came to my hearing," said the technician.

"To be sure," agreed Randuhar, also sitting. "And you have been faithful to that charge."

The technician humbly lowered his eyes. "I believe you will find the contents of this tape quite informative," he said, extending his hand, a labeled audiocassette in his palm.

"Let me hear it," Randuhar said, indicating the cassette player he had only recently brought into his office.

The technician stood, inserted the tape, and pushed the "play" button.

"Uncle?"

Randuhar leaned forward and steepled his hands together.

"Michael, is that you? Where are you?"

The tape played through to the end, the voices of Michael Del Rio and Cardinal Roca sounding clearly in the Secretary's office.

When it had finished, Randuhar flicked off the cassette player, then walked around and placed his hand on the technician's shoulder.

"You're doing the right thing," he said. "Keep me informed."

The technician nodded, then stood and left the room.

Alone again, Randuhar played the tape through one more time. So Father Del Rio was headed to Paphos, and Roca planned to send him a passport and an airplane. Within hours Roca might have the Mary scroll in his possession, a document the scholar Del Rio thought might be authentic. A most disturbing possibility!

Randuhar punched a button on his speakerphone. An assistant answered immediately.

"Find Cardinal Marchino for me," Randuhar said. "Bring him here. Do it quickly."

Shutting off the phone, he stood by the tape player and steepled his fingers once more. So far, everything had gone well. But this complicated matters more than he liked to consider. Only one reasonable thing to do—get someone to Paphos and find Michael Del Rio before Roca did.

THIRTY-TWO

Valerie Miller dreamed she was in the middle of a wheat field, seated on a bench before a piano. An undecorated Christmas tree sat beside the piano, and a man without a face stood beside the tree.

In her dream, Valerie knew what she wanted to play, and she knew exactly how to play it. But when she placed her fingers on the keyboard, they refused to work correctly. A hot sun beat down on her head one minute, frozen snow the next. Her fingers pounded on the piano keys, but she missed all the notes. A wind at her back became harsh, gusting higher and higher, threatening to blow her off the bench. But she continued to bang on the piano, refusing to quit, refusing to give up. The piano jangled louder and louder now, and the harsh notes clanged faster and faster, faster and faster, so fast she couldn't stand it anymore. Her head was about to explode into a million pieces. Valerie screamed over and over again, a long wailing screech.

"Valerie!" a voice shouted. "Wake up, Val, you're okay, you're home, it's okay, wake up, sweetheart, it's okay."

Valerie opened her eyes, her shoulders shaking, her head wet with a cold sweat. Seeing her dad sitting on the bed beside her, she threw herself into his arms, her body quivering all over, a fever baking her forehead like a gas grill.

"I was trying to play the piano," she cried. "But I couldn't do it, couldn't do something I've done all my life. I kept missing the notes. I couldn't do it, couldn't do it . . ."

"It was a dream," her father said, stroking her forehead. "That's all it was. You were having a bad dream. But you're home now, you're all right."

Valerie coughed and it rattled her from head to toe.

"You've got a phone call," her father said, holding up a port-able phone. "I wasn't going to wake you." He smiled and her head cleared a bit. "But since you're already awake . . ."

"A phone call? Now?"

"Yeah, right in the middle of your last scream."

She sagged down in the bed. "Take a message. I don't want to talk to anyone."

"I don't think I should do that."

"Why not? Who is it?"

"Some man. He didn't give his name and I didn't ask. Aren't you proud of me?" He smiled at her with his big blue eyes the way he always did when he teased her about men, which was every time she came home.

Valerie rubbed her forehead and hoped the ache in her skull would disappear soon.

"I don't know if I can talk," she said. "I feel like a bug on a windshield."

"The man sounds anxious." Her father waved the phone.

"Michael?" Valerie sat up quickly, her thoughts suddenly busy as the notion hit home. Could it be Michael?

"I'll take it," she said, grabbing the phone.

"Your mom's working on some soup," he said, standing and walking to the door. "Holler when you're done. You can tell us who Michael is."

Ignoring his tease, Valerie cupped the phone to her ear. "Yes, this is Valerie Miller."

"Hold please," said an efficient male voice.

It wasn't Michael. Disappointed, Valerie fluffed her pillow.

"Miss Valerie Miller?"

"Yes."

The caller identified himself and Valerie sucked in her breath.

"Have you heard anything from Father Michael Del Rio?" the man asked, dispensing with formalities. "Has he contacted you at all?"

Valerie froze for an instant, too confused to speak. But then the meaning of the question hit her. "How could he?" she stam-mered. "He's unable . . . Is he okay? Do you know something about him? Has something happened? Is he—?"

"I can't answer all of your questions right now, Miss Miller," interrupted the caller. "But I can tell you he is no longer a prisoner. He has escaped, and we're all grateful for that. Has he contacted you?"

Valerie threw her legs onto the floor, her suspicions suddenly aroused. What did this man want with Michael?

"How do I know you're who you say you are?" she asked.

The caller hesitated and Valerie could almost hear him thinking.

"Don't you recognize my voice?"

"You could fake a voice."

"Look, Miss Miller, I can't prove anything to you that you don't want to believe. But you're a woman of faith, aren't you?"

Valerie shrugged. "Yeah, sure, but that's no guarantee of much, at least not lately."

"I know your last few days have been difficult. Death isn't easy to see."

Valerie coughed. The man continued. "I need you to trust me, Miss Miller. I have no motive to lie about this."

"You've got plenty of motive. Lots of people are trying to find Michael right now. And most of them aren't friendly."

"You care for him, don't you?"

Valerie shivered. "That's my business, isn't it?"

The man chuckled. "You're right about that."

Valerie stayed quiet. The caller didn't press her. Her guard dropped a bit. If he was who he said he was . . .

"Okay," she said. "I guess it can't hurt anything for me to tell you he hasn't contacted me. I've been home since late Friday but haven't heard anything. You say he's safe?"

"No, I said he had escaped. That's not the same as safe. In fact, I'm still quite concerned about his well-being."

"So am I."

"Here's what I'm asking you to do. If he contacts you in any way, please advise him to stay away from Rome."

Valerie nodded. A number of competing factions in the Vatican wanted the document. It made sense to stay away from that confusion until things settled down some.

"Sure, sure I can do that. I'll tell him to come here, back to the—"

"No, not that either, not yet. Things are not ready. Too much like Rome, too many people wanting the document for the wrong purposes. The minute he shows up in customs, he'll lose control of the document."

"Then where—"

"I don't know where, not yet. When he contacts you, get back to me. Here's a private number. I'll make some arrangements, then we'll bring him home."

Valerie jotted down the number. The plan sounded reasonable. She took a deep breath. If the caller was telling the truth about his identity, his idea made more sense than anything she had heard in days. If he wasn't, then she hoped her faith was strong enough to face even more turmoil before life settled down again, if it ever did.

THIRTY-THREE

A steady stream of hot tears swept down Hans Walter's chin. His head reeled and his body shook with grief. He held Alfred's body close to his chest and cried out against the injustice of the world that had brought such misfortune to him. Murphy's law to the worst extent—a brother, three years his junior, dead in his arms and a gray-headed, wheelchair-bound mother in Germany who would want an explanation for her youngest boy's death.

And what could he tell her? That Alfred had brought his demise on himself? That he had obviously mismanaged the simple task of guarding the prisoners entrusted to his care? That her son was a poor excuse for a soldier and a general failure at everything he ever tried?

She would, of course, give no heed to any of that. She would blame it on Hans instead, just as she had always done when Alfred found himself in still another self-created catastrophe.

You are the elder, she would remind Hans. *You should look out for your brother. You should protect him.*

But how do you protect a man who constantly disgraces himself with his own immature choices? Walter had no answers.

Still crying, he did what all good soldiers eventually do—he accepted the responsibility for the mess his brother had made. He should have known better than to leave Alfred alone, to give him that much leadership. He had made the mistake, not his incompetent brother. But Alfred had been making progress it seemed, and what better way to encourage his development than to give him more important work?

Walter's shirt was now wet from his tears, and his chest was heaving with sadness. His brother was dead, and the scroll he had gone to such lengths to acquire had disappeared. He felt a touch on the back of his head. Turning, he saw the remainder of his men—four professional soldiers—waiting to do his bidding. Sonji's hand rested on his shoulder, but Walter sensed it wasn't from any effort to comfort him.

"We need to move quickly," said the square-jawed Asian, his voice sharp with the accent of his homeland. "The one who did this will disappear if we don't find him soon. And he has the document your kinsman died to protect."

Walter blinked as if waking up from a long nap. Father Del Rio, of course. The priest had done this—the priest had killed his brother. The priest now forced him to face his mother, a woman who had survived the worst of the deprivations of World War II as the daughter of a soldier of the Third Reich, and tell her that her baby was dead. To compound his transgression, the priest had also stolen the scroll—his own personal ticket to freedom, his last best chance to clean up his gambling debts and drive the dark cloud of his angry debtors from his life.

Walter hugged Alfred one more time, then laid his brother's head on the floor and stood up. His face, now cleared of tears, glowed with rage. Del Rio had done all this to him! That made it personal. Hans not only wanted the document, but he also wanted revenge. So far as he could see, ending the life of the accursed priest was the only way to get it.

Quickly scanning the room, Walter grabbed a bed sheet and spread it over Alfred. Sonji did the same for McAuley. The other guard, burly Hispanic, lay unconscious on the bed, his head wrapped in a white bandage.

"What shall we do with them?" Sonji asked, pointing to the now-covered bodies.

Walter bit his lip. "Call the Turkish police but give them no name. We'll claim Alfred's body later, then see to it that it's well buried."

Sonji nodded, obviously satisfied with the decision.

"Del Rio has at least an hour's head start on us," Walter said. "I have no doubt he has already left Limassol."

"He will leave Cyprus as soon as possible," Sonji said.

"He can't do that from here very well," Walter said. "He'll need to go to an airport—Larnaca or Paphos. Both are easily accessible, less than fifty miles."

"We'll need to split up to cover them both," Sonji said.

Walter nodded. "You come with me to Paphos," he said, "and you also." He pointed to a blond man to his right.

Sonji nodded and pointed to the other two men. "You go to Larnaca, should be there in an hour, call us when you arrive."

Walter pulled a cellular phone from his shirt pocket and checked the battery. Sonji did the same.

"They're good," Sonji said, tossing his phone to one of the men going to Larnaca.

"Del Rio has no passport and no money," Walter said. "Someone will have to come for him."

"Who could that be?"

Walter rubbed his head for almost thirty seconds. Then he knew the answer to Sonji's question. "He came from Rome," he said. "So surely that is where he will want to return. Someone from Rome will come for him."

"The Vatican wants the document," agreed Sonji.

Walter smiled ruefully. "Oh yes, the Vatican wants the document. But so do we, and we will see to it that they don't receive it unless they pay us the price we deserve."

————

Twelve miles west of Limassol, Michael Del Rio jumped into the back of a rusted out pickup truck and threw a thumbs-up sign to the snaggle-toothed driver, who smiled back at him through the broken window behind the cab. The driver, a bearded man who had to be at least seventy years old, wore a battered safari-style hat, a worn out pair of brown wool slacks, and a navy sport coat with patches on the sleeves. But he had a smile as wide as a boat paddle, and his truck engine sounded smooth, even if the vehicle looked awful. Turning to face the road, the driver eased his truck back into the traffic.

Stretching his feet out, Michael exhaled a huge breath and stared up at the sky—a blue canopy of sheer beauty. In spite of McAuley's death and the guilt that weighed on him like a manhole cover around his neck, he felt a huge sense of relief. If nothing else, he had managed to escape, at least for the moment.

Finding that many of the Cypriots spoke at least a smattering of English, he had used Alfred's money, Cypriot currency it turned out, to pay a bus fare for the first ten miles of his journey. At the end of the bus line, he had hurriedly climbed off, thanked the driver, and started to walk. About two miles later, the truck came by and Michael flagged it down.

"Airport?" Michael asked, hoping this man also spoke some English.

"Yeah, yeah," the man said, sticking his head out and pointing west.

"Are you going to the airport?" Michael asked again.

"Yeah, yeah, live near airport."

"I ride with you?" Michael pointed to the back of the truck, his eyebrows arched with the question.

"Ride, you ride?"

"Yes, to airport, I pay you." Michael waved the money he had left, unsure if it was a little or a lot.

The man jogged his head up and down, the gap in his front teeth bouncing.

Michael handed over the money, placed Walter's bag in the back, and climbed in after it. The truck rattled off, its engine steady, if not particularly fast. A constant succession of traffic passed it as it chugged along.

Using the bag as a cushion, Michael leaned back and closed his eyes. Images from the morning spilled out into his head. The knife plunging into McAuley's throat. The back of Alfred's head as he twisted it. The sound of the man's neck snapping, like kindling wood broken to start a fire.

Like a mouthful of snake venom, the bile he had managed to swallow earlier returned to him now, pushing up from his gut and into the area behind his tonsils. Fighting off the sickness, Michael rolled up onto his knees, leaned over the side of the truck and sucked in huge draughts of air, one after the other in a desperate attempt to control the awful taste of regret that threatened to overwhelm him. To his surprise, he managed once more to get control of his emotions, and he swallowed the sensation and started to lean back into the truck again. But then, from out of nowhere, a new series of images suddenly flooded his thoughts and merged into those from the morning. These images came from the day of his seventeenth birthday, the day his family died.

For what seemed like the millionth time in the past twenty-two years, Michael heard again the sound of car wheels on pavement, smelled again the acrid aroma of gasoline, watched again the explosion of the car—the sky twisting and twisting and turning black from the smoke. Then everything became black that day, and Michael had awakened to find himself alone, everyone else dead—mother, father, and brother dead. Only he survived. . . .

And now McAuley was dead too, but he had survived once more. Mother, father, brother dead, but he was alive—alive and alone. Just like today, right now, he was all alone and carrying the weight of the world on his shoulders. He had killed a man, and the guilt was a raging torrent now, its poison almost sulfuric in its heat and nuclear in its power. The river of guilt surged once more, and this time Michael didn't even try to hold it back. Throwing his body to the side of the truck, he retched out his torment as best he could, his stomach and throat and shoulders constricting in one thunderous effort to expel the overwhelming self-loathing he felt in his soul. Oh, how terrible the stain he carried, the sin he had tried to repress all these years. But now it all poured out of him, at least for the moment, the grief and bitterness and regret like a black cascade crashing out of his spirit and onto the road beneath the wheels of the truck.

Within seconds, the deed was finished, the sickness passing as quickly as a Texas tornado. Wiping his face and breathing deeply several times, Michael sagged back again and closed his eyes. Though he felt better for the moment, he knew the guilt wasn't gone forever. It would surface again as it always did, unbidden and uncontrollable.

The wind whipped around Michael's head, and he rubbed his chin. He hadn't shaved in days. The beginnings of a beard covered his face. He knew he looked a sight, anything but the clean-cut professor of New Testament studies he had been in his other life. Michael shifted and stared down at the road as it moved away from him. His old life at Notre Dame seemed a long way off now, a fairy tale of safety and comfort.

The scroll had changed all that, had thrown him into danger beyond his wildest dreams. A half dozen people had died because of the document, maybe more. The Vatican was in an uproar, and people all over the world were searching for him. So far the document had been more of a curse than a blessing, had created more evil than good, more suffering than healing.

As unbidden as the attack of guilt, more questions suddenly came to Michael. For several moments, he chewed on them, not sure what to do with them. Did the scroll really hold some secret to divine healing? he wondered. McAuley thought the document had taken the pain from his broken fingers and caused him to lose weight.

Michael flexed the knee injured at the Ceylan Hotel—it had felt better the instant he touched the canister. And his headaches had disappeared too, and the pain from his ribs, all at the same time he touched the scroll. Or so it seemed now as he looked back on it.

The truck hit a pothole and Michael's head bounced against the back of the cab, and he told himself he was being ridiculous— speculating about something that made no sense. He was a fast healer, that's all, and that, plus the intensity of his emotions, explained the disappearance of the pain from his injuries.

But then he remembered a passage from the document. The words came to him almost verbatim, describing a time when the baby Jesus had taken a fever.

In the evening, his face burned with the heat of sickness and he wept. Mary held him in her arms, touched her hand to his forehead, and pulled him close to her breast. Then she prayed unto the Lord, the Holy One of Israel.

Her hand became warm at the touch of Jesus' skin, and she felt a quickening in her inner being. Then she kissed the forehead of her son. In the next moment, she looked again into his face, and he looked up at her and smiled. His skin suddenly cooled, and the fever disappeared as quickly as morning overtakes night. Never again did she know Jesus to suffer sickness.

Michael thought through the words once more. Did they signify that Mary was a healer? Had she healed Jesus? Had God used her then, and did God use her now—her hands, her eyes, her words as conduits of divine power to the world? Was she somehow a sacramental agent, a conduit of holy grace? Had any of the visions of Mary that people had reported over the centuries actually occurred? Or were they cases of religious fervor gone astray? He shook his head—no way to know, no way to know. Questions, questions, always questions. But no clear-cut answers.

He thought of Willard Madden's granddaughter. What if she had made it to Costa Rica before Hans Walter stole the scroll? What if he had read the passages about healing over her? Placed her hands on the scroll? Prayed for her? Would anything have happened?

Michael sighed. More questions without answers.

The truck bounced hard again, and an even more disturbing thought came to him. For a couple of seconds, he rolled the idea around in his head, but then dismissed it as too implausible. But it didn't go away. He rubbed his scratchy face. Maybe there was a way to find out once and for all. The scroll had caused so much death, but maybe there was a way for him to use it to save a life. Maybe there was a way to get some answers to his questions. It wouldn't be easy, but nothing had been easy the last few days, nothing had gone according to plan. Why not take a shot at it and give himself the opportunity to find out, one way or the other. The idea suddenly made sense, the only thing that did at the moment. He didn't know where to go from here, certainly not to Rome or the United States. So why not go. . . ?

Michael rubbed his chin, his fingers working the black stubble like a farmer digging at a garden row. Roca expected him in Paphos. No doubt his uncle had some ideas about what he should do next. But maybe his uncle was wrong. Maybe he should try his own idea first, see where it led. If nothing happened through that venture, then fine, go back to Roca in Rome. But what if something did happen? Well, if something did happen, then everything changed. Everything.

The wind picked up and Michael snuggled back against the cab of the truck. The trip seemed to be taking forever. If Hans Walter had returned to the hotel in Limassol within an hour or so of his escape, and if he figured out where he was heading, he might already be ahead of him. He might be waiting for him.

Pushing away the thought, Michael scrunched lower in the pickup. The edge of Walter's leather bag nudged into his spine.

To follow his instincts like this was no simple choice. He chewed on his lower lip. The course of action he was considering challenged everything he had ever been, the system that had supported him, the institution that had trained his intellect, nurtured his hopes, and sustained his faith, such as it was. To do anything but go back to that institution meant he had to act alone. He had to become one single man aligned against all the authority of his beloved Church. But if he wanted any answers to his questions, he knew he had to do it, regardless of the risks.

He hung his head. But how? He had no passport, no money, and no allies. How could he refuse the help Roca was sending? To do that was dangerous. Walter was still out there and Alfred was dead, and he, a simple professor from Rolla, Missouri, had stolen what might prove to be the most significant manuscript in the history of modern Christendom. A recipe for danger if ever there was one.

Michael sighed and knew his idea wouldn't work. He had to go with Roca, no way around it. He had to give up the scroll and leave his questions where they were, unanswered, untested.

He shifted the bag behind his back. The lump from the canister inside jabbed into his spine like a bony finger. Grunting, he pulled the satchel into his lap, unsnapped the fastener, and flipped open the satchel. There, in the bottom of the leather pouch and sitting beside the canister, he saw four wallets and passports.

Though surprised, he quickly dumped the contents of the pouch into his lap. His eyes widened when he saw his own wallet. Flipping it open, he found everything in place—almost four hundred dollars in traveler's checks, plus his credit cards, his driver's license—everything. His hands shaking, he checked the three other wallets—Madden's, Cashion's, and Valerie's. Between them he added up almost two thousand dollars, fifteen hundred of it from Madden. His spirits lighter now, Michael put all the money into his wallet, thumbed through the passports and found his, most recently stamped with his entry into Turkey.

Pocketing his wallet and passport, Michael looked up into the sky. His getaway vehicle looked like a reject from a junkyard, but the engine purred smoothly. He had his passport and a pocketful of money. He had everything he needed to take a shot at the one thing that he now wanted more than anything else—a chance to find out if the God he said he followed did indeed work in mysterious ways His wonders to perform. Most importantly, he had a chance now to see if he could save a life to replace the one he had just taken.

Michael rubbed his chin. Maybe all this didn't add up to a miracle, but it came as close to one as he had seen in a long, long while. As far as he was concerned, it met the criteria pretty well. Leaning back in the truck, he cradled the canister containing the scroll close to his stomach and decided he'd take his miracle any way he could get it.

THIRTY-FOUR

It took Michael just over an hour to get to Paphos. About a mile from the airport, the driver stopped at a small store to buy some gas. Hopping off the back of the truck, Michael pulled a stack of bills from his wallet and approached the driver.

"A hundred dollars for your clothes," he said, waving the money at his new friend.

"My clothes? But what I wear?"

"These," Michael said, indicating his slacks and jacket. "A hundred dollars and my clothes."

"Crazy American," said the man, smiling widely. "A good deal for me, yeah?"

"Yeah," agreed Michael, handing him the cash. "Good deal for you."

The Cypriot took the cash. "I fill up," he said. "We change clothes. I take you where you want."

Five minutes later Michael walked out of the restroom, dressed in his new togs. The pants were too short, and the old jacket had holes in the elbows. But they did offer him at least some measure of a disguise. Pushing the man's tattered hat down on his head, Michael searched the station for a telephone and found one on an outside wall. But the phone didn't work. Placing the dead receiver back on its cradle, Michael considered his options. Though he didn't want to go to the airport, he didn't see any choice. He had to have a phone, and he didn't have much time to find one. Hans Walter would regroup quickly and come for him; he knew it in his bones.

He hurried back to the truck. His Cypriot friend sat inside, ready to go.

"Take me to the terminal?" Michael asked, another roll of money in his hand.

"Sure," said the man, still grinning. "Here, you sit in front with me. Right here." He indicated the tattered seat to his right.

Clutching the carry-on bag, Michael jumped in. Less than ten minutes later, the battered truck taxied to the gates of the airport.

"You wait for me?" Michael asked. "Just a few minutes? I will pay you for it." He took out another wad of bills.

"Sure, no problem. I'm for you. I wait, then take you another place."

"Good, that's what I need," Michael said, climbing out. "Just wait here. I need to make a phone call, then I'll be right back."

"Good, right back, phone call, right back, I wait."

Tapping the passenger door, Michael adjusted the bag on his shoulder, then turned and rushed off, his head low, his hat down. Seventy-five feet inside the terminal, he spotted a bank of phones and stepped to it. His stomach churning, he turned his back to the terminal, picked up a telephone, and quickly dialed international information.

"Charlotte, North Carolina, in the United States," he said.

Waiting, he glanced back at the airport walkway beside the phone bank. A steady stream of people moved past, some headed toward outgoing flights, others just arriving in Paphos. No one seemed to be paying any attention to him. Good.

"Yes, this is information for Charlotte, North Carolina, what listing please?"

"Miller, Tyrone Miller," he said. He hoped she had followed through with her notion of going to her parents' home to get a grip after the events of the last few days.

"One second please."

His eyes as busy as a cat watching a tennis match, Michael stared up and down the terminal, ready to dart away at any sign of Walter or his accomplices. About a hundred yards to his right, he spotted a face that looked vaguely familiar headed toward him from the gated area. He hunched his shoulders and pivoted sideways, away from the man.

"Here's the number," said the operator.

Repeating the number, Michael pulled up his jacket collar and keyed the phone. "Come on, Valerie!" he whispered, his toes bouncing with anxiety. "Be home and answer the phone. Answer the phone!"

The phone rang once, twice, three times. Michael glanced

over his shoulder. He saw the man in the terminal again, obviously just arriving in Paphos. An entourage followed him, a moving flood of at least ten people sweeping through the airport like a small tidal wave. The man and his crowd were less than fifty yards away now and moving steadily right at him. How in the world did he get here?

"Hello."

Michael ducked his head and focused as best he could on the phone.

"Valerie?"

"Yes."

"Valerie, it's Michael . . . Del Rio, you know? I'm sure glad you're home!"

"Michael? Is it you? Where are you? Are you—?"

"Just listen, Valerie," he said breathlessly. "I've only got a second. Call Madden. Tell him to bring his granddaughter Katie to Costa Rica. I'm headed there—if I can make it."

"You're okay?"

"Yeah, fine, I'm okay."

"McAuley?"

Michael hesitated, but then knew he couldn't hide it. "He's dead."

"But how? What hap—?"

"Look, Valerie, I can't talk any longer! Just get Madden to Costa Rica. I'll explain later."

"Michael?"

"Yeah."

"Can I come to Costa Rica?"

"If you want," he said. "I'd like that."

"Okay. Good. I'm praying for you."

"Thanks, I need it."

Michael dropped the phone and ducked his head as the entourage passed the phone bank—a swoosh of humanity, marching almost in step. From the corner of his eye, he saw the point man of the group glance his way, his black eyes two bullets aimed right at him. Cringing, Michael froze in place, his heart thumping so loudly he knew everyone in the airport could surely hear it. Had the man recognized him? Or had his scruffy beard and strange clothes thrown him off? To Michael's relief, the man kept walking, his entourage in his wake.

Breathing again, Michael tugged his hat even lower and slunk slowly away in the opposite direction, doing everything he could to make sure the flat-faced man walking through the airport terminal didn't recognize him and take offense at his presence.

––––––––––

Sitting by the security checkpoint that led into the area reserved for departing international flights, Hans Walter almost dropped his ice cream cone when he spotted his leather carry-on bag rapidly making its way down the airport walkway toward him. Slowly tossing the cone into a trash can by the baggage security x-ray, he calmly studied the man shouldering the prized pouch. The clothing was strange—ragged and ill-fitting. Walter smiled slightly at the obvious effort at a disguise. His eyes drifted to the man's feet and he felt the blood rush to his head. Click, click, click—the black boots clicked quickly on the floor, coming his way at a rapid pace. Alfred's boots!

For several seconds, Walter watched the boots approach, step by step. But then his stare raked up from the boots, his anger growing with each step. This was the accursed priest Del Rio! How dare he wear Alfred's shoes! This was an outrage!

His jaws grinding, Walter rubbed his head and told himself to calm down. Then he rolled his shoulders, stood, and joined Sonji and his other man. With a nod, Walter indicated Del Rio, now less than fifty feet away.

"We have to do this gently," Walter said quietly. "A scene of any kind will get the local authorities involved. We don't want that."

The men nodded. "If we can get him in there," he said, pointing to a nearby men's room, "we can do what is necessary."

His men nodded again and moved off without a word. Walter followed them, his calves flexed. He could almost feel Del Rio's throat in his hands, a throat he planned to twist until it turned blue and snapped.

––––––––––

Tehraq, the flat-faced man, had taken at least twenty steps past Michael Del Rio before he suddenly came to a halt. Behind him, the entourage also braked sharply, a couple of its members actually bumping into each other. His neck bowed, Tehraq pivoted and stared back down the way he had come, his head bobbing left and right as he searched the terminal for the man he had just passed.

"Tehraq, what is the meaning of this?" shouted the man in the middle of the group, a man exquisitely dressed in a tan suit and immaculate white shirt and holding the arm of a blond woman with emerald eyes.

"Mr. Azziz, I saw a man from the hotel," Tehraq said fiercely, stalking back toward his employer. "From Istanbul, one of the men who obtained the scroll from Yoseph."

"Are you sure of what you say?" Azziz asked, pulling away from the woman.

Tehraq bit his tongue against the sarcasm he felt. "One does not forget such a thing, Mr. Azziz," he said. "He and his companion almost killed me."

Azziz pivoted toward the terminal again. "Which one is he?" he asked. "Is he still here?"

"I don't see him now," Tehraq said. "He was there, at the telephones."

Azziz beckoned the woman, then started walking toward the exits, his entourage automatically following. "It's quite possible he's here, my dear Martha," he said hurriedly. "We investigated the names on the list Tehraq took from Yoseph. One of the men on the list, a German named Hans Walter, works out of Cyprus. Last night, this Mr. Walter called me, told me that he now holds the scroll, and that two experts have examined it. Walter asked me to make a bid on the document. As with all my communications, I had a tracer on the call, and tracked it to Limassol, a port city just a few miles from here. So we came today to meet Walter and inspect the document."

Ten feet from an exit door, Azziz braked and faced Tehraq again. "You say the American who took the scroll is here. Has he taken the document from Walter? Is that possible?"

"Why not?" interjected Hinton. "Walter messed up somehow."

Azziz pivoted to his followers. "We're looking for an American," he called.

"He has a brown carry-on," added Tehraq. "And he's wearing old clothes, a brimmed hat."

"Find him!" shouted Martha Hinton.

"I want that bag!" yelled Azziz. "A new home and my undying gratitude to the person who finds me that bag!"

———

Leaving the telephones, Michael had taken only a few steps when he heard the commotion behind him. Without stopping, he glanced over his shoulder and spotted the flat-faced man less than a hundred yards away, his big body pushing people aside as he threaded his way forward. Behind the black-bearded bodyguard, the rest of his troupe followed, elbowing their way through the crowded corridor.

Grateful for the human obstacles slowing his pursuers, Michael ducked around the corner, his legs churning. Dead ahead he spotted an exit and sprinted toward it. The sliding glass doors pushed open, and he hustled into the sunshine outside. On the sidewalk, he quickly spotted the rusted truck of his Cypriot friend and ran to it. Five steps away, he stopped, yanked the silver canister from the leather bag on his shoulder, slipped it under his coat, and tossed the bag against the wall by the electric doors. Jumping into the front seat of the truck, he nodded to his elderly friend.

"Drive!" he said, trying to stay calm. "Quickly!"

A gap-toothed smile lit up the old man's face as he flipped the ignition. The truck started immediately, and the man pulled smoothly away from the curb. Twisting around, Michael saw the flat-faced man rush through the electronic doors, scanning up and down the road trying to see where he had gone. A blond-headed woman sprinted up behind him, her ponytail bouncing. Suddenly, the woman squatted and picked up the leather satchel by the wall.

The rusted truck slid around a corner, and both the flat-faced man and the blond woman disappeared from Michael's view.

"I need a boat," Michael said to his friend. "A boat to take me to . . . to," he thought a second, "to Lebanon."

"Quickly?" his friend asked, still beaming.

"Yes," agreed Michael. "Quickly."

———

At the airport, Addam Azziz rushed through the exit doors, his black tasseled shoes sliding on the concrete sidewalk as he skidded to a stop and looked hurriedly around. To his right, Martha Hinton picked up something beside the wall of the terminal.

"Hey," Hinton shouted. "It's the leather bag. He dropped it!"

Before she could open it, Azziz jerked the bag from her hands and pushed her roughly against the wall.

"Is the scroll here?" he shouted, tearing at the closures.

"I don't know!" Hinton grunted, her teeth clamped.

Azziz stared into the bag, his black mustache almost disappearing inside as he searched it. He brought up a piece of pottery, his fingers hooked into a looped handle. His entourage gathered around him, their attention centered on their master. A small group of bystanders paused too.

"Is it in here?" Azziz shouted again, this time to no one in particular.

He studied the pottery for only a second, then handed it to Hinton. He stuck his hand back into the bag and came up with a nearly identical piece of pottery.

"It's a jar!" called Hinton, seeing the second piece. "No doubt the container for the scroll!"

From the left of Azziz, a square-jawed Asian man stepped gently through the crowd.

"But where is the scroll?" Azziz asked, still riffling the carry-on bag. "Where is the scroll?"

No one answered. The Asian was no more than five feet away now. One of Azziz's bodyguards moved toward the intruder, his hands balling into tight fists.

Ten feet away from the entourage, Hans Walter ducked behind an airport trash can, pulled a pistol from his waistband, and calmly fired four shots into the air. The crowd panicked. From left and right, most of the people ducked and fell, or ran and screamed. The bodyguard beside Azziz dropped to the ground, apparently forgetting his responsibility toward his employer.

But not everyone panicked. As steady as a concrete pier in the middle of a hurricane, Addam Azziz closed the leather bag and began to ease back toward the entry to the terminal. Fifteen steps from Azziz, Tehraq dropped to his knees and squeezed off a round of cover fire in the direction of the four shots.

Still crouched, Hans Walter scurried away from the trash container, his angle carrying him to a spot to cut off Azziz before he reached the airport door.

Two steps from Azziz now, Sonji moved in sync with his prey, a knife the length of his forearm tucked by his side.

Azziz took one more step toward the electric doors into the terminal. Beside Azziz now, Walter stood and pointed his pistol at his chest. His eyes on Walter's weapon, Azziz twisted back toward the street. But Sonji blocked his path.

"Do it, Sonji," whispered Walter.

The command wasn't necessary. As if inserting a key, Sonji slipped his knife through Azziz's silk coat and shirt.

His eyes as round as saucers, Azziz sagged forward. For a millisecond his lips opened, and it seemed that he wanted to speak, almost as if he wanted to greet him. But then his dark eyes glazed over and he slumped to the sidewalk.

As Azziz fell, Walter grabbed the bag from his hands, threw it over his shoulder, and pointed his gun at the bodyguard's back, less than twenty feet away. Two shots erupted. The man turned slightly, then toppled over, the black eyes in the center of his flat face wide with surprise.

Sonji extracted his knife from Azziz, wiped the blade on the thigh of his victim's pants, and slipped it back into his waistband. Inside the terminal, a fire alarm went off, and the chaos at the airport notched even higher. Walters other man had done well. The diversion was in place.

Moving hurriedly, but without panic, the two assassins pushed through the frantic scene to a utility van thirty feet away. Rejoining their companion, Walter climbed into the back, and Sonji took the wheel, speeding away from the curb.

Taking a deep breath, Walter laid the bag in his lap and flipped it open. He had taken a big risk to recapture the scroll. One wrong step and he might have been the one lying on the sidewalk in a pool of blood. But he had to do it. No way could he let someone else have it now, not after it had cost him the life of his brother. Regardless of the danger, he had to reclaim what rightfully belonged to him.

His fingers digging through the bag, Walter thought of his next steps—sell the document, pay off his gambling debts, use the rest of the money to track down Michael Del Rio, twist the man's throat until his head snapped, twist . . ."

He had finished searching the satchel, but he had found no scroll. He thumbed through the contents again, this time more slowly, checking every compartment, every nook and cranny. But still no document. His temper rising, he pushed back against the seat and cursed loudly.

"Stop the van!" he commanded.

Sonji braked hard.

"It's not here!" Walter screamed, tossing the leather bag against the window. "That murdering priest still has the scroll!"

Dressed in a night robe, Valerie Miller placed the phone in the cradle. Madden, though obviously weak, had readily agreed to fly back to Costa Rica to meet Michael.

"I've got nothing to lose," he said. "Me or Katie. I'll call ahead to get things ready for you. I'll get there as soon as I can and bring Red with me."

"I don't think he'll leave his wife," she said. "I went to see him Friday, to ask him to help me find Michael. He said no."

Madden grunted. "I'll talk to him. He'll come for me. I introduced him to Margaret. Right after we came back from Vietnam. She worked for me."

Valerie almost smiled. Even sick, Madden still talked like an automatic pistol firing.

"I'm sure Red will come for you," she said.

"If she knows it's me, Mags will make him."

A bowl of cold soup sat in the center of the kitchen table beside her. Twenty feet away, a fireplace crackled, sending the warm smell of woodsmoke into the house. Beside the fireplace, a wooden manger scene sat on the floor, its carved figures silent reminders of the season.

Valerie coughed but noticed that some of the rattle had cleared up in her chest. She touched her forehead. It felt cooler. Apparently her fever had broken.

Feeling a little better, she pulled a wadded piece of paper from her pocket. Staring at the number on the paper she wondered if she should call it.

The man who had given her the number had the power to help Michael. But Michael hadn't asked for his help. Should she place the call anyway? Michael hadn't specifically told her not to call anyone else. And how did he think he could do this all by himself? Fly to Costa Rica, protect the document, get it in the right hands at the right moment? If she had learned anything from the last few days, she had learned she couldn't do everything by herself. She needed assistance like everyone else, and so did Michael. Going it alone had almost gotten them both killed.

The paper in her fist, she punched in the number. Three rings later, the man who had called her came onto the line.

"This is Valerie Miller," she began. "You said for me to call."

"Yes I did and I'm glad you took my advice. I want to do anything I can to help. Has Father Del Rio contacted you?"

Valerie cradled the phone under her chin and shoved her hands into the pockets of her robe. "Well, yes, just a short time ago."

"And is he well?"

"Yes, okay for the moment, but he didn't talk long."

The man paused a second. Valerie jammed her hands deeper into her pockets. "He may need you," she nearly whispered. "He's in danger."

"I am aware of the risks. That's why we need to get him to safety."

"You can do that?"

"I'm sure of it. But I do need to know where he is."

Valerie coughed and wrapped her arms around her waist. Could this man hurt Michael in any way? Would he, even if he could? Was the world so evil that one such as this would choose to do wrong for his own selfish purposes? The last few days suggested it was. The violence she had witnessed told her not to trust anyone, no matter how safe they seemed. More problematic, her own failures told her to mistrust even her own judgments, to question her assumptions, to place her faith in nothing and no one, not even God. But was that any way to live?

"I know you're not sure about me," said the man, as if reading her mind. "But I'm asking you to trust me. I am who I say I am."

Out of nowhere, a rush of grief overcame Valerie and she sagged against the wall. What kind of life was it to live without faith? Certainly not one she wanted to experience. But she couldn't deny the pain of the last few days, couldn't erase it like a second grader erasing bad penmanship. So what choice did she have? Let the reality of death and evil destroy her faith in everything? Or deal with reality, come to grips with it, and find a way to trust in spite of it?

Valerie stared across the room. The fireplace cracked, and a log fell as the heat consumed it into ashes. Her eyes moved to the manger scene, to the still figures that surrounded the baby Jesus.

For the first time in her life it suddenly dawned on Valerie that God had never promised anyone, not even one as blessed as she, that faith meant the absence of suffering. Nothing in the life of Jesus suggested anything of the sort. What God had promised was strength and comfort—a divine assistance to see the believer through the pain that inevitably comes. To survive life meant walking through the dark clouds of trouble to the sunlight on the other side—not avoiding the clouds altogether. That was the story of Jesus more than anything else, life after death, not life without death.

Valerie licked her lips and took a deep breath. "He's headed to Costa Rica," she said. "To Willard Madden's estate. It's on an island a mile or so off the northwest coast, near a peninsula, a place called Golfo del Papagayo."

"I will make the necessary arrangements," said the man. "Though it may take longer than I'd like. Things get complicated around here, if you know what I mean?"

Valerie smiled slightly. "Tell me about it."

"Stay safe, Ms. Miller. Perhaps I will see you soon."

Valerie hung up the phone and ran to her bedroom to get dressed. Though her parents wouldn't understand it right here at the holidays, she had a plane to catch and she didn't want to miss it.

Sitting with Sonji at a coffee shop less than five miles from the Paphos Airport, Hans Walter squeezed the top of his head with both hands and cursed yet again. "We have to find Del Rio!" he seethed. "He killed my brother!"

"And he has the document," Sonji said, much cooler in his demeanor. "A document worth millions of dollars, money that men such as you and I must have to survive."

Walter gritted his teeth. "Yes, the money," he said. "But it's beyond that. Now it's personal."

Sonji grinned. "We will find him," he said. "And when we do, I will cut out his liver for you and hand it to you upon a silver tray."

Walter rubbed his head, his mind reeling. Where was Del Rio? Where had he gone? Walter's fingers balled into fists, and he began to pound on his temples, first with one hand and then the other. Rocking out and back against the seat, he popped himself again and again, his rage mounting with each blow that fell. As his seat rocked with his fury, a man and woman at a table a few feet away stood and eased out of the small restaurant, casting furtive glances over their shoulders as if they thought him disturbed.

For at least thirty seconds, Walter continued his pounding. But then, as suddenly as it had come, his fury dissipated. His fists fell to his side, and for a moment he stared blankly into the wall behind Sonji. Walter heaved a big sigh and then looked directly at Sonji.

"It's so simple I didn't see it," he said.

"What do you mean?"

"I have approached this the wrong way, trying to figure out where Del Rio will go. The man who hired me in the beginning possesses the resources to find Michael. Perhaps he will aid us in our efforts to reclaim the document."

"After our betrayal of his wishes?"

Walter stood and pulled a phone from his jacket pocket. "He

still wants the document. I have no doubt of that."

"But what will you tell him? How will you explain your decision to keep the scroll for yourself?"

Walter shrugged and keyed in a number. "Like the Americans say, 'Murphy's law.' I'll tell him things came up. If he wants the scroll as desperately as I think he does, and he believes I'm the guy who can get it for him, he will not ask too many questions."

"But couldn't he hire another to find it for him?"

"Sure, but that takes time, time he doesn't have. And I know more about Del Rio and the scroll than anyone else. He'll stick with me. I'm sure of it."

The phone clicked.

"Yes, this is Hans Walter. Calling from Cyprus."

The man on the other end didn't sound surprised. "Ah, Mr. Walter, I have wondered about your welfare."

"I'm fine, but others have not fared so well. My brother Alfred is dead. And another of my men as well."

"You have my sympathies. Father Del Rio is quite resourceful, it seems."

"Then you're aware of him?"

"Yes, very much so. An intelligent man, physically stout. And more innovative than either of us expected."

"He's disappeared."

"So I've gathered. Quite remarkable really. I suppose you're searching for him."

"I am." Walter paused, not sure how to go further. His benefactor picked up on his uncertainty.

"Are you asking for my assistance?"

"I am. I need money, more men."

"And you need the location of Father Del Rio, am I right?"

"Yes."

The man paused, and Walter wondered about the hesitation. Was the man having second thoughts? Had his conscience gotten to him? Would he back away from his ambitions at this most crucial moment?"

"Del Rio must believe in the authenticity of the document," Walter suggested, any attempt at subtlety jettisoned. "Otherwise he would not have taken it with him when he ran. I suspect this scroll is vital to you. And if you want it, I'm the guy who can get it for you. I did it once. I can do it again. Certainly, I need your assistance to make this happen, but you also need me."

"I'll transfer money to Paphos," he said, obviously convinced by Walter's arguments. "More than enough to supply all your needs. There's a bank just off the airport, on the main road to Larnaca. You hire the men. I know nothing about such matters."

"I'll handle it."

"You need to hurry. Everything is moving quickly."

"I'm on it."

"Del Rio is on his way to Costa Rica."

"Back there?"

"Yes. Ironic, isn't it? But he doesn't have a lot of choice. I don't know what he plans to do once he arrives, but the billionaire Madden will almost certainly meet him there. And the Miller woman as well."

"Madden is still alive?"

"Surely no thanks to you."

"His injury was unfortunate, not my intention, but things do happen."

"I regret the violence, but I'm not naïve. Now that we've gone this far, just get me the scroll. Get it, no matter what it takes."

Walter smiled at Sonji and hung up the phone. "I like what the Americans say," he told him.

"And what is that?"

Walter stared at the phone. "Politics makes strange bedfellows!"

————

Less than an hour after Hans Walter closed his cell phone, Michael Del Rio, still dressed in the garb of a Cypriot peasant, handed five hundred American dollars to his gap-toothed friend and shook his hand. Behind him, a cruise ferry made its last preparations for departure from Cyprus.

"Thank you," Michael said to the Cypriot. "You have been a good man to me."

The man smiled hugely and waved his new money at Michael. "You the good man," he said. "Crazy American."

Michael patted his front coat pocket. The Cypriot had taken his passport to an officer at the pier of Paphos. For a fee of two hundred dollars, the officer had stamped it for him. Now he had not only officially visited Cyprus, but he could also legally enter any country he chose. And he still had over a thousand dollars in his wallet, plus his credit cards.

"God bless you," said Michael, stepping onto the ferry.

"And you, my friend."

A horn sounded and Michael waved at the Cypriot as the

cruise boat pulled away from the pier. He took a deep breath and turned away from Paphos. He didn't know what had happened to the men chasing him. All he knew was that he had one more journey to make—a ferry ride to Lebanon and a flight from there to London, and on to Costa Rica. Then he would learn more about the scroll. Unless he missed his guess, he would learn more about a whole lot of things.

———

Though too busy to eat much, Nelson Randuhar had managed to shove down an orange and drink a glass of fresh tomato juice for lunch. Finished with the orange, he trashed the peelings and unwound himself from his desk chair. Holding his sticky fingers out as if to let them dry, he stepped to the bathroom that adjoined the office of the Secretariat and turned on the water.

Marchino had just left his office. Things were getting more and more complicated.

The warm water washed over Randuhar's hands, and he scrubbed them clean. If Michael Del Rio suddenly appeared on television somewhere claiming that he had a document written by John from the life of the Holy Mother, the whole world would go mad.

Randuhar splashed water over his face. He couldn't let Del Rio do that, no matter how complicated things became. He had to stay in control.

Pulling a towel from the rack beside the sink, he dried off his hands and face and stared into the mirror. He had made some decisions over the last few days, decisions that required some tough choices, choices that he might not have made at other times, under other circumstances. But a man did not always get to choose his circumstances. More often than not, they chose him. All he could do then was decide how to respond.

Randuhar studied the face in the mirror. The face of a giraffe, his boyhood friends often said to him—so long and so grave. He had not minded the childish kidding, but had seen it for what it was, a sign of affection.

Turning from the bathroom, Randuhar sighed and steepled his fingers. Not all of his recent decisions pleased him, but given the same circumstance, he knew he would make the same choices again. How could he do anything else? He had obligations, responsibilities no one but he could understand, burdens to bear that no one else carried.

He stepped back to his office and slumped into his chair. Sighing heavily, he stared at the set of pictures on the wall to his right. The pictures were similar to the ones in his personal quarters, pictures of distended stomachs, fly-covered children, cramped and squalid refugee camps. Randuhar placed his hands over his eyes and tried to block out the memories. But they refused to disappear. Instead, they stayed as fresh as ever, gaping wounds cut into his very soul, wounds that demanded that he do everything in his power to alleviate the suffering he had left behind when he departed his homeland.

To his left Randuhar felt a subtle movement, a stirring of the air. Surprised, he rocked forward and jerked to the right, his lean frame banging into the side of his desk. A shot of pain ripped through his hip.

A man he had never seen jumped at him. The man had forearms like a brick mason, legs as bowed as any he had ever seen, and a birthmark the shape of Italy on his nose. From the right, two other attackers grabbed him, their hands pulling at his throat, his wrists, and his ankles.

Randuhar tumbled to the floor, his body falling like a tall pine in the forest. His head rapped the corner of the desk as he fell, and Randuhar felt the room swirling. A pinprick of hurt jabbed into his right arm, and he realized that someone had injected him with a hypodermic needle. Within seconds everything faded toward black, and before he could stop it, Nelson Randuhar, Secretariat of the Curia of the Roman Catholic Church ceased to worry about the choices he had recently been forced to make.

THIRTY-FIVE

It took Michael almost thirty hours to make his way to Madden's island. Off the cruiser in Lebanon, he took a taxi to the Lebanese airport. Then, using his credit card, he paid for a quick change of clothes at an airport haberdashery and a ticket on the first available flight to Costa Rica, one that routed him through London.

Dressed now in khaki slacks, light hiking boots, and a burgundy, long-sleeved turtleneck, he bought a shoulder bag for a computer, stepped into a bathroom stall, and pulled the scroll from the canister that had kept it safe thus far. Knowing that airport security would automatically search any metal sphere going through their x-ray machines, he gingerly placed the scroll in the plastic sack the clerk had given him when he bought the computer bag. Placing the sack into the computer case, he threw away the canister, shouldered the computer bag, and left the bathroom. His heart in his throat, he passed through the nondeclaring line at customs, cleared the security checkpoint, and boarded the plane without a hitch.

Wolfing down the deli sandwich, apple, and cookie provided on the flight, he felt a fresh surge of energy. So far, so good.

In London he suffered through an anxious four-hour wait for his connection and another security checkpoint, but everything unfolded nicely. He caught a first-class seat on a wide-bodied jet that would take him to San Jose, capital of Costa Rica. To his relief, the seat beside him was vacant. Placing the computer bag in the unclaimed seat, he tried to get some rest but quickly found that impossible.

Though he tried, he simply couldn't unwind. As the hours

and hours of the flight droned on, his mind buzzed with a million scattered thoughts, and he couldn't doze off. A couple of times he almost slept, but the feeling that someone was watching him prevented him from relaxing enough to sink away into slumber. So he stayed awake, his head spinning, his eyes searching his fellow passengers for any signs that one of them recognized him. None did so far as he could tell.

The airline provided a substantial meal—grilled chicken and rice, mixed vegetables, roll, and lemon pie, which he swallowed with relish. Unfortunately, though, the food didn't make him any less tense. Too much had to happen in the next few hours for him to relax.

Using the back of an airline magazine and a pen he borrowed from a flight attendant, he jotted down a number of outlines for what he hoped to do. But none of them seemed certain, none completely foolproof. So he continued to plot as the airliner raced through the night sky, the stars outside the window going mostly unnoticed as he schemed. Around him others slept, but he couldn't bring himself to join them. Later, after it ended, he would sleep, but not until then.

As the plane landed, he stared out the window at the early morning and checked his watch. If he had the time zones figured out, it was about six A.M. Costa Rica time. A gray haze hung over the sky, a sharp contrast to the clear weather the last time he had come to this tiny country.

Michael rubbed his eyes. He felt as though someone had plowed over him with a tractor. As the jet reached the gate, though, he pushed his fatigue aside, shouldered the computer bag, rocked up from his seat, and climbed off the plane.

In the terminal, he bought a toothbrush, toothpaste, and shaving products. In the bathroom, he checked himself in the mirror. After almost five days without shaving, his stubble had already changed to fuzz. Within a few more days he would be well on his way to a full-fledged beard. On a whim, he tossed the shaving materials into the trash can. A beard might look good.

Finished with his teeth, he washed his face and pushed his hair back from his forehead. The mirror stared back at him once again. Can you do this, the face in the mirror asked? Can you make it stick?

Michael wrapped his toothbrush in a paper towel and shoved it into a side pocket of the computer bag. No way to know what he could do until he tried.

He took a rental car northwest to a small village near the

Golfo del Papagayo, where he hired a small charter boat to carry him the last mile and a half to Madden's island. Overhead, the sky seemed even bleaker than when he landed—a dull canopy the color of bad chalk. Gazing upward, Michael's spirits faltered as he suddenly sensed an air of gloom hanging over his head. The water was calm, but had taken on the same dead gray as the sky overhead. He leaned against the railing of the boat, and a sense of loneliness worse than any he had experienced in years draped on him like a cold blanket. It all felt so hopeless. But the boat ploughed on through the Pacific waves, its small engine puttering like a lawn mower, and Michael knew he had no choice. It was too late to turn back. Dead ahead, Madden's island loomed large on the horizon.

At the dock, a security guard dressed in black shoes, white shirt, red-and-blue tie, and gray slacks greeted the boat. Michael immediately recognized the guard.

"Hey," he yelled, climbing out of the boat. "You're Rick, aren't you?"

The guard smiled and nodded. "Yeah, back here again."

Michael pumped the man's hand. "Hope you're doing okay."

"Sure, fine. I'm a fast healer. No luggage?"

Michael shook his head. "Just me. I travel light."

Behind them, the chartered boat turned around and headed back to Costa Rica.

"Who else is here?" Michael asked, following Rick up the stone path that led to Madden's estate.

"Me and one other guard," Rick said. "Mr. Madden is on the way. Seems there's a holdup of some kind with his granddaughter. Red Cashion and Dr. Brown are with him. He sent us on down to open up the place. No one's been here since . . . well, since we were here a few days ago."

"And Valerie Miller?"

Rick cleared his throat. "Oh yeah. She's already here, taking a nap. Arrived a couple of hours ago."

Michael nodded and tried to hide his excitement. He had a lot to tell Valerie before . . .

"You want me to wake her?" Rick asked, pausing at the top of the stone path.

"Oh no, don't do that. Let her rest."

Standing on the cobbled walkway, Michael stared once again at the imposing sight of Willard Madden's Costa Rican home. A variety of lush ferns draped a green silhouette over the white exterior. Fresh-water fountains bubbled to the left and right of the expansive front porch, and a number of exotic fish floated in the pools created by the cascading water. Though he didn't know many of the names, more birds and insects than anyone could count twirped and twittered and crawled and crept and soared in the thick vegetation that surrounded the grounds. The estate literally pulsated with life.

"This place is paradise," Michael said, his voice soft.

Rick grunted. "Not today," he said.

Surprised, Michael turned to him.

"Look at the sky," Rick said, directing his eyes upward.

"Yeah, I noticed, but everybody gets a cloudy day now and again," Michael said.

"That's ash," Rick said. "From Rincon, a volcano about twenty, thirty miles east of here. It's been acting up the last couple of days."

Michael studied the sky for several seconds. "Is it dangerous?" he asked.

Rick shrugged. "Don't know exactly. But Costa Rica is a hot bed of volcanic activity. At least nine big ones, several of them pretty active. Lava, ash, earthquakes—volcanoes stir all of them up. No one has been hurt in years, I don't think, but a volcano can sure ruin a pretty day when one belches off."

Michael nodded. "I felt something last week," he said. "While I was studying the document. A quiver in the ground."

"Maybe a small earthquake," Rick said, moving onto the front porch. "They come and go. Come on in. Let's get you settled."

Following Rick up the steps, Michael took one last look at the sky. With a volcano rumbling in the distance and Valerie Miller sleeping nearby and a crazy notion churning around in his head, he felt anything but settled.

At just past five P.M. Cyprus time, Hans Walter drew himself to his full height, rubbed his head, and inspected the twelve men standing at attention before him. He knew only half of them and that made him nervous, but he had no choice but to hire the first men available. It had already taken longer than he wanted to pull everything together, and time didn't allow him the luxury of bringing in his favorite troops. In truth, he had to admit, he had been fortunate to find so many in a proximity close enough to get them in place as fast as he had. Thankfully, the political instability of the Middle East seemed to produce such men in abundance, and if one didn't care about ideology, one could recruit them pretty easily.

His hands clasped at his back, Walter paced up and down, his mind churning through the events of the last thirty plus hours. The money—more than he had imagined—had arrived at the bank as promised. With Sonji's help he had contacted these new mercenaries, prepared the airplane, thought through a plan of attack. Now it was nearing the time to launch. Walter smiled at his men and began his speech.

"You men are the best of your kind," he said, acknowledging only to himself the lie he had just spoken. "And I'm glad for the opportunity to lead you."

The men nodded. They knew the reputation of Hans Walter and were undoubtedly proud that he had called on them.

"I've already told you the purpose of our mission," Walter continued. "We're after a document—a document worth more than you can imagine."

He studied them for their reaction, but they showed no emotion. Good, they were professionals, not given to giddy outbreaks.

"Security should be minimal," he continued. "And we should have the element of surprise on our side." Walter glanced at Sonji, who nodded his agreement. Neither Del Rio nor Madden had any reason to anticipate their return to Costa Rica. For all Del Rio probably knew, no one but those he had told knew of his destination when he left Cyprus.

"We will time our departure in order to arrive in darkness," he said. "We will fly straight to our drop-off point. Under the cover of the night, we will execute a low parachute drop into the surf off an island. We will gather on the beach, consolidate our gear, then make our way to our target."

He nodded to Sonji, who killed the lights and turned on a video screen. "Here is the place," Walter said, pointing to the image of Willard Madden's home that beamed off the screen. "We will enter the house from the front side, quietly if possible, and secure the people inside. Then we will take the object we're after."

Walter paused. "Any questions?" he asked as Sonji flipped on the lights.

No one moved. But then Sonji raised his hand.

"Yes?" said Walter.

"What if we cannot enter quietly?"

Walter rubbed his head and took a deep breath. "Then we go

in, as the Americans say, 'With all guns blazing.' "

About two hours after a hearty lunch of fresh fruit, French bread, and tangy spaghetti that Rick had made, Michael heard the sound of feet on the floor. Rolling over on the sofa where he had been trying to nap, he saw Valerie Miller enter the room. She wore a pair of soft tan slacks, a navy pullover sweater, and tennis shoes. Though she seemed paler and a bit thinner than when he last saw her, she still looked stunning.

Jumping up, Michael brushed back his hair and stood at attention, his hands at his sides. Valerie came to a stop too, and for several awkward moments they just stood there and stared at each other. Michael started to speak but found he was tongue-tied. To his relief, Valerie finally broke the silence.

"You need a shave," she said, her eyes dancing.

Michael scratched his chin. "It's my new look. Do you like it?"

"Are you going for Jeremiah Johnson? Mountain man and all?"

"I don't know. I thought it looked more like Moses, you know . . . the Charlton Heston version. You don't like it?" he asked, his lips in a mock pout.

"I don't know for sure," she said, stepping toward him. "Let me see." She rubbed a hand against his cheek. "It's soft enough," she said. "I can handle it."

Michael opened his arms, and Valerie snuggled up against him, her head on his shoulder.

His hands quivering, Michael touched her cheek and lifted her face toward his and almost kissed her. But then the implications of such a thing hit him squarely between the eyes, and he looked away quickly and coughed. Apparently unaware of his discomfort, Valerie nestled deeper against his chest, her breathing soft and warm on his neck. For several long seconds, they held each other that way, two people who cared about each other gaining strength and comfort in one another's arms.

Michael closed his eyes and let the sensation of the moment wash over him, its intimacy more intense than anything he had ever experienced. His heart thumping, he forgot his reservations and gave himself to the experience, to the joy of a woman's embrace. If his plan unfolded like he imagined, his days as a priest would end anyway. So why not give his feelings free reign for once? The opportunity to hold Valerie this way would probably never come again either. So why not revel in her warmth for these few short moments?

Inside his head, Michael knew he had crossed a line somewhere, had violated, at least in his emotions, a part of his priestly oath. But, for the life of him, he didn't feel guilty about it. Though he was a priest, he was also a man, and the feelings he had for Valerie Miller were as pure as any feelings he had ever had about anyone or anything. Would God condemn him for the love he now felt for the first time in his life?

Though feeling extremely awkward, Michael inhaled it all, the smell of her perfume, the softness of her skin, the rhythm of her breathing. He knew he shouldn't, yet he imagined himself with her for the rest of his life, sitting in a rocking chair on a big porch, changing the diapers of their children, taking long walks as the sun dropped lower in the sky. . . .

He sighed as his imagination settled down, and he came back to reality. The truth was that none of that could ever happen— no way, no how. Too many hurdles to jump. Michael released her and stepped back a pace.

"It's hard to remember you're a priest," she said softly, smiling at him.

"Not as hard as being one sometimes."

They stood silently a moment, but then before Michael changed the subject, "You get any rest?"

She smiled again. "Yeah, and I needed it. Getting over a bad cold."

"I thought you looked a little tired."

"I'm better. Slept like a newborn baby for about three hours."

"It's your clean conscience," he teased. "Nothing to keep you awake."

Valerie rubbed the stubble on his face. "Nothing but worrying about you. It's been crazy the last few days, not knowing what happened, how you were, whether you were—"

Michael pressed his fingers to her lips. "It's okay," he soothed. "I'm alive and well."

"But McAuley?"

Michael lowered his gaze. "Let's walk," he said. "We've got a lot to talk about." He led her out the back door and past the pool at the rear of Madden's home. Stepping through the shrubs at the edge of the yard, he came to a spot the size of a racquetball court almost totally secluded from the house by a high stand of dark green hedges. The clearing overlooked the cliffs and the ocean below.

"I found this place earlier today," he said, taking a seat on a flat rock in the center of the open space. "Seemed like a good place to do some thinking."

Valerie took a seat beside him. "I guess you've got a lot to think about," she said.

Michael grinned slightly. "More than you can imagine."

"Tell me about it."

"You sure you want to hear?"

"Nothing in the whole world I'd rather do," she said. "Nothing in the whole world."

Michael stared up at the overcast sky. "I've got the scroll," he began. "But McAuley is dead because of it. As are Yoseph and his bodyguards. Plus one or two of the creeps that Red Cashion ran into at the Ceylan Hotel might be dead too. I don't know. And Madden, though he's alive, has been badly hurt. And I heard shots fired at the airport in Cyprus. Who knows how many were killed or injured there? Everything is a mess, a sick, sad deadly mess. I feel like I'm in the middle of a movie or something. People keep dying. Good guys, bad guys, it doesn't matter. The effort to find this document has led to nothing but bloodshed. Something that should be a blessing has become a curse."

"You can't blame the killing on the scroll," Valerie said. "It's the people involved with it."

"But they kill for *it*," insisted Michael. "So it really is the scroll. If the document didn't exist, none of this would have happened. It's brought nothing but pain and suffering."

He leaned down, picked up a rock, and tossed it over the cliffs.

"There's nothing you could do to stop any of it," Valerie said. "Sometimes things just happen. It's nobody's fault, really. It's like one of those waves." She pointed to the ocean. "They come our way and we're powerless to stop them. All we can do is react."

Michael stood and walked to the edge of the cliffs. The breeze from the ocean whipped through his hair, pushing it off his face and collar.

"I killed a man," he said to the ocean. "Walter's brother. I took his head in my hands, and I twisted it hard, and his neck snapped like I had broken a pretzel."

Valerie stood too, eased over to him, and stroked the back of his hair. "I'm sorry you had to do that," she said. "But I'm sure you had no choice. He would have killed you. You know that."

"It's not the first time," Michael said.

Valerie withdrew her hand. "Not the first time?" she asked.

"No, not the first time. And the other time it *was* my fault." The wind picked up against Michael's face and thinned out his voice. He seemed to be speaking into a vast expanse now, his vision blurred as he stared at the sky, his voice tiny against the cliffs and the water beyond them.

"I was seventeen at the time, and I hadn't been driving long. My whole family was headed out to eat after my brother's baseball game, a birthday dinner for me. I had spent most of the game in the parking lot with a few of my friends, smoking . . . you know . . . marijuana. I was high, 'spaced out' as we used to say."

"Your parents didn't smell it on your breath?"

Michael sighed. "Guess not, but that's not surprising. In those days, a lot of parents hadn't ever smelled the stuff, didn't know it when they sniffed it. Plus, my folks thought I was perfect, a good Catholic boy, a straight A student. They never dreamed I would do anything like that! I chewed some gum, ate some popcorn. They didn't have a clue."

He eased a step closer to the cliffs, leaving Valerie two paces behind. For several seconds, neither spoke. Michael stared out over the cliffs. At his feet he noticed a steel cable hooked into the rock at the top of the escarpment. He squatted and touched it, then noticed that it led down and over the rocks toward the ocean. A low rumble sounded from the east, and Michael glanced up and squinted through the haze toward the sound.

"Must be the volcano," he said, standing and facing Valerie again.

"Is there one active?"

"Apparently so," he said, indicating the sky. "That's why we have all this haze."

"Finish your story," Valerie said. "That's what you came out here to do."

Michael nodded, walked back to the rock in the clearing, propped a foot on it. "Like I said, I was spaced. And it had just rained, not hard, but like you get in late spring—a gentle little shower that had come and gone. Since I had just started driving, my dad put me behind the wheel. He wanted me to get experience on wet roads."

"And you—"

Michael threw up his hand to stop her interruption. "We came to a curve, not too bad, but sharp enough. I was doing about fifty-five, the speed limit, nothing out of line. I saw a car coming from the opposite direction, headed right at me. He was passing another car and was in my lane across the yellow line. I swerved to the right, had a pretty good shoulder on the highway. My car lost traction on the slick road. The other car missed me on the left. I fought to get control of the car, but everything went crazy then. My wheels kept sliding and the car dipped off the shoulder of the road, then skidded toward an embankment. I jerked the wheel to the left but couldn't stop the crash—the dope had slowed my reactions. The car dove downward . . . I wrestled it as hard as I could, but nothing happened. It just kept going—down the hill, down through the trees. The car hit a deserted house at the bottom of the hill and ploughed straight into the brick of an old chimney. I slammed into the steering wheel; it knocked me out. When I came to, I was on the ground, twenty feet away from the car. I smelled smoke and tried to get up, tried to get to the car, tried to help . . . I heard someone screaming, and I crawled through the grass. My face was bleeding . . . I smelled gas. I crawled toward the car . . . but then it exploded. I saw smoke and fire rising out of the car, then I lost consciousness again. The next time I woke up the screaming had stopped. I was in the hospital, the only survivor."

Valerie walked over and patted his back. "It wasn't your fault," she soothed. "The other car caused the wreck. You did all you could. . . ."

"But if I hadn't been high, my reactions would have been faster, clearer!" Michael protested, moving away from her. "I could have controlled the car . . . could have . . ." His voice trailed away.

"You were just a kid. Kids make mistakes, even good kids!"

"But the car exploded!" he shouted, his face at the ocean again. "They burned to death. . . ." He started to sob. "All because of me . . . all because of me." Tears ran down his cheeks now, and his body shook with grief. From behind, Valerie came to him and encircled her arms around his waist. He turned to her and laid his head on her shoulder and poured out his sorrow. For several minutes, she just held him, her hands stroking the back of his head.

"You did all you could," she soothed. "You were just a kid. You did all you could . . ."

Slowly, his sobs subsided to a trickle of tears and he raised his head. "I almost killed myself that summer," he said. "Probably would have if not for my uncle, Cardinal Roca. He flew to Missouri and stayed with me for weeks, and then took me back to Rome. Gradually, over the weeks and months that followed, I began to come out of the depression that had settled over me. In the rigors of the Church, I found a home again, a structure that gave me a reason to live. I didn't realize it then, but the Church became my family, the mother and father and brother I no longer had. And, again not recognizing it at the time, I intuitively decided that serving the God my parents loved so much might, in some small way, offer some atonement for my sin."

"So you became a priest."

"Started the process that fall," he said. "Seemed the right thing to do. And up until now"—he stepped back and smiled at her—"I've never doubted the decision, never looked back."

"But now you have some questions," Valerie said.

"That's an understatement if I ever heard one. I'm in a full-blown crisis."

"Join the club."

"You too?"

"Sure, Norman Rockwell, remember? He's not hanging on the wall anymore. Someone ripped down the frame, pulled out the painting, and tore it up."

"Seeing violence and death isn't easy, is it?"

"That's just part of it. The broken engagement plays in too. It hurt more than I've let myself admit. And remember Ambassador Bremer?"

"Sure."

"Well, he fired me."

"Fired you?"

"Just like that, he took me off the job the minute I came back to Rome."

"But that's not—"

"Not fair? No it's not. But my problems seem pretty lame compared to some others I've seen in the last few days. Madden's cancer, his granddaughter's leukemia. How's that for bad family genes? Then there's Red Cashion's wife."

"What's wrong with Cashion's wife?"

"She's paralyzed from a horse that threw her. It's all too much. There's tragedy everywhere I look. Puts a dent in the faith, if you know what I mean."

Michael sat down on the rock again, and Valerie joined him.

"I've never had Norman Rockwell," he said. "At least not since my seventeenth birthday. Must have been nice."

"It was. But then reality sets in, and it's shown for what it is—fake, superficial. And a faith built on it is just as false, a cotton candy religion. It looks good, but when you bite into it, there's no substance."

"So now you're trying to adjust," he said.

"I'm trying to find out what God has to say about all of this . . . this death and dying."

"If you get an answer, let me know—"

From behind, Michael suddenly heard a familiar, but still dim sound. He swiveled around and stared at the sky for several seconds. The sound came closer and he recognized it now—the *chomp, chomp, chomp* of a helicopter approaching. Squinting into the haze, he saw a speck in the sky headed their way. "Must be Madden," he said, facing Valerie again.

"I called him and Cashion like you asked me," she said.

Michael took her hand and squeezed it. "Thanks for helping me," he offered. "And thank you for coming too."

"I wouldn't dream of doing anything else," she said. "I'm in this almost as deep as you are."

Michael watched the helicopter approach.

"What are you going to do?" Valerie asked. "Why did you bring us all here?"

Michael stood and kissed her hand. "I think you know the answer to that," he said. "I'm going to see if I can bring some relief to some of the suffering. Going to see if this scroll can do something besides get people killed."

"You think the scroll can heal—?"

"I don't know," Michael said. "I don't know what it can do. But I think it's time we found out, don't you? If I can keep one person alive, then who knows, maybe there was a reason that McAuley died and I didn't, my family died and I didn't. It's survivor's syndrome, a need to know that I haven't lived in vain."

Valerie stood beside him. "I don't know what will happen with Katie," she said. "But if she gets healed, it's not the scroll, not really."

"What do you mean?" Michael asked.

The chopping of the helicopter drew nearer.

"Healing is the Lord's work," Valerie said. "Anything else— a person, a vial of oil, a document from the heart of Mary—any of that is only an instrument of God's power, a tool of Jesus."

Michael nodded. "I can go with that," he said, remembering the moment he found his wallet and passport in Walter's leather bag. "If she gets healed, I'm willing to give God the credit."

"God's not interested in getting credit," Valerie said, her voice edging higher to be heard over the increasing noise of the chopper. "God is interested in people, in you."

"You *are* a good Baptist girl, aren't you?" Michael shouted, smiling at her.

"I do try."

"Well, I tell you what!" called Michael, stepping away from the clearing. "Right now I'm as interested in God as God is interested in me! This whole episode has made me take a closer look at the whole notion of faith, what it means, how it works. I want to know what God can do with Katie!"

"But what happens then?" pressed Valerie. "What happens after you know?"

"I don't know what happens after that," he shouted, the helicopter hovering over the landing pad in the backyard now, the breeze from it blowing toward them. "But somehow, I believe I'll do the right thing when the moment comes! I've got to trust that somehow, someway I'll know what to do, what course to follow!"

The helicopter touched down on the pad, and Michael and Valerie stepped out of the secluded clearing. As he left the area by the cliffs, Michael suddenly thought of the steel cable hanging from the rocks and a flash of insight hit him. Hans Walter and his men had left the cable there after they used it to scale the rocks to invade Madden's home!

Ducking to greet the group climbing out of the helicopter, it also came to Michael that just as a man could use a cable to climb up and invade, so also could a man use a cable to descend and disappear.

THIRTY-SIX

The group gathered in the great room in the back of Madden's house at just after five P.M. Dr. Cindy Brown wheeled Madden in on a hospital bed, and Red Cashion took up a spot like a guard dog at his right shoulder. An intravenous fluid line snaked down into Madden's left arm from a bag attached to a metal pole beside his bed. Brown, holding Madden's hand, stood beside her patient on the same side as the bag, her blue eyes alert. Madden, at least ten pounds lighter than the last time Michael saw him, seemed practically transparent, his skin as thin as Saran Wrap. To Michael's surprise, though, the billionaire's granddaughter wasn't with him.

Punching a button, Madden brought the bed to a sitting angle, cleared his throat, and addressed the group, his words fired as usual in rapid fashion.

"I'm not the one who brought you here this time," he began, his voice noticeably weaker than the last time Michael heard him. "You can thank Father Del Rio for that. He's had quite an adventure since we saw him a few days ago."

Everyone turned expectantly to Michael, who sat on the leather sofa next to Valerie. Rubbing his palms together, he stood and walked to the center of the room. "I called Valerie," he said, "after McAuley and I escaped from Walter. We were in Cyprus. McAuley . . . McAuley didn't make it. I had to leave . . . leave him there." He paused, cleared his husky throat, then continued. "At first I didn't know what to do, where to go. But then an idea began to evolve—a strange idea for a guy like me, a person so tied to . . . well, so unaccustomed to acting spontaneously, doing anything as an individual. As you know, I'm tied to a system to the Church. I'm not prone to making decisions on my own . . . decisions like this.

"But anyway, I got this idea. I wanted something good to come from all of this, something better than all the killing. So I asked Valerie to call Madden and tell him to bring his granddaughter."

He propped a foot on the fireplace hearth, then began to speak quietly again, almost as if talking to himself, trying to convince himself.

"Maybe it's stupid, I don't know, but I wanted Mr. Madden to bring Katie here so we could . . . I don't know . . . it does sound stupid now when I say it, but I've come to the conclusion that the scroll might really be authentic. Of course I don't know that for sure, but maybe it does convey some kind of unusual power, some kind of—" and here he paused and stared at Valerie— "some kind of power from God." He left the fireplace now and walked to the back of the room, his eyes staring out the wall of glass.

"I mean, think about it—all the signs. Remember how I couldn't speak right after I read it? And there's the sensation you get when you touch it. It's like a hot water bottle or something . . . warm and tingling." He turned back to the group.

"Pain disappears too. You saw McAuley's fingers, all broken and everything." He held out his left hand, fingers pointed to the ceiling as if to demonstrate. "But McAuley said they didn't hurt anymore, said nothing hurt anymore, not his arthritic knees, not his head, nothing after he touched the document. He thought it was probably just the effects of adrenalin, but I experienced the same thing—my headache, my ribs where Walter kicked me— all the pain disappeared when I touched the scroll."

He walked back to Valerie and stood behind her, facing the rest of the group. "I know it sounds crazy, but the document seems to hold some kind of energy in it. Maybe it's my imagination, maybe it's what I want to believe . . . I don't know, but it radiates this force, and that force seems to energize the body and eliminate pain."

"It's the power of faith," Valerie said, her voice no more than a whisper. "Maybe God is using this scroll as an instrument of holy grace. And you wanted to see if it could help Katie."

Michael nodded and the room fell silent for several moments. Michael stepped back to the fireplace. "The scroll speaks of healing in several passages, and I wanted to try to read from it and let Katie touch it. It's the wildest thing I've ever done, totally out of character, but somehow, at the time, it seemed the right thing to do—bring her here, see what might happen. But now . . ."

"But Katie's not here," Madden said, his head resting on his pillow. "Her parents wouldn't let her come." He sounded defeated. The group looked stunned. "Can you believe that?" he continued. "They said she was too ill to travel. They couldn't take the chance. I told them she was too ill not to take the chance. But they wouldn't budge. So I came without her. Thought maybe I'd take the scroll back to her." He stared at Michael, his expression obviously seeking a positive response to his suggestion.

"I don't know about that," Michael said, recovering from his surprise at Katie's absence. "This was my best shot, and it didn't work out. So I don't know where to go from here, what to do. Maybe I should just go back to the Vatican and turn it in to the Church." He sat down on the edge of the hearth and dropped his head into his hands, his confusion palpable.

"You can use it for Mr. Madden," suggested Cindy Brown. "See if—"

Madden held up a hand, cutting her off. "No, I don't want to do that," he said, patting her gently on the arm.

"But why?"

"No, Cindy, it's okay. I've done a lot of thinking about this since our first episode a few days ago. If this document is real, if it truly is what it claims to be, then I guess it's holy, spiritual, or whatever you want to call it. And if that's the case, it shouldn't be used for the wrong purposes. Father Del Rio is right about that. Trying to help Katie is fine. That's, you know, an act of love. But to use it like some magic bottle with a genie inside for purely selfish reasons, well . . . I don't want to do that. Maybe I'm crazy, but the closer I get to dying, the less ego-centered I am. If that big *IT*, whatever that is, wants to keep me alive, then okay, I'll accept that gladly. But it just seems wrong for me to use this scroll to save my own sorry backside. Probably wouldn't work anyway if you come at it from such a selfish motive."

He closed his eyes, obviously weary from the effort of speaking. Outside the house, a low roll of what sounded like thunder filtered through the ground.

"Why not take it to Katie?" suggested Red Cashion, ignoring the rumble from the volcano. "Take Father Del Rio and the scroll to San Francisco."

Madden waved his hand over the group. "Only if Father Del Rio agrees," he whispered. "He did his best to try to help my

granddaughter, risked his own life to give her this chance. I respect that. So I'll do nothing with the scroll he doesn't want me
to do. He's suffered too much, risked too much for me to force him
to do anything. If he doesn't want to take it to San Francisco,
then we'll all just spend the night here, then head in our different directions tomorrow morning. He can do with the scroll
whatever he wants. I don't want it on my conscience that I kidnapped a holy man and forced my will on him. Not good karma
for a man about to die, know what I mean? It's up to the padre."

Again, everyone turned to Michael. Valerie stood from the
sofa, crossed the room, and took his hand in hers, not bothering
to hide her affection for him from the rest of the group. But Michael didn't speak. This time, though, his failure to talk wasn't
because he couldn't. This time he didn't respond because the
idea that had just popped into his head completed the puzzle he
had been trying to work out ever since he escaped from Hans
Walter. If it worked, it would mean that everything changed,
everything he knew and trusted, everything he had previously
been. He closed his eyes for a moment and felt the warmth of
Valerie's hand in his. If his idea worked, it changed that too, ir-
revocably and forever.

But he had no doubt that his idea was a good one. In fact, in
spite of how it would alter his life, the idea that had come to him
felt so right that for the first time in his life he felt confident that
God had spoken to him. For the first time in his life, he believed
God had given him a direct, personal word about what he should
do. And the sheer fear of that belief and what it called him to
risk left him tongue-tied and speechless.

THIRTY-SEVEN

Michael trudged quietly up the stairs at just past midnight. For the last two hours he had been alone, walking up and down the well-manicured paths that surrounded Madden's estate, trying to come to a final decision about his next step. Though an increasingly noticeable cloud of volcanic ash had finally obliterated the last light from the moon, and the ground occasionally trembled a bit with another distant eruption, Michael hardly noticed. Too many confusing ideas swirled in his head for him to pay much attention to anything else.

In the hours after the earlier meeting broke up, everyone encouraged him to return to San Francisco with Madden, to go to Katie and try to help her. But Michael hesitated. It wasn't that he didn't want to do everything possible for the little girl. Anyone with any compassion at all would want to do that. But he feared what would happen in America if and when he landed there. Could he and Madden even get the document to Katie? Or would American officials, surely alerted by the State Department to watch for him, take the scroll into their possession the moment he landed on United States soil? For that matter, the authorities might arrest him as well. At least one death in Cyprus, maybe two, could be blamed on him—to say nothing of the mayhem he had witnessed in Istanbul—and who knew how American authorities treated international incidents like that?

Madden had assured him he could prevent tie-ups like those, but Michael wasn't confident he could. When the government got involved all bets were off, even the bets made by one of the richest men in the world.

At the top of the stairs, Michael paused and admitted one

more reason for his hesitance to go to San Francisco. He feared what he might find out there. If the scroll did somehow lead to Katie's healing, what would he do then? Turn the document over to the United States government? But for what purpose? Or should he give it to the Church? That possibility raised the same question.

As the only man alive who had read the scroll, neither of those solutions appealed to him. In fact, he finally concluded, neither was a viable option at this point. If the document truly possessed healing powers, was the world ready for it? Was he? Or would it cause more problems than it solved? But what if it wasn't authentic? Well, that raised some questions too. If it did nothing, and someone later proved it a hoax, then he could probably go back to what he had been—a teacher of the New Testament, a scholar of some international reputation, a Catholic priest in the safe environs of the Holy Church.

But what sense did that make? He had already admitted his lack of faith in any kind of personal God. Yes, he had been reevaluating that conclusion over the last few days, but if the scroll proved false . . . well what did that do to his considerations? Was this new search for spiritual truth tied completly to the scroll? Or was something else going on in him? But if he couldn't settle his doubts, how could he teach the New Testament anymore? How could he articulate something he didn't accept as true? And what about the fact that he had killed Alfred? Would the Church, his university, even take him back?

His head down, Michael turned left, away from his room, and slumped toward the set of double doors at the end of the hallway, near the back of the house. As he reached the doors, Rick stepped forward to greet him.

"You're up late, aren't you?" asked the security man.

"Yeah, tough to sleep," Michael said.

Rick nodded. "It's all pretty crazy, I guess. Trying to figure out what to do."

"You got that right. Is Mr. Madden asleep?"

"Don't know. He's up and down at odd hours these days. The medicines he takes keep his system pretty messed up." He shook his head. "I hate cancer."

"I know what you mean. Think I could see him for a few minutes?"

Rick shrugged. "Let me see if he's awake." He disappeared through the doors. Michael stroked his stubbly beard and waited. A moment later, Red Cashion stuck his head out.

"You want to see Mad?" he asked.

"Yeah, if it's possible. Is he awake?"

Red stepped back and indicated that Michael should enter. Rick passed him on the way out. Michael nodded to the guard, then walked farther into Madden's personal suite—a series of several rooms that ran left and right off the main living area, where he now stood.

"In here," Red said, leading Michael into a bedroom on the right. "He's pretty alert, but I don't think you should stay long."

"I'll be quick," Michael said.

In the bedroom, he saw two beds. Dr. Cindy Brown sat on the end of one, still dressed in her wrinkled white doctor's coat. Michael nodded to her, then gave his attention to Willard Madden. The billionaire lay prone on a bed twenty feet from Dr. Brown's, his gray hair splashed out on his pillow, his face thin and haggard. The ever present plastic bag hung to his left.

Madden had DEATH written on him like a bad tattoo, and Michael wondered if he should bother him in his weakened condition. But Madden's eyes were open, and he stared at Michael with an intensity that belied his illness.

"Father Del Rio," Madden said. "Shouldn't you be resting?"

"Shouldn't you?"

"Oh, I expect I'll get a good long rest soon enough." He chuckled slightly. "What's on your mind?"

Michael glanced at Dr. Brown. "I don't know how to say this, but . . . well, this is something not everyone should hear."

"Cindy has my total confidence," Madden said. "She hears what I hear."

"But it could be dangerous for her," countered Michael. "I don't think you want that."

Madden punched his bed controls and raised himself to a sitting position.

"How dangerous?"

Michael shook his head. "She doesn't need to get involved."

Madden turned to Cindy. "Go on," he said. "I'll call you back in a few minutes."

For a moment, Michael thought she might argue, but then she seemed to change her mind. Yielding to Madden's wishes, she stood and kissed him on the cheek with an affection that was obviously more than professional. "I'll be right outside," she said. "Call me if you need me." She stalked out of the room, casting a less-than-appreciative glance at Michael as she left.

"Does Red need to leave too?" Madden asked Michael.

"I'm not leaving," Red said, his jaw set. "I don't care what you say."

Michael grinned sheepishly. "No, he needs to stay. If you accept my proposition, he's going to be very much involved."

Madden's eyes widened, and his body took on a heightened sense of energy. "You got a proposition for me?" he asked, sitting up straight.

"Oh yeah," Michael said. "It's quite a deal, maybe the biggest one you've ever considered."

From somewhere deep within, Madden summoned a fresh reserve of energy. "Help me up, Red," he grunted. "I don't want to hear this lying down."

With Red's help, Madden put on a robe and took a seat in a high-backed chair. He motioned Michael and Red to a nearby sofa. Leaning forward, Madden winked and said. "Now tell me your idea. Then I'll be the judge of whether it's the biggest deal I've ever considered or not."

Michael rubbed his palms together and began to talk, unfolding all that had happened to him and what he wanted to do about it. Beside him, Red Cashion bit off a chew of tobacco and softly began to hum. This time Michael recognized the tune. "Like a bridge over troubled waters, I will lay me down . . ."

For some reason the humming soothed Michael as he described his idea, made him remember the times his dad had sung him to sleep as a boy, the strong arms that used to hold him, back before he became a teenager and started to drive, back before the awful night of the wreck. Red moved seamlessly from one song to another, over and over again as Michael spoke. After a while the humming became as much a part of the background as the roll of ocean waves on the beach, the kind of constant, comforting, resonant presence that filled up the empty spaces in a person's very soul. Minutes became ten, then twenty and thirty before Michael came to the summation of his outrageous notion.

"So that's it," he concluded. "That's the proposition." He leaned back and crossed his legs, glad to have shared with someone else what he had held within himself for too long. For several interminable seconds, no one said anything else. Even Cashion's humming came to a stop. But then Willard Madden pushed his emaciated body up from his chair and came to stand beside Michael. Placing a bony hand on Michael's shoulder, Madden bent over and hugged his neck.

"I don't know if it'll work or not," he whispered. "But you're right about one thing. It is the biggest deal I've ever considered."

Emotionally drained, Michael stared at the floor for what seemed like an eternity, thinking through for one final time what he had just suggested. So far as he could see, it was the only thing that made sense, and it came to him then that perhaps this idea would fulfill his destiny somehow, that it would bring his entire life since the tragic night of his family's death to full circle. Maybe this was why God had created him, why God had brought him safely to this point.

He couldn't help but smile at the thought. Apparently, Valerie was rubbing off on him. He hadn't even questioned whether or not God had created him, and he had actually assumed that God had played a part in his escape from Walter and his safe return to Costa Rica.

He looked back up at Cashion and Madden. Madden patted him on the back and eased back to the edge of his bed. Michael inhaled and exhaled slowly as he watched the sick billionaire. His whole life depended on Madden's answer to his next question. Madden pulled his robe tighter around his waist and shivered slightly. Michael didn't see any reason to wait any longer.

"Will you help me, Mr. Madden?" he asked.

Madden grunted, then smiled widely. "Oh yeah," he said. "You've made me an offer I can't refuse." He turned to Cashion. "You with me on this, Red? I can't do it without you."

Cashion dribbled tobacco into his ever present cup. "I'm here for you, Mad," he said. "Always have been. Mags would kill me if I said no."

Cashion turned to Michael. "This is a good thing you're saying," he offered. "The kind of thing a man should do."

"Does it make you feel better about priests?" Michael teased, glad for the chance to ease his tension.

"At least one of them."

Michael nodded and turned serious once more. "I don't know why this has fallen to me," he said. "I'd give anything if it hadn't, if it had come to someone else, someone more prepared. But it didn't, so I've got to deal with it. Whether I'm up to it or not, I don't know. But somehow, and this sounds insane for me to say, somehow I sense in my gut that God is in this. And that's not easy for me to admit. It's not the way I've always thought God worked. But the last few days, well, things I can't explain have happened, things that seem, well, I don't know, almost supernatural. If God is in this, then it'll work. If not . . ."

"If not, then we haven't lost anything," Red said.

"Except maybe Michael's life," Madden said. "Lots of people want this scroll."

"Yeah, well, I'm supposed to protect him," Red said.

"I'm counting on you to do that," Michael said, grinning. "I'm counting on it big-time."

Red spat into his cup again, then stood and walked to Michael, extending his hand. Michael stood to meet him, taking his hand in both palms. Madden pushed up from his bed once more, holding the side to stay balanced. Now the three men stood in the center of the room—one a billionaire with perhaps only a few days left to live, one a broken down detective with only a few reasons for living, and one a frightened priest who had just decided on a new way of life. Arms around one another's shoulders, they started to laugh and to cry all at the same time—a sense of relief and anticipation driving them to momentary insanity. Though each of them knew that Michael's suggestion was a longshot, it was enough to give them all hope.

Outside the window of Willard Madden's suite, an orange splash suddenly flickered into the eastern sky. No more than twenty-five miles away, the Rincon de la Vieja Volcano pushed its hot lava higher and higher into the air as if to celebrate the pact made by the three men. But the men, too wrapped up in the companionship of the moment, failed to notice the fiery display.

THIRTY-EIGHT

At ten minutes after two A.M., Hans Walter led his men onto the uninhabited beach just less than a half mile down the sloped, cobbled walkway that led to Willard Madden's home. The moon, blanketed by a sullen cloak of volcanic ash, offered no light to those who might have seen him, even if they had been watching for his coming.

"Stow the rafts," Walter quietly commanded as he slipped out of his wet suit. "We may need them later."

"Only if we can't commandeer Madden's helicopter," whispered Sonji, his hands busy unwrapping a cache of automatic weapons from their waterproof packaging.

"Or a couple of his boats," agreed Walter. "But no reason to get careless. If things go wrong, the rafts can get us back to the mainland." Our pilot will refuel and wait for us there," continued Walter, almost as if to reassure himself.

"Everything is as it should be," Sonji said, now dressed in a tight black body suit and light boots, his face covered with liquid darkness. "The men made the flight well. All is in readiness."

Walter slipped an AK–47 over his shoulder and examined the troops now assembled on the beach, their gear ready, their nerves on edge. For a hastily assembled crew, they had meshed well through the long night. After a final briefing on board the aircraft that had carried them over the ocean, they had dropped their properly encased weapons and dry clothing into the water. Within seconds, they also tossed in three rafts. The men followed the rafts. Now they were dressed and poised.

"You know what to do," Walter said quietly, his chest jutted forward as he slowly walked up and down through his men. "I will go first, survey the area, make sure all is quiet. Sonji will lead the rest of you five minutes later. You will come in from all sides and surround the house. If all stays calm, we'll go in with two groups, one from the back, one from the front. Once in the house, half of you will follow me up the stairs to the sleeping quarters on the third floor, and half will stay down with Sonji to handle Madden's security forces."

"What about electrical surveillance?" asked a tall man from the rear of the group. "Automatic alarms?"

Walter choked back his impatience and came to a dead stop. He had already covered this. "We put them out of commission last week," he said softly. "I'm certain Madden has had no opportunity to repair them. They will have no warning. Now, are we ready?"

The men stood up straighter, their faces resolute. Each man signaled his readiness.

Walter took a deep breath. If all went according to plan, the evil priest Del Rio would be dead within the hour.

————

His hands shaky but resolute, Michael Del Rio folded the note he had just written and slipped it into an envelope. Standing from the desk in his bedroom, he licked the envelope, sealed it, and patted it against his thigh for a second. Exhaling a quick puff of breath, he slipped the envelope into his back pocket, stepped to the bed, and unzipped the black computer bag he found lying there. Inside the bag, he saw the Ephesian document, now wrapped carefully in a white cloth and encased in a triple layer of zippered plastic bags.

Closing the computer bag again, he grabbed a lightweight backpack from the closet, shoved the computer bag into it, slipped the backpack over his shoulders, and moved out of his bedroom into the hallway. An ankle level nightlight cast a yellow glow onto his face. For a second, he stood still, his ears pricked for any sound. But he heard nothing. The place was as quiet as a graveyard at midnight. Michael grinned. Cashion had taken care of everything, including security.

Stopping at Valerie's bedroom, he bent down and started to shove the envelope under the door, but then hesitated. Was this the right way? The fair thing? Maybe not. Maybe it was dangerous. He pulled back the envelope and studied it in the glow of the hallway. Maybe it was better if she never knew.

Upright again, he slipped the envelope into the pocket of the

navy warm-up suit he was wearing and stepped quietly down
the hallway and onto the spiral staircase. Beneath his feet he
felt a slight tremor, then heard a low rumble. He paused for a
split second as another small tremor from the volcano quivered
through the house. The rumble rolled through his feet but
stopped within seconds. His breath quicker now, Michael eased
down the stairs and through the kitchen at the back of the house.
Still no security, just as Red had promised. Nothing and no one
to keep him from taking care of the business at hand.

In the backyard, he flicked on a small flashlight and turned
back toward Madden's house for one final look. His eyes moved
to the balcony on the left side just over the pool, the balcony
where he had had his last conversation with Valerie. . . .

———————

A light breeze blew through Valerie's auburn hair as he held
her in his arms, his heart heavy with the weight of his upcoming
actions. She told him more about her mom and dad, about her
childhood living in exotic places all over the world. She told him
about the time she played Mozart for the first time and how it
blew her away, and the time she failed her first calculus test at
Duke. She told him about the man who asked her to marry him,
and how she said yes at first because she so loved the idea of love,
but how she broke it off a few months later because neither of
them loved the other enough to spend any real time together.

As Valerie talked, Michael became quieter and quieter. He
listened to her words like a starving man picking apples and
stuffing them into a sack to hoard until a day when he knew he
would have no tree from which to gather them. He listened to
her talk and wished for all his soul that he had a tape recorder
to capture her cadences, the rhythm of her laughter, the tone of
her enthusiasm. But he didn't, so he said nothing lest he miss a
single syllable that fell from her lips.

After a while, she stopped her own talking and turned toward
him, her eyes sparkling.

"You've been awfully quiet tonight," she said.

"I'm the strong, silent type, remember?"

"You and Moses, right?" She reached out a hand and rubbed
his beard.

They fell silent again. Michael stood and walked to the
balcony, resting his elbows on the railing. A sense of heaviness
came over him, and he lowered his head and stared out toward

the cliffs past the backyard. He heard Valerie stand up behind him, and he turned to face her.

"You okay?" she asked, reading his emotions far better than he liked.

He shrugged and swallowed hard.

"What is it, Michael?" Valerie pressed. "What is it you're not telling me?"

He shook his head. "It's a lot of things, a lot of things I've got to settle."

She stepped to him and both of them leaned over the balcony, staring out at the backyard.

"I'm just confused," he said. "So much has happened."

"Don't bottle it all up," she said. "Maybe I can help."

Michael shook his head. "It's complicated," he said. "I've got to work it out myself."

Valerie touched his shoulder and pulled him around to face her. "You're not alone in this," she said. "You've got me. You've got other friends here. And you've got the Lord too. I know you expect me to say that, but it's true. God wants to guide you through this."

"I thought you weren't sure about the Lord right now," Michael said. "All the suffering and everything."

Valerie pinched him on the hand. "Well, sure, all this raises some questions, but you don't stop flying just because one airplane crashes. At least I don't. I've got some adjustments to make in how I see God acting in the world, but you're not the only one doing a lot of thinking the last few days." She leaned her elbows once more on the railings. "I know I'm no theologian or anything, but it's occurred to me recently that no matter how you slice it, faith is always going to hold a few mysteries to it, a few loopholes you can't quite close, a few questions you can't quite answer. But you know what? Those without faith in God have trouble explaining a few things, too. Take creation for example, the design of it all. The unbeliever says it's all chance. They trace it back to some cataclysmic event eons and eons ago. But they don't know the origin of the material for that cataclysm. That's a mystery to them. They just accept by faith it was all there. But from where? Or from whom? Seems to me there's a better chance for a monkey to sit down at a keyboard and type out a dictionary than for life to have happened without some Divine Designer behind it all."

"You sound like a theologian to me," Michael said, grinning.

"Well, maybe I am." She faced him again, a challenge in her

voice, her chin jutting out. "So here it is, my theological confession. You ready for it, Moses? Ready to hear my take on it all?"

"Lay it on me, Sister Valerie," he teased.

"It's a matter of the heart," she said, her eyes dancing as she spoke. "Either way you come down, it's sheer faith. Faith to believe or faith to disbelieve. Somewhere or other, somehow or other, you have to make a choice, and that choice has to be the one that feels right to you, the one that makes your soul sing when you think about it, the one that makes your heart beat a little faster. That choice gives you peace in the midst of chaos, joy in the midst of sorrow, hope in the midst of death. That's what I believe. That's my theology. It may sound simple and naïve, but it makes as much sense as anything else I've heard, and I've heard a lot. So in spite of the fact that suffering is real and it hurts and I can't explain it all, that's my story, and I'm sticking to it until someone can show me something that makes more sense than that does." She took a deep breath, and laid her head on his shoulder and neither of them said a word for several seconds.

"That's quite a speech," he said, breaking the silence.

She looked up at him. Tears fell from her eyes. "I know something is going to happen to you," she sobbed. "I can feel it in here." She tapped her chest. "I don't know what it is, and I know you can't tell me, but I know what I'm saying is right. I just want you to know what I believe before . . . before . . ."

Her tears overwhelmed her then and though Michael knew he shouldn't, he could no longer keep himself from it. He kissed her. He tasted the salt of her tears, and he felt the softness of her lips. They were warm and tender and sweet. She wrapped her arms around his neck, and he wanted the moment to last forever. He wanted a future with this woman. He wanted what almost everyone else wants—a hand to hold while strolling on the beach, the sound of a baby waking him at three in the morning, Sunday dinners with all the family gathered at the table. He wanted . . . he wanted . . .

But it wasn't about what he wanted. Everything was changing—his service as a priest, his understanding of faith, his connections to all he had ever known. So he would have to enjoy this moment for what it was, one isolated oasis of tenderness and love, but he could never visit it again.

He broke off the kiss and stepped back a half step and wiped away the tears from Valerie's cheeks. His fingers moved to the scar below her right ear, the scar he had noticed the first time he ever saw her.

"I've always wanted to ask you about this," he said, touching the spot.

"I . . . I climb trees," Valerie said, her sobs receding.

"And you fell out of one," Michael said, guessing where the story went.

"Yeah, a big magnolia as tall . . . as tall as my house."

"Did you stop climbing trees after that?"

Valerie took his hand and kissed it lightly. "Oh no," she said, her tears drying up. "I still climb trees every chance I get."

"Good, don't ever stop, no matter how many times you fall. You promise me that, okay?"

Valerie stared at him for a moment, as if realizing his words had a double meaning, but she didn't question him as to what the second meaning was. Instead, she simply nodded and looked at him expectantly. Michael took a deep breath. When he spoke, his voice had a tremor in it.

"I love you," he said. "No matter what happens in the next few days, don't ever doubt that. I've never said that to any other woman."

"I guess not," Valerie said, a tiny smile now replacing her tears. "It's not exactly a priestly thing to say." Then her voice became serious again. "I know it's crazy, but I love you, too. I love a priest, a man I can never marry, a man who can't give up his vows . . . not even for love, not even for—"

"Shush," Michael said, placing a finger over her lips. "Don't worry about any of that. Let's just hold this moment, enjoy it, accept it as a gift." He pulled her close again, and she laid her head on his chest. The ocean rolled in and out below the cliffs, and Michael held her as long as he could. He kissed her once more and then led her back into the house and left her in her room. Her tears came again, and so did his, but there was nothing he could do about it. It was time to go.

———

Now, pivoting smartly before he changed his mind, he stepped past the pool and into the clearing where he and Valerie had talked earlier in the day. Ten feet past the clearing, he directed his light at the edge of the cliffs. Spotting the cable, he squatted and pulled it up from the cliffs, his hands working quickly but quietly in the darkness. Within seconds, it lay at his feet, a coiled black cord, about two hundred feet long by his estimation.

His hands sweaty, he wrapped the cable around his waist and secured it to the front of a thick black beltlike harness that Red Cashion had jerry-rigged for him after their conversation in Madden's suite. Then, pulling a metal clasp from his pocket, he tied off the cable and hooked it with the clasp so the loop wouldn't come loose.

Taking a pair of gloves from the backpack, he zipped it back up, slipped on the gloves, and threw the backpack over his shoulders. Tugging on the cable to make sure it was secure, he took one final breath and stood up straight. Ready now, he turned his back to the ocean, faced his feet toward Madden's house, and eased his body over the edge of the rocks. Down he went, one foot, two feet, five feet, the cable playing out gradually through his gloves as he descended.

Though he had done some rock climbing on a couple of occasions, he didn't have the normal equipment this time and no one to help if he got in trouble. So, too afraid to go any faster, he moved like a turtle down the craggy incline, his feet acting as a prop against the rocks to keep him stable. Blackness stared back at him as he faced the side of the precipice. Sweat poured down his chin.

Pausing, he found a good foothold, regripped the cable, and licked his lips. So far, so good. He started to ease down again. But then he felt a tug at the cable.

He stopped and leaned out, trying to see back up and over the cliffs.

He heard a grunt, then felt a harder pull at the cable. Someone was trying to haul him back up!

"Hey, Red!" he shouted.

The cable became taut, but no one answered him. Confused, he braced himself and pushed upward, his feet balanced on the wall of the incline. As he crested the edge of the precipice, he saw a pair of black, tie-up military-style boots.

A hand like a vise grabbed him by his jacket and hauled him roughly onto the ground. Though still prone, Michael recognized the boots and lunged at them, his fingers digging into the man's ankles, his biceps jerking to pull the attacker down. The man fell on him and knocked his breath out, but Michael kept moving, rolling to the right. A thick hand grabbed at his throat, but Michael dodged away and righted himself to his knees, facing his tormenter. Three feet away, Hans Walter sprang to his feet, his legs wide and balanced, his right hand holding a knife the length of a hammer handle. Walter's eyes were lively, his face a grim mask.

"You thought to escape me?" Walter asked, his breath even, his knife held at arm's length as he inched closer to Michael.

Michael didn't answer. He felt a slight tremor under his feet.

"I saw your light," continued Walter, even closer now. "So stupid of you to use it."

Michael took a half step backward. His heels were on the edge of the cliffs. Walter crouched at the waist. A sound like a distant freight train sounded off to the east, and the air seemed to shift and quiver around him.

"I've got the scroll," whispered Michael. "Leave everyone else alone and I will give it to you."

Walter grinned crookedly. His eyes glowed as if on fire. "You killed my brother," he said. "So, I will kill you—snap your neck as you snapped his. Then I will take the scroll off your cold dead body." He rolled his knife in his fingers like a gunslinger doing tricks with a pistol.

Watching Walter's expertise with the knife, Michael knew he stood little chance against the huge professional in a fight. But if he surrendered, Walter would kill him anyway, no doubt about it. Gritting his teeth, Michael moved without warning, lowering his head, and charging the mercenary.

Beneath his feet, the ground suddenly shifted and bucked up at him. Michael tripped and fell as the earthquake rolled by, his charge coming up short of his adversary. Like a fullback throwing a block, Michael crashed sideways into Walter's shins.

From the corner of his eye, he saw Walter's knife darting down at him, and he rolled to the right. The ground roiled up again, stronger this time, and a rumble as deep as a bear growling poured from the earth. The knife blade dipped at his back and grazed him just below his right shoulder blade.

The earthquake shook the ground violently now, and the soil cracked beneath Michael's feet and opened a fissure the width of a man's leg that ran into the distance toward Madden's house. A palm tree as tall as a basketball goal toppled and fell into the crack. The noise from the ground boomed through the night, a deafening crash and scrape and thunder.

Walter drew back the knife to stab him again. Michael twisted to the left and the blade missed him this time. He rolled to his feet once more, his back no more than two feet from the precipice.

Staggering against the still trembling earth, Michael grabbed Walter's wrist and forced it backward, but the mercenary didn't drop the blade. Instead, he wrapped his left arm around Michael's waist and jerked him close to his chest, squeezing him with every ounce of power in his thickly muscled torso. Michael tried to call for help, but Walter's embrace cut off his breath, and the roaring of the earthquake now drowned out everything else anyway. Like a wrestler executing a head butt, Michael jerked back his neck and hammered his forehead into Walter's nose and mouth. Still the massive man didn't fall.

Lifting Michael off the ground like a rag doll, Walter pulled back his knife one more time, its blade aimed at Michael's throat. With a last burst of strength, Michael did the only thing left to do. He deliberately yanked backward, and his body, like a two-hundred-pound ballast, pulled Walter with it. In that instant, the earth bucked one more time, a huge and vicious heave against the two humans fighting on its surface.

Walter stumbled forward, his mouth and nose bleeding, his weight tilted against the moving earth, his knife dipping into Michael's right bicep. Michael held on to Walter now, his weight completely backward, his feet now leaving the ground, his hands gripping Walter like sharp talons. Behind his back, he felt a swirl of emptiness surround his body. He remembered the parachute jumps he had once made and realized he had fallen off the cliff now and that the ocean rushed up at him from below. Above him the sky receded farther and farther, and a whoosh of air whistled around his neck and legs. Walter stared at him with wide-eyed wonder, a look of frozen fear in his eyes as the two of them catapulted straight down.

With a sudden jerk, Michael rolled Walter over, tossing the big man underneath him, his back to the water, Michael's toward the sky. And so the two men fell, their bodies attached to each other like twins in the womb as they hurtled downward toward the ocean.

From out of nowhere, time seemed to suspend itself. Michael stared down at the ocean and the milliseconds seemed to slow to minutes. The minutes became like hours, and the ocean seemed a thousand miles below and the sky a million miles above. From deep in his soul Michael breathed a silent shout as the murky waters reached up for him, a wordless acceptance of his impending death. In that instant, he realized he had just prayed, had just yielded himself to the source of all life, had just made a personal statement to the God of all that existed. It wasn't a prayer for God to rescue him. No, it was simpler than that, a prayer only to say that he knew that God was real, that God had made the stars and the sea and everything in between, including him. With that prayer a strange calm overcame Michael, and as he looked once more at the black ocean below, he yielded himself now to the God in whom he believed—the God who might let him die but who gave him peace even as he faced his own demise.

He and Walter hit the water with a massive whomp, the mercenary first, then Michael on top of him. The impact rattled Michael's brain, and a searing pain cut through his face as his body ploughed deep into the salty spray. His arms fell limp as Walter dropped away into the foaming surf, and Michael fought to stay conscious. Blinded by the black water, he twisted side to side, trying to find the surface, but not knowing up from down. A push of water jerked him to the right, and he felt a tug at his waist.

Remembering the cable that attached him like an umbilical cord to the cliffs, he reached for it, his fingers grasping for the last hope he had, the last chance to fight his way out of the deadly water and back onto the narrow strand of beach. A sense of electricity ran through his body as he realized the cable could take him back to the top. The cable could keep him alive. As his hands latched on to it, he yanked as hard as he could and felt himself moving upward. He reached for the surface of the water, his fingers arching upward ... upward ... upward. But the ocean grabbed him then, grabbed him before he reached the top, grabbed him and threw him up and out in a giant whirlpool of white spray. The spray tossed him into a rocky mass on the surface of the water, and the mass crunched into his face and his fingers let go of the cable. He gave up his struggle and closed his eyes and let the water have its way with his body.

THIRTY-NINE

Keeping watch in the hallway just outside Willard Madden's bedroom suite, Red Cashion jumped out of his chair the instant the earthquake began to shake. Grabbing the wall for balance, he stumbled to Madden's suite and kicked open the door. The walls shook as if battered by a jackhammer. Red flipped on the lights. A lamp bounced off a nightstand and shattered on the floor. The next thirty seconds seemed to last forever.

"Get him up!" he shouted at the top of his lungs to Cindy Brown, who sat transfixed in the middle of her bed, apparently shocked into inactivity. "Get Mad downstairs!"

Rushing from the room, he pounded on the other doors in the hallway, his voice bellowing to be heard over the rumbling of the quake.

"Out!" he yelled. "Everybody out!"

The ceiling in the hall started to crumble, and a split ripped down the side of the wall.

Behind him, Red saw Valerie Miller run from her room, her eyes wide, her hair wild. A split-second later, Cindy Brown appeared with Madden in tow, two bodyguards on either side of him.

"Move it!" Cashion commanded. "Downstairs!"

"Where's Michael?" shouted Valerie.

"No time to wait!" shouted Red. "Follow me!"

A crystal chandelier crashed from overhead, and the pieces broke into shards at Red's feet. The stairs rocked as he stepped on them, but he didn't slow down. Behind him, he heard a crack. Glancing over his shoulder, he saw the top of the stairwell separate from the hallway above. A gaping hole appeared between the two, and the stairs bucked like an angry bull. Four steps from the bottom, the bucking tossed Red Cashion up and outward. His body flipped threw the air, and he landed on his back at the bottom of the stairs. Scrambling up, he ignored the pain in his hips, jerked Valerie down the last step, grabbed Madden by the belt loops, and sprinted toward the front of the house.

Rounding the corner to the entryway, he pushed open the double doors and rushed outside. The sidewalk slithered at his feet, and he pulled Valerie and Madden to the ground. Cindy Brown fell down beside the three of them, her face ashen with fear.

Hitting the ground, Red heard gunfire popping over his head.

Confused, he rolled to one knee, his eyes searching the shadows of the yard. The ground seemed to have stabilized for a second, and he used the respite to his advantage, darting behind a column on the front porch. A hail of machine gun fire suddenly erupted to his right, and the column splintered near his right ear, a sliver of wood jamming into his neck.

"Back inside!" he shouted to Brown. "Get Mad back inside!"

Jerking his Glock from his waistband, Red stretched prone behind the column and peeled his eyes in the direction from which the shooting had come. The earthquake suddenly stopped. To his left, he saw Valerie and Cindy Brown haul Madden back through the front door.

The sound of automatic weapons took the place of the ground's rumbling. Crawling backward, Red pushed his feet, then his shoulders and head back inside the house. To his left and right, Madden's three bodyguards fanned out and took up spots on his flanks, each of them hunkered low. At his shoulder, Valerie Miller also appeared—her jaw firm. The gunfire from outside slowed for a moment to a light peppering of the front door.

"Do you think Michael is out there?" Valerie asked, tilting her head toward the door.

Red dropped his eyes. "Don't know where he is," he said. "But there's nothing we can do about it. He's smart. He'll do okay."

"But why would he—?"

Red threw up a hand and cut her off. "Don't ask me where he is," he insisted. "I told you I don't know."

Valerie gritted her teeth and changed the subject. "Who do you think is out there?" she asked.

"Don't know that either, but this place sure seems to draw a crowd."

"You think Walter came back?"

"It's possible, but who knows?"

"What are they doing now?" she asked, staring at the front door.

"Getting situated. I'm sure the earthquake threw off their timing when it woke all of us up. They didn't expect that."

"What are we going to do?"

Red shrugged. All the shooting had momentarily stopped. "We've got four guns," he said, indicating Madden's bodyguards. "From the volume of fire out there, I'd guess at least ten men, maybe more. We need to call for help, stall until someone can get here."

"That could take hours," Valerie said. "With this earthquake, who knows what's happened on the mainland."

"You got a better idea?"

Valerie shook her head.

"Okay, then," Red said. "Grab a phone, then take everybody to the basement, to the vault. It's solid steel. Call the authorities, then wait for the cavalry. Unless the bad guys have some pretty heavy artillery, the vault should hold them out for a long time."

Valerie nodded. "What are you going to do?"

Red licked his lips. "I'm going to see if I can slow down the nasty boys. Now get moving."

Valerie put a hand on his forearm. "Your wife is married to a good man."

"Tell her that when you meet her."

"Take care of yourself."

He patted her hand. "That's the plan. Now move."

Valerie nodded and pivoted back toward Madden. Red whistled toward the bodyguards. "Get everyone to the vault," he said. "Wait on me there."

"I'll go with you," Rick said.

Red shook his head. "No, stay with Mad. He needs you more than I do. Stay with him. You got that?"

Rick nodded, and the group headed toward the basement stairs. Red started to hum. Ten seconds later, he picked his way back up the splintered staircase, jumped the four-foot span that separated it from the third floor hallway, ran through Madden's bedroom suite, climbed onto the roof, and hustled to the trellis on the back of the house. Then, holding his Glock over his head like a torch, he slithered down the trellis and into the backyard, his eyes alert for the sight of anyone who might want to challenge him.

The earthquake caused Sonji to attack before Walter had ordered, but he didn't hesitate once it began. Sprinting the last twenty yards toward Madden's front door, he squeezed off a round of machine gun fire, certain that it would signal the men in the back to initiate their assault as well. Ten feet from Madden's porch, he saw the door pop open, and he dropped to the ground behind a shrub, his arms hugging the trembling earth even as he fired another burst at the house.

Recognizing Cashion as he darted onto the porch, Sonji aimed and clicked the trigger, but the earthquake rattled his accuracy and he missed, the bullets spraying the column near Cashion's head. Before he could aim again, Cashion and the others had backed into the house once more.

Cursing under his breath, Sonji stopped firing, glanced quickly to his left and right, and spotted three men on either side of him, spaced behind trees or shrubs at about ten-foot intervals, each of them apparently in one piece, unharmed by the earthquake that had now ceased. A couple of them kept popping rounds at Madden's house, their eyes intense with concentration.

To his surprise, Sonji heard nothing from the back, no gunshots at all. Pulling a walkie-talkie from a pouch at his waist, he whispered, "Walter? Sonji, here. I await your orders."

Walter didn't answer.

Sonji tried again but received no response.

Beckoning to his left, he called one of the men, a slender Arab named Ragib, to his side. "You okay?" he asked.

"Yeah, fine, ready."

"Everybody else?" Sonji indicated the rest of the men.

"Counting you, six of us are here, one is missing, six went to the back. I don't know about them."

Sonji nodded. The earthquake had knocked everything out of sequence. One man was probably injured, and Walter might have lost his communications. Murphy's law, as Walter often said.

"Check the back," he told Ragib. "Find Commander Walter, get a status, then get back to me."

Ragib darted away, and Sonji rubbed his head and took a deep breath. He didn't like the way things had started out here, the element of surprise gone, his leader failing to check in as expected, the earthquake erupting from nowhere. Things were in chaos and chaos was dangerous.

For several seconds, he remained in place, his eyes darting left and right, his mind busy trying to figure his next move. Instinctively, he knew that Cashion wouldn't go down easily. The man had too much experience, too much courage to do that. What he didn't know was how many men Cashion had with him. His best guess said no more than four to six. Sonji rubbed his head and tried to calculate the odds. If Cashion had more men than that, things could become troublesome in a hurry.

To Sonji's right, Ragib suddenly reappeared, breathing heavily as he dropped to a knee. "Five men are in place in the back," he said. "Commander Walter is missing."

Sonji pulled at his pigtail, stroking it as it lay on his shoulder. The earthquake? Had something happened to Walter during the earthquake? No way to know. But what should he do now? Without Walter, he was in charge. He threw his ponytail back behind his head. He knew what Commander Walter would do.

"The men are ready to move?" he asked.

"They're ready," Ragib said. "They stopped advancing when the shooting ceased, and Commander Walter didn't show. Didn't want to overreach."

"Okay," Sonji said. "That makes sense. Go to the back. Tell them when I go, everyone goes."

"Fire at will?"

Sonji grunted. Without the element of surprise, people had to die tonight. In such a situation as this, his only hope was that he wasn't one of those people.

"Yes," he said. "Fire at will."

———

Easing off the trellis, Red Cashion crawled across the yard, taking up a position on his belly behind the barbecue pit about twenty feet from the back door and to the left of the swimming pool. Anyone trying to enter the back of the house had to go right past him. Comfortable with his spot, he paused and let his eyes adjust to the dark. To his right, he saw a dull orange glow in the sky, and he realized that the volcano at Rincon had erupted again, this time with more ferocity than anything he had ever seen. Exhaling quietly, he wondered for a second about Michael, then realized he had done everything he could for him. If Michael made it, he made it, as simple as that. If not, well, nothing to do but hope he did.

His eyes searching the yard, Cashion started to hum silently.

To his left, he thought he heard something move. He tucked his shoulder under his chin and aimed his Glock in that direction, but he didn't fire. About a minute later, something moved again, and he caught a glimpse of a man darting through the undergrowth toward the front of the house.

Red licked his lips. A runner, no doubt, carrying messages from back to front. Okay, his enemies were split up—good in one way, bad in another. If he held his fire until they were almost on him, he could probably count on hitting three or four of them before they picked him off. If he could get four or so, then maybe Rick and the others could hold the rest of the attackers at bay until help could come.

Red squeezed his Glock a bit tighter and thought of Mags back in Wyoming. If things didn't go well he might not see her. . . .

He shut off the thought and brought himself into a crouch and began to hum, this time not quite to himself, but not quite loud enough for anyone to hear either. From the front of the house, he heard the sudden eruption of machine gun fire, and he braced himself against the barbecue pit.

For some reason he couldn't understand, the words of an old hymn came to his lips this time, words his Lutheran grandmother had drilled into him in the summers when he went to visit her as a boy.

"O God our help in ages past, our hope for years to come . . ."

From his left, a man sprinted toward Madden's house, and Red took dead aim at him. The mercenary fell in a heap as Red cut him down, and two more followed before the others figured out the danger and came to a sudden halt.

"A shelter from the stormy blast . . ."

Machine gun ordnance bounced up and down the chimney of the barbecue pit now, and bits and pieces of brick and mortar splashed down onto Red's head.

"And our eternal home . . ."

A ricochet clipped him in the neck and he began to bleed.

"A thousand ages in they sight . . ."

It wasn't a direct hit, and he jammed his hand over the wound, rolled to his right, and sprinted toward the bathhouse beside the pool. Halfway across the yard, he spotted another attacker. Red fired on the run and the shot clipped the man's left leg and knocked him to the ground. Without stopping, Red slid belly first behind the bathhouse and came up ready to fire. To his surprise, though, nothing happened.

He eased his head around the corner of the bathhouse. But he saw no one, and the only shooting he heard came from the front yard. Apparently he had blunted the assault from this side.

Jerking off his shirt, he wrapped it around his neck and tied it as tightly as possible without cutting off the circulation. Then, his breath slightly altered, he checked the yard again but again saw no movement.

He had taken down four men, leaving no more than three or four more out here. Maybe the best of the men were around front. Maybe the guys in back were hesitant, leaderless. He'd seen the type. Show them a bit of expertise, knock off a couple or three and they lost the heart for it all.

Red pushed his shirt into his neck again, hoping to slow the bleeding. But then he heard shooting from the front and knew he had to move. If he had blunted the attack from the back, he had to do what he could to slow down the assault from the front.

"Pretty woman," he began to sing softly. "Walkin' down the street, pretty woman, kind . . ."

Moving in a crouch, he shifted away from the bathhouse, his legs moving like pistons around the corner of the house toward the front. Ducking behind a large fern, he spotted a dark figure just to his right. As he raised his Glock to a firing position, a bullet hit Red full in the chest, its force knocking him down and back into the wet grass that bordered the edges of Madden's palatial estate.

———

Sonji stood on the hearth of the fireplace in the great room as the men under his control moved quickly through Madden's house—third-floor bedrooms first, second-floor office area next, then first-floor study, library, rec room, kitchen, dining room, and great room last.

Sweat poured off Sonji's neck, and his ponytail lay across his shoulder as he stroked it. Things were not going well. Everything had gotten knocked off balance. Commander Walter and five other soldiers were missing. Worse, his men hadn't found Del Rio and the scroll. For that matter, they hadn't found anyone else either—except for Cashion. Ragib had taken him down outside the house. But that was the only good news he had.

Sonji rubbed his hair and walked his thoughts through the possibilities. If everyone had disappeared from the house, then where were they, where had they gone, where—?

"The basement!" he yelled to Ragib, remembering the obvious. "That's all that's left."

Leaving two men to guard the upstairs, he led the others down into the cavernous underbelly of Madden's house. At the bottom of the stairs, it suddenly dawned on him where everyone had gone.

"The vault!" he shouted to no one in particular. "Second room on the right. Check the vault!"

Ragib darted ahead of the rest, his lithe body disappearing down the hall. Five seconds later, he reappeared, his face a bright smile.

"The vault is locked," he said. "But I found this." He held up a leather bedroom slipper and handed it to Sonji.

For several seconds, Sonji examined the slipper as if studying a diamond.

"An expensive shoe," he said, his eyes gleaming. "A man's expensive shoe."

Ragib nodded. The rest of the men waited patiently, their weapons ready.

The shoe still in hand, Sonji led his troops to the vault, tested the door, found it locked, then stepped back.

"They're in there," he said. "No doubt of it. I suspect they've called for help, hoping it will arrive before we can extricate them. Cashion stayed outside to slow us down. It's a classic strategy, quite admirable really."

He inhaled slowly, then did a gradual turn around the room. The men stood in place, awaiting his orders. He liked the feeling of authority. He stroked his ponytail. "We have no heavy weaponry," he said. "They realized that."

"What shall we do now?" Ragib asked, his shoulders slumped.

Sonji took a quick deep breath. "Burn it down," he said calmly.

"The house?" asked Ragib.

Sonji stepped back a pace and glared at the man. "Of course, the house, you imbecile!" he screamed. "If they want to hide in the vault, so be it! Let them hide! And let them cook!"

"But the document?" Ragib asked, taking the insult in stride. "Will it not destroy the document?"

Sonji shook his head. "I think not," he said as if talking to a child. "There's a small safe in the vault. They will put the scroll in the safe. The heat will bake those who hide the document, but the safe will preserve it from the same fire that kills its protectors."

Ragib smiled widely, and Sonji patted him on the back. "Let's get out of here," he said. "Then burn it down!"

Outside on the ground, Red Cashion's shirt was caked with coagulating blood, and a wound the size of a thimble in the upper right quadrant of his chest still bubbled with the red ooze. Beneath his back and legs, the ground stirred again, and the leaves of the fern under which he lay began to shake. Like a giant muscle vibrator, the earth slowly rocked him side to side, its movements massaging his body. As if revving up an engine, the quake grew stronger and stronger and louder and louder until it seemed that the whole world had started to move and bounce and rattle.

Red's head rocked forward off the ground, then clubbed back down again, his skull rattling into the wet grass. The shock of the quake jarred through his back and chest, and his right eyelid fluttered against it. The ground burped loudly once more, and Red's right eye opened first, then the left.

Above his head, he saw a crack appear in the wall of Madden's home. A second later, a second crack appeared. The cracks widened to the width of a shoe and ran down the side from top to bottom.

His eyes fully open now, Red heard another noise over the sound of the earthquake. He threw a hand over his face to shield himself as a rush of heavy wind buffeted him. The noise swerved to Red's right, and then a blinding light pierced the darkness. A piece of stucco from the house fell on his shoulder, but he hardly even felt it. The light completely blinded him, and the noise romped through his ears. The wind threatened to blow him away, and the ground still shook under his back. He rolled up into a fetal position and wondered what monster would attack him next.

But then the noise seemed to steady, and the light darted off his face and straight down to the ground, and the wind shifted toward the back of Madden's house. Underneath him, the ground stopped shaking too, and he realized that the quake had ceased for the moment.

Covering the chest wound with the palm of his hand, he gritted his teeth, pulled up into a semi-crouch, picked his Glock off the grass, and watched the movement of the light as it settled just past the pool in the backyard. Half-crawling, half-crouching, he inched his way around the corner of the house. The noise and light settled on the ground, and Red saw a bow-legged man in a blue uniform and beret jump out of a helicopter and sprint to the rear entry of Madden's place. Behind the man, ten others followed, each of them in identical attire. By the time that group reached the back door, two other helicopters had joined the first one, and more soldiers had piled out. Some of them followed the bow-legged man through the back door while others rushed toward the sides of the house to encircle it.

Seconds later, more shooting erupted, and Red realized that the troops in blue were firing on someone inside Madden's home. His hands shaky, he propped himself against the wall, barely able to hold his weapon. He felt blood dripping from his neck, and he took a deep breath and heard a rattle in his throat.

A soldier in navy rushed around the corner of the house, a flashlight in hand. Red tried to raise his Glock to protect himself but discovered he couldn't. His arms were too weak to lift his weapon.

The soldier pointed his light into Red's eyes, then raised a rifle, and pointed it at his face.

The battle in the house intensified, and Red heard the *ack, ack, ack* of machine gun fire ripping through the night.

Red's legs crumbled now and he sagged to the ground. Taking a short breath, he began to sing, but it was little more than a whisper. "A mighty . . . fortress is our . . . our God, a bulwark never . . . never failing . . ."

A look of confusion crossed the soldier's face.

"Our helper he, amid the . . . amid the flood of mortal ills pre . . . prevailing . . ."

"Hey!" shouted the soldier to his comrades. "I got one over here!"

Red opened his mouth to sing some more, but then he gave out. Though his lips kept moving, nothing came out of them.

He saw Mags then, and she was walking toward him, her long black hair tied in a knot behind her head, her legs willowy under a flowing dress.

A smile came to Red's face and he spoke her name. "Mags," he said. "Mags . . ."

"English?" asked the soldier, squatting in front of him. "You speak English?"

Red tried to nod his head but couldn't tell if he did or not.

"Stay silent," said the soldier, a lilting accent in his voice. "We will get you to a doctor."

The fighting in the house suddenly ceased.

Red raised his eyes at the soldier. "A doctor," he mumbled. "A . . . a doctor is . . . good."

Two other troopers rushed up to him, one of them the bow-legged man. The bow-legged man crouched at Red's side. He had a strange marking on his nose.

"You okay, my friend?" he asked.

"Been better," moaned Red.

Two men holding a stretcher rushed up to the group.

"Take care of him," the bow-legged man commanded the men with the stretcher.

Treating him gingerly, the soldiers laid Red on the stretcher and rushed him toward one of the helicopters. Directly ahead, he saw Valerie Miller, then Cindy Brown behind her, the two of them wrapped in blankets and headed toward one of the choppers. Behind them, two more soldiers had Willard Madden on a stretcher as well, a clear plastic tube in his left arm.

Using his last reserve of strength, Red raised his head off the stretcher and turned to the bow-legged man.

"Who . . . are you?" he asked.

The man chuckled gently. "It may surprise you," he said.

"I like . . . like surprises," said Red.

"My name is Luggio," said the soldier. "I work for the Big Guy."

"The president?"

"No, my guy is bigger than the president."

Red dropped his head. "Who's bigger than the president?"

"The Big Guy is," said the soldier. "I'm captain of the Swiss Guard. I work for His Holiness, the Vicar of Christ."

"The pope?"

"You got it."

Red grinned, then closed his eyes. "I . . . like the Church . . . better all the time."

PART SIX

When wisdom enters your heart, and knowledge is pleasant to your soul, discretion will preserve you, understanding will keep you, to deliver you from the way of evil, from the man who speaks perverse things, from those who leave the paths of uprightness to walk in the ways of darkness.

Proverbs 2:10–13

I keep six honest serving men, they taught me all I knew; Their names are What and Why and When and How and Where and Who.

Rudyard Kipling

FORTY

Her shoulders slumped, Valerie Miller followed the pope as he led her down the tiled hallway of the tenth floor of the Gemelli Hospital. Six members of the Swiss Guard escorted them to the end of the corridor, pushed open a double set of swinging doors, then stepped back and indicated they should enter.

"I was here myself just a few days ago," said the pope, his white cassock swishing as they walked through the doors and into the hospital suite. Two of the guards followed them inside and took up positions by the entryway. "I had a seizure, a mini-stroke, if you recall."

He smiled slyly and Valerie stared into his copper-colored eyes and understood once more why so many people loved him so devotedly. The man had such charisma you could almost feel it. But even that wasn't enough to make her smile today. Her heart hurt too much for that.

She glanced quickly around the room. It contained two recliner chairs and a tiny window on the far wall but no bed. A sink hung in the left corner, and a set of double doors split the wall a few feet from it.

Valerie stared at the floor and wanted to cry again. Though the pontiff had rescued her and the rest of her friends and safely brought them all back to Rome, she felt as though her whole world had crumbled. Michael had disappeared, and no one knew what happened to him. The Swiss Guard had searched Madden's home and yard with a fine-tooth comb but had found no sign of him. Extending the search to the whole island yielded the same devastating result—no Michael anywhere. He had vanished like a puff of smoke into thin air.

They had found one body, though. Hans Walter had washed up

onto the rocks below the cliffs on the back of Madden's estate. Apparently the earthquake had tossed him over.

"Sit here," said the pope, indicating one of the chairs. "I want to explain a few things to you."

Her emotions drained, Valerie obeyed, her arms wrapped around her waist. Though she wore a long-sleeved tan blouse, a pair of blue jeans, and sandals with socks someone had brought from her apartment, she felt chilled and her chest hurt. Maybe her cold was coming back.

The pope turned to the guards and nodded. One of them walked to the double doors by the sink and knocked. A second later, the doors swung open, and two men in green gowns wheeled two rolling beds toward Valerie and the pontiff.

Seeing the patients in the beds, Valerie jumped up and ran to them, her arms open. Yielding to her grief again, a cascade of tears ran down her face into her mouth.

"Red!" she cried, standing between the two beds, grabbing one hand of each man and twisting from one to the other. "And, Mr. Madden. I'm so glad to see you, to know that . . . that you're both okay, you're—"

Madden threw up a hand and cut her off. "I'm not okay, but I am still here, at least for now. Too rich to die I guess."

She faced Red again and he winked at her. "I'm going to make it," he said. "But Mags may kill me when I get home. I've been gone a long time, and I haven't even bought her a Christmas present. You all right?"

She nodded quickly, her spirits momentarily raised by the sight of the two men. "I'm okay," she said. "Tired, but . . ." She thought of Michael again. "I'll be okay . . . maybe . . . someday."

Still standing, the pope eased to her side and took her elbow. "Here, my child," he said gently. "Sit down for a moment."

Her eyes moist, Valerie allowed him to guide her to the chair. He took the seat next to her and patted her hands. The guards pushed Red and Madden closer to them, then stepped out of the way. The pope cleared his throat and leaned over to Valerie.

"I'm sorry about Father Del Rio," he began. "We're still looking for him, and will continue to do so as long as there's any hope for his survival."

"I appreciate that," Valerie said, drying her eyes. "Thank you. I know you'll do all you can."

For several moments, silence fell on the room. The pope shook slightly as he waited, his age suddenly becoming more evident. But his eyes were clear, and his hand on Valerie's hand felt warm, vital.

Red cleared his throat and broke the quiet. "Well, are you going to tell us what's going on or not?" he asked, his tone not as respectful as Valerie thought appropriate.

The pope stared at Red for a moment, then grinned just a bit. "You're the detective," he said, as if explaining Red's outburst to the others. "You need to solve the riddle."

Red nodded and sat up straighter.

"That's why I brought you all together," said the pope. "I thought I might explain it to you all at once." He licked his lips and leaned back.

"I had a seizure on Sunday, December 8," he began. "It left me incapacitated—paralyzed and unable to speak—for about half a day. Thankfully, though, my mind cleared up even quicker, within a couple of hours after the attack. As I lay paralyzed in bed, not knowing that I would regain my capacities, it came to me that if I did recover, I had a unique opportunity to discover something about the men who might succeed me, to learn how they might react to crisis. Who would act in Christ-like ways? Who would become selfish? Who would show himself worthy of perhaps becoming pope someday, who would not? Then, thanks be to God, my body recovered within a day, and the effects of the seizure disappeared completely."

"But you didn't tell anyone!" Valerie said, her mind jumping ahead. "You pretended you were still gravely ill!"

The pope smiled. "Exactly, my child. No one but my private doctor and the head of my security knew. And they are sworn to secrecy."

"You lay in the bushes and watched," Red said, admiration in his voice. "Pretty sneaky for a holy man."

The pope shrugged. "The Lord Jesus tells us to be 'as wise as serpents and as innocent as doves.' I did what I believed prudent to protect the Church. I didn't want a power monger to ascend to the Holy Seat. If I sinned in my actions, at least they came from a pure motive. I'll let God judge me for what I did."

"So you knew when Michael went to find the document?" Valerie asked.

"Yes, I knew. The captain of my Swiss Guard put recording devices in the Vatican offices about two years ago. I didn't like it at the time, but he convinced me we should do it. Not in personal quarters, mind you, but official offices. So I knew that Cardinal Roca sent Father Del Rio to Turkey. But that didn't particularly bother me. It made sense to do so."

Valerie stood, walked to the window, and stared out. A thin morning sun blinked back at her. "Did you know when the two of us went with Mr. Cashion to Costa Rica?"

"Yes, again Cardinal Roca's communication with Michael kept me informed."

"But you didn't think it dangerous?" She faced the pontiff again, a touch of challenge in her tone.

The pope rubbed his hands together. "I suspected it carried some danger, yes. But how much, I didn't know, not at the time. Remember, I was getting bits and pieces of information, not enough to see the whole picture, to understand the entire situation. When Hans Walter took Father Del Rio and Dr. McAuley, I lost track of him, as you did." He stood and eased over to Valerie and stood by her. Though Red and Madden listened from their beds, the pope's words were directed at Valerie.

"You have to believe me," he said, his eyes pleading. "I wanted no harm to come to him. But I am only human like you. I make miscalculations like everyone else. I had much to consider during all of this, much to confuse me. And I was taking medication to prevent a recurrence of my seizure. I still am, for that matter. Blame me if you wish for the tragedy with Father Del Rio, but know as you do so that I would trade my own life for his right now if I could. I would do anything to bring him back to us. But I can't do that and I'm sorry."

For several seconds, Valerie stared into the pope's eyes, her anger wanting to find some deceit, some insincerity lurking in them. But she didn't. Instead, she saw nothing but compassion, nothing but love. The man did care about Michael. He did genuinely grieve over what had happened to him.

She nodded her understanding. The pope took her hands and steered her back to the chairs.

"I am still weak," he said, speaking again to all of them as he sat back down. "But I need to finish this story."

Valerie sat opposite him and leaned forward. "So when did you pick up Michael's trail again?" she asked.

"I had my man Luggio working on it, but with little success until Father Del Rio called Cardinal Roca," he said. "Only then did I discover he had escaped from Mr. Walter on Cyprus. But I didn't know where he was going."

"And that's when you called me?"

"He called you?" Red asked, interrupting the conversation.

The pontiff smiled. "Yes, I reached her at her home in North Carolina, though she was somewhat skeptical of my identity."

"Wouldn't you be?" Valerie asked. "The media said you were in a coma."

The pope smiled. "We never lied to them, you know. Just let them write what they wanted to write anyway."

"And when Michael called me to tell me he was headed back to Costa Rica, I called you and told you," Valerie said, continuing the explanation.

"Exactly. And I put my Guard to work planning a rescue operation. Not exactly its normal line of expertise, but I didn't want any other authorities involved. It would have been too complicated that way. It would have taken too much time."

"So you rescued us from Hans Walter, right in the nick of time," Red said. "Not bad for amateurs."

The pontiff clapped his hands together, enjoying the left-handed compliment.

Valerie tried to soak it all up, yet for some reason, something didn't make sense to her. The pope had rescued them from Hans Walter, but somehow that didn't seem to be the end of the story. Unless she missed her guess, Walter almost certainly worked for someone else, someone with more authority than he had, someone with more at stake in the search for the document than simple dollars. Other than the scroll, what else was at stake here? The pontiff had gotten involved in the search for the scroll because Roca had sent Michael to find it. But that wasn't his first motive for keeping his physical condition a secret. His first motive had been to monitor his potential successors, to see how they responded to his condition. Did that hold the key to all this? Something the pontiff had learned about the men in the Vatican?

Valerie wrinkled her brow. "You haven't told us everything, have you," she asked the pope.

"Not everything, no."

"You wanted to see how your potential successors might react," she said, deciding to explore the line of reasoning. "Just as you monitored Michael's actions, you also watched theirs."

"True," said the pontiff. "I knew nothing of the scroll when I first had my seizure."

Red suddenly dropped his legs over the side of his bed and wrapped his gown tighter around his waist. "Cardinal Roca wasn't the only one in the inner circle who learned about the document, was he?" he asked, his mind obviously as busy as Valerie's.

"And other people started searching for the scroll!" said Valerie, knowing she had hit the right button. "Others were desperate to find it because of what it might say about Mary and Jesus, particularly given your deliberations about naming Mary the Co-Redemptrix!"

"You know the Church well," said the pontiff. "Many had speculated I would make such a declaration in time for the New Year's Day Mass."

"Some within the Curia want you to do this," Valerie said.

"And others do not," said the pope.

"But both groups needed the document before they could press their point either way," Red said. "If the Church decided it was authentic—"

"Then what it said about Mary would bring incredible power to anyone who possessed it," Valerie interrupted, her eyes bright. "Regardless of his position on the Marian Decree, the document could give him enough leverage to elevate himself or one of his allies to the papacy!"

The pope clapped his hands again. "You two are smart," he said. "But now let's see how intelligent you truly are. Who went after it? Who hired Hans Walter?

"So it really was one of your inner circle?" Red asked, almost in disbelief.

The pontiff sighed. "Tragically, yes. Sin invades even the holiest of conclaves."

"But I've heard nothing from the media," interjected Valerie. "No one has been arrested for all this, for Michael's . . . well . . . Michael's disappearance."

The pope smiled ruefully. "The Church keeps her dirty laundry out of the public eye whenever possible," he said.

No one spoke for several seconds. Valerie sorted through her memory, trying to recall the most prominent names mentioned as possible successors to the pope. Whoever hired Walter had to be one of them. Why else would anyone go to such lengths?

Two names came instantly to her—Severiano Roca and Antonio Marchino. But why would Roca hire Walter at the same time he sent Michael out? Was Walter a second option in case Michael didn't find the document? But wouldn't Roca have ordered Walter to protect Michael at all costs? To back off once Michael found the scroll? Why would he send Walter after the document once Michael had it in his possession after Istanbul? That made no sense. Unless . . . unless Walter had gone off on his own, become a renegade bent on taking the scroll for himself!

Confused, Valerie faced the pope again. "It had to be Roca or Marchino," she suggested. "They're the men most often mentioned as your possible successors."

The pope nodded slightly but didn't let on either way.

"You're missing one other guy," Red said.

"Who's that?" asked Valerie.

"The guy at the head of the table right now, can't recall his name, but the papers described him as the Secretary. Shouldn't he be one of your suspects too?"

Valerie considered it for a second. "Randuhar?" she asked, staring at the pontiff. "But no one thinks he'll succeed to the papacy."

The pope stayed quiet. Valerie chewed on at the notion. Everyone knew Randuhar as a capable man, but not a charismatic one. He was a bureaucrat with an uncanny ability to manage internal affairs, but not a leader. But had they misjudged him? Had his position as Secretary gone to his head? Had he decided that he wanted to become pope? Had he sought the document in an effort to rise to a position no one thought he could ever achieve? Valerie had to admit it was a possibility she had overlooked.

"Randuhar?" she asked, though not convinced.

The pope nodded. "Not just Cardinal Randuhar, but he was involved. I know it doesn't make sense," he said. "But power does strange things to people. Cardinal Randuhar learned that Cardinal Roca had sent Father Del Rio to find this document. But he wanted it for his own purposes. As I could have predicted, however, he didn't have the courage to go after it alone. He needed someone else to fortify his intentions when the going got more difficult."

"Marchino?"

"Yes, I am sad to say." The pontiff hung his head. "The two struck a bargain. Cardinal Marchino would support the Secretary in the holy conclave when the time came to elect a new pope. This would almost assure Cardinal Randuhar the papacy, a position from which he believed he could do the most for his people, a people desperately in need of more help than even the Church can offer."

"It's a good motive," Valerie said, struck by the way people often did bad things for good reasons.

"But the end doesn't justify the means," said the pope.

"And what does Marchino get from this?" asked Red, just a touch sarcastically.

"He gets a papal decree naming Mary Co-Redemptrix," Valerie said, figuring it out immediately. "The one thing he wants more than anything else, even the papal crown."

"So they hire Walter to do their dirty work," Red said, his disgust obvious.

"Yes," said the pontiff. "As sorry as I am to say it."

"And they were willing to kill for this thing?" Valerie asked.

The pontiff shook his head. "Not at first. Cardinal Randuhar ordered Mr. Walter to hurt no one, even offered him double payment if he managed the job without injuries."

"But after they got into it, they didn't know how to back out," Red said.

"Exactly," agreed the pontiff. "Circumstances overcame them. Walter decided to keep the scroll for himself. Sin has a way of doing that, pulling us down bit by bit, leading us by the hand into deeper and deeper shadows. Their desire for power led to deceit, their deceit led to danger, the danger led to death. Dr. McAuley, Mr. Walter and several of his mercenaries, three people at the airport in Cyprus . . . and others in Istanbul. They even tried to kill me."

"They came after you?" Red asked, his tone skeptical.

"Yes, they made an attempt. They hired a cleaning man at the hospital, telling him it was a merciful act, since I was already so near to death anyway."

"They didn't know you were very much alive."

"Exactly."

"But why didn't you stop them before they got that far?" Red asked.

The pope shrugged. "Again, I didn't know all their plans. I had to react as they acted."

"And now Michael," Valerie said. "I just wish I had made him come back to Rome . . . give the stupid scroll to Roca. Or he could have come to America . . . I should have insisted. . . ." She lowered her eyes.

The pontiff folded his hands in his lap. Red climbed out of bed, gingerly made his way to Valerie's side, and touched her shoulder. "You couldn't have stopped him," he said. "Michael did what he wanted to do. He went to Costa Rica to see if he could help Katie. You know that. He wanted something good to come of this, something more than the death that seemed to follow the document. He wasn't going to change his mind either, no matter what you might have said. I know that for a fact. If you think about it, I think you'll know it too."

Valerie took Red's hand and held it to her cheek. "I'm sure you're right," she said. "But it doesn't help much right now, you know?"

Red placed a hand on her shoulder. The pope stood and nodded to his guards. One of them stepped over and took him by the elbow.

"I need to go," the pontiff said. "The business of the Church never ceases."

"What about Randuhar and Marchino?" Valerie asked, facing the pope. "What happens to them?"

The pope shrugged. "We'll talk with the Italian police about them," he said. "Work out an agreement. I don't want this tragedy to become fodder for the tabloids. I think the Italian authorities will work with us on this. The two cardinals will disappear into the prisons somewhere, quietly put away where they cannot engage in such deadly activities again."

"And Roca?" asked Red.

The pope shrugged. "Technically, he did nothing wrong. I could question his judgment about sending a singular priest out on a dangerous mission, but I might have done the same thing. He's devastated about his nephew."

"I need to see him," Valerie said.

"He would welcome that," said the pontiff, easing toward the door. "You're the last one to see Father Del Rio alive."

"One more thing," interjected Red, stopping the pope in midstride. "The scroll," Red said. "Did your guys ever find it?"

The pope lowered his eyes for a moment, then rubbed his hands together. "No," he said. "We interrogated each of the mercenaries who survived and inspected every inch of Mr. Madden's estate. It is not there. I am sure of it. I suppose it is with Father Del Rio, wherever he is."

"He's got a hunch that it may be authentic," Valerie said.

The pontiff nodded. "I heard him tell this to Cardinal Roca. But now I suppose we will never know."

Red glanced quickly at Madden but said nothing else. The pope cleared his throat as if to speak again, but then didn't. With a short nod, he headed again to the door.

"I'll walk with you," Valerie said, standing. "I've got a lot to do before I leave for Charlotte." She hugged Red, then walked to Madden's bed and kissed his forehead. "I'll check on you two before I go," she said.

"We're leaving late this afternoon," Madden said. "If I don't get Red back to Mags by Christmas Day, she's going to kill both of us."

"We don't want that," Valerie smiled. "See you before you go."

With that, she turned and walked out, the pope and his guards leading the way.

———

As Valerie left the room, Red stepped to Madden's bedside and took a seat on the corner. "You think he made it?" Red asked.

Madden shook his head. "No way to tell. But my best guess says he and Walter got mixed up together before he left. Rick says they found the German's body at the bottom of the cliffs."

"Yeah, real near the spot where you and I know Michael should have touched down on the beach."

"Rick say anything to you about the cable?"

Red thought a moment. "Nope, nothing. Wonder if it's still there?"

Madden shrugged. "Maybe not. Rick said the earthquake caused a lot of damage. A good bit of the cliff wall crumbled into the water."

For a couple of seconds, both men fell quiet. Then Madden raised himself slightly. "You get the money transferred?" he asked.

"Yep, just like you said. Gave him fifty million instead of the five he asked for. Shifted it to a Swiss account and gave him the number."

"And the harness and clasp for the cable?"

"Gave him all the equipment just before he left."

"The boat?"

"Tied at the bottom of the cliffs. All he had to do was climb down, unhook the cable, and take the boat to the mainland."

"New identification papers?"

"I called a guy in Miami, and he went right to work on them. Said he'd bring them to San Jose. Michael was to pick the papers up there, assume his new identity, then take off. He keeps the scroll, and everyone presumes he's dead and the scroll is lost in the ocean. He's got enough money to stay out of sight for a long time, and no one's the wiser until he decides to go public with the document."

"Did anyone pick up the false papers in San Jose?"

"Can't find out yet. The earthquake destroyed the telephones into Costa Rica. Everything's in a mess over there. I haven't heard from my man in Miami, either."

"Did they find the boat?"

"Nope, but the earthquake might have dislodged it. I don't know."

Madden laid his head back and took a deep breath. "I hope he made it," he said. "I really hope he made it."

"Me and you both," Red said, standing and shuffling to the window. "It ticks me off to say it, but I had started to like the guy."

Madden smiled and closed his eyes. If Michael didn't make it, poor Katie had no chance, no chance at all.

FORTY-ONE

At just after four A.M. San Francisco time, a bearded man in a pair of baggy khakis pants, a denim shirt, and a pair of tan hiking boots leaned quietly against the hospital wall outside an intensive care unit and sucked in his breath. Thirty feet away, an attractive but drawn woman stepped out of one of the rooms, hugged her arms around her waist, and trudged away from him down the hallway. As the woman disappeared around the corner, the man limped quickly into the room the woman had just left. Passing by the mirror over the room's sink, the man took a brief look at himself. A gauze patch the size of a computer disk hung over his left eye, and his right arm hung at a slightly odd angle by his hip.

Moving with as much dispatch as possible given his limp, the man walked to the bed in the corner, slipped a navy backpack off his shoulders, plopped it onto the edge of the bed, and opened it. The patient on the bed stirred and turned to the side but didn't waken. The man exhaled softly and peeked over his shoulder at the door again. Everything was still clear.

He laid the contents of the backpack on the bed, then became as still as a monument. Several seconds passed, but the man still didn't move.

The patient, a young girl with curly blond hair and ears that stuck out like miniature saucers, lay still too, one tube snaking from her left arm, another from her nostrils. Her bones stuck out of her joints, and her skin was thin and drawn. Her breathing was choppy, and a glint of perspiration rimmed her upper lip.

The man stared at the little girl for several more moments, his breathing becoming more and more regular as he focused on what he had come to do. Everything in his life seemed to have led to this room, to this moment, to this opportunity. Now the time had come, the time to discover.

His hands busy now, the man snapped open the metal container he had taken from the backpack and pulled out the document that lay rolled up in a soft linen cloth within it. Taking a deep breath, he held the document to his chest with his left hand and touched the forehead of Katie Madden Riggs with his right. Her skin felt clammy from fever, and he shuddered at the sensation. Closing his eyes, the man began to speak, repeating words he had memorized from his many readings of the scroll.

"And Jesus, on the night before His arrest in the Garden, said unto Mary, *'I grant unto you the gift of faith.'*"

Nothing happened. The man waited several more seconds and repeated the same words a second time.

"I grant unto you the gift of faith."

Still nothing. He moved on with the passage.

"The faith that moves mountains, that removes darkness from light, death from life, sickness from health."

No response from Katie. The room seemed as empty as a tomb, a waiting room for death. The man grunted, then rubbed his beard. He cleared his throat, then started to speak again. But this time, he didn't repeat anything from the scroll.

"Eternal God," he said. "I beseech thee . . ." He paused and closed his eyes. "I beseech thee to hear the humble words of this unworthy servant."

As the man prayed, he felt a strange sensation of energy tingling in the fingers of his left hand.

"I ask thee to look with mercy upon this little child." The tingling felt warm and began to spread throughout his arm.

"I ask thee to . . . to . . . to move through thy Holy Spirit and heal this girl." The heat traveled up his left arm, across his chest, out into his right arm, and finally to his fingers. He moved from his prayer and back to the words of the scroll.

"And Jesus, on the night before His arrest in the garden, said unto Mary, 'Unto you I give the gift of faith,' He said.

" 'The faith that moves mountains, the faith that removes the light from the darkness, the life from death, the sickness from health.'

" 'But I am unworthy,' Mary said.

" 'The one who believes in his own worthiness is already unworthy of the gift,' Jesus said. 'The gift is from the Father and is to be used only for the children of the Father. As the Father gave

the gift to me, so I now give the gift to you. And the gift flows as
the Spirit does and no one knows where the Spirit flows.' "

Katie stirred as the man whispered, and her lips opened and closed as if gasping for air. His hand on her forehead tingled and pulsated, and the heat from his fingers seemed to surge into her body, too, and she turned her face away from it. But he kept his hand on her forehead, his fingers light on her skin.

The heat in the man's arms seemed to increase now, and the warmth felt like a torch firing through him, a blue flame of something he could neither understand nor contain. His face became hot, and his breathing became ragged. His mind reeled, his fingers burned, and he stood dead still. For several seconds, he didn't move, couldn't move even if he had desired. The heat in his body had intensified to the point that it welded him to the floor, and he felt certain he would disintegrate at any moment into a heap of charred ashes. His fingers arched, his chest heaved, and he felt surely that he would soon die. But then the force of the sensation knocked him backward, and he staggered against the wall as the metal canister on the bed clattered to the floor.

Braced against the wall, he waited for several seconds to catch his breath. The whole experience seemed unreal, more mysterious and frightening than anything he'd ever known. The power he had sensed wasn't rational, and it wasn't controllable. He certainly didn't know yet if it was from God or some other, much less holy, source. But it *was* real.

His heart slowing to a normal beat again, the man straightened up, touched the bandage over his eye, and realized he had done all he could. He had kept his part of the bargain. No matter what happened now, it was time to go.

Quickly gathering up the fallen canister, he wrapped the document in the linen cloth again, placed it inside, grabbed his backpack, and shoved the canister into it. Then, shouldering the backpack, he walked to Katie's bed one final time and fingered her forehead. It seemed cooler than before, but he couldn't know for certain.

"Merry Christmas, little one," he said. "May God give you the gift of life. In the name of the Father and the Son and the Holy Spirit, Amen."

Katie's eyelids fluttered but didn't open. The man sighed, pivoted, and headed to the door.

At the door, he turned back for one last look. Katie still lay quietly on the bed, her body unmoving.

"Your granddaddy loves you," he whispered. "I know he does because he told me so." With that, the man pivoted and limped out. At the corner of the hallway, he saw Katie's mom headed back to the room, and he nodded in greeting. She smiled briefly at him, and he studied her face—Mrs. Riggs looked a lot like her father.

Moving quickly away from Mrs. Riggs, the man headed into the shadows of the hospital hallway, his left leg dragging as if he carried a sack of rocks upon his back.

———

Inside the intensive care room, Katie's eyes fluttered again, and the fingers of her right hand twitched. She moaned softly and rolled onto her back. A single beam of moonlight slid through the window to her right and landed on her cheekbones. Her eyelids fluttered several more times, and then she lifted her head two inches off her pillow and licked her lips.

"Katie?" Her mother rushed to her side.

The little girl moaned slightly and lay back down, her eyes still closed.

Her mom grabbed a washcloth from the sink, wet it, rushed back to Katie, and swabbed her forehead with the damp cloth.

Katie's eyes fluttered again, then blinked open.

"Katie?" her mom said, not believing what she saw. "Katie, can you hear me?"

Katie raised her head again. "Mommy?"

Pushing a button on the side of the bed, Mrs. Riggs summoned a nurse. The doctors had said Katie would never come out of her coma again. They said she would just drift away now.

"Yes, sweetheart," she said. "Your mommy is here, right here! Are you okay? Are you—"

A nurse popped through the door, and Katie dropped her head back to the pillow.

"You doing okay here?" the nurse asked Mrs. Riggs.

"She's awake!" Mrs. Riggs said. "For the first time in a week!"

The nurse stepped to Katie's side, then leaned over her.

"Can you hear me, Katie?" she asked.

Katie stared at her but didn't speak. The nurse touched Katie's forehead. "She seems cooler," she said. "Maybe her fever has dropped."

"That's a good sign!" Mrs. Riggs said. "She's been so hot. That's a good sign!"

Katie blinked and opened her mouth. "Can I have some ice cream?" she whispered.

"She wants ice cream!" exclaimed her mom, turning to the nurse. "That's a good sign! Isn't that a good sign?"

The nurse looked puzzled. "Yeah . . . she's responsive," she said. "First time in days . . . that's good, but I don't think you should jump to any hasty con—"

"I know," Mrs. Riggs said, throwing up a hand to interrupt. "I know not to get my hopes up too high. But she looks better— don't you think? Just look at her, look at her!"

The nurse faced Katie and touched her forehead again. "She is cooler, and she wants something to eat. Those are good signs but—"

"No buts!" Mrs. Riggs said. "We'll take what we can get."

"Ice cream," repeated Katie, her eyes closed again.

"Let me get a doctor," said the nurse. "This is really surprising."

"You do that," Mrs. Riggs said. "Get a doctor."

As the nurse left, Mrs. Riggs eased onto the side of Katie's bed, slid her hands under her daughter's bony shoulders, and pulled her close to her chest. Katie's head rested on her shoulder, and she felt the warm breath of her precious daughter tickling her neck.

"You want ice cream?" Mrs. Riggs asked.

"Strawberry," whispered Katie. "A big bowl of strawberry ice cream."

Her mom began to laugh then—a laughter oiled with tears, a wild, hilarious out-of-control laughter that rolled out of the room and down the hallway and over the whole hospital floor.

"I'll get you ice cream!" she roared. "I'll buy you an ice cream store!"

Katie's green eyes opened, and she smiled up at the ceiling of her room. She licked her lips again. Obviously, buying an ice cream store sounded really good to her.

FORTY-TWO

Valerie Miller sat in the middle of her bed, still in her pajamas and green robe, her hair covered with a Braves baseball cap. Her feet were bare. A yellow candle burned on the mantel of the fireplace on the wall opposite her bed, and the aroma of lemon filled the air. At least five logs crackled in the fireplace. But Valerie felt anything but cozy.

Grabbing a book from her nightstand, she tried for a few minutes to read, to make herself sleepy enough to conk out again. But her mind wouldn't let her relax enough to concentrate on the page. Too many images kept rushing through her thoughts, too many memories. Giving up the effort, she tossed the book on the floor and walked to the window that overlooked the backyard. A squirrel darted from the ground and up the barren maple tree that grew thirty feet past the window.

Valerie pressed her forehead against the window. She had visited briefly with Cardinal Roca in his private quarters on Tuesday morning, agreed with him they needed a long time together sometime soon. Leaving there, she had gone to the embassy, packed her personal effects, and said good-bye to Arthur Bremer. Red Cashion, Willard Madden, Cindy Brown, and the rest of Madden's entourage flew out on his private jet early that afternoon, and she followed within the hour on a commercial flight.

Arriving in Charlotte at just about ten P.M., she had pushed aside her weariness and attended Christmas Eve services with her mom and dad. At just past midnight, she crashed into bed. Waking at six, she had eaten breakfast with her parents, exchanged Christmas presents, had a glass of juice, and made telephone calls to a number of relatives, near and far—all pretty routine. It was now almost nine A.M. But Valerie felt anything but routine.

She turned from the window and walked to her desk. Sitting down in the chair, she threw her bare feet onto the desktop. For a few seconds, she fiddled with her Rolodex, thinking she might call someone. Perhaps she would get together with some friends later in the day. But no name in the address file came up as someone she really wanted to see, and it was really too early to bother anybody on Christmas day.

Agitated more and more by the second, she stepped to the corner of her room, sat down at the piano bench, and began to play. Her fingers ran easily over the keyboard, and she started into a jazzy rendition of "Rudolph the Red-Nosed Reindeer," but stopped halfway through it. Nothing felt right, nothing. Some Christmas this was!

Standing, she tried to decide what to do next, but then realized that was her problem. She was thinking about what to do in the next few minutes, when the reality was, she had questions about her whole life.

She adjusted her Braves cap and plopped back down at the desk again. Before Michael Del Rio, everything had seemed so simple. Even the breakup of her engagement had happened cleanly, without complications. But now all that had changed. Nothing seemed simple now—not her career, not her love life, not her faith. But she had to deal with it.

Exhaling quickly, she leaned forward and switched on her computer. Might as well send a few Christmas e-mail messages and let a few friends know she had come back to the States. It would be better than sitting at home moping all day.

Tucking her feet under her, she clicked on her e-mail icon. The computer whirred, and moments later another blinking icon indicated that she had mail.

Pleased that someone had thought of her, she opened the mail—one message. To her surprise, it had no return address. And only one word was typed in the "Message" area of the screen.

FAITH.

Just like that, in capital letters, all by itself.

Confused, she studied the word for a moment. "FAITH." Okay. But who sent this to her? And why?

She rubbed the scar under her ear and rolled the word over

in her head again. Was this one of her dad's tricks? Some kind of cryptic Christmas message?

She started to stand to go downstairs and ask him, but then she noticed the message had an attachment on the bottom she needed to open. Even more confused now, she clicked on the attachment icon, and a small picture popped up. For several seconds, she studied the image, trying to determine what it was.

A slender man in a pair of red pants, black boots, bow tie, and Santa Claus hat stood with his right foot propped up on a white bench. A woman on her knees tugged at his left arm. A waterpot sat by the woman.

Her brow furrowed in concentration, Valerie clicked the "print" icon and made a copy of the picture and held it up to the light overhead. But the image was too small to clearly determine what it was.

Intrigued now, she took the printing, stepped downstairs to the kitchen, and laid it on the kitchen table where her mom and dad were sitting.

"What you got?" asked her dad.

"An e-mail message," Valerie said. "Some kind of picture. Thought you two might know what it was. Or did you send it to me?"

"Not me," said her father, his hands up in surrender. "I don't know what this is."

Her mom leaned over the table, lowered her glasses from her nose, and picked up the image.

"It's a copy of a painting," she said, holding it up. "Looks familiar." Her mother studied the picture for a few more seconds. It's fuzzy," she said, "But it looks like a Rockwell."

"A . . . Rockwell?"

"Yeah," said her mom, standing and walking to a bookshelf in the sitting area just past the kitchen table. "As in Norman Rockwell."

Valerie hustled after her mother, her heart skipping a beat. Her dad followed her.

"What you doing?" Valerie asked.

"I've got a book here somewhere," she said. "Copies of the Rockwell collection. If it *is* one of his, we can find out what it's called."

It took her mom about a minute to find the book. "Here it is," she said, pulling the volume off the shelf and sitting down on the sofa.

Valerie and her dad sat down beside her. Her mom fingered

through the prints in the book, her thumb hurriedly flipping pages. Sandwiched between her parents, Valerie found it hard to breathe, and it wasn't because they were too close. Her mom stopped turning pages and pointed to a picture.

"I was right!" she said triumphantly. "It's a Norman Rockwell."

"What's it called?" Valerie asked, trying to see the title past her mom's finger.

"Cute," said her mom.

"Cute?"

"No, that's not the title. It's called 'Christmas Surprise.' Does that mean anything to you?" She looked from the picture to Valerie.

Valerie just sat there, too confused to speak. She sagged back into the sofa and tugged at her baseball cap, trying to figure it out. It didn't make sense, but she didn't know anyone who could have sent this e-mail to her but Michael Del Rio! No one but Michael knew about Norman Rockwell!

Sure of her conclusion, Valerie jumped up and ran to the front door of her house and threw it open. A cool nip hit her in the face, but she paid it no attention. Who cared about cold at a time like this?

She stepped onto the porch. Her toes touched the cold of the stones underneath. Her breath poured out in white wisps. On either side, her mom and dad joined her as she stared down the street.

"He's out there," Valerie said, her voice a whisper. "He's alive."

"Who's out there?" asked her dad. "Who's alive?"

Valerie bit her lip but didn't answer. If Michael was alive, why didn't he come forward and let everyone know he was okay? But then she immediately knew the answer—he wanted to protect the scroll. Until he knew for certain about its authenticity, he couldn't let it fall into the wrong hands. Why else would he not come back?

She took a deep breath and considered the irony. The man who saw himself as a tiny cog in the larger body of the Catholic Church had become a lone individual protecting a document that he believed might be the story of Jesus as told by Mary, the beloved Mother of the Lord. Even better, this same man had sent her the one word she had given to him when she told him it all came down to a matter of the heart, a matter of faith. One way or the other, it came down to that, and the man she loved now told her he had it. Faith. That was his Christmas Surprise to her.

Valerie felt herself beginning to grin. Michael had given her the best present she had ever received.

"You okay?" asked her mom, wrapping an arm around Valerie's waist.

"I am now."

"But what's with the 'Christmas Surprise'?" asked her dad.

"It'll take a while to explain it," Valerie said.

"We've got time," said her mom.

Valerie smiled again at her, then stomped her feet up and down on the porch. "My toes are freezing," she said. "Let's go inside by the fire. Then I'll tell you both a story."

"Is it a true story?" asked her dad.

Valerie chuckled. "I'll let you be the judge of that."

On the sofa again, Valerie tucked her feet under her, took a big breath, and closed her eyes before starting. She didn't know where she was headed with her life. But Michael was alive. That much she knew. Whether she would ever see him again was still a mystery. But she could live with that. As long as Michael was alive, she'd leave the rest to God.